Building IBM

Memories That Shaped an Industry, Emerson W. Pugh, 1984

The Computer Comes of Age: The People, the Hardware, and the Software, R. Moreau, 1984

Memoirs of a Computer Pioneer, Maurice V. Wilkes, 1985

Ada: A Life and Legacy, Dorothy Stein, 1985

IBM's Early Computers, Charles J. Bashe, Lyle R. Johnson, John H. Palmer, and Emerson W. Pugh, 1986

A Few Good Men from Univac, David E. Lundstrom, 1987

Innovating for Failure: Government Policy and the Early British Computer Industry, John Hendry, 1990

Glory and Failure: The Difference Engines of Johann Müller, Charles Babbage and Georg and Edvard Scheutz, Michael Lindgren, 1990

John von Neumann and the Origins of Modern Computing, William Aspray, 1990

IBM's 360 and Early 370 Systems, Emerson W. Pugh, Lyle R. Johnson, and John H. Palmer, 1991

Building IBM: Shaping an Industry and Its Technology, Emerson W. Pugh, 1995

Building IBM
Shaping an Industry and Its Technology

Emerson W. Pugh

The MIT Press
Cambridge, Massachusetts
London, England

© 1995 Massachusetts Institute of Technology

This book was set in Baskerville by DEKR Corporation and was printed and bound in the United States of America.

Library of Congress Cataloging-in-Publication Data

Pugh, Emerson W.
  Building IBM : shaping an industry and its technology / Emerson W.
Pugh.
    p.   cm. — (History of computing)
  Includes bibliographical references and index.
  ISBN 0-262-16147-8
  1. International Business Machines Corporation—History.
2. Computer industry—United States—History. I. Title.
II. Series.
HD9696.C64I4867   1995
338.7'61004'0973—dc20
                                                    94-21609
                                                    CIP

Contents

17
Legacy 243

Naming the industry. Some early business practices. Patent policies. Dominating the industry. Settling the antitrust suit. Domestic competition. The World Trade Corporation. Competition abroad.

18
Gambling on System/360 263

Organizing for growth. Impact of the IBM 1401. Seeking compatibility. The SPREAD Task Group report. Saved by emulation. Announcing System/360

19
Commitment and Delivery 279

Entering the components business. Developing SLT. Memory and storage. Achieving manufacturing goals. Stress at the top. Software support. Market impact.

20
Onrush of Technology 301

Going after monolithics. System/370. The FS failure. Strategic concerns. The IBM PC. RISC architecture.

21
Demands of the Future 317

New leaders. Antitrust issues. Coda.

Foreword

Beginning with the company's origins in the punched-card technology of the late nineteenth century, this well-researched volume tells how IBM became so rapidly the dominant company in the computer industry. In doing so, it provides refreshing new insights on the origins and development of that industry.

The unique circumstances under which this book was written have contributed to its remarkable qualities. It was begun as an internally funded project to document research and development at IBM and, as such, benefited from access to all people and records within the company. However, with the downsizing intended to make the company more competitive in the 1990s, the project was divested and became the private property of the author. Taking advantage of this opportunity, the author has gone well beyond a technical history, adding insightful discussions of internal business and cultural factors as well as external market forces.

The author brings great knowledge and experience to this book. Employed by IBM for thirty-five years, he has functioned in a broad range of assignments including research scientist, product development manager, and corporate executive. For nearly a decade, beginning in 1983, he participated in IBM's Technical History Project, heading it since 1985.

He is the author of three previous books published in this series: *Memories That Shaped an Industry* (1984) and two volumes written with others from the Technical History Project: *IBM's Early Computers* (1986) and *IBM's 360 and Early 370 Systems* (1991). In reviewing the first of these books, the *Boston Globe* said, "Pugh's book is to good business magazine journalism as Jane Austen is to *New Yorker* fiction." That accolade seems even better deserved by the author's most recent effort.

From its beginnings in punched-card technology through the heyday of computer mainframes, this book dispels many myths held within IBM and the larger computing community about the origins, personalities, and operating structures of the company and, as such, is a good antidote to both external journalistic assessment and internal corporate lore. And the book offers insight into how actions taken as early as the 1970s contributed to the company's predicament today. For all these reasons, this book will undoubtedly stand as one of the major sources on IBM well into the next century.

I. Bernard Cohen
William Aspray

Preface

When I joined IBM in 1957, its major products were punched-card accounting machines, time recording equipment, and electric typewriters. The rapidly growing commercial electronic stored-program computer segment accounted for only about 10 percent of the company's gross revenue, whereas military contracts still accounted for more than 15 percent. The company's popular electric typewriters were making IBM better known to the general public, but several years would pass before IBM would be as familiar a name as DuPont, General Electric, General Motors, RCA, U.S. Steel, and many others. The company was well known to the investment community, however, because of its sustained rapid growth.

My first year's salary of $11,000 seemed enormous compared to the small stipend I had received while working toward a doctorate in solid-state physics. Within a year I was promoted to manager of a small research group. I wore a suit, white shirt, and necktie to work as did all managers and most other employees. We joked about the singing of IBM songs by salesmen at meetings they occasionally held in a small conference room in the building. But we did not joke about the policy on alcohol. It affected all of us. Managers even worried about serving alcoholic drinks at parties in their homes. It was good to have non-IBM employees in attendance to be sure a private party could not be classed as a company function.

Like most young people, I was cynical about such policies and quick to criticize the manner in which the company was managed. But as I gained experience managing projects in several of the company's laboratories and advanced to executive positions with companywide responsibilities, I came to appreciate how difficult it is to manage any large organization and how well managed IBM was. The enormous management problems I observed made me increasingly interested in the company's history, and especially in its product development efforts. I published my first book on the subject, *Memories That Shaped an Industry*, in 1984.

Since then I have had the privilege of working with others in producing two volumes that cover major product developments between 1945 and 1975: *IBM's Early Computers* and *IBM's 360 and Early 370 Systems*. Published in 1986 and 1991, respectively, these books were sponsored by IBM for the purpose of documenting the company's technological developments as accurately as possible. They were written to appeal to specialists in the field and to those desiring a reliable source of information about IBM and its early computer products.

Now I have chosen to write a book that is relatively short, covers a longer time frame and a wider range of topics, and is intended for anyone with a desire to learn about the origins of IBM and the computer industry. Although no longer employed by IBM, I have been granted the use of certain facilities and access to corporate archival materials. Without this access I could not have written the book. I am indebted to the corporation for placing no constraints on the manner in which I tell the story and for renouncing any right to review the manuscript prior to publication.

The quality of the book has been aided by three people with whom I have written books in the past: Charles J. Bashe, Lyle R. Johnson, and John H. Palmer. They have read and commented on the chapters as they were written and have offered numerous suggestions and corrections. John A. Armstrong, William Aspray, James W. Cortada, Martin Campbell-Kelly, Robert A. Myers, Arthur L. Norberg, and Charles E. Pankenier read early versions of the manuscript and offered many helpful comments. So many others have provided personal recollections and documents, given me tutorials on specific topics, or read and commented on individual sections that it is impractical to list them all here. Although I take full responsibility for the content of the book, I am indebted to all of these individuals for helping me make it better.

The book has also benefited from the availability of many recently published books. In particular I want to acknowledge the use I have made of *Father, Son & Co.: My Life at IBM and Beyond* by T. J. Watson, Jr., and P. Petre; *Herman Hollerith: Forgotten Giant of Information Processing* by G. D. Austrian; and the books I myself wrote with C. J. Bashe, L. R. Johnson, and J. H. Palmer. Finally I would like to express my gratitude to Robert H. Godfrey and John F. Maloney of the IBM Corporate Archives for helping me locate historical documents and photographs, to Phillip D. Summers for helpful discussions and a preliminary draft of one of the sections, and to Carolyn C. Coppola for her consultation and assistance with text processing.

Emerson W. Pugh

Introduction

No company of the twentieth century achieved greater success and engendered more admiration, respect, envy, fear, and hatred than IBM. This book tells the story of that company—how it was formed, how it grew, and how it shaped and dominated the information processing industry.

Challenging the widely held perception that the origins of the computer industry lie in specialized electronic devices created during World War II, the book reveals how punched-card equipment created the market into which early electronic computers were placed and defined many of the processes by which computers did their work. It tells how the technologies of IBM and its industry evolved from electromechanical devices and punched cards to integrated semiconductor circuits and magnetic disk storage devices of previously unimagined capabilities. Finally it reveals conditions and events of the 1970s that led to the severe difficulties IBM experienced more than a decade later.

The emphasis is on the development of new technologies and their application in products. Maintaining leadership in these activities was crucial to IBM's success. Other topics such as manufacturing, marketing and sales, customer service, education, personnel practices, and organizational structure are sufficiently discussed to provide a general overview of the evolution of the company and its practices. Although the primary focus is IBM, the background coverage of other organizations provides a broad view of the origins and development of the information processing industry.

Rather than accepting the popular myth that Thomas J. Watson, Sr. (1874–1956), founded IBM in 1914, this book shows how a business established a quarter of a century earlier by Herman Hollerith (1860–1929) provided the primary basis for IBM. The story begins shortly before Hollerith first learned about the difficulties of processing census data. It progresses through his inventive and entrepreneurial efforts that created punched-card equipment for processing data from the census of 1890 and that led to improved systems and wider applications.

Chapter 2 finds Hollerith reaching the limits of his managerial capabilities and welcoming an opportunity to sell his company. In 1911 his business was combined with two others to create the company Watson was hired to manage three years later. Chapters 3 through 9 provide the background of the new manager and describe how he transformed Hollerith's small entrepreneurial organization into the vertically integrated IBM Corporation. These chapters emphasize Watson's efforts to strengthen research and development and to couple them closely with manufacturing. They tell how IBM secured a dominant position in its industry during the Great Depression and World War II.

The problems facing the company in the postwar and cold war years are topics of chapters 10 through 17. Of particular note is IBM's response to the rapid transition from electromechanical to electronic technologies. Key elements of this story are the reluctance of Watson to participate in government-funded development projects and the manner in which he and his older son interacted. Making use of a variety of evidence, including minutes of engineering meetings chaired by him long before his son returned from service, the book challenges the widely accepted view that he was slow to move into electronics.

Bringing out the company's first large-scale electronic computers was a major test of Thomas J. Watson, Jr. (1914–1993). Trained at the knee of IBM's legendary leader and driven by a strong competitive spirit, the young Watson rose to the task and guided the company through an era of unprecedented technological change. His crowning achievement, discussed in chapters 18 and 19, was development and introduction of the IBM System/360 line of computers during the 1960s. Adopted as an industry standard, System/360 provided the basis for sustained growth of IBM and the industry for nearly two decades.

Topics of chapters 20 and 21 include IBM's response to the onrush of technology during the 1970s and 1980s and the underlying causes of the severe problems faced by the company during the 1990s.

Building IBM

1
Hollerith: Inventor and Entrepreneur

"*To all whom it may concern:* Be it known that I, Herman Hollerith, a citizen of the United States, residing at New York city, in the county and State of New York, have invented certain new and useful Improvements in Apparatus for Compiling Statistics."

These opening phrases preceded several pages of text and figures describing the invention, followed by the all-important assertion: "What I claim as new, and desire to secure by Letters Patent, is . . . ." Then came a series of specific invention claims. This first of Hollerith's many patent applications was filed in September 1884. He later divided it into two applications and renewed it twice before it was finally issued as two patents (simultaneously with a third patent) in January 1889.[1]

Not yet twenty-nine, Herman Hollerith had been granted three patents covering inventions essential to punched-card equipment that was to tabulate data from the U.S. Census of 1890 and would later provide the basis for the information processing industry. The path was not easy, however. It required all of Hollerith's entrepreneurial skills, severely strained his family life, and ultimately required new management to ensure the survival of the enterprise he had created.

Getting Started

Hollerith's family background, education, and early work experience flowed so naturally toward his lifetime career as an inventor and entrepreneur that only the level of success he achieved can be considered surprising. He was born in Buffalo, New York, in February 1860. His father, a teacher of Latin and Greek, died in an accident when the boy was only seven. His mother came from a family whose members had been skilled locksmiths in Europe prior to establishing themselves in the business of designing and manufacturing horse-drawn carriages in America. Left to raise her five children alone, she was guided by values that emphasized industriousness, integrity, thrift, education, and self-reliance. Refusing to ask her family for financial help, she turned her hobby of making ladies' hats into a successful millinery business in Buffalo.

Except for a difficulty in spelling that plagued him throughout life, Hollerith was a good student. His mental processes tended to be visual rather than abstract, and he had a remarkable ability to assimilate and logically organize large quantities of information. He attended the College of the City of New York and the Columbia School of Mines, from which he received perfect grades in drawing, geometry, graphics, and surveying, and was graduated at age nineteen.[2]

In the fall of 1879, soon after graduating from the Columbia School of Mines, Hollerith moved to Washington, D.C., to begin work as a special agent for the U.S. Census of 1880. The job was offered by one of his professors who had been appointed a chief special agent. Hollerith's assignment was to collect and analyze statistical information on the use of steam and water power by the iron and steel industries.[3] His academic record alone would have qualified him for the job, but the ease with which he engaged in discussions with his professors and the enthusiasm he showed for each new task were important factors. Indeed the pleasure he derived from the companionship of older men was an important asset throughout the early part of his career.[4]

As originally conceived, the census was relatively simple. Article I, Section 2, of the U.S. Constitution requires the Congress to conduct an enumeration of population every ten years, "in such Manner as they shall by Law direct." Its purpose was to ensure fair representation and taxation among the states. The first U.S. Census in 1790 revealed a population of just under 4 million. By 1870 the population had grown tenfold and the questions to be asked of each person had increased manyfold to include age, sex, race, place of birth, occupation, and more.

Responding to congressional interest in the country's growing industries and the movement of people from farms to cities, the census increased yet further the range of information it collected and analyzed. The census had become a tool for policy-making well beyond its original purposes. Because of their political significance, census results had often been challenged. But as the amount of information grew and the analyses became more complex, it was increasingly difficult to achieve results that were meaningful and accurate. Clearly some improvement was needed in the error-prone manual methods used for collecting, recording, and analyzing the information.

Francis A. Walker, superintendent of the census of 1870 and 1880, was committed to improving the process. He increased the number of staff members in the Washington office for the 1870 census and tripled that number to almost 1,500 for the 1880 census.[5] His quest for expert assistance in the classification of diseases for the census of 1870 led to the assignment of two assistant surgeons by the surgeon general. One of these was John S. Billings, a talented young physician who continued his involvement with the census and headed the Division of Vital Statistics for the 1880 census. Walker's policy, that agents hired to analyze data on the country's industrial activities must have scientific and technical knowledge, led to the hiring of many qualified men for the 1880 census. Among them was Herman Hollerith. Billings was in his early forties when the nineteen-year-old Hollerith arrived. Nevertheless the two became acquainted and quickly learned to respect each other's capabilities and knowledge.[6]

To enhance the friendship and as a diversion from his other work, Hollerith says he "computed a lot of life tables for Dr. Billings." It was the beginning of a long relationship with profound significance. In particular Hollerith credits Billings with starting him thinking about solutions for the census problem: "One Sunday evening at Dr. Billings' tea table, he said to me there ought to be a machine for doing the purely mechanical work of tabulating population and similar statistics. We talked the matter over. . . . He thought of using cards with the description of the individual shown by notches punched in the edge of the card."[7]

Encouraged by Billings and Superintendent Walker, Hollerith began spending part of his time seeking ways to improve the processing of census data. To better understand the requirements, he even took a temporary assignment in the population division, working as "a clerk reporting for duty." After studying the problem, Hollerith recalls, "I went back to Dr. Billings and said I thought I could work out a solution for the problem and asked him would he go in with me." But the older man was well established in his own profession and responded that he was "not interested any further than to see some solution of the problem worked out."[8]

In the fall of 1882, Hollerith moved to Boston to become an instructor of mechanical engineering at the Massachusetts Institute of Technology (MIT). The position was urged upon him by Walker, who had left the census a year earlier to become president of the institute. Hollerith thrust himself enthusiastically into his new role and soon gained the respect of his students. But before the year was out, he knew teaching would not interest him in the long run. He had no desire to repeat the same material for the next group of students.

Even more important, he wanted to solve the census problem. During his spare time, he had made use of MIT laboratory facilities to conduct his first real experiments. The results were encouraging, but even if he failed with the census problem, he now knew he wanted to be an independent inventor. He had all the tools he needed except one: knowledge of patent law and practice.

With help from colleagues at the census, Hollerith obtained an appointment as an assistant examiner in the U.S. Patent Office in Washington, D.C. He reported for work as soon as his obligations at MIT had been fulfilled. His new duties offered him the opportunity to study the structure and wording of patents and to learn how to use the patent processes to enhance the quality and duration of patent protection. He also reviewed the patent art in areas pertaining to his own ideas. In less than a year he had accomplished his objectives.

He resigned from the Patent Office in March 1884 and went into business for himself as an "Expert and Solicitor of Patents." Helping other inventors with their patents would provide sufficient income while he worked on his own inventions.[9]

Addressing the Census Problem

It is impossible to reconstruct with certainty the inventive steps by which Hollerith conceived the equipment used to tabulate the census of 1890. His recollections and those of others leave little doubt, however, as to what got him started. It was Billings who first urged him to work on the problem, and it was Billings who suggested using cards to store data. There were many problems to be solved, however, and several false starts before a practical solution was achieved.

The difficult problem of handling individual cards led Hollerith to consider using a long roll of paper tape that could be

Figure 1.1. Herman Hollerith
Photographed in Washington, D.C., in 1888, Herman Hollerith had already
invented equipment that would be used to tabulate the census of 1890. He
was born in 1860 in Buffalo, New York. Hollerith's punched-card tabulating
equipment altered forever the way government and business records were
kept and was the basis of the early data processing industry.

moved forward and back by simple rollers. Ten years earlier the
chief clerk of the census had proposed using a continuous roll of
paper, threaded over many rollers to facilitate the manual writing
of information so as "to form condensed tables of figures or
characters." The invention, according to his patent, "consists in
the method of bringing the widely separated columns or parts of
the paper into close proximity." Data collected in convenient
tables in this manner were subsequently analyzed by hand.[10]

In contrast Hollerith proposed storing information by means
of round holes punched in a roll of wide paper tape. Each line
of holes across the width of the tape would represent information
about one individual. To tabulate the information, Hollerith proposed that the tape be passed between a metal drum and a set of
wire brushes. Electromechanical counters, associated with specific hole locations, would be advanced one unit each time the
correspondingly positioned metal brush made electrical contact
with the metal drum through a hole in the tape.[11]

Hollerith's decision to use electrical signals rather than mechanical methods to detect the holes is somewhat surprising. He was well versed in mechanical devices, but he had taken no courses in electricity. Indeed Thomas A. Edison had developed his incandescent lamp only a few years earlier, and the supporting electric power system was still being developed. There was a solid precedent or basis for Hollerith's approach, nevertheless. The automatic telegraph system, developed about two decades earlier, made use of perforations in paper tape to represent information to be transmitted electrically. Like Hollerith's proposal, the tape was drawn over a metal cylinder, and electrical signals were created as the perforations passed under electrical contacts.[12]

As his experiments and studies progressed, Hollerith became increasingly aware of the disadvantages of paper tape. Once information was punched into the tape in some predetermined order (for example, people listed alphabetically by name) all further use of the information had to proceed in the same order. If one wanted to study characteristics of one age group or ethnic group, the entire tape would have to be scanned again and again.

Returning to Billings's original speculation, Hollerith decided to use one card to hold all information pertaining to each individual. A group of cards could be ordered in any desired sequence, and groups of cards could be combined into larger groups or subdivided into smaller groups, for statistical analyses. The idea of representing the characteristics of an individual by holes punched in a card was suggested by a "punch photograph" he observed being used in the West for identifying railroad ticket holders. On each ticket were locations for the conductor to punch out holes to identify the individual as having "light hair, dark eyes, large nose, etc. So you see," Hollerith modestly observed, "I only made a punch photograph of each person."[13]

It seems likely that he was also influenced by an automated loom invented by the Frenchman, Joseph Marie Jacquard, about eighty years earlier. Jacquard looms in Hollerith's time routinely produced very intricate patterns guided by a sequence of thousands of punched cards, each with holes punched so as to specify one step of the process. If not from other sources, he would surely have learned about the Jacquard loom from a brother-in-law who was involved in the silk-weaving business.

The planned function of what came to be known as the Hollerith card was of course different from either of these uses. Its function was to facilitate the statistical analysis of large quantities of information. A closely related use of punched cards had been proposed half a century earlier by the British mathematician, Charles Babbage. Data and instructions stored on punched cards were to operate "analytical engines" devised by him for carrying out mathematical computations. Hollerith was apparently not aware of this work—probably because Babbage never completed a working model.[14]

The First Practical Test

With the help of Billings, Hollerith arranged for the first practical test of his equipment in 1886. The task was to record and tabulate vital statistics for the Department of Health in Baltimore. Hollerith recorded each death on a $3^{1}/_{4}$-by-$8^{5}/_{8}$-inch (8.26-by-21.9-centimeter) card by selectively punching out hole locations in three rows along each of the two long edges of the cards. Each hole represented information about the deceased, such as age, place of birth, occupation, and cause of death.[15]

To tabulate data from the cards, Hollerith provided a flat work surface behind which were several rows of dials, each dial being associated with a specific hole location in a card. Dials could record numbers from 0 to 9999 by means of two hands that rotated in a manner analogous to the minute and second hands of a clock, each hand pointing to one of the one hundred marked positions on the circumference of the dial. The operator began the tabulation process by placing a punched card on a hard rubber surface that contained an array of tiny cups of mercury, so spaced that there was a cup directly under each of the possible hole locations. Then as the operator pulled down the handle of a hinged "pin box" that held an identically spaced array of spring-loaded pins, each pin either passed through one of the punched holes into a cup of mercury or was restrained by the card. Pins that contacted mercury closed an electrical circuit that advanced the corresponding counting dial by one unit. After a number of cards were processed, the operator wrote down the dial readings and reset the dials to zero.

Hollerith also devised an entirely new apparatus for sorting cards into categories. It consisted of a wooden box with many compartments. Each time a card was tabulated, the electrical signals that advanced counter dials (based on which holes had been punched) were also used to open the lid of one of the compartments. The operator manually removed the card from the rubber surface, placed it in the open compartment of the sorter, and closed the lid. He then placed the next card on the rubber surface and repeated the process. Using this equipment it was possible to perform a variety of statistical analyses. For example, it was possible to sort cards according to types of occupation and then determine the most common causes of death for people in different occupations.[16]

The results of the test were very encouraging not only for the young inventor but also for Billings who took pride in having initiated the activity. In describing Hollerith's equipment and its capabilities in a paper published by the American Public Health Association in 1887, Billings enthusiastically asserted: "I have watched with great interest the progress in developing and perfecting this machine, because seven years ago I became satisfied that some such system was possible and desirable, and advised Mr. Hollerith who was then engaged on census work, to take the matter up and devise such a machine. . . . I think that he has succeeded, and that compilers of demographical data will be glad to know of this system."[17]

Obtaining Patent Protection

Storing information by punching holes in cards was not new, nor was Hollerith's proposed electrical method for detecting the holes. Still he could obtain patent protection if he could show that his combination of well-known devices created a new device with useful capabilities not obvious to those "skilled in the art." He also needed a workable embodiment of his invention.

Since no one before him had used punched cards in conjunction with electromechanical means for detecting holes and tabulating data, and because the result was useful, Hollerith could surely obtain a patent. The challenge for him was to obtain broad patent protection that would hold up against any future challenge. The embodiment he chose for his first patent application made use of paper tape rather than cards, but the wording of his claims was broad enough to cover the use of cards as well. Filed in September 1884, only six months after he resigned from the Patent Office, this patent application was divided by him into two applications in October 1885. There were nine invention claims

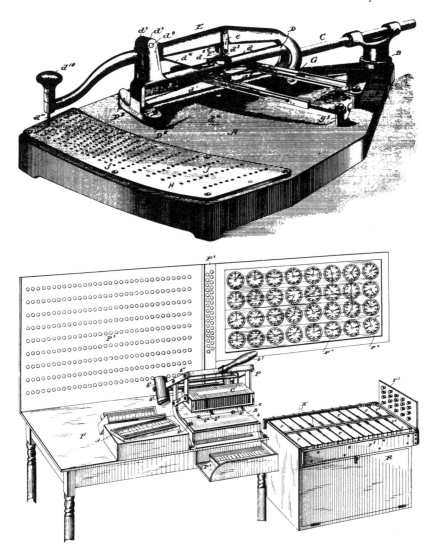

Figure 1.2. Early Hollerith Inventions
Top: Pantograph punch as depicted in U.S. Patent 487,737, filed by Hollerith in March 1891. Bottom: The tabulating apparatus as illustrated in U.S. Patent 395,781, filed by Hollerith in June 1887. The 1890 census was mechanized by apparatus similar to that illustrated here, except that there were 26 rather than 22 compartments in the sorter and 10 rather than 8 counter dials in each of the four rows. Also the boards of electrical posts (P^3 and P^7) were out of sight, and the array of counter dials was directly behind the table.

in the two patents. Each claim was broadly written to cover as many different implementations as possible.[18]

Hollerith's third patent was not filed until June 1887 after he had built fully operable equipment and tested it in the Baltimore study. The description of the equipment is therefore quite detailed. There are twenty-one invention claims in the patent, ranging from very broad ones to some that are quite specific to the embodiment shown. This patent was issued in January 1889, simultaneously with the two earlier patents, applications for which Hollerith had renewed twice in the interim. By delaying the patent process on his first two applications, Hollerith was able to give himself the longest possible protection (17 years from date of issue) on all three patents. The more detailed claims of his third patent would prevent others from simply copying his equipment, even if some of his broader claims were rejected or successfully challenged at a later date.[19]

A critical flaw in the equipment was painfully revealed to Hollerith during the tests in Baltimore. To punch holes in the cards, he had used a small hand-held punch of the type employed by train conductors. Although the conductor's punch was satisfactory for intermittent use, it was not suitable for punching thousands of holes in cards. Hollerith's hand and arm became nearly paralyzed after spending a day continually punching holes in cards.[20] To solve the problem, he devised a new punch, commonly called a pantograph punch because large motions of a manually moved stylus were mimicked by smaller motions of a punch that cut round holes in the card.

Near the operator was a large flat plate with holes corresponding in their locations to possible hole locations in the much smaller card. By moving the stylus by hand and pushing it into the selected hole in the plate, the operator caused a punch on the levered arm to create a similarly located hole in the card. Ready for the next test of Hollerith's system, this device permitted an operator to punch an estimated 500 cards per day with good accuracy and little physical strain.[21] Although the improved punch was crucial to the efficient use of Hollerith's system, it would be impossible to get broad patent coverage because there were already many types of punches in use. He therefore delayed filing for a patent on the punch until March 1891 after he had tested it in practical applications, modified it, and used it in processing data for the census of 1890. The patent was issued in December 1892.[22]

Entrepreneurial Setbacks

Shortly before filing his first patent application in 1884, Hollerith requested a loan from his sister's husband to finance the development of experimental equipment. It was not the first time the two men had considered joint business opportunities. Their previous discussions had involved possible improvements in silk-weaving equipment used in his brother-in-law's business.

Concerning the tabulating equipment venture, Hollerith assured his brother-in-law, "I can secure what is technically known as a "foundation patent" covering the ground broadly and, therefore, all subsequent improvements would be subject to my broad patent."[23] He also advised him that the new superintendent of the census was willing to assign clerks to test an experimental model of his tabulating equipment on unprocessed data from the previous census. Hollerith estimated the cost of an experimental machine at $1,500. Another $1,000 should cover all other costs, including the securing of domestic and foreign patents. He offered to pay his brother-in-law 6 percent on the loan plus half of the profits up to $12,000.

It was an attractive offer, and Hollerith soon received enough money to get started. Less than a year later, however, the deal had soured. No longer convinced it would be a profitable venture, the brother-in-law refused to supply additional money. Hollerith protested, but to no avail. When his efforts to secure funding from other family members also failed, he became so embittered that he broke off all further relations with them.[24]

The loss of financial support for developing tabulating equipment only increased the urgency with which he pursued his newest venture. On the last day of April 1885, he had filed three separate patent applications with the same title: "Electro-Magnetically-Operated Air-Brake for Railway-Cars." All three patents were issued on the same day in January 1886. Although no models were provided, the patent examiner was evidently convinced of their operability and uniqueness.[25]

The patents list Hollerith's address as St. Louis, Missouri. He had moved there to work on railway brake improvements as an employee of an older cousin, an accomplished engineer, who had already acquired seven patents of his own on electromagnetic devices for railway brakes.[26] Electrical devices offered the possibility of activating brakes on all cars nearly simultaneously, rather than waiting several seconds for air pressure from a single tank in the locomotive to make its way through long air hoses and tubes that ran from car to car in the system George Westinghouse had introduced more than a decade earlier. The newness of the technologies and the complexities of the systems left considerable uncertainty, however, as to the best solution.

During railway tests conducted at Burlington, Iowa, by the Master Car Builders' Association in 1886 and 1887, electrically activated air brakes proved to be superior to purely pneumatic ones. Moreover it appears that a system using Hollerith's inventions was superior to all others. But that is where his superiority ended. The benefits of rapid standardization across the industry, combined with the dominance of the Westinghouse Air Brake Company, pushed Hollerith and other independent inventors and entrepreneurs out of the field. Westinghouse offered to purchase Hollerith's patents, but he refused to sell. He believed Westinghouse would have to pay him more later, but that never happened.[27]

Deeply discouraged, even embittered, Hollerith returned to Washington. He now had no option other than to pursue his inventions for compiling statistics on a full-time basis. It proved to be a fortunate circumstance.

Winning the Census Business

Successful use of his equipment by the Department of Health in Baltimore and the enthusiastic support of Billings helped Hollerith gain other opportunities to demonstrate his equipment. New Jersey adopted the system soon after Baltimore, and the Surgeon General's Office of the War Department contracted for a system late in 1888. During the spring of 1889 Hollerith exhibited his equipment in Berlin and in Paris, and in July he installed a system in the New York City Health Department.

Adding to the good news that year was the appointment of Robert P. Porter as superintendent of the upcoming census. Porter, like Hollerith, had worked on the U.S. Census of 1880, and the two were quite friendly. During the intervening years, Porter had become editor of the *New York Post* as well as an enthusiastic advocate of Hollerith's equipment. He had even written in the *Post* that the next census might well "be tabulated by electricity."[28]

One of Porter's first actions as superintendent was to appoint a commission of three experienced statisticians to evaluate equipment for improving the census process. Headed by Hollerith's good friend, the widely respected Dr. Billings, the commission limited its evaluation to Hollerith's system and two others. Using 1880 census enumeration data from four districts of the city of St. Louis, it was determined that the transcription of data with Hollerith's system was at least 50 percent faster and tabulation was more than eight times faster than with the second place contender. More than two times faster overall in the test, Hollerith's system was expected to be far superior in meeting the growing requirements for analyzing the same data in many different ways. On the basis of the commission's report, Hollerith's equipment was selected and used for the census of 1890.[29]

Even before the commission's final report had been submitted in November 1889, Porter authorized the installation of six Hollerith machines for the Division of Vital Statistics. Another one hundred machines were expected to be needed to process all census data. At $1,000 rental per year per machine, the cost seemed enormous. To reduce the costs, Porter insisted on the right to use the equipment day or night. In this way only fifty machines would be needed. Furthermore Hollerith was to forfeit $10 per day for any machine that was not repaired (or replaced with an operable one) within twenty-four hours after notification of its malfunction. When working at night proved to be undesirable for all parties, Hollerith agreed to install another forty machines for an annual rental of only $500 each. To compensate for the lower fee, Porter agreed that no machine would be used outside of normal office hours.

Hollerith was fortunate in his choice of manufacturers. The Pratt and Whitney Company manufactured the pantograph punches and the rest of the equipment was made by the Western Electric Company. Partly because of the quality of their construction and partly because of Hollerith's personal commitment and penchant for detail, he never had to forfeit the stipulated $10 per day for malfunctioning equipment.[30]

There was good reason to question the impartiality of those who selected Hollerith's equipment for the 1890 census, and the press of the time enjoyed printing abusive stories. In retrospect, however, its superiority over previous methods is beyond dispute. It saved both time and money. But the system's most significant achievement was that it made possible the analysis of data in many different ways and with far fewer errors than had been previously possible.

Two features are particularly worthy of note. First, the counters and sorting box lids could be wired to be activated either by a single hole punched in a predesignated location or by combinations of several preselected holes. Thus it was just as easy to tabulate information based on several parameters as it was on a single parameter. Second, the machine could reject cards with many types of punching errors. For example, a card failing to have either the "male" or the "female" locations punched would result in the monitor bell just to the left of the press, refusing to give "its cheery signal of correctness." As reported in 1891 by a publication devoted to theoretical and applied electricity, "the apparatus works as unerringly as the mills of the Gods, but beats them hollow as to speed."[31]

Commercial Applications

Even while Hollerith was preparing for the U.S. Census of 1890, he had received inquiries from several foreign countries about using his machines in their census work. Austria, Italy, Norway, and Canada were among the first to adopt the equipment. With few exceptions, the equipment was hailed for its performance and accuracy. The director general of Italy's Imperial Bureau of Statistics evinced remarkable vision by predicting, "The time will come when the railroads, the great factories, the mercantile houses, and all the branches of commercial and industrial life will be found using the Hollerith machines as a matter of not only economy but necessity."[32]

Accomplishing this prediction would not be easy, however, because new techniques would have to be developed for commercial applications. On top of the technical problems, a decline in Hollerith's business following completion of the U.S. Census in the early 1890s forced him to lay off all but four employees and move his family into his mother-in-law's home.[33]

Hollerith's initial commercial thrust was into railroads, which during the mid-1800s had led the way in using sophisticated accounting techniques.[34] His primary target was the New York Central, which had become the second largest railroad system in the United States. Nearly 4 million freight waybills per year were processed by hand. Hollerith's goal was to automate this process so that freight movements and revenues could be handled more economically and monitored on a weekly rather than a monthly basis. He redesigned his cards and his equipment for railroad use.

Unlike cards used for census work in which punched-hole locations represented personal characteristics such as age or marital status, the new cards were entirely numeric; a single digit could be recorded in each column by a hole in one of ten positions. To help operators read the cards manually, each column was printed with the numerals 0 through 9 from top to bottom, and groups of vertical columns reserved for particular classes of information were set off from other columns by printed lines. A region between two lines was called a field, a term that endured for decades. A field of several columns was allocated to each class of information. For example, Hollerith allotted five columns for the weight of shipments to permit values up to 99,999 pounds. When an amount of money was recorded, the right two columns indicated cents and the adjacent columns indicated dollars up to the largest number anticipated. A three-column field, for example, could record values up to $9.99.

No longer did simple counting suffice. Hollerith made substantial modifications to his tabulating equipment to perform addition—that is, to add a number recorded in a field on one card to those in the same field on preceding cards. The dials were replaced with accumulators having sufficient digit positions to handle sums from the assigned fields. Each digit position was represented by a ten-position wheel with visible numerals. The sizes of the fields and associated accumulators were selected for the needs of the New York Central.[35]

A significant innovation that helped reduce the cost of this new function was introduced soon after Hollerith replaced the pin-box card reader with an automatic card feeder. The new method for performing addition made use of the distance between punched holes to represent number size. Represented by holes punched in a row near the top of the card were 0s, and holes representing 6s, for example, were six times further from the 0s than were holes representing 1s. This arrangement made it possible to advance each digit in the accumulator by the desired amount using an electrically actuated clutch that mechanically coupled the rotation of the ten-digit wheels of the accumulator to the motion of the cards.[36]

Hollerith had moved his business from downtown Washington, D.C., to a former cooper's shop in Georgetown in 1892. The two-story brick building, to which a third story and other expansions were subsequently added, served as the card manufacturing plant, final assembly plant, repair shop, and development laboratory. Subassemblies were obtained from numerous suppliers. The shop also served as a training facility for salesmen, whom Hollerith trained by requiring them to take apart and reassemble equipment. In September 1896 Hollerith signed a contract agreeing to supply the New York Central with sufficient punched-card equipment to process up to 4 million waybills during the next year. That December he incorporated his business as the Tabulating Machine Company.[37]

Success in the commercial field came slowly, partly because desk-top calculating machines were more easily absorbed into standard business routines than were tabulating machines. Hollerith was therefore grateful for a large order for census equipment from the Russian government that helped carry the business until the next U.S. Census. Tabulators used in the 1890 census again served in the 1900 census of population, but tabulators of the type developed for the New York Central Railroad were needed to process farm crop data. For these newer tabulators, Hollerith also developed an automatic sorter. His manually operated sorter was becoming impractical owing to the large volume of cards being processed.[38]

Entering Foreign Markets

Despite the rapidity with which Hollerith's equipment was adopted for census purposes by several foreign governments, the broader development of foreign markets progressed slowly. Then in 1901 Robert Porter fortuitously came back into Hollerith's life to create his first permanent business relationship outside the United States. Porter, it will be recalled, had first met Hollerith when they worked together on the U. S. Census of 1880. Later as editor of the *New York Post*, he had promoted Hollerith's system. Appointed superintendent of the census of 1890, Porter not only supervised the first significant use of the equipment, but he had been instrumental in its selection.

Leaving the census in 1893, Porter was appointed special fiscal adviser and tariff commissioner for Cuba and Puerto Rico. He also arranged to join Hollerith in giving presentations on tabulating the U.S. Census to the Royal Statistical Society in London. Porter's professional credentials were no doubt sufficient to warrant this opportunity, but the fact that he was a naturalized U.S. citizen of British birth added interest to the presentations and contributed to the warm reception the two men received.[39]

Hollerith preceded this event with an arduous tour of European capitals to promote his system. He arrived in Berlin in November 1893 and then went on to Rome, Paris, and London, where he joined Porter. When his tabulating equipment failed to arrive in time for his presentation, Hollerith spoke extemporaneously using lantern slides prepared for such an emergency.[40] Porter's wife, who attended the event, graciously wrote to Hollerith's wife, telling her how brilliantly her husband had overcome the unexpected problem. "You would have been proud of Mr. H's appearance before that scientific and august bald-headed body," she wrote. "He rose to the occasion and in the easiest possible manner and in the most lucid language gave his distinguished audience a clear idea of the machine."[41] Hollerith was subsequently elected a member of the society—one of many honors he sought and received throughout his life.

Despite this favorable introduction to the British scientific community, Hollerith failed to find suitable backers for a permanent outlet in Britain for several years. Then in 1901 President William McKinley was assassinated, bringing to an end Porter's political career. Porter accepted an offer to return to England to become the first editor of the Engineering Supplement of the *Times*.

Very likely Porter had already given thought to establishing a British outlet for Hollerith machines. In any event he acquired an exclusive option to establish one from Hollerith in February 1902. The British company was finally incorporated as the Tabulator Limited in June 1904. Porter was chairman and Raleigh Phillpotts, a thirty-year-old specialist in commercial law, was general manager. Phillpotts's most relevant prior experience was three years as secretary of the British Westinghouse Company. Another important asset, especially for a businessman in England, was that he came from a prominent family.

Progress in getting equipment accepted by customers was slow, in part because of the inexperience of the company's management. For example, it was about a year before they realized that the equipment's decimal counters could not handle the nondecimal British currency then in use. Since they had raised only 10 percent of the 20,000 pounds specified by the original agreement, operating funds were in short supply. To solve this problem, Phillpotts negotiated a new agreement that replaced a one-time payment of 10,000 pounds for use of Hollerith's patents with a 25 percent royalty on all future revenues. These high royalty payments were later viewed as a primary reason for the relatively poor success of the British firm.[42]

In 1905 the company established its first machine installation with the Vickers company, and Porter used his influence with the general manager of the Lancashire and North Yorkshire Railway to arrange for a trial installation. A large installation resulted, involving five tabulators and many key punches. Now the company needed more money to purchase equipment to place on rental. With its better business prospects, it was able to sell enough shares of stock to solve the immediate problems, although friends and relatives again had to be solicited. To make the company more attractive to investors and customers, its name was changed in October 1907 to the British Tabulating Machine Company (BTM).

The selling of each new installation continued to require considerable effort, and business expanded slowly. In 1910 BTM still had only five employees when a major effort was undertaken to win the contract for the British census. Trials that summer indicated modified equipment with thirty-six counters would be required. Despite the short time available to make these modifications, the contract was signed in December. Calling for eight counting machines, fifteen sorters, and sixty punches, the contract represented more revenue than all previous installations combined. Inevitably problems were encountered, but the census was successfully tabulated during a two-year period beginning in mid-1911.[43]

In 1910 a German businessman obtained from Hollerith the right to establish a firm to serve the German market. Headquartered in Berlin and named the Deutsche Hollerith Maschinen Gesellschaft, the new company was more commonly referred to by the acronym Dehomag. Like BTM, Dehomag paid the American company 10 percent over the cost of the machines plus a royalty of 25 percent of gross rentals. Perhaps learning indirectly from the experiences of the British company, the German company was quickly funded and profitable. Soon it was paying Hollerith's Tabulating Machine Company an additional annual fee to operate in Denmark, Norway, Sweden, and Switzerland as well.[44]

2

Origins of IBM

After tabulating the U.S. Census of 1900, Hollerith enjoyed considerable success in the commercial market. He had also established an outlet for his equipment in Great Britain and Germany by the end of the decade. His pleasure in these achievements, however, was undercut by growing problems with his primary customer, the Bureau of the Census.

More an inventor and entrepreneur than a businessman or an executive, Hollerith had never been able to remove himself from the details of his entire operation. His devices were his personal creation. Their successes and failures were his own. When machine parts did not arrive on time, he became an expeditor. When money was needed, he sought a loan. When there were legal problems, he handled them with his attorneys. His health suffered from the strain, and he longed to have more time with his family. Nearly overwhelmed by his many problems, Hollerith accepted a merger proposal in 1911 that made him a wealthy man. The merger also triggered a series of events that were destined to propel his small business into one of the larger and more successful business enterprises of the century.

Business Stress

In spite of the intensity with which Hollerith pursued his intellectual and business interests, he had always devoted some time to social activities. Frequently this took the form of discussions with older men or women, but he also participated in leisure activities with others his age. His first fiancée died of typhoid fever in 1886, one year after their engagement was announced. Two years later he became engaged again, this time to Lucia Talcott, a young woman whose widowed mother had been married to an engineer. Estranged from his own family, Hollerith derived considerable comfort not only from Lu but also from her mother who had much in common with his own.

For nearly two years Hollerith and Lu were formally engaged, but he continually postponed the marriage, hoping he could first get out from under his business uncertainties and pressures. Winning the contract for the census of 1890 reduced the uncertainties, but it dramatically increased the pressures. Ordering, installing, and servicing so many machines allowed no time for a wedding. So great was Hollerith's stress that he suffered from severe headaches, inability to sleep at night, and an uncontrollable temper by day. When his doctor ordered him to leave town for a complete rest, he concluded there could be no rest for him without Lu. He contacted her immediately and a wedding was hastily arranged. Three days later he and his new wife headed off for *their* honeymoon and *his* complete rest. It appears to have been a good marriage—strong enough to withstand the vagaries of Hollerith's business as well as the peaks and valleys of his emotions.[1]

Except for its sharp ten-year cycle, the Census Bureau work provided an ideal beginning for his business. All of the equipment was installed in the same geographic location and all of the systems were essentially identical. Hollerith, the one-man entrepreneur, could supervise their installation and maintenance, while leaving Hollerith, the inventor, time to work on major improvements. With business customers by contrast, he had to spend more of his time learning about diverse applications and making minor modifications to his equipment rather than making more basic improvements.

To reduce the burden of managing his business, Hollerith needed more employees on whom he could depend, but he lacked the personal skills to attract and retain them. His relationship with his first employee, Edmund Talcott, who was also his wife's younger brother, is particularly revealing. Soon after the contract for the 1890 census was signed, Hollerith hired him to install and service machines and to rewire them for different applications. Rewiring consisted of unsoldering selected copper wires from one set of terminals and resoldering them to others. Servicing the equipment included a daily recharging of two-foot-high storage batteries, using Edison power lines that came into the building. Batteries were used to power the equipment because of the uncertain voltage levels and continuity of service of the power lines.

Ned Talcott learned to perform all chores with diligence and was essential in achieving the rapid buildup of equipment required by the Census Bureau. He was also exceptionally loyal. Termination of the census work in 1894 coincided with a nationwide financial depression, forcing Hollerith to lay off all but Ned Talcott and three other employees. When Ned obtained another job so his brother-in-law would have fewer people on the payroll but did not explain the move to Hollerith, the latter became so furious that the younger man felt obliged to abandon his new job.

Two years later an angry dispute erupted over Ned Talcott's lack of initiative—and his wages, which Hollerith had been unable to pay. In a fit of anger, Hollerith fired him. It was a decision the two regretted almost immediately and for years to come, but neither one was able to bring about the mutually desired reconciliation.[2]

Battling the Census Bureau

Probably no events were more frustrating and emotionally draining for Hollerith than those that followed creation of a permanent U.S. Bureau of the Census in 1902. Simon Newton Dexter North, its newly appointed director in 1903, became concerned that the government might be paying Hollerith excessively high prices.

As the record revealed, the cost per capita of the 1870 census had been 8.8 cents; of the 1880 census, 11.5 cents; and of the 1890 census with Hollerith's equipment, 18.4 cents. The increased costs do not seem unreasonable in view of the larger amount of data collected and analyzed per capita.[3] From another perspective, however, the rates were high. The rental Hollerith charged was based on the number of cards processed: 65 cents per 1,000 cards tabulated and 18 cents per 1,000 cards sorted. Using the old machine, an operator could typically tabulate 8,000 cards per day, resulting in an annual rental of about $1,500 per machine. The new automatic machines could process four to five times more cards, yielding an annual rental greater than $6,000. This was more than the cost of building a machine. Hollerith was also the sole supplier of the cards. The faster his machines worked, the more cards he sold.

The potential political embarrassment for North was heightened in 1904 when his predecessor accepted the position of president of the Tabulating Machine Company. Any future contracts between the company and the Bureau of the Census might well come under considerable scrutiny.[4]

To break the hold Hollerith had over the Census Bureau, North obtained a $40,000 appropriation from Congress in July 1905 to cover experimental work to develop new tabulating machinery. Almost simultaneously all of Hollerith's machines were removed from the Census Office. Explaining this event, North cited the failure to reach a mutually acceptable rental agreement, whereas Hollerith cited his company's reluctance "to leave its patented devices where they could serve as models for experimental work."[5]

As events unfolded, North established a machine shop in the Bureau of Standards (later moved to larger quarters in the Census Bureau) and staffed it with people, several of whom had previously worked for Hollerith. Learning that Hollerith's primary patents would soon expire, North set the objective of copying the basic designs and then improving on these in ways that would circumvent more recent patents.

Meanwhile Hollerith was becoming increasingly incensed by the government's effort to prevent him from profiting from his inventions. Even if he could show that the Bureau of the Census was infringing his patents, the laws of the time made it doubtful that he could stop the bureau or collect damages as he might from a private company. Almost more galling was a new policy that permitted Census Bureau employees to acquire patents in their own name for their own use, so long as the government also had free use. In addition to driving Hollerith out of the census business, the government was in effect paying to develop patents that could be used by individuals or private companies in direct competition with him in the commercial market. Hollerith believed the practice was grossly unfair. He lobbied influential friends and congressmen, and he took his case directly to President Theodore Roosevelt and later to President William Howard Taft.

His activities contributed to the ouster of North as director of the Bureau of the Census. He even obtained a temporary court injunction in January 1910 to prevent the bureau from making equipment modifications essential to carrying out the constitutionally mandated census of that year. Ultimately his efforts failed. The census of 1910 was taken using equipment built by the Bureau of the Census. Hollerith received no compensation for patent infringement—if indeed his patents had been infringed. Even before his suit against the government ended, Hollerith decided not to seek damages in the Court of Claims. He preferred to concentrate on new business activities rather than spending his limited resources seeking an uncertain outcome.[6]

"After my row with North," Hollerith stoically recalled some years later, "I devoted my attention entirely to commercial work. However, I always have regretted that I could not stay in census work long enough to carry out my ideas regarding verification machines."[7] It was the lament of a man whose driving motivations were to solve engineering problems and create useful inventions. He enjoyed his business primarily because it was a means for proving the worth of his inventions. Increasingly, however, he saw his business obligations as preventing him from doing interesting work.

The Proposed Merger

In the past Hollerith had turned down offers to sell his business. But in 1911 any reluctance he had to sell the business was overcome by his frustration with the actions of the Bureau of the Census and by a very attractive proposal presented by the financier Charles Ranlett Flint.

Born in Maine in 1850 to a family in the shipping and shipbuilding industries, the young Flint graduated from Brooklyn Polytechnic at age eighteen. Declining his father's offer to send him to college, he began his career as a dock clerk in New York City. Four years later he was a partner in the W. R. Grace and Company shipping firm. By the time he was thirty, he had become an independent businessman, procuring and shipping munitions to Peru and Brazil and serving as consul for Chile in New York, among other activities. His diverse involvements included an unsuccessful effort, as president of the United States Electric Company in 1880, to become part of the national surge in business consolidations by combining major elements of the electric light and power industries. Attributing his failure to his position as president of one of the involved companies, Flint decided to pursue future consolidations in the role of adviser and facilitator.[8]

Many organizational structures were available, ranging from loose federations to a full merger of the operations of two or more companies. Among the structures in use in the 1880s was the "trust," a device in which several companies turned their stock

Figure 2.1.   Charles R. Flint
Known to the press as "the father of trusts," Charles Ranlett Flint was entering his sixties when he merged Hollerith's company with two others in 1911 to form the Computing-Tabulating-Recording Company. The name of the company was changed to the International Business Machines Corporation in 1924.

over to a board of trustees in return for "trust certificates" of equal value. The board of trustees was empowered to make operating and investment decisions on behalf of the companies within the trust. Large financial resources, and control of major industry segments, provided trusts with opportunities to squeeze out smaller companies and ultimately gain monopoly power.

Exploitation of monopoly powers by the railroads and other industries had caused the federal government to become involved in protecting local regions and small companies from ruthless exploitation. The Interstate Commerce Act of 1887 and the Sherman Antitrust Act of 1890 were intended to stop undesirable monopoly practices, but they had only limited effect until President Theodore Roosevelt initiated his aggressive "trust-busting" activities in the early 1900s. Thereafter business consolidations had to be carefully structured to reduce the likelihood of antitrust action by the government.[9]

By the time he approached Hollerith in 1911, Flint was among the better-known speculators and promoters of industrial mergers. Well on his way toward a lifetime total of two dozen industrial consolidations, Flint had socialized and negotiated with many of the country's leading inventors, entrepreneurs, financiers, and industrial leaders. He had also found time to become a skilled aviator, to own and operate one of the fastest racing yachts in the country, and to join with six others in founding the Automobile Club of America.

Flint favored large corporations because they had economies of scale that created profits needed to improve products and production methods and to expand business. He derided competition as a destructive influence that forced manufacturers to lower the quality of products in order to meet competitive prices. Among companies created by his mergers were the United States Rubber, American Woolen, and American Chicle companies. Flint obtained substantial profits from mergers by selling stock at prices well above the tangible assets of the corporations. For example, in the case of American Chicle, "the chewing gum trust," the tangible assets of the six merged companies were $0.5 million, whereas Flint capitalized the corporation at $9 million based on his estimate of the value of their trademarks.

The plan Flint offered Hollerith and his fellow owners of the Tabulating Machine Company was a merger with the International Time Recording Company and the Computing Scale Company of America. It would be Flint's first consolidation of manufacturers of similar but not identical products.[10] A ten-year series of mergers and acquisitions, facilitated by Flint, had helped the International Time Recording Company dominate its industry with annual sales throughout the United States and Europe exceeding $1 million. Flint had also been involved in creating the Computing Scale Company of America, but its business was less successful. By merging the two firms, Flint hoped the marketing and financial resources of the former would strengthen the latter.

The subsequent decision to include Hollerith's Tabulating Machine Company could be rationalized by the company's chronic shortage of funds to support its growth—a shortage exacerbated by Hollerith's policy of renting machines rather than selling them outright. Flint also believed there would be marketing benefits since the three companies produced products sold directly to other businesses. Finally, there was some hope of technological synergism because all three companies were dependent on new inventions. Each could trace its origins to patents issued and entrepreneurial activities begun in the latter half of the 1880s.[11]

The first of these patents was issued in 1885 to Julius E. Pitrat of Gallipolis, Ohio, for a scale equipped with a chart to enable clerks to determine an item's price at the same time it was being weighed.[12] Through the efforts of those who bought his patent, the world's first computing scales were manufactured in Dayton, Ohio, beginning in 1889, and the Computing Scale Company was formed. In 1899 the Moneyweight Scale Company was organized to serve as the selling agent in the United States and Canada. Under Flint's guidance in 1901, the Computing Scale Company of America was incorporated to take over the properties and businesses of the Computing Scale Company, the Moneyweight Scale Company, and the Detroit Automatic Scale Company.

The second corporate entity to be merged with Hollerith's company began operations in September 1889 when the Bundy Manufacturing Company was incorporated through the efforts of Harlow E. Bundy. Its product was a time clock invented by his brother, Willard L. Bundy, a jeweler of Auburn, New York. Willard Bundy's patent on time clocks had been issued in 1888.[13] To use the Bundy device, each workman was given his own key bearing his number. To check in or out, he inserted his key in the mechanism and gave it a quarter-turn. This action printed his number and the time on a roll of paper that became the plant time record.

In 1896 Harlow Bundy persuaded George W. Fairchild, a self-made businessman and publisher of a small-town newspaper in upstate New York, to become a substantial stockholder and active participant in the affairs of the Bundy Manufacturing Company. Three years later, the Bundy company acquired the Standard Time Stamp Company. Then followed a series of structural changes that by 1907 had created the International Time Recording Company as it was when the three-way merger was proposed. The restructuring had included acquisition of the Willard and Frick Manufacturing Company in 1900, the Chicago Time Register Company in 1901, and the Dey Time Register Company in 1907. The Willard and Frick company manufactured the world's first card time-recorder, and Dey Time Register Company manufactured a popular dial time recorder that did not require each worker to be issued a key. These products were based on patents issued in 1894 and 1888, respectively.[14]

Hollerith's patents and business formed the third component of Flint's proposed three-way merger. Eventually all parties agreed to the plan, and in June 1911 the Computing-Tabulating-Recording Company (CTR) was incorporated. Its name was derived from the three companies whose businesses were merged: the *Comput-*

ing Scale Company, the *Tabulating* Machine Company, and the International Time *Recording* Company. The value Flint ascribed to CTR was $17.5 million, only $1 million of which was based on tangible assets.[15]

Reaping the Rewards

The price set for the stock of the Tabulating Machine Company was $2.3 million. Hollerith received just over half. In those days majority stockholders often negotiated more for their own shares than was subsequently received by others, but Hollerith insisted that all stockholders receive the same amount per share. Among those benefiting from Hollerith's fairness was Eugene A. Ford, an engineer and inventor who had helped Hollerith implement some of his designs and who later played a key role in the merged organization. To Hollerith he wrote: "Please accept my thanks for procuring me the same price for my stock as for your own. I have been wondering how much more you could have gotten for yours if you had let the minority make its own deal, and also how many men there are who would have acted as you did."[16]

After the deal was consummated, Hollerith took advantage of his new freedom and wealth to build a home for his family in Georgetown and to establish a small farm in Virginia. But he was not yet prepared to give up his involvement with the Tabulating Machine Company. He negotiated a contract to work for the company as a consulting engineer for ten years at the large salary, for the time, of $20,000 per year. The contract stipulated that Hollerith "shall not be subject to the orders of any officer or other person connected with the Company and shall be allowed to perform his services in such manner and at such place as [he] may decide." In return Hollerith agreed "to devote his best energies to the development" of new product features, to "assign to the Company all inventions and improvements . . . without further expense to the Company," and to refrain from engineering in "any business competing with business of the Company."[17]

The chairman of the board of the new company was George Fairchild, who had played an important role in the series of mergers that had created the International Time Recording Company and now had created the Computing-Tabulating-Recording Company. A member of the U.S. Congress since 1906, Fairchild was not expected to take an active part in the business.[18] The first president was an associate of Flint who served only one month to get the company started. Fairchild reluctantly took over as acting president until April 1912 when Frank N. Kondolf, formerly chief operating officer of the International Time Recording Company, was chosen.

In May 1914 Thomas J. Watson was hired as general manager of CTR, becoming president in March 1915. Nine years later, in February 1924, Watson changed the name of the company to International Business Machines Corporation, a name that had grown in favor following its adoption in 1917 by CTR's Canadian subsidiary.[19]

Watson had the greatest interest in the products of the Tabulating Machine Company, which he had observed in operation long before he was approached to manage CTR. Products of the Computing Scales Company interested him the least, and under his leadership this part of the business failed to prosper. In 1935 the scales business was sold to the Hobart Manufacturing Company in exchange for shares of Hobart stock. Much to Watson's chagrin, the scales business almost immediately began making money after it was sold.[20]

Although the time equipment business was reasonably profitable, it became an ever smaller segment of the company's business and was finally sold to the Simplex Time Recorder Company in October 1958.[21] Long before then the product line initiated by Hollerith dominated all other sources of IBM's revenue combined. Thus the two businesses that were merged with Hollerith's in 1911 can be viewed primarily as catalysts for a process that provided the Tabulating Machine Company with financial backing and experienced management at a critical time.[22]

It is traditional in IBM to honor Watson by equating the founding of the company with his arrival as general manager of CTR.[23] From a historical perspective, however, the founding of IBM might better be dated to the founding of Hollerith's business. Although other candidates for the "founding event" exist, winning the contract in late 1889 to process data from the upcoming census literally put Hollerith in business.

3

Watson: A Man with a Mission

"I only want a gentleman's salary and a part of the profits when I am able to make the company a success," Watson told the directors of the Computing-Tabulating-Recording Company (CTR) when queried about the compensation he would expect if hired as general manager. Asked why he had left the National Cash Register Company (NCR), Watson responded, "Because Mr. Patterson asked for my resignation." These straightforward answers, combined with Watson's outstanding record as a salesman and manager, satisfied the directors, and they hired him as general manager of CTR beginning in May 1914.[1]

Being dismissed by the idiosyncratic John H. Patterson of NCR was in some ways a tribute. Patterson had a reputation for firing those who had risen far enough to challenge his authority. In spite of his forced departure from NCR, Watson never complained or lost his respect for the man about whom he would later say, "Nearly everything I know about building a business comes from Mr. Patterson." The father of modern salesmanship, as Patterson has been dubbed, made his salesmen memorize standardized sales pitches, motivated them at emotionally charged meetings, and set challenging goals.[2]

Patterson had created arguably the best sales organization of the time, but from him and NCR there was far more than salesmanship to learn about business. In the mid-1880s the company had begun to establish a vertically integrated structure in which all facets of its business were centrally managed. At that time manufacturers of office equipment typically sold their products through independent sales agents. Remunerated primarily by commissions on sales, these agents generally had little incentive or capability to provide advertising and technical support for salesmen or credit and other services for customers. Manufacturers were also likely to contract out much of the manufacturing

Figure 3.1. Thomas J. Watson

Watson is shown (top) in his office soon after he was appointed general manager of the CTR in 1914. He was photographed as president (bottom, left) in 1920 with board chairman George W. Fairchild. Thousands of copies of the photo-portrait of IBM president Watson, created by Yousuf Karsh in 1948 (bottom, right), were displayed throughout company buildings for many years.

process and to hire independent engineers to devise improved products. By placing all of these functions under one central management, NCR was able to expand its size substantially and dominate its industry. Vertical integration could provide increased profits because of the interdependence of mass production and mass marketing and the economies of scale available in both.

The successful methods of NCR and of the Remington Typewriter Company (which had created an integrated business structure at about the same time) were soon followed by others in the office equipment business. A. B. Dick & Company, developers of the mimeograph machine, and the Burroughs Adding Machine Company had integrated business structures by about 1900.[3] Thomas J. Watson, starting with CTR in 1914, was to become one of the more successful followers. At NCR he had learned just about everything there was to know about structuring and managing such an enterprise.

A Gifted Salesman

Even before he joined NCR in the Buffalo office in 1895, Watson had demonstrated his natural gift for salesmanship. He had come to Buffalo to seek his fortune after spending two years selling organs, pianos, and sewing machines for a local businessman in the small town of Painted Post, about twenty miles west of Elmira, New York. At his father's insistence, he had also enhanced his basic eighth-grade education by studying business and accounting for a year at the Miller School of Commerce in Elmira. Watson had lived and worked in and around Painted Post all his young life. He regarded it as his hometown although he was born in the nearby village of East Campbell on 17 February 1874. His father, a man of Scottish and Irish descent who derived only a modest living from farming and lumbering, was ambitious for his son and urged him to leave Painted Post to improve his prospects.[4]

His first job in Buffalo was much like his job in Painted Post, selling sewing machines off the back of a wagon. One day he followed the custom of many of his cronies by going into a roadside saloon to celebrate a sale. He had too much to drink, and when the bar closed, he found that his horse, buggy, and merchandise had been stolen. His employer dismissed him and dunned him for the lost property. Word got around, and Watson had difficulty finding another job.[5] He was reduced to sleeping on a pile of sponges in the basement of a drugstore and having the only suit he owned cleaned and pressed while he waited in a back room.

His next job was as an assistant to a man selling shares of stock in the building and loan business. Investors paid for the stock in installments, and the salesmen kept the first installment as commission. Watson made so much money that he decided to go into business for himself by opening a butcher shop. His employer in the stock business turned out to be a cheat, who abruptly left town with the result that Watson was forced to sell his butcher shop to pay his debts.[6]

Desperate for a job, young Watson talked his way into one at the Buffalo office of the National Cash Register Company. It was October 1895; he was twenty-one years old. If he could prove himself, he was told, he would become a regular salesman. At NCR he studied the *Primer,* reportedly the first fully structured sales pitch in America and the brainchild of the company's president, John Patterson. Watson learned how to use the canned pitch, how to vary it, and how to combine it with his own natural enthusiasm and sincerity. He succeeded so well that, at age twenty-five, he was put in charge of sales for the Rochester office. The sales performance of the office, as measured against its sales quota, was near the bottom for NCR offices when he took over. Three months later, it ranked near the top.

In October 1903 he was summoned to the head office in Dayton, Ohio, to meet the fabled president of NCR. Watson was now twenty-nine years old. The proposition Patterson put before him was challenging. The company had produced such reliable, long-lasting machines that the market for secondhand machines was encroaching seriously on the market for new ones. Having a near monopoly of the market for new machines, Patterson had decided to expand the company's revenues by entering the secondhand market. The proposed business was to be financed by NCR, but this relationship was to be kept secret.

Watson was put in charge of the entire operation. As described by his biographers: "It was rough business. Watson established stores next to successful competitors, copied their successes, discarded their failures, hired their salesmen, undersold them, eventually put them out of business. His experiences during those years Watson always regretted and rarely mentioned."[7] Not until three years after the surreptitious activity was begun did NCR publicly announce that Thomas J. Watson was in charge of its secondhand business. One and a half years later, in August 1908, Watson was named assistant sales manager, and the secondhand business was gradually absorbed into the regular sales offices. In effect he was the sales manager because the nominal sales manager was spending most of his time on other company matters. In May 1910 Watson became sales manager in name as well as fact.

During his years in the secondhand business, Watson learned a great deal about the inner workings of cash registers. Far more than in selling new equipment, secondhand equipment sales depended on a salesman's ability to explain how the mechanical structure of the machine provided superior function and durability to those machines he was selling against. Because of this knowledge, Patterson asked Watson to attend meetings of his Future Demands Department, which had responsibility for anticipating future customer demands and translating them into products. Through this activity Watson gained considerable experience and responsibility for NCR's engineering effort at the same time that he was head of the sales organization. In Patterson's view it was more important for the people responsible for engineering to know what was needed than it was to know how to achieve it.[8]

A Lesson in Antitrust Law

The manner of entering and running the secondhand business is indicative of the vigor with which Patterson sought to preserve the cash register business for the only company he believed deserved to have it. It is perhaps not surprising therefore that in February 1912 Patterson and twenty-nine other officials of NCR, *National Cash Register Company* including Watson, were indicted and brought to trial in the Federal Court for the Southern District of Ohio for violation of the Sherman Antitrust Act. According to the prosecuting attorneys, the company had used "unfair, oppressive, tortuous, illegal, and unlawful means" to create its near monopoly of the industry. Reportedly NCR had over 90 percent of the cash register business. One year after the suit was filed, the jury reached its verdict. All but one of the defendants was guilty. Watson, Patterson, and one other were given the maximum sentence of one year in jail.[9]

While the case was being appealed, tensions mounted between Watson and Patterson. The latter perceived that Watson was overstepping his bounds and "developing quite a following among the rank and file."[10] Patterson made Watson's position increasingly unpleasant until November 1913 when it was announced that Watson had resigned.[11] About to turn forty, out of work, and his first child due in less than two months, Watson was nevertheless very selective about his next position. He turned down several opportunities before accepting the position of general manager of CTR.[12]

Through his experiences he had become a man with a mission. He wanted to be an entrepreneur like Patterson with a share in his company's profits. Having been fired by Patterson, he wanted his business to become even bigger than NCR. Although Watson was convinced that the criminal charges against him would not stand, he was remorseful about many of his past actions. He vowed that he would never again take any business action that could be considered illegal or unfair—nor would he allow any of his associates to do so. And alcohol, which had cost him his first job in Buffalo, would never be permitted at business functions for which he was responsible.[13]

The impact on Watson of his youthful incident with alcohol and the later criminal indictment can be inferred from the strong stand he took on related issues throughout the rest of his life. Almost more revealing is the fact that his older son was unaware of either of these events until long after he had joined IBM. Even then, he learned about them from others.[14] The events apparently had been too painful for his father to discuss.

In March 1915 the appeals court set aside the earlier verdict and granted a new trial. The decision indicated the government would not be able to make the criminal charges stick. Watson was jubilant. "This decision," he told a close friend, "has lifted a great load off my shoulders."[15] Two days later the CTR board of directors elected him president of the company. When Watson had been hired as general manager in May of the previous year, the board had chosen not to appoint him president until he could clear his name of criminal charges. With this accomplished, he could now assert his leadership with full confidence.[16]

The Man

The Tabulating Machine Company had been the means by which Hollerith proved the worth of his inventions. Its growth had been driven by him, and it was also limited by him. Developing associates and working through them did not come easily for Hollerith.

By contrast Watson was not trained as an engineer and had little interest in personally creating new devices or ideas. His gift was in recognizing and adopting the good ideas of others. He measured his own success by that of the organization he led, and he knew that its success was dependent on the contribution of others.

To drive home the importance of individual contributions, Watson liked to stand before an easel at company meetings and write a series of job titles, one under the other: "general manager," "sales manager," "salesman," "factory manager," "factory man," "office manager," and "office man." Then crossing out all but the word "man" in each line, he would observe, "We have different ideas, and different work, but when you come right down to it, there is just one thing we have to deal with throughout the whole organization—that is the MAN."

To be successful, Watson believed men had to be well trained and well dressed, and feel good about themselves and their company. "You cannot be a success in any business without believing that it is the greatest business in the world," he asserted. To help create an image of success, he instituted an unwritten but rigidly adhered-to dress code, held evangelical sales meetings, and had songs written about the company's products, its employees, and himself. He commissioned one of these songs to be written to the stirring music of Hammerstein and Romberg's "Stouthearted Men." The result was "Ever Onward," IBM's best-known company song. "We're big, but bigger we will be," asserted the song that hailed the corporation, its pioneers, and "that "man of men," our sterling president."[17]

Gifted as he was in dealing with people, Watson could not achieve a good working relationship with Hollerith. Part of the problem lay in the personal loss Hollerith suffered when he sold his business. His sense of loss was intensified by Watson's very different management style. Antagonism was particularly generated by Watson's emphasis on increasing the sales effort. Hollerith believed his equipment should sell itself. In his view the company should select from among potential customers only those that would clearly benefit from the equipment and then work closely with each customer to assure satisfaction.[18] "It is a good deal better never to have the machines put in than to have them fail," he emphasized to Watson.[19]

During the years after he sold his business, but prior to Watson's arrival, Hollerith had vigorously pursued his inventive activities on behalf of the company. His most important patent filed during these years described a means for controlling tabulator operations automatically using information stored in punched cards. First used by the company's engineers in coupling a printing mechanism with a tabulator, this patent represents an important first step in the evolution of punched-card systems that performed complex information processing tasks and mathematical computations long before the advent of electronic computers.[20]

Whether primarily for reasons of health or out of personal animosity, Hollerith substantially reduced his involvement with the company soon after Watson arrived. Indeed Watson got so little cooperation that he came to believe Hollerith wanted CTR to fail so he could buy back his business at a low price.[21] Despite Hollerith's failure to help him, Watson was outwardly generous in his praise of the man who had founded the company. When Hollerith died of heart failure in November 1929 at age sixty-nine, Watson was prominent among those who attended the funeral.[22]

As Watson advanced in age and his business grew, he became increasingly committed to the methods that had brought him success. He was more aloof and less flexible. Regrettably it is his later years that are best remembered, in part because no effort was made to document his life until quite late. His official biography, *The Lengthening Shadow,* was not published until more than five years after he died.

Watson is of course destined to be remembered for dress code, company songs, alcohol prohibitions, paternalistic policies, authoritarian practices, and salesmanship. But as we shall learn in later chapters, he should be remembered even more for his ability to adapt to changing times. He successfully modified the company's products and business methods to prosper during two world wars and the Great Depression. He pioneered professional careers for women in his industry. And contrary to popular mythology, he showed remarkable ingenuity and flexibility as he readied the company for its post–World War II thrust into electronic computers.

4
Building an Engineering Organization

It is ironic that Watson, who was hired for his sales and management skills, found his greatest early challenge at CTR to be in product development. This is not surprising, however, since the company consisted of three quasi-independent, high-technology business units. To help meet the challenge, he asked the Guaranty Trust Company for a $40,000 loan, $25,000 of which was to be allocated to engineering studies. Three years earlier the Guaranty Trust had provided $4 million to get CTR underway, but now it refused to extend additional money until business improved. In what Watson regarded as one of his finest sales pitches, he responded, "Balance sheets reveal the past; this loan is for the future." The Guaranty Trust reversed its decision and provided the money.[1]

Competition Emerges

The genesis of Watson's problems in product development lay in the lengthy battle between Hollerith and the Bureau of the Census. Out of this battle had arisen the first competition in punched-card equipment in the person of James Powers. According to the records of the bureau, Powers was born in 1871 in Odessa, Russia, and was educated at the Technical School of Odessa. He subsequently helped fashion scientific instruments for the university's physical laboratory before emigrating to the United States in 1889. For eighteen years prior to joining the Census Bureau Machine Shop in July 1907, he held positions in which he worked on improvements to a variety of devices including cash registers, typewriters, and adding machines, and he had acquired a number of patents. Although North hired him primarily to work on the sorting machine, Powers made contributions in many areas. Resigning from the Bureau of the Census in April 1911, he established the Powers Accounting Machine Company to compete directly with Hollerith.[2]

Powers's primary competitive edge was equipment that provided a printed output. This made unnecessary the manual recording of numbers registered in dials or counters. Printed output is a feature Hollerith had apparently considered for many years, but failed to patent or implement. The reasons for this are not clear. As early as 1899, for example, he had written to his patent attorney proposing a printing feature on a tabulator.[3] A few years after the CTR merger, however, he is reported to have "severely reprimanded" an engineer for attempting to attach a printer to a tabulator.[4] Hollerith's decision not to pursue the printer attachment and Powers's decision to do so at the Bureau of the Census gave Powers the competitive edge he needed to challenge the better established Tabulating Machine Company.

By the time Watson took over CTR, Powers had developed a range of machines for the commercial market. There were three basic units: the "slide punch" based on a punch he had developed earlier at the Bureau of the Census; a horizontal sorter that was functionally identical to Hollerith's vertical sorter except that the operator did not have to stoop or stretch to remove cards; and the all-important printing tabulator. The Powers equipment used the same size cards but had a mechanical rather than an electrical hole-sensing method. Mechanical sensing was apparently faster and more reliable as originally implemented. Powers also devised a very attractive feature: linkages between machine parts were localized in an interchangeable mechanical "connection box" that made it possible to change rapidly from one application to another.[5]

Changing applications on the original Hollerith tabulators had required tedious rewiring—changing the interconnections among electrical terminals. This burden was alleviated at first by the provision of a plugboard whereby terminals were more easily connected by plugwires. Later, to compete more effectively with Powers, the plugboard was moved from the back of the machine to a more accessible position at the front. The third improvement was the introduction of the so-called automatic plugboard that could be quickly removed from or inserted into the machine with its plugwires in place. A customer might well have dozens of these prewired plugboards stored on a rack, ready for use. Although the plugboards were more than a foot on a side, and somewhat cumbersome to handle, they were easier to insert and remove than were the mechanical connection boxes of Powers. Plugboards also had the advantage that they could be wired or rewired by the customer.[6]

Initially Watson lacked technical resources with which to meet the challenge from Powers. Under Hollerith's direction the design and construction of machines had been carried out on a contract basis by several firms. The Western Electric and Pratt and Whitney companies had supplied most of the equipment used in the 1890 census. After that Hollerith sought out smaller companies with specialized skills, such as the Taft-Peirce Company of Pawtucket, Rhode Island, and the Frederick Hart Manufacturing Company in Poughkeepsie, New York. The Taft-Peirce Company had devised improved tabulating and sorting machines, card-feeding mechanisms, and accumulators; the Poughkeepsie-based company had primarily contributed designs for keyboard-controlled punches.[7]

Even had Watson chosen to continue working with vendors, he could not count on Hollerith to provide the necessary technical guidance and coordination. After selling his business in 1911, Hollerith increasingly found contentment with his family and his farm in Virginia. A year before Watson was hired in May 1914, Hollerith had resigned from the CTR board to avoid the inconvenience of traveling to New York. Three months after Watson's arrival, Hollerith asked to resign from the Tabulating Machine Company's board as well. Watson reacted quickly. Citing the value of Hollerith's advice, Watson urged him to remain. But Hollerith was not deterred from his decision. His resignation was accepted with regret in December 1914.[8]

Hiring Creative Engineers

Aside from Hollerith, the only senior technical person in the Tabulating Machine Company was Eugene A. Ford. His laboratory was located in Uxbridge, Massachusetts, not far from the Taft-Peirce plant with which he had worked closely in the past. Within months of taking over CTR, Watson prevailed on Ford to move to New York City to establish the company's first full-time engineering department for the development of tabulating machines. Bringing three draftsmen with him, Ford soon had activities underway in a huge room Watson rented on the top floor of a twelve-story building on Sixth Avenue and Thirty-first Street. A model shop was equipped and ten model makers were hired.[9]

Watson selected this location near Pennsylvania Station, hoping that Hollerith would upon occasion make the train trip from Washington to contribute to the development effort—but this hope was never realized.

The first senior technical person to be recruited by Ford was Clair D. Lake, a machine designer employed to design automobiles in the Locomobile plant in Bridgeport, Connecticut. Lake had no previous experience with tabulating or time-recording equipment when he joined CTR in 1915. His only education past eighth grade was in manual training, but he was highly recommended to Ford by a mutual friend. In the following year Watson hired Fred M. Carroll, an experienced inventor who had previously worked on cash register designs for NCR.

Watson assigned both Lake and Carroll the task of independently developing printing tabulators that would meet the competition from Powers. Carroll pursued the design of a wholly new tabulating machine that incorporated a novel rotary printer, whereas Lake chose to build a more conventional printer that could be attached to an existing tabulator. Watson selected Lake's design to keep development and manufacturing costs low and to reduce the time required to develop the product. Even so the printing tabulator was not introduced until 1920, partly because of difficulty in achieving good reliability and partly because of the interruption of World War I. The military establishment was apparently well satisfied with nonprinting tabulators because of their simplicity and reliability.

During 1917 Watson took two significant actions concerning the company's research and development activities. First, he closed the Sixth Avenue shop in New York City and moved Lake and Carroll with seven others to Endicott, New York, to facilitate interaction with the Time Recording Division's development group. This move also brought tabulating equipment development and manufacturing together in Endicott, where manufacturing had been consolidated soon after CTR was established.[10] Second, he hired James W. Bryce as supervising engineer of the Time Recording Division in Endicott.[11]

Of all the people hired by Watson, none contributed more to the company's success than James Bryce. Born in New York City in September 1880 to parents of Scottish descent, he has been described as taciturn, humble, dry-humored, and intensely proud of his ancestry. He attended the city's public schools, but spent much of his spare time with his brother performing physics and

Figure 4.1. James W. Bryce
Shown addressing an IBM group in 1939, James Bryce had been hired by
Watson as supervising engineer of the Time Recording Division in 1917 and
appointed chief engineer of the CTR in 1922. He served as Watson's primary technical adviser until shortly before his death in 1949. By then he had
acquired more than five hundred U.S. and foreign patents.

chemistry experiments at home. When he was eighteen, he contracted to do the bell wiring in a new apartment house.

Bryce studied mechanical engineering at the College of the City of New York, but he quit after three years to take a position as a draftsman and designer. In another three years he joined an inventor with whom he designed what may have been the first front-wheel-drive automobile. In 1904 he was employed by Harry W. Goss, an engineer and patent designer, with whom he soon formed a partnership. One year later the firm of Goss and Bryce contracted to assign all patent rights for its time recording developments to the International Time Recording Company—an activity that later brought Bryce to the attention of Watson who determined to hire him.

Shortly after he joined CTR, Bryce initiated development of a self-regulating electric time system. It was a major factor in the wide adoption of the company's master-clock-controlled time system. In an era of direct-current electric power systems—before 60-cycle alternating current was used to keep clocks synchronized—this innovative system caused clocks and time recorders throughout a building to register the same time. Prominently mounted in the rooms and halls of major buildings, IBM clocks became a familiar sight throughout the country. Bryce also helped develop a system that printed a record of when and by whom any door in a building was locked or unlocked. The system additionally recorded the time and the initials of watchmen as they punched into each station while making their rounds.

Bryce was also interested in card-controlled machines, and he filed for a number of patents on combinations of time recording and punched-card equipment. Even before joining CTR, he had invented a punched-hole-reading, elapsed-time recording machine. Through interferences declared by the U.S. Patent Office between his patents and those of Hollerith and an independent inventor, J. Royden Peirce, Bryce became familiar with Peirce's patents and urged Watson to acquire rights to them.[12]

Obtaining Crucial Patents

The importance of patents had been brought forcibly to Watson's attention several times before he hired Bryce. Within three months of joining CTR, for example, he had been approached by representatives of the Powers Accounting Machine Company requesting a licensing agreement to use some of Hollerith's patents. "You are in a position to put us in business or put us out of business," Watson recalled them saying.[13]

Watson, who was still facing criminal antitrust charges for his activities at NCR, chose to set terms that would permit Powers to remain in business. Nevertheless the licensing fees were substantial. Set at 25 percent of gross machine rentals and 18 percent of gross receipts from the sale of cards, these fees contributed to the Powers company going into receivership during the recession of 1921–1922. The licensing agreement also limited Powers to the use of Hollerith's patents for mechanical equipment only, thus forestalling any shift by Powers from mechanical implementations to electrical ones that proved to be far more versatile in the long run.[14]

The CTR's upper hand in patents was severely challenged in January 1917 when an interference was declared by the U.S. Patent Office between patent applications of Hollerith and Powers. The issue involved the use of "stop cards" versus "automatic group control." Hollerith had designed his tabulators to stop whenever a stop card was encountered. These were inserted between card groups in the deck of cards by the operator to indicate when selected subtotals should be copied and accumulators reset to zero.

An alternative means, known as automatic group control, had also been conceived by Hollerith and described in a patent application filed in March 1914, two months before Watson joined CTR. As described in the patent, two sets of wire brushes were used to read each card twice. The second reading of a card occurred at the same time as the first reading of the subsequent card. Whenever the identification fields in adjacent cards failed to match, the tabulator paused to signal that the last card of a group had been read.[15] Believing the stop-card method was too cumbersome for a printing tabulator, Clair Lake proposed to use Hollerith's automatic-control feature. The plan was jeopardized, however, by an interference with a related patent of Powers.

Just as the interference proceedings appeared to be going in Hollerith's favor, the patent examiner called attention to patents of C. A. Tripp and J. R. Peirce that also had claims pertaining to automatic control. Interferences with these patents were declared in 1921, and the process of determining who had priority in the claims progressed simultaneously with efforts to negotiate a settlement. It was a serious situation. According to the patent attorneys retained by CTR, "It took only a glance at the claims in the

Tripp application . . . to reach the conclusion that whoever prevailed in these interferences would be in possession of the claims which would completely dominate the automatic printing tabulator field."[16]

In 1921 a license agreement with royalty payments based on usage was negotiated with Tripp. Problems in accurately determining royalties led to a new contract in January 1924 in which CTR made a one-time payment of $212,500 plus some interest. The payment corresponded to nearly 10 percent of the company's earnings or 2 percent of its gross revenue for the year. Early in 1922 Watson also obtained Peirce's patents. Simultaneously he acquired the laboratory and services of Peirce and some of his co-workers, who by then had been designing and building innovative punched-card machines for the Metropolitan Life Insurance Company. The price paid for Peirce's company and patents was $261,000—even more than was paid to Tripp.[17]

Also in 1922 the patent licensing agreement with the Powers company was modified to reduce by half the fees paid to CTR. This helped return the Powers company to profitability. Small royalties were better for CTR than none at all, which would have resulted had the Powers company been forced out of business. Furthermore some competition was necessary to forestall antitrust action by the government.[18]

A Drop in Revenue

The decline in patent licensing revenue and the huge price paid for Peirce's company and patents came at a difficult time for the company. Its three major divisions had projected continuing revenue increases for 1921, but a severe (albeit brief) economic recession had caused a downturn in all three. Particularly hard hit was the Computing Scales Division. Having projected a doubling of sales during the year, its revenues actually dropped by half. A strike at the Dayton plant was a contributing cause, but severe competition and a less-than-satisfactory product line were primary factors. The only part of the business whose revenues held reasonably steady was tabulating machines, largely because its equipment was rented rather than sold. To offset the huge companywide drop in revenue from $14 million to $9 million, Watson cut his own salary and that of other executives by 10 percent. A similar reduction was made in the wages of factory workers. Many employees were laid off, particularly those with the greatest skills and highest wages.[19]

Seeking ways to avoid such a catastrophe in the future, Watson made particular note of the stabilizing benefits of renting rather than selling products. He had always believed tabulating equipment had the greatest potential, but his emphasis on that part of the business was now reaffirmed. To overcome problems of poor engineering in the scales product line and to assure top-quality engineering in tabulating equipment, he appointed James Bryce of the Time Recording Division as chief engineer for all of CTR. Watson also created a Future Demands Committee (discussed in chapter 9) to provide Bryce with guidance in the selection of product development objectives.

Managing Engineers

"Mr. James W. Bryce has been appointed Chief Engineer of the Computing-Tabulating-Recording Company," Watson advised his key executives in June 1922. "He will be in direct control of all phases of engineering and development work, reporting directly to me." Bryce's office was moved from Endicott to CTR headquarters at 50 Broad Street, New York City. At the same time, the Peirce facilities at 37 East 25th Street were enlarged to provide for expanded engineering activity and a research laboratory. Carroll and his group were moved from Endicott into these facilities so that he could work more closely with Peirce and Bryce on longer-term research and development projects.[20] Convinced that Hollerith's equipment provided the best basis for company growth, Watson spent more than ten times as much on high-risk development projects for it as he did for the other product lines.[21]

Appointment of a chief engineer was intended to supplement, rather than replace, Watson's own involvement with the company's inventors. Excerpts of correspondence between Ford and Watson in February 1924 typify that involvement. After assuring Watson that all product requirements were "perfectly satisfied" by his horizontal sorter, Ford asserted: "I have been perfecting the mechanical details relating to the new rotary card feeding, the brush shifting mechanism, and the electrical connections and now have it practically just as I should like to see it manufactured. . . . I think applications for patents covering the new sorter and alternative constructions should be immediately made. The fundamental principle of direct sorting, without the intervention of tripping mechanism that all sorters have heretofore used, can be applied to a mechanical machine, and the Powers Company should be forestalled along these lines. I should like the pleasure of demonstrating the new sorter to you and your Board of Directors."[22]

Watson responded promptly: "It is a great pleasure for me to congratulate you upon the outcome of your experiments and developments in the building of a horizontal sorter. I have heard something of it from Mr. Bryce and am looking forward with a great deal of anticipation to seeing the exhibition of the completed models now under construction. . . . The matter of patenting your new machine has been taken care of as the work progressed and you may be sure that it will all be covered."[23]

Some two years later, after the sorter had demonstrated its utility and reliability in customer use, Ford received a $5,000 bonus from the board of directors. In expressing his appreciation to Watson, he wrote: "I thank you still more and am made happier by the kind expression of approval of my efforts in behalf of our Company. At times I have felt discouraged when my recommendations have been turned down and opinions overruled but now that I know you have not looked upon my defects as evidence of incompetence, I shall strive harder to justify your good opinion."[24]

Ford's reference to "opinions overruled" and his intent to strive harder to justify Watson's good opinion give a glimpse of the authority and influence Watson wielded. As a manager of the Endicott laboratory observed some years later, "Many, many times, the engineers have been reasonably satisfied with a machine development, and it is only because of the dissatisfaction and the criticism which Mr. Watson has presented that the engineers renewed their efforts and came out with something far superior."[25]

Handwritten letters to Watson expressing appreciation for salary increases or other favors were common. "I am proud to have some part in this important work and glad to remember that this could not have been, had you not some confidence in my fitness for the job," Carroll wrote Watson in April 1925. "It is a matter of pride and ambition with me to make this undertaking a great success, but it would not be human to under-value that part of your kind letter which refers to an increase in salary. Coming as it does at a time when our expenses will be much greater, Mrs. Carroll and I doubly appreciate the favor."[26]

So it was that Watson involved himself in the company's product development activities from his first days at CTR. He hired and promoted key technical people and took an interest in their assignments. As an experienced salesman, he was sensitive to the needs of customers, and he became adept at expressing these needs in terms inventors understood. Often he gave similar tasks to two or three inventors and then selected the result he liked best.

Internal Competition

The first of a long series of such competitive assignments was the previously mentioned one given to Lake and Carroll to develop a printing tabulator.[27] After Watson selected Lake's approach, Carroll turned his attention to other challenges. His most important contribution was the rotary punched-card press. More commonly called the Carroll Press, it manufactured punched cards in one continuous process involving printing, cutting, and corner trimming. One young engineer recalls how impressive it was "for those of us who were working for sixteen dollars a week to see a machine printing a thousand cards a minute that sold for a dollar a thousand. In sixteen minutes it made as much money for the corporation as I earned in a week."[28]

In the case of the printing tabulator, Lake and Carroll were aware of each other's assignment, but competing assignments were frequently made by Watson without informing the inventors. This policy increased the pressure to excel and the sense of urgency. Inventors never knew whether Watson might have assigned the same product objectives to someone else. Intense rivalry developed, and inventors jealously guarded their work. Those who worked for an inventor were careful not to be seen talking with people from other departments lest they be suspected of passing secrets. Aside from the obvious disadvantage of not sharing ideas internally, the system of internal competition seems to have served the company well.

Egged on by Watson, an intense rivalry developed between Lake's group in Endicott and Peirce's group in New York City, following the latter's move in 1927 to an expanded facility on Varick Street. Both groups were attempting to respond to Watson's request for a way to store more information on each punched card. This was required by many accounting applications. A forty-five-column card was then standard for IBM products, as well as for those of Remington Rand, Inc., which had acquired the Powers Accounting Machine Company in 1927.

Working in secrecy from each other, the Lake and Peirce groups took different approaches. To enhance the value of their solutions, each group intended to provide additional functions. Peirce was placing his emphasis on developing machines capable of handling alphabetic as well as numeric information. His approach was to increase storage capacity by using a multihole, combinational code for each character, while continuing to use the standard card format with hole locations arranged in an array of 45 columns by 10 rows. With the proposed multihole (binary) code, 6 adjacent hole locations in each column provided 64 possible combinations—enough to store any one of the 26 letters of the alphabet or of the 10 digits and have 28 additional combinations for special symbols. The remaining 4 locations for punched holes per column provided 16 possible combinations. This was 6 more than needed to store any one of the 10 digits. By changing from the standard code, in which the location of 1 hole per column provided storage for only 1 digit, Peirce's group had provided the ability to store twice as many characters, half of which could be alphanumeric.

Meanwhile Lake's group was taking a more standard engineering approach. His group chose to use smaller holes so that each card could accommodate more columns. This required the development of new punches and readers, but (unlike Peirce's approach) the coding of the holes and the underlying numerical operations were not affected.

After reviewing the competitive designs, Bryce selected Lake's simpler approach. It could be implemented more rapidly and would retain the long-established machine timing methods for reading numbers on cards. Another factor in the decision was possible patent interference with Powers relating to the multihole card punch. To Peirce's utter amazement and disappointment, the ability to store alphabetic information in addition to numbers was judged to have little value to customers.[29]

The IBM Card

In 1928 IBM introduced the Lake-developed 80-column card system. It offered nearly twice the storage capacity per card as the previous system. The most obvious feature of the new card was its rectangular holes. Rectangular instead of round holes had been

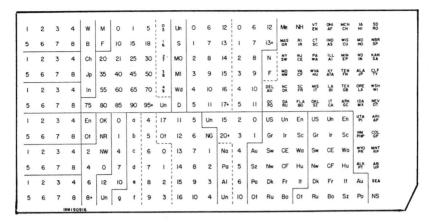

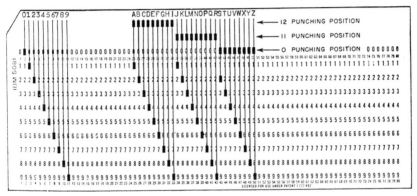

Figure 4.2. Punched Cards

Top: The punched card used in the U.S. Census of 1900 (unlike the card used in 1890) had information printed on the surface to facilitate visual reading of punched information. In both cases punched holes were round, and the card size was $6^5/_8$ inches by $3^1/_4$ inches. Bottom: The IBM 80-column card, with rectangular-shaped holes, replaced the then-standard 45-column cards in 1928. By the early 1930s, the two additional rows shown here were introduced to facilitate alphabetic coding. Holes in these rows were punched using the 11th and 12th punching positions of a 12-key punch. The 80-column card and the earlier 45-column card were both $7^3/_8$ inches by $3^1/_4$ inches.

proposed by Lake and Bryce because they provided better space utilization for wire brushes that electrically detected the holes. Cards with rectangular holes also proved to be mechanically stronger, making the new design patentable. Perhaps most important, the rectangular holes gave punched cards a distinctive appearance that could not be copied by others. Recognizing the marketing value of this patented appearance, Watson began promoting it as the "IBM card." It was not *just* a punched card anymore.

To help customers convert their records to the new 80-column cards, a "reproducer" was offered that punched 80-column cards from existing decks of 45-column cards. The value of being able to reproduce cards became evident through this experience, and reproducers to copy from either 80-column or 45-column cards became standard products.[30]

Remington Rand countered IBM's 80-column card with a 90-column card in 1930. Like the IBM card it was the same size and shape as the 45-column card previously used by both companies. The 90-column card used a multihole code that was similar, but not identical, to the one Peirce had proposed at IBM. Physically the card had 45 columns and 12 rows, but it was logically divided into two sets of 45 columns of 6 rows each, one set above the other. Using one-to-two holes to code a digit and two-to-three holes to code an alphabetic character, there were more than enough possible combinations to provide for full alphanumeric coding. Remington Rand's 90-column card thus provided the customer with more storage capacity for numbers than the IBM card, and it offered alphabetic capability as well.[31]

Peirce's engineering group at the IBM Varick Street laboratory had already switched its efforts from developing its own multi-hole-coded card to finding an acceptable way to provide alphabetic capability on the newly introduced 80-column card. But when Remington Rand's announcement was made, the pressure from IBM's sales organization for alphabetic capability was so great that the company hastily introduced a machine from Peirce's group that provided only a subset of the full alphabet. It used two punched holes for each letter, one of which was in one of the two rows above the ten rows used for numbers. Known as the ATB (Alphabetic Tabulating Model B), it was offered to customers beginning in 1931. Model C, offered soon after, provided full alphanumeric capability. A hole punched in one of the top three rows (X, Y, and zero) combined with a hole in one of the bottom nine rows was used to designate alphabetic characters. This form of alphanumeric coding survived to the end of the punched-card era.[32]

The 80-column and 90-column cards were roughly equivalent in their capabilities. The slightly greater storage capacity of the 90-column card was offset by the greater ease with which operators could visually read information on the 80-column card—especially the numbers, which were still represented by a single hole for each digit. Using today's terminology, one would say the IBM card was more user friendly.

Competition between these cards was influenced by a new factor: they were incompatible. No longer could cards prepared by an IBM system be processed by a Remington Rand system, or vice versa. Not only did each installation now have to chose one system or the other, but communication between two installations was possible only if they used the same system. The benefits of compatibility among installations within an organization—and even among those in different organizations—led inexorably to greater domination of the market by IBM.

Only a major improvement in machine function and reliability and in the service provided by Remington Rand could have saved it from continued decline. But this did not happen: IBM maintained its generally superior reputation for product reliability and service; in advanced function, where its conservatively structured product line was often behind the competition, IBM pushed forward with numerous product enhancements.

Significant among new products introduced in 1928 was the Type IV tabulator. Designed by Clair Lake's group, it offered direct subtraction capability. Negative numbers were identified by a hole punched in an appropriate column in row 11 of the 80-column card. When this so-called "X-punch" was detected, the tabulator carried out the indicated subtraction automatically. Previously negative numbers, called "credits," and positive ones, called "debits," were punched in separate card fields and separately summed by the tabulator. The sums were then manually subtracted. (Alternatively, the complements of negative numbers were manually determined and then key-punched in the same field as the positive numbers so as to achieve subtraction through addition of the complements.)

The company's first product to perform multiplication, the Type 600 multiplying punch, was added to the line in 1931. Based on pioneering work of Bryce and others, it could take two factors from a single punched card, multiply them, and punch the result into a blank field of the same card. Two years later it was superseded by the Type 601 electric multiplier that, among other improvements, could perform "cross footing," a term used by bookkeepers for summing a table of numbers by row rather than by column.[33]

5

Responding to the Great Depression

The largest ever one-day drop in New York stock market prices occurred on 24 October 1929, a day that became known as Black Thursday. Following years of unbridled speculation and business excesses, the drop triggered—but was not the root cause of—the most serious business recession ever experienced in the United States. By 1932 one-third of the labor force was unemployed, and the value of shares on the New York Stock Exchange had dropped to about one-tenth of the peak value in 1929.

The depression was disastrous for most businesses. The revenues of NCR, for example, dropped from $58 million in 1929 to $16 million in 1932.[1] The impact was less severe for IBM because of increased marketing efforts and because its equipment was rented rather than sold. Unless returned, equipment on rental continued to provide revenue. The company's revenues dropped from $18 million in 1929 to $17 million in 1932—less than 10 percent (appendix A).

Taking advantage of the relatively strong financial condition of IBM during the depression, Watson consolidated its market position and strengthened its technical capabilities. Numerous product improvements were made, culminating in the Type 285 Numeric Printing Tabulator introduced in 1933 and the Type 405 Alphabetic Accounting Machine introduced in 1934. Both could tabulate 150 cards per minute or tabulate and print from cards at 80 cards per minute. The more expensive Type 405 provided greater versatility in its control features and could print alphabetic as well as numeric information. It was the company's flagship product until after World War II.[2] Even more important than specific product improvements, however, was the strengthening of research, manufacturing, and employee education activities.

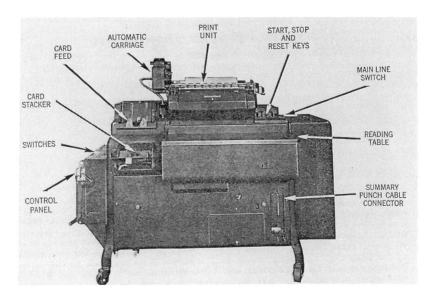

Figure 5.1. Type 405 Alphabetic Accounting Machine
Top: Arrows point to key functional elements of the Type 405 Alphabetic Accounting Machine, which offered considerable functional versatility through its removable (automatic) plugboard, labeled "control panel." Bottom: Pictured here when it was introduced in 1934 is the Type 405 Alphabetic Accounting Machine (center) with a key punch (left) and a horizontal sorter (right).

Coupling Engineering to Manufacturing

In 1933 Watson moved most of IBM's research and engineering activities to Endicott, New York, where the company's primary manufacturing operations were already located. A new building known as the North Street Laboratory was constructed to house the engineering activities of the manufacturing and product development organizations. Close proximity of these two activities permitted the sharing of common resources and was expected to facilitate the transfer of new products from development to manufacturing.

The reception room of the North Street Laboratory was known as the Hall of Products. It shared the first floor with the manufacturing engineering department. On the next two floors, seven of Watson's highest-ranking inventors—among them Carroll, Ford, and Lake—occupied seven of the eight corner offices. Each had his own cadre of draftsmen and technical support people. Elsewhere in the building was a variety of common service functions, such as the blueprint room, machine shop, tool crib, electrical shop, industrial design shop, and the patent attorney's office. A technical library was located in the penthouse. Unusual for the time, the building was fully air-conditioned.[3]

At the ground-breaking ceremony for the new laboratory in July 1932, Watson asserted, "We have realized from experience that the future of our business largely depends on the efforts, brain, and ability of our engineering department. . . . That is why today we are breaking ground for this new building, which will be devoted entirely to research and engineering work."[4]

Even with manufacturing and engineering consolidated in Endicott, the number of IBM employees was small compared to that of the major employer in town, the Endicott-Johnson Shoe Company, whose employees were mostly first- or second-generation immigrants from eastern Europe. To help them adapt to the new country, their employer provided them with company housing, a hospital, a cafeteria, and a variety of recreational facilities. Initially IBM provided none of these, but its employees enjoyed the use of facilities offered to city residents for a small fee by the shoe company.[5]

Convinced that the economy would soon recover, Watson produced tabulating equipment and stored it in warehouses during the depression. It was a policy that won him high marks among

Figure 5.2. North Street Laboratory
Ground was broken for the North Street Laboratory (top) in July 1932. One
year later it was occupied by about 250 employees, who carried out most of
IBM's research and development activities. Photographed in 1937 is the electrical laboratory (bottom) within the North Street Laboratory.

his employees. Broader vindication of his policy came with passage of the Social Security Act in 1935. The record-keeping and data-processing requirements of this law created a huge demand for punched-card equipment. Many businesses as well as government agencies installed equipment just to carry out tasks mandated by the law, and IBM machines built and stored during the depression were brought out to help satisfy the needs.[6] All Social Security checks for unemployed and retired workers were printed on IBM punched cards and mailed to the recipients. For those who received these benefit checks, the punched-card era had happily arrived. For IBM the depression was over.

Emphasis on Education

In May 1932 Watson formally established an Education Department to manage the company's many educational activities for employees and customers. An IBM schoolhouse devoted entirely to the education of employees was built in Endicott in 1933. For the first time, the company offered a formal engineering education program. The first three engineers were graduated in 1934.[7]

Previously, newly hired technical employees had been assigned to experienced engineers for a training period that was similar to an apprenticeship. Several of the company's leading inventors got their start this way, but as the company grew and its products became more diverse and complex, the apprenticeship form of training was judged to be inadequate for engineers. As the new program evolved, the curriculum included electrical and mechanical operating principles of the company's machines, temporary assignments in development laboratories or factories, field assignments to service machines in use, experience in sales applications, and lectures by the company's inventors describing the underlying concepts of the machines. The entire course lasted from six to fifteen months.[8]

The expanded education program for the manufacturing organization offered courses in blueprint reading, shop mathematics, measuring instruments and techniques, modern milling and grinding practice, and electricity. Courses were typically scheduled one evening a week, after work, and lasted for thirty-six weeks. Taking courses was not mandatory. Nevertheless in 1937, approximately half of the 3,200 factory employees in Endicott were enrolled in fifty-two classes, studying twenty-four subjects.

Particularly important was the tool-making apprentice program. By the mid-1930s the company was hiring approximately fifteen candidates for this program each year, selecting high school graduates with high scholastic standings in such subjects as drawing, shop practice, science, and mathematics. "Character, personality and evidences of ambition" were all used as the basis for selection. A new apprentice was placed on probation for six months. If he demonstrated good mechanical ability, he was enrolled in the course. The first year and a half was spent in the apprentice machine shop learning the fundamentals of tool making. This training was supplemented by practical experience in the heat-treatment department, the physical laboratory, and the machine repair department. The apprentice typically spent another year and a half in the tool room before completing his apprenticeship.

There was also a "supervisor's school" that all factory supervisors and executives were required to attend. It was divided into three sections to serve the special needs of executives, supervisors, and foremen from the various departments. Deeply committed to growth from within the company, Watson believed there was "no saturation point in education."[9]

In 1935 Watson established an educational program that must have surprised even him. It began with a speech he presented before the Institute of Women's Professional Relations. When members of the audience said they were distressed by the limited opportunities for women, Watson expressed surprise. "I would be willing to hire twenty women immediately," he advised them. Inundated by applications, Watson challenged his personnel department to create an appropriate program.

The resulting plan was to train women in the operation of IBM equipment so they could assist salesmen in analyzing the needs of potential customers and in developing a system solution. Once equipment was installed, they were to teach the customer's employees how to use it. The first group of trainees consisted of twenty-five women selected from top colleges such as Bryn Mawr, Cornell, Smith, and Wellesley. It was an emotional and intellectually stimulating experience. They were presented with flowers and attended a welcoming formal dinner dance hosted by Mr. and Mrs. Watson during the first week. More social events followed, and the young women delighted in writing and singing their own songs about IBM and its leaders. The women were trained at the

Figure 5.3. The First Systems Service Women
This graduation photograph, taken in front of the IBM schoolhouse in Endicott in 1935, shows the twenty-five college graduates who attended the first class for systems service women together with their three instructors.

Endicott schoolhouse for three months, taking essentially the same classes as the seventy-five male sales trainees. After graduation they were designated systems service women and assigned to branch offices.

The program provided IBM with an invaluable source of talent for its expanding business, helped it meet wartime challenges when many men were drafted into military service, and pioneered the entry of women into professional positions in the data processing industry. In November 1943 Ruth M. Leach, a graduate of this program, became IBM's first female corporate vice president. She had been manager of the Systems Service Department since 1942.

In describing the opportunity to women in the first training class, one vice president told them it represented a new concept in business, "which emanated from the powerful brain and keen intellect of our president, Mr. Watson." Another said, "I am sure that you will meet this responsibility with energy and intelligence and that you will make an outstanding success of this work, thereby opening to a large number of college women, who will follow you, an important and productive field of endeavor which did not exist before."[10]

Research for Current Needs

Research in Endicott emphasized immediate product needs rather than fundamental studies. The electrical laboratory, for example, was primarily responsible for approving electrical features of products under development. It also carried out research for product improvements and devised test equipment. Considerable research had been done in evaluating insulated wires to find those most suited for electrical interconnections and for winding electromagnets. Similarly the metallurgy and chemical laboratories carried out studies of materials and chemicals planned for use in new products or in production equipment and processes, and research in manufacturing engineering was limited to improving processes such as drilling, grinding, turning, hobbing, die pressing, welding, heat-treating, plating, and assembly.[11]

The paper-testing laboratory was particularly important. Its job was to analyze incoming paper stock—or proposed new types of stock—for the lucrative business of manufacturing and selling punched cards. By 1937 IBM had 32 Carroll presses at work in Endicott printing, cutting, and stacking 5 to 10 million standard and special cards each day. The company derived less than 10 percent of its revenues, but more than 20 percent of its profits, from the sale of these cards.

A significant problem was caused by occasional inclusions of conductive material, such as carbon specks, in the card stock. A conducting inclusion in a card could produce a false reading by permitting electricity to flow through it almost as if the inclusion were a punched hole. A unique testing method had been devised to find these inclusions. As the roll of paper stock entered the machine that cut it into strips, the sheet was passed between a metal plate and wire brushes to which 220 volts was applied. Whenever a conductive inclusion permitted current to pass through the paper, a thyratron-tube detector activated an automatic ink dauber that stained the defective portion of the paper with a red dye. After the paper strips were run through the Carroll presses, visual inspection was used to locate and reject cards with red ink on the back sides.[12]

Quality and Production Control

"Believing that tools are the basis of quality, IBM provides for tooling as it plans its products," a trade publication reported in the mid-1930s. Although IBM was not entirely alone in this approach, the publication indicated that its emphasis and methods were well ahead of those in most other companies.[13] Each part of a new product was subjected to a manufacturability analysis during the design stage to determine if changes were needed in order "to conform to modern shop methods." The product itself was subsequently "scrutinized by a tool analyzer" to determine what manufacturing tooling was required. Prior to the depression IBM purchased most of its manufacturing tools, but by the mid-1930s it was making all of its special tooling. Only standard tools such as drills, reamers, and milling cutters were purchased.[14]

To ensure that quality was built into each product, an independent quality control department was established under the factory comptroller. Its task was to inspect purchased parts and materials, tools, subassemblies, and completed products to be sure they met specifications. Emphasis was placed on inspection of individual parts and subassemblies so as to avoid the large scrap and rework costs associated with problems discovered after final assembly. Although the statistical models now used for sample testing were not then available, inspectors were authorized to move simple parts directly to stock whenever "experience on periodical checks" indicated inspection of each item was not warranted.

The factory comptroller was also assigned responsibility for the operation of a pioneering production planning and control system that made extensive use of accounting and tabulating equipment. The system included inventory control and used machine-written records and requisitions for all except raw material and tool requisitions. Punched cards followed and recorded the progress of all parts and subassemblies from inventory to final product.[15]

Standard punched-card equipment was used as much as possible, not only to support manufacturing operations but also to provide an applications research facility. New uses for punched-card equipment in manufacturing could be tested and improved before they were made available to customers. It was a fertile source of new ideas because IBM's production control problems were particularly challenging. Each inventor had his own machine shop and had little incentive to use parts already in production. Once Watson was shown a working model, he was likely to want it placed in production so rapidly that there was insufficient time to convert parts specified by the inventor to standard ones.

Each new product thus added many new parts to be cataloged and tracked during production and throughout the product's life. Parts ranged from mundane items such as studs, clips, screws, and bolts to complex assemblies. Subsequent model releases might employ a higher percentage of standard parts, but each release added yet more parts to the overall inventory because of functional enhancements and because both models now had to be serviced in the field. The policy of renting machines and continually refurbishing and upgrading old machines exacerbated the problem.[16]

Methods Research

During the years following the stock market crash of 1929, IBM salesmen needed considerable ingenuity just to forestall the return of rented equipment. A return to clerical processing of data was attractive for many customers in an economy in which wage rates and business volumes were decreasing. Nevertheless Watson continued hiring salesmen. Many people of superior quality were available. New salesmen were schooled in the company's products and their applications before being sent into the field. Among those hired in 1929 was Felix J. Wesley. After graduating from sales school the following year, he went to work in New York City as an assistant salesman. His primary duty was to render technical assistance to salesmen whose accounts were in jeopardy. "Only through technical tricks was it possible to hold a customer's rental at a minimum figure and yet accomplish the required tasks."[17]

In September 1931 Wesley obtained a transfer to the newly formed Methods Research Department at corporate headquarters. The department's mission was to formalize the acquisition and centralization of data-processing "methods know-how" and to investigate field requirements for new applications and new machines. Such know-how had been created in a relatively unstructured manner over the years by individual salesmen, servicemen, and customers. Often there were several different solutions for similar problems. Electrical interconnections and plugboard control of IBM's punched-card machines provided greater versatility than was available in Remington Rand's mechanically controlled machines and encouraged innovative data-processing methods.

Ingenious plugboard wiring arrangements were distributed by the new department in a news bulletin called "Pointers." Most of the wiring schemes were devised and contributed by branch office people, but some were provided directly by customers. By collecting and disseminating methods information and introducing some standardization, the new department contributed significantly to IBM's success in retaining its customers during the depression.[18]

By 1937 the growing business resulting from President Franklin D. Roosevelt's New Deal programs encouraged even greater emphasis on standardization and dissemination of know-how. To accommodate this, the Methods Research Department was enlarged. Its name was changed to Commercial Research and Wesley became its manager. The department was also given responsibility for specifying desired machine functions, consulting with engineers about new products, and writing product manuals.[19]

These responsibilities were not easy to fulfill, in part because IBM's key engineers reported directly to Watson who thought of them as *his* inventors. If a disagreement between an inventor and Commercial Research was escalated to Watson, he was likely to side with the inventor. Indeed there were cases in which an inventor complained to Watson that members of the Commercial Research Department were "bothering" him, and Watson showed his support by ordering them to "let up" on the inventor.[20] Nevertheless under Wesley's guidance, the department got many of its ideas introduced in new products.[21]

Some ideas that originated in the department were quite sophisticated. Others were seemingly obvious, simple to implement, and yet critical to product success—as in the case of a change made to collators used in the Social Security system. The collator was used to merge new information, punched in cards of a "secondary" deck, into a "primary" deck of similar but older information. Both decks were arranged in order of Social Security number. The collator was designed to compare the Social Security number of the next card in the secondary deck with the next card in the primary deck to determine when a card from the secondary deck should be inserted. Unfortunately, if a Social Security number was incorrectly punched, the information on the new card would be assigned to the wrong person forever. There was no provision for avoiding such an error by checking that the names on the two cards matched.

The comparing mechanism that made the high, low, or equal comparison needed for collating was designed to read only numeric information. What was needed, ideally, was another comparing mechanism capable of handling alphabetic characters, which were stored in punched cards by two holes (rather than one hole) per column—one hole always being either in the 0's row or in one of the two rows above that. The methods expert assigned to the problem quickly recognized that a comparison of two names based solely on the holes punched in the rows normally used for numbers would be almost as good as a comparison that used holes in the upper rows as well. This insight, combined with knowledge of the mechanical and electrical operation of the collator, permitted the methods expert to correct the problem with only minor changes.[22]

Hiring Good People

Crucial to the success of Wesley's department was the quality of its people. Their backgrounds were diverse, encompassing sales, service, engineering, manufacturing, and ex-customers. "Together this group worries each problem as a dog a bone—or better perhaps, as a lot of dogs, one bone. Sometimes the ex-salesman is vanquished by the engineer, and sometimes the ex-customer-service man has a bit of an awkward time at the hands of the ex-customer," Wesley asserted. "But eventually all differences are resolved in a joint opinion, which is the survival of the fittest opinions. This, briefly, is the department's working platform—on every problem that comes within its range, to seek out all the evidence, to examine all possible opinions and to recommend, among them, the fittest for survival." This description of his department's activity was one Wesley thought "might pass muster as a definition of 'research.'"[23]

Among those who joined Wesley's department in 1938 was Stephen W. Dunwell. His uncle, who had developed the moving assembly line for mass production of automobiles at the Ford Motor Company, served as his father figure and mentor following the death of his own father when he was ten.[24] Dunwell's IBM career began in Endicott in 1933 on a work-study program with

Antioch College. During this program he alternately spent ten weeks at college and ten weeks at work.

His first assignment was as an errand boy, obtaining missing parts for the production groups in the plant. His second assignment was in production control, and his third in wiring machines in final assembly. So adept was he at the third task that he was given "special engineering" work in which he began with a fully assembled and tested machine, partially disassembled it, and then wired in special features. Learning of the young man's talents, a manager from the development laboratory offered him a full-time engineering job. To accept the job, he would have to give up returning to college for his senior year. "I thought on that about ten seconds before saying, 'Yes,'" Steve Dunwell recalls. "A college degree didn't seem so important in those days."[25]

His job in the laboratory was to prepare retrofit kits with instructions for installing new features to machines already in the field. So long as he handled requests promptly, no one cared how he spent his time. "I had access to everything in the laboratory," Dunwell recalls. "I could place an order to do anything and nobody would question it. . . . So I did a certain amount of experimenting." As a result, he was selected to build a variety of special devices, including a calculation control switch proposed by Wallace J. Eckert at Columbia University (see chap. 6).

Having a strong interest in electronics, he was also given the assignment to put together a display for Watson to show how electronic devices were used, or being considered for use, in the company's products. This was 1937. The only uses planned for electronics involved photocell detection of marks or holes in cards, and the only product already using a photocell was the Social Security bill-feed machine. Each time a line entry was made on a ledger card, a hole was punched to indicate that the line had been used. The photocell detected the holes as the ledger card advanced and thus determined when the first unused line had been reached. This product, one proposed product, and several electronic test devices used in production became Dunwell's small display for Watson.[26]

6

Support for Academic Research

Bryce and Watson became aware, during the late 1920s, that the company's equipment was being used increasingly for scientific calculations. Particularly noteworthy was the work of Leslie J. Comrie, a New Zealander, who had studied mathematics and astronomy at Cambridge University and taught college briefly in the United States before joining the Nautical Almanac Office of the Royal Naval College in England in 1926. By 1928 Comrie had begun reporting on the use of Hollerith machines for the construction of mathematical and astronomical tables.[1]

Mathematicians in the United States had also begun to use the equipment to reduce the labor and errors in lengthy computations. A paper published in 1928 by a professor at Iowa State College (now a university), for example, reported on the use of Hollerith equipment for correlating various attributes. He had, for example, correlated the college grades of students to their high school grades, and in another study the "cost per hundred pounds gain in swine as related to season, feeding system, average daily gain, and initial weight."[2]

Educational Testing Studies

In the same year these papers were published, Professor Benjamin D. Wood, head of the Bureau of Collegiate Educational Research at Columbia University, wrote to leaders of ten office machine companies, seeking help in creating an automatic means for scoring and analyzing the results from large-scale testing programs. Some did not respond. Others expressed interest but offered no help. Only Watson showed sufficient interest to meet with Wood.

The appointment was set for one hour. A secretary, assigned to advise Watson when the time was up, was subsequently waved away every hour on the hour. Excited by Wood's enthusiasm and ideas, Watson kept him talking the entire afternoon. Soon after, he appointed Wood an IBM consultant and ordered three truckloads of IBM equipment sent to a location in the basement of Hamilton Hall, where the Columbia University Statistical Bureau began operations in June 1929.[3] Watson donated the equipment because he saw in Wood's request an opportunity to support an important educational activity and, at the same time, to achieve a means for keeping abreast of this new field.

Soon after this equipment was installed, Wood approached Watson with two more requests. The first was for modified tabulating equipment to carry out certain calculations more efficiently. This request was quickly fulfilled when, in December 1929, Watson donated to the Columbia University Statistical Bureau a one-of-a-kind difference tabulator that had been designed for Wood by Bryce and others. It was equipped with ten accumulators of ten digits each that could be operated in the standard mode of conventional tabulators. But by changing the manner in which the plugwires were connected so as to pair accumulators, it was also possible to follow the normal card cycle with a special cycle in which the content of one accumulator was summed into an accumulator with which it was paired. Among the probems devised to test the so-called Columbia Machine was calculating the fifth powers of integers by the method of progressive totaling.[4]

Wood's second request was received by Watson just as enthusiastically as the first, but it turned out to be far more difficult to fulfill. What Wood wanted was an automatic means "to reduce the cost, inconvenience, and errors of scoring objective tests." It was a need of which he had become acutely aware in the spring of 1928 while serving as technical adviser to a study conducted by the Carnegie Foundation for the Advancement of Teaching. During this study 200,000 tests had been administered and graded by hand. Wood joined others in a study of the test scoring problem, finally concluding that "the design and construction of a satisfactory scoring machine could be accomplished, if at all, only with the aid of talented and experienced engineers and with the facilities of a large and well-organized research laboratory." Upon learning of the need, Watson agreed to make the solution of the problem "a major project of the engineering staff and research laboratory" at IBM.

Seven years passed before a satisfactory solution was found. "The record of the succeeding long years of expensive research, of costly models laboriously designed, built, and abandoned, of high hopes and discouraging disappointments, would make an interesting story in itself," Benjamin Wood recalled, "but the essential point of that story is that Mr. Watson and his engineers carried on in the face of repeated disappointments and mounting costs during a major economic depression until the problem was solved in a way that goes far beyond the fondest hopes that any of us entertained when we first appealed to Mr. Watson to undertake the task."[5]

An Innovative Science Teacher

Wood failed to note that Watson would not have been able to provide the solution as soon as he did—or perhaps at all—had it not been for the ingenuity and persistence of Reynold B. Johnson, a former high school science teacher and part-time inventor from Ironwood, Michigan. Johnson had received his bachelor's degree from the University of Minnesota in 1929.

Prior to joining IBM, Johnson had begun work on a similar problem on his own. Noting that many textbooks printed in the 1920s had multiple choice tests in them, he decided to devise a way to grade student answers more easily. He began by creating an answer sheet from which students tore out tabs from the partially perforated paper sheets. The sheets, with the tabs thus removed at points corresponding to the selected answers, were each placed over a board containing many wires that were used to complete electrical circuits and turn on a light wherever a hole appeared at the correct place in the paper. Since each of the lights so energized drew equal current, a meter in the circuit read directly the number of correct answers.

His first model was built with the help of two children who, having been caught stealing a radio from the school, had been assigned by the judge to assist Johnson after school. Johnson next had an improved model built by a firm in Minneapolis. A company that published tests ordered twenty-five of these. The device also received publicity in 1932 through an article written for the local paper by a young woman who was then Johnson's teaching associate and who subsequently became his wife. Her article was picked up by the Associated Press, and thus came to the attention of IBM. The idea was not pursued by the company, however, in part because Watson had already assigned his own inventors the task of building a test scoring machine.

Meanwhile Johnson decided to attempt to detect pencil marks on separate answer sheets using their electrical conductivity. He had learned that pencil marks conducted electricity from the then-common prank of short-circuiting the ignition on automobiles by making a pencil mark down the porous side of the porcelain spark plug insulator. Using the conductivity of pencil marks worked well enough that Johnson revised his equipment and again attempted to sell his invention.

Failing to interest IBM, Remington Rand, or any other company—and being now jobless because of the depression—he and his wife went on the road to sell silk hosiery. When they returned home, they found a message from IBM asking them to come to New York. A model he had shipped to the company had been given to Benjamin Wood at Columbia University for evaluation. Wood's evaluation was positive.

Johnson and his wife were provided $50 per week expenses to stay in New York City during the six weeks in which he helped complete the evaluation. The conclusion of the IBM engineers, which the board of directors endorsed, was that Johnson's invention was incomplete. Among other problems, pencil marks appeared to be unreliable conductors. Johnson was told that the company would like to see the invention again if it could be made more reliable. When Wood learned of this, he telephoned Watson, who was on vacation, and urged him to reverse the decision.[6] Watson did, and Johnson was hired two days later in September 1934. He was paid $4,000 for his patent and a salary of $4,000 per year.[7]

One year later, after considerable engineering work, the test scoring machine was placed in experimental operation in the IBM school and the public schools in Endicott, New York. Then followed more trial uses as well as an evaluation by the Columbia University Bureau of Collegiate Educational Research. According to these evaluations, the machine could score tests about thirteen times faster than trained clerks and with substantially fewer errors. "I have received a very encouraging letter from Dr. Ben D. Wood, of Columbia, as to the results accomplished by your machine," Watson wrote Johnson in March 1936, "and I wish to take this opportunity to let you know that I am personally very much interested in the work which you are carrying on."[8]

Students using the equipment were provided with soft lead pencils and advised: "Blacken each narrow space between the pair of [vertical] red lines numbered the same as the answers in the test that you consider correct. Make your mark as long as the red lines. Use the special pencil only and move the point up and down firmly two or three times." An important feature of the machine was its ability to determine a student's score based either on the number of correct answers or on the number of correct answers minus the number of wrong answers—or minus any fraction of the number of wrong answers. Lacking digital circuitry, Johnson had implemented this arithmetic function by passing the electric signal from wrong answers through an electric meter in the opposite direction to that from correct answers.[9]

The system was announced for rent as the IBM Type 805 International Test Scoring Machine in 1937. Within five years, rental revenues were approaching $100,000 per year and the sale of supplies for it produced nearly twice that amount. Because this was only about three-tenths of one percent of the company's revenue, the Test Scoring Machine was generally considered to be a minor product. But Watson's primary interest with this product was to help education. In that sense it was very successful. The test scoring method it introduced was widely adopted and is still in use today, albeit with dramatically improved electronic sensing and calculating means.[10]

Johnson subsequently adapted the concept to more conventional and profitable punched-card applications. But his most significant contributions were achieved two decades later when he and his colleagues created the world's first magnetic disk storage devices for computers (see chap. 16).

Automatic Computation

Watson's support of Wood's educational research and statistical bureau at Columbia University attracted many to the field of automatic computation. Particularly important among these was Wallace J. Eckert. With a bachelor's degree from Amherst in 1926, he joined the Columbia University faculty as an assistant in astronomy. After taking courses at Columbia, the University of Chicago, and Yale, he received his doctorate from Yale in 1932.[11] Returning to Columbia, he became deeply involved with the Statistical Bureau, using IBM punched-card equipment to perform mathematical computations in the field of astronomy.

Like Wood before him, Eckert recognized that his computational work could be speeded by specialized equipment. Watson obliged by having his engineers build a Calculation Control

Switch designed by Eckert. Operational in 1936 this switch permitted a dozen different modes of operation of an interconnected system consisting of a Type 601 electric multiplier, a printing tabulator, and a summary punch. In describing the benefits of the control switch, Eckert noted that lengthy punched-card computation processes were normally set up so that one numerical operation could be done on many cards before shifting to the next operation. But in numerical integration, for example, "different arithmetical operations must be done in succession for the first step before proceeding to the next." Solving this type of problem was greatly speeded by the Calculation Control Switch, which permitted the standard electromechanical punched-card equipment to perform a sequence of computation steps between reading in a number and punching out the result. To provide simplicity of construction, cards were moved manually from one unit to another when necessary and the shaft was rotated manually. Nevertheless this cam-sequenced calculator was a pioneering early step toward stored-program digital computers.

As described by Wallace Eckert in his classic book, *Punched Card Methods in Scientific Computation*: "The calculation control switch contains a row of electric contacts each of which is operated by a rotating cam. The cam is a circular fiber disk which is notched at various points around the circumference. A series of about twenty of these disks are attached to a common shaft to form a sort of player piano roll. When this roll is rotated from one position to the next, the various contacts open and close according to the notches in the disks. The circuits from the contacts are used to operate the various control switches on the tabulator and multiplier, and also a number of multicontact relays which effectively change the wiring of the plugboards."[12]

The computational facilities established by Eckert began as part of the Columbia University Statistical Bureau and were later administered as part of the Department of Astronomy. In 1937 these facilities were named the Thomas J. Watson Astronomical Computing Bureau and were made available to other astronomers through the joint sponsorship of the Columbia University, IBM, and the American Astronomical Society.[13]

In the same year that IBM made its equipment widely available to astronomers for mathematical computations, the Monroe Calculating Machine Company rejected the opportunity to design and build an electromechanical supercalculator envisioned by Howard H. Aiken, a graduate student in physics at Harvard University. The purpose of Aiken's proposal was to provide scientists and mathematicians with an innovative sequence calculator capable of a broad range of functions: performing basic arithmetic on positive and negative numbers in any desired sequence; supplying and utilizing a wide variety of transcendental functions (e.g., trigonometric, elliptic, Bessel, probability, etc.); providing for storage of intermediate results; and carrying out a long series of operations without operator intervention.[14]

The person Aiken approached was George C. Chase, the chief engineer of the Monroe Company. A pioneer in the development of key-driven calculating machines, Chase had begun his inventive work more than ten years before joining the company in 1917. In 1932 the Monroe Company was awarded the John Price Wetherill Medal by the Franklin Institute in recognition of its implementation in mechanical desk-top calculators of "the four basic rules of arithmetic: addition, subtraction, multiplication, and division as attained through Mr. Chase's inventions." According to Chase, Aiken's proposal for the construction of an electromechanical machine was quite general and not restricted to any specific type of mechanism. He urged support of the project in spite of the large anticipated costs because he believed the experience of developing such a sophisticated calculator would be invaluable to the company's future.[15]

But top management of the Monroe Calculating Machine Company rejected the proposal. Chase then urged Aiken to contact IBM through an intermediary at the Harvard Business School. Aiken did so, following which he wrote to Bryce in November 1937, saying, "Professor Brown of the Graduate School of Business Administration tells me that he has discussed with you my interest in automatic calculating machinery for use in computing physical problems. If possible I should like to come to New York early next week to call on you and discuss this matter in some detail."[16]

Bryce and Chase had much in common. Both were chief engineers who had joined their companies in 1917, and both had previously been established inventors. Bryce, however, enjoyed greater management support and had no trouble convincing Watson of the merits of the project.

The Mark I Computer

At Bryce's suggestion, Aiken received education in the operation of IBM equipment similar to that given to the company's customers and servicemen.[17] Bryce believed such training was essential. He wanted to be sure that Aiken had some understanding of the capabilities and limitations of the devices available for implementing his ideas. Following this Aiken made his first visit to IBM's Endicott laboratory in February 1938. It was the beginning of a cooperative effort that produced the IBM Automatic Sequence Controlled Calculator (ASCC), which became better known as the Mark I computer, in part because Aiken followed it with Mark II, III, and IV at Harvard. In February 1939 Bryce advised Lake, whom he had put in charge of the project, that Watson had given his approval for building the proposed machine at an estimated cost of $100,000. Its final cost was more than twice that amount.

Aiken spent the summers of 1939 and 1940 in Endicott, but he was unable to spend much time on the project after assuming his duties as a Naval Reserve officer in April 1941. The work of Lake and others in Endicott was also interrupted by higher priority projects of World War II. Nevertheless the Mark I was sufficiently completed in January 1943 to solve practical mathematical problems that required multiplication, division, addition, subtraction, and the computation of logarithms and antilogarithms. In February of the following year, the machine was completed and shipped to Harvard. Men from Lake's department installed it, tested it, and improved its operation for several months prior to its formal presentation to Harvard in August 1944.[18]

The Mark I was 51 feet long, 8 feet high, contained 530 miles of wire, and weighed five tons. It is the largest electromechanical calculator ever built and the first machine able to exploit the ideas proposed one hundred years earlier by the British mathematician and inventor, Charles Babbage.[19] Although Aiken and Bryce were both aware of Babbage's earlier work, it appears to have had minimal influence on their efforts.[20] A key design feature of the Mark I contributed by Aiken was its ability to perform many mathematical operations in a sequence defined by instructions punched in a paper tape. The "paper tape" was made of IBM card stock to provide sufficient width and ruggedness to supply instructions at the required speed. Computation with an accuracy of up to 23 digits was provided by 72 accumulators, each

Figure 6.1.   Mark I and Its Creators
Clair D. Lake (top, center) and Howard H. Aiken (top, right) are pictured
in front of the Mark I, for which they served as chief engineer and chief architect, respectively. Francis E. Hamilton (top, left), who provided daily supervision for the project, later led the development of the IBM 650, which
became the most widely used computer of the 1950s. The Mark I is shown
(bottom) at the IBM North Street Laboratory about ten months before IBM
presented it to Harvard in August 1944. At the right are the typewriters,
card feeds, and card punch. To the left of these are the paper-tape storage
units, then the multiplying-dividing unit and counters used in computing
logarithmic and trigonometric functions, then storage counters, and (at far
left) dial switches.

consisting of 24 electromechanical counter wheels, one of which was used to represent the algebraic sign.

Design and construction of the Mark I was a major engineering feat. Howard Aiken, who initiated the project, specified the functions of the computer such as the algorithms by which complex functions were computed. In today's parlance it would be said that he served as chief architect. Clair Lake, IBM's best hands-on engineer and most prolific inventor after Bryce, served as chief engineer. Numerous inventions, which had been modified or specifically devised for the machine, were incorporated in it. These included improved relays and counters and means for high-speed multiplication and division invented by Bryce, Dickinson, Lake, and others.[21] Bryce, whom Aiken called "a very astute inventor" and "a valuable senior adviser," played both of those roles throughout the project. "If you started down a road that didn't look very practical," Aiken said of Bryce, "he could put his finger on it just about that quick."[22] With Aiken frequently inaccessible because of war-time activities, Bryce found himself making many decisions that otherwise would have been handled by Aiken.

IBM paid the entire cost of building the machine, approximately $200,000, and donated an additional $100,000 to Harvard to cover costs of operation. All patents associated with the project were assigned to IBM. The primary patent for the calculator was filed in 1945 and issued in 1952 with 127 claims. The inventors were listed as Clair D. Lake, Howard H. Aiken, and two associates of Lake.[23]

Watson's support of academic research helped the company establish itself in the new and vital field of automatic computation. It brought corporate leaders in contact with members of the academic community who provided new insights and later helped in the hiring of technical people for the post–World War II thrust into electronics. By 1934 it had already led to the hiring of Rey Johnson, who became one of the most creative research leaders of the post–World War II era. It also attracted Wallace Eckert to the field of automatic computation and paved the way for his decision in 1946 to join IBM to establish the company's first laboratory devoted to automatic computation and pure science.

7

Research for Patents and Devices

Watson frequently intermixed the titles of engineer, scientist, and inventor when referring to his key technical people. Although this may reveal some confusion on his part, it also reflects the fact that each of these terms properly applied to activities of his chief engineer, James Bryce. Not only was Bryce a trained engineer and an accomplished inventor; he had the inquiring mind of a good scientist. He was able to perform the functions of chief scientist and research director at the same time that he served as chief engineer. There was no written job description for Bryce, but the record speaks for itself. As chief engineer he devised products to satisfy customer needs, and he made sure the company had rights to all necessary patents. As chief scientist he was alert to technological advances and scientific discoveries that might affect the company, and he initiated appropriate research projects.

Patents were Bryce's principal concern. If the company did not own critical patents, it had to acquire rights to them or undertake the costly and risky process of engineering around them. Bryce worked closely with Watson to gain the rights to many patents. Purchase of the Peirce company and its patents was the most visible action, but numerous other patents were purchased. Included in the company's early patent portfolio for tabulating equipment, for example, were fifty-nine patents that had been issued during Watson's first ten years with CTR. Only twenty-six of these had been issued to the company's employees. The remaining thirty-three had been purchased from others.[1]

A Prodigious Inventor

Increasing the number of patents created by the company's own inventors was a major thrust of Bryce, who was himself a prodigious inventor. During his first twenty-five years with the company, he acquired U.S. patents at an average rate of nine per year. Over half were improvements to tabulating equipment, one-third to time recording, and many of the remainder related to computing scales.[2] Bryce was honored as one of the ten "greatest living inventors" by the U.S. Patent Office during its centennial celebration in 1936. By the time he died in 1949 at age sixty-eight, he was credited with more than five hundred U.S. and foreign patents. Next to Bryce, the company's major early inventors were Lake, Carroll, and Ford. Peirce places well among these, although many of his inventions were made before he joined CTR.[3] (See appendix B.)

Some of these patents related to inventions used in current products and were a necessary part of product development. Others covered inventions for products not yet conceived and can thus be thought of as resulting from the company's research activities. To stimulate new ideas, Bryce initiated the development of a "universal tabulator" with arithmetic and control features not available in current or planned products. The resulting "Jumbo Machine" was designed, constructed, and subjected to numerous engineering tests in Endicott during the mid-1920s. It was not released as a product because its manufacturing costs were judged to be too high. Many of its capabilities, however, especially its control features, were covered by patents issued to Bryce, Lake, and their associates, and a number of these capabilities appeared in later products.[4]

A particularly significant aspect of Bryce's work was his self-taught knowledge of electrical phenomena and applications. At IBM he continually sought ways to increase the use of electrical devices and to enhance the benefits of electrical control of equipment. The value of this emphasis was not universally recognized, as evidenced by Powers's decision to use mechanical implementations to compete with Hollerith. Even inside IBM, many inventors favored mechanical solutions. Royden Peirce, for example, who was brought into the company in 1922 primarily to obtain his patents, strongly favored mechanical devices and resisted using electromechanical relays in any of his designs until well into the 1930s.[5] Another key inventor who favored mechanical devices was Frederick L. Fuller, whom Watson hired from NCR to develop a key-operated proof machine for use by banks. This highly successful product was strictly mechanical. Having worked on NCR cash registers that used cylindrical tubing (one tube inside another) to control their operation, Fuller always referred to the

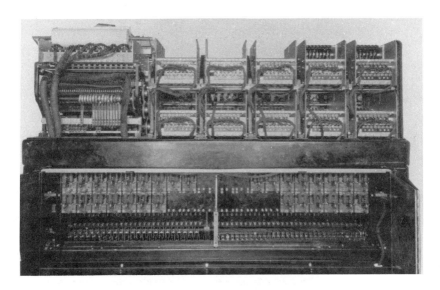

Figure 7.1. Jumbo Machine
Work on the Jumbo Machine, also known as the Universal Tabulator, was initiated by Bryce and carried out by Fred Carroll, Clair Lake, and others beginning about 1925. The back of the machine is shown (top) with printing
mechanism at the upper left. A gate is swung open (bottom) to reveal the internal wiring. A key feature was the use of a large "universal" accumulator
that could be used to store the separate sums resulting from adding numbers in separate fields rather than allocating an individual accumulator to
each field. As was customary at IBM, the Jumbo Machine was not revealed
outside the company even after many of its innovative features had been incorporated in products.

electrical control wiring of IBM machines as the "tubing." He could think of electrical control only in mechanical terms.[6]

In 1926 Bryce formally organized and headed the IBM Patent Department. Its functions were to help inventors obtain patents, to maintain records of the company's patents, and to determine if the company's products were likely to infringe on patents held by others.[7] Preferring to leave administrative matters to others, Bryce had his former assistant appointed head of the department in 1930 so he could "devote his entire time to invention and development work."[8] With Watson's enthusiastic support, Bryce began looking for an assistant to help him create patentable ideas. In 1932 he hired A. Halsey Dickinson. Bryce had become acquainted with Dickinson eleven years earlier in Endicott, quite by chance, when he rented a garage for his car from the young man's father.

Inspired by the well-publicized work of Charles Steinmetz at General Electric, Dickinson had enrolled in the electrical engineering department Steinmetz headed at Union College in Schenectady, New York. There Dickinson obtained his bachelor's degree. Expecting to enter the public utility field, he obtained a master's degree from the Massachusetts Institute of Technology in fuel and gas engineering in 1930. Unable to find work in his chosen field during the depression, he contacted Bryce who hired him. Dickinson was Bryce's first assistant in an activity that became known as the Patent Development Department. Its function was to create and patent new ideas.

Dickinson's job, for several years, was to begin with Bryce's hastily drawn sketches and discussions and create working embodiments that could be patented. "As time went on, I had some of my own ideas," Dickinson recalls, "but it proved to be that most of them had been done before. Nevertheless, Mr. Bryce gave very considerable encouragement." According to Dickinson, Bryce's management style was very informal even after the department grew in size:

Bryce held no meetings. There were no deadlines, and his securing of a certain number of patents had no bearing in his thinking whatsoever. He plowed the field every day. By that I mean he came around to see us or other people. Sometimes he would talk about the business. Sometimes he would talk about personal things that he was doing. If he had an idea or was thinking about something, he would discuss it. Usually he would make a sketch or a drawing, which was sufficient to establish what he was thinking about or what he wanted to do. Since he explained it to me, I would witness it.[9]

Much of the initial work pertained to enhancements for the Type 601 multiplying machine, which had been introduced in 1933. Bryce invented numerous ways to handle more complex arithmetic functions—for example, utilizing three factors rather than just two. Bryce himself placed little emphasis on implementing these inventions in products. His primary purpose was to provide the company with patent protection—that is, freedom to use any idea its engineers might need in future products.

Pioneering in Electronics

Bryce's interests carried him well beyond extensions of existing technologies to entirely new ways of doing things. Even before he joined CTR he had studied electron tube devices to see how they might be applied in practice. At IBM he was continually on the lookout for cost-effective uses for electronics. By 1936 serious inventive activity was underway in Halsey Dickinson's laboratory in Bryce's Patent Development Department. Describing this work to Watson early in 1939, Bryce said, "We have been carrying on an investigation in connection with the development of computing devices which do not employ the usual adding wheels, but instead use electronic effects and employs tubes similar to those used in radio work. Since these devices operate approximately with the speed of light, it will be possible to compute *thousands* of items per second. Patent work only and some few experiments have been done so far, but it appears to look very promising for certain fields of work where extreme speed is either desirable or necessary."[10]

In January 1940 Dickinson made what is believed to be the first patent filing for an electronic computer circuit. The circuit was capable of adding and subtracting multiple-digit numbers and displaying the result on a cathode-ray tube. The next earliest patent filings are believed to be two by NCR workers later that same year and two by RCA workers more than two and a half years later. (See appendix C.) The inventions were quite different from one another even though they all related to electron tube circuits for performing arithmetic. Dickinson, for example, used a sawtooth oscillator whose phase, relative to the controlling clock, indicated the decimal digit stored in that oscillator. The early work at NCR used ten thyratrons (gas-filled tubes) connected in a ring for digit representation. Progressing from addition only, the NCR group had demonstrated subtraction and multiplication by 1942. The RCA effort was apparently directed toward electronic fire control for antiaircraft guns and involved both analog and digital circuits.[11]

Another engineer with early interest in electronics was Ralph L. Palmer, who had joined IBM in January 1932 with a bachelor's degree in electrical engineering from Union College. Like Dickinson before him, Palmer was attracted to electrical engineering and Union College by General Electric's advertising campaign that characterized Steinmetz as the wizard behind its advanced electrical products. Palmer took all the math and physics courses he could. He thought "Maxwell's electromagnetic theory of light was one of the most beautiful things that you could run across." Because of the depression, he was unable to get a job with GE, RCA, or other companies that were known for their work in electronics. So he returned to Union College to begin graduate work.

When IBM offered him a job working on electromechanical equipment, he eagerly accepted. Assigned to the electrical laboratory in Endicott, his primary mission was to support product development work by measuring the electrical characteristics of new devices and by offering suggestions for their improvement. As the first engineer in Endicott with training in electrical and electronic engineering, he taught a number of courses for the other engineers. He also began building specialized test equipment to measure the mechanical and electrical characteristics of relays and other devices. Among these was an early oscilloscope built to display device characteristics on a cathode-ray tube. The necessary electronic components were not available in Endicott, so he purchased them at radio supply stores in New York City during a business trip to IBM's headquarters. The managers in Endicott had so little understanding of the value of an oscilloscope that Palmer had to use his own money to pay for the components. When they saw what an oscilloscope could do, however, their attitudes changed. In 1937 Palmer was promoted to supervisor of the electrical laboratory.[12]

At Bryce's urging, Palmer undertook numerous small research projects in such areas as photodetection of printed spots on cards and in the storage of information in magnetic media on cards, tapes, and drums. The type of research Bryce encouraged was tolerated rather than supported in Endicott. "There was a tremendous gap between that kind of experimental work in the laboratory and the product," Palmer recalled. By and large IBM engineers believed in achieving product design objectives in the most conservative manner possible.[13]

Building Electronic Calculators

By early 1941 Palmer had become sufficiently enthusiastic about the possibilities of using vacuum tube circuits for high-speed counters that he assigned the task of building one to Byron E. Phelps, a member of his department. Phelps had received his electrical engineering degree from Union College in 1935, just three years after Palmer. The immediate stimulus for Palmer's suggestion was a 1939 article on counters published in the periodical *Electronics* by a professor at the University of Illinois. The counters made use of bistable vacuum tube circuits similar to ones proposed two decades earlier. Originally called "triggers," bistable vacuum tube circuits were soon more commonly known as "flip-flops."[14]

Because flip-flops have only two stable states, usually described as "on" or "off," their initial use in counters was to represent binary numbers, in which each digit is either a 0 or a 1 rather than ranging from 0 to 9. These binary counters, with one flip-flop per binary digit, found growing favor for scientific applications, for example, in radiation particle counters in which each particle caused an electrical pulse that advanced the counter by one. Binary arithmetic was little known outside academic and scientific communities, however, and was completely foreign to accounting practice. What Phelps needed was a circuit with ten stable states to replace the mechanical counting wheel in which each of ten rotational positions was used to represent one of the ten decimal digits.

The most obvious way to replace a decimal counting wheel with flip-flops was to use ten flip-flops arranged in a ring. Only one of the ten was "on" at one time, and they were connected so that an input pulse turned the "on" flip-flop "off" and the next one in the ring "on." This simplistic approach was selected a year or so later by the designers of the ENIAC, the world's first large-scale, programmed, electronic computer.[15]

Wishing to make his design more economical for a commercial product, Phelps devised a flip-flop circuit using only one vacuum tube (a twin triode), and he sought ways to represent the decimal digits 0 through 9 with fewer than ten flip-flops. He believed this must be possible because in binary notation 8 digits can be represented by only three flip-flops, and 16 digits by four. In December 1941 he hit upon a method of interconnecting five tubes so that a sequence of nine pulses caused four of the interconnected tubes to progress from the 0-state to the 9-state, but the 10-state was blocked by the fifth tube so that the tenth pulse caused the first four tubes to return to the 0-state. Simultaneously, it generated a carry pulse that could be transmitted to the set of tubes representing the next higher order digit. Although Phelps didn't think of it in those terms at the time, he had invented the subsequently much used "binary-coded decimal" representation.[16] He had also devised an electronic circuit for representing decimal numbers that required half as many vacuum tubes as the circuit subsequently designed for ENIAC.

He and Palmer began planning for a complete electronic multiplier based on the new circuit. With the help of one technician, construction began before the end of 1941. Almost immediately, Phelps recalls, "there appeared to be a commercial demand for a "cross-footing" keypunch—that is, a keypunch that could add or subtract two or more numbers as they were being punched into a tabulating card, and automatically punch the result in another field of the same card. Such a cross-footing punch, using modified binary counters identical to those in the multiplier and combined to form a 10-position accumulator, was built at the same time as the multiplier and actually finished first." Completed in March 1942, the unit's test results were good enough that a second cross-footing unit was completed with improved components intended to meet formal product test requirements.

The multiplier, which was larger and more complex, was completed by the end of the year. It was capable of multiplying two 6-digit numbers and placing the product in a 12-digit accumulator. Numbers read from a card could be multiplied and the product punched in the same card at speeds greater than needed by the fastest card-handling equipment. By December 1942 the electronic multiplier routinely executed five hundred random multiplications without error. The multiplication process consisted of repetitive additions of the number in the multiplicand register into the product accumulator.[17]

Because of Palmer's departure for the navy early in 1943 and Watson's decision that company resources were to be devoted to

Figure 7.2. Electronic Arithmetic Circuits
Top: Decimal digit counter built in the IBM Endicott laboratory near the end of 1941. Only $4\frac{1}{2}$ tubes were needed to store one decimal digit; two digits could be stored in this 9-tube unit. The small box of ten neon bulbs is shown plugged into a test socket to reveal which of ten digits was stored in the back row of tubes. Bottom: The electronic multiplier pictured here with a card reader-punch in December 1942 was able to read two numbers from a card, multiply them together electronically, and punch the resultant product into the same card at a rate of 50 cards per minute. These electronic circuits were the basis of circuits used in the IBM Type 603 Electronic Multiplier, the first commercial product to offer electronic arithmetic capability.

the war effort, the electronic computing circuits developed in the Endicott laboratory were not considered for use in products until near the end of World War II. They were then used in the company's first electronic product as discussed in chapter 10.

Contacting Outside Researchers

Bryce's primary research thrust was to increase the number of patents generated from within the company. He recognized, however, that many crucial ideas and patents would always be created by others, especially in areas new to the business. Accordingly he and other top technical leaders were continually on the alert for new developments.

It was in this context that the Endicott laboratory manager wrote to John W. Atanasoff in May 1942 concerning Atanasoff's effort to develop an electronic computing machine. "When your development work has proceeded to a point where you feel that it is proper for representatives of our Company to look over your machine, we would appreciate an opportunity to do so," the laboratory manager wrote. "Naturally, we do not wish to accept any confidential disclosures."[18] The Endicott laboratory manager had apparently learned of this project earlier that year when Atanasoff requested electrical contact brushes from IBM.

More than four years earlier Atanasoff had become interested in devising an electronic means for solving mathematical equations encountered in his research work. As a professor at Iowa State College (later Iowa State University), he had very limited financial or technical resources. He was, however, able to obtain the help of a graduate student, Clifford E. Berry, to carry out some preliminary circuit design studies. To reduce the complexity of their vacuum tube circuits, they elected to use binary arithmetic. For Atanasoff this was an easy decision. A book given to him by his mother had introduced him to number systems in bases other than ten during his childhood.

By December 1939 Atanasoff and Berry had enough confidence in their results to begin constructing a special-purpose electronic computer. A grant of $650 from the school in 1940 left only $200 for materials after paying Berry the modest stipend of $450. Significant progress was made in 1941 when a $5,000 grant was received. The electronic computing device was still not fully operational in 1942 when Atanasoff and Berry left for wartime assignments. Like the first of the two IBM electronic arithmetic units completed in 1942, the Atanasoff-Berry computer was designed only for addition and subtraction because that was all the application required. Its arithmetic unit contained about 300 vacuum tubes. Approximately the same number were used for system control and regeneration of information stored capacitively on two rotating drums, each of which could hold up to 30 numbers of 50 bits each.[19]

No response was received by IBM to its inquiry, presumably because of the departure of Atanasoff and Berry to their wartime assignments. Thus one can only speculate as to what type of cooperative effort, if any, might have resulted. Furthermore, their pioneering electronic computing machine was never fully completed, bringing it perilously close to having no impact whatsoever on future developments. It was saved from this fate only because Atanasoff showed John W. Mauchly the partially completed computer and a written description of it in June 1941.

Fourteen months later at the Moore School of the University of Pennsylvania, Mauchly proposed building what became the ENIAC. Exactly what Mauchly learned from his discussions with Atanasoff has been a matter of dispute, but there can be little doubt that these discussions helped Mauchly formulate his belief that an operational electronic computer could be built. For a time he even considered constructing an Atanasoff-type computer at the Moore School. Gradually his plans changed, however, and ENIAC was dramatically larger, faster, and quite different in design from the Atanasoff-Berry computer.[20]

8

World War II Activities

The decade of the 1930s was satisfying for Thomas Watson. He had strengthened the company's R&D activities and its product line during the early depression years, and he had watched these efforts bear fruit as IBM's data processing equipment became essential administrative tools for governmental programs. Revenues, which had stagnated in the $17 to $19 million range during the first half of the decade, doubled to $38 million during the second half after passage of the Social Security Act in 1935. The number of employees followed a similar pattern, changing little during the first half and then nearly doubling to 11,315 by the end of the 1930s. (See appendix A.) The company's leadership over its nearest rival, Remington Rand, had increased from eight- to tenfold when measured in number of units shipped.[1] President of IBM since 1915, Watson was gaining ever more recognition as a successful businessman and civic leader.

Like many others he believed Hitler would stop short of a major war once his initial goals were achieved. It seemed self-evident that far more could be accomplished through peace than through war. Coining the phrase "world peace through world trade," Watson vigorously promoted the concept as president of the International Chamber of Commerce, a post to which he was elected in 1937. He changed his view, however, following Hitler's invasion of Poland in September 1939 and the entry of France and Great Britain into the war. Soon Watson was devoting his efforts to winning the war as fervently as he had been to maintaining the peace.[2]

Organizing for War

Watson placed all IBM facilities at the disposal of the government in July 1940, just ten months after the National Emergency Proclamation found IBM to be a potential supplier of war matériel. Manufacturing space was expanded with new facilities in Endicott and Poughkeepsie, New York, in Washington, D.C., and in California. To operate these plants, the number of manufacturing employees was increased from 4,712 in 1940 to a peak of 12,238 in 1943.

The largest new facility was in Poughkeepsie, where the company previously had no facilities at all. A new IBM subsidiary, the Munitions Manufacturing Corporation, was created in March 1941. Frederick H. M. Hart, of IBM's longtime supplier, the Frederick Hart Manufacturing Company of Poughkeepsie, was elected president. That April the new subsidiary purchased 215 acres of property adjacent to the Hudson River from R. U. Delapenha and Company. On the property were two small buildings previously used in processing specialty foods. Just two months after the December 1941 bombing of Pearl Harbor brought the United States into World War II, a new 140,000-square-foot manufacturing facility had been completed; over 250 people had been hired; manufacturing tools had been installed; and the first product, a 20-millimeter aircraft cannon, began coming off the assembly lines.[3]

By the end of the war, thirty-two different ordnance items had been mass-produced at IBM's manufacturing sites. These included aircraft and naval fire-control instruments, 90-millimeter antiaircraft gun directors and prediction units, Browning automatic rifles, 30-caliber carbines, supercharger impellers, and bombsights.[4] Not wanting to profit from wartime production, Watson took the unusual step of freezing his own compensation at the 1939 level. He also voluntarily limited corporate profits on munitions to less than 1.5 percent, setting aside that amount as a special fund for the benefit of widows and for the education of children of employees killed in service. Watson was proud of the wartime record of IBM. It never missed a delivery date and never had parts rejected because of poor quality.[5]

Immediately after the United States entered the war, Watson instructed his senior engineers and inventors to devote their entire effort to wartime needs. Normal engineering duties were to be handled by their subordinates, who were also to be assigned to wartime projects whenever possible. At that time approximately 350 of IBM's 10,000 domestic employees worked in the company's research and development laboratories.[6] Ninety-nine separate research and development projects were undertaken for the military during the war.[7]

Watson also terminated the Commercial Research Department at corporate headquarters so its members would be available for assignments in support of the war effort. For example, the department's manager, F. J. Wesley, who had previously devised the army's personnel accounting system, became a technical adviser to IBM's Washington Federal office to assist in developing new punched-card procedures for the military services and government agencies.

Among the challenges was that of writing checks for payment of dependency allowances to families of service personnel as mandated by the Dependency Allowance Act of 1942. Wesley worked with IBM engineers to develop a check-writing collator specifically for this task. Simultaneously he provided technical guidance in establishing the U.S. Office of Dependency Benefits (ODB), which came to have the largest single installation of punched-card machines of World War II. Inducted into the army in August 1942 with the rank of major, he directed the accounting and check-writing aspects of the family allowance program of the ODB.[8]

To coordinate the company's wartime activities, Watson created the Department of Logistics in February 1942, placing it under the direction of Frederick W. Nichol, who had begun his IBM career as Watson's secretary in 1914. Nichol, who had served in the army in World War I and had been placed in charge of IBM's foreign activities in 1930, was now the company's vice president and general manager. "Major Nichol is eminently fitted for this important work by reason of broad executive experience in industry, combined with military knowledge," Watson asserted. "He has intimate knowledge of foreign industrial methods and resources."[9]

Munitions production and special research and development projects were important, but so were the company's regular products for which 85 percent of the orders were on government priority schedules. Emphasizing this point, Watson told the employees, "One of our machines just recently was given priority of shipment by the Government over a certain munitions product. . . . Two of our machines were taken to England on a bomber recently at the request of the British Government."[10] At the IBM school in Endicott, some 1,300 members of the armed services were trained during the war in the use of EAM equipment for accounting and statistical control. Spoken as the three letters of the alphabet, EAM stood for electric accounting machines and had grown in favor for identifying all IBM punched-card equipment.[11]

"Production of American industry is going to startle the world by the end of this year," Watson asserted. "This is no time for us to think in terms of 'I' or 'We,' whether we are in the factory, the offices, or the field force. We must think only in terms of WE-All for victory." Then showing a remarkably perceptive view of the distant postwar era, he said, "After we have won the war, we must win the peace by establishing sound economic policies between nations so that raw materials, food and clothing, and other comforts of life will be fairly distributed throughout the entire world."[12]

Mobile Machine Record Units

Early in 1940 the Adjutant General's Office (AGO) became interested in the possibility of developing mobile punched-card processing units to travel with combat units for the preparation of personnel status records, reports of change, casualty lists, and strength summaries. Following preliminary discussions in the lecture rooms of the IBM schoolhouse in Endicott, twelve IBM systems engineers and consultants were dispatched to Washington in June to assist the War Department in determining its requirements. It was quickly determined that mobile units could not be successful unless their record-keeping methods were compatible with those of the entire AGO. All parts of the AGO record-keeping system needed to be modernized.

The first phase of the modernization effort began with the development of punched-card procedures for preparing and processing the desired reports. Machine record units for implementing these procedures were then established in the nine corps areas and in the headquarters commands at Fort Knox and Bolling Field beginning in November 1940. Similar AGO installations were soon operational in Panama, Puerto Rico, Hawaii, and the Philippine Islands as well.

The second phase began in July 1941 when three IBM engineers in Endicott were assigned the task of initiating the design of a mobile EAM unit. A truck was purchased with a twenty-foot van body, and special rubber mountings for punched-card equipment were devised. Preliminary tests at the army's proving ground in Aberdeen, Maryland, were followed by more severe tests of the mobile unit during military maneuvers in Louisiana. The equipment performed well even under adverse road and weather conditions. Requests for radio operators, truck drivers, and other specialists were handled expeditiously by machine processing of cards in the mobile unit.

A second and larger mobile unit using a thirty-foot trailer van with a $2^1/_2$-ton tractor was designed to overcome limitations revealed in the smaller unit. Less than two months after the army successfully completed tests of the larger unit, the Japanese attacked Pearl Harbor. A number of mobile units were immediately ordered by the Adjutant General's Office. The Endicott Engineering Laboratory built and delivered sixteen by the spring of 1942. A total of 274 had been built and delivered by the end of the war.

When U.S. troops landed in Tunisia, Sicily, Italy, and Normandy, the mobile machine record units were pulled up onto the beaches along with guns, ammunition, ambulances, and other mobile equipment. Frequently they followed the initial assault by only a few days. Eager to learn the secrets of this new application for data processing equipment, the German High Command issued instructions for their capture. The American Fifth Army in Italy, for example, came into possession of the orders of a German commander instructing his troops to capture intact an IBM mobile records unit with all of its machines, records, and personnel. But none of the equipment or personnel was ever captured.[13]

Teleprocessing with Punched Cards

Mobile record units plus modernized EAM facilities at fixed strategic locations solved many record-keeping problems for the military. But for some information, the time required to transport decks of punched cards from one location to another was too long. The Army Air Corps had the most severe problem. Its operations would involve continual rapid movement of planes, flight crews, fuel, replacement parts, and other supplies throughout the world.

Just prior to World War II, the Army Air Corps monitored its stock by a system of machine-posting in duplicate of stock record cards at stations and depots. Once a year the duplicates were sent in to the Air Matériel Command headquarters at Wright Field, Dayton, Ohio. There they were manually transcribed to IBM tabulating cards, which in turn were used for preparing reports for purchasing and distributing new stock. Once-a-year balancing of supplies against use had been satisfactory in peacetime, but would be totally inadequate in a global war. To make inventory balances available daily, telegraphic transmission of data was envisaged, but such data could not be processed without manual transfer from teletype tape to punched cards. The anticipated volume of information was staggering. Transactions would approximate 40,000 per day from each depot for inventories estimated at 300,000 items. A manually operated system seemed doomed to failure.[14]

The Army Air Corps approached IBM late in 1940, seeking a machine that would read holes in telegraphic paper tape and automatically transfer the data to punched cards, thus avoiding the laborious and inaccurate manual transcription. Fortuitously the IBM Commercial Research Department had already made a preliminary design of such a machine following inquiries by the National Analine Company in the spring of that year. But business considerations had impeded implementation. Among these considerations was the type of relationship required between IBM and the American Telephone and Telegraph Company (AT&T), which owned the telephone lines and telegraph equipment.[15]

With business issues now set aside for reasons of national security, the Endicott laboratory personnel obtained technical information from AT&T concerning its equipment and had a prototype machine completed within a few months.[16] Initial operation was established between Wright Field and the Pacific Overseas Air Service Command Headquarters in Oakland, California, using an AT&T leased wire circuit. In August 1941 the IBM Type 40 tape-to-card punch began coming off an Endicott production line. Using this device, information transmitted over telephone lines and punched into a teletype tape could be punched automatically into IBM cards. In another six months the Type 57 card-to-tape punch was also available for converting information stored on punched cards into the same information on teletype tape.[17]

With five punched-hole locations across its width, the standard teletype tape offered thirty-two different combinations of punched and unpunched holes—sufficient to encode the twenty-six alphabetic characters, with six combinations left over. Three of these were used for spacing, carriage returning, and paper feeding. Two more were used to signify whether the subsequent entries were alphabetic or numeric; this was needed because there were not enough combinations in one row to accommodate both alphabetic and numeric characters. At the standard spacing of ten rows per inch, a single eight-inch-diameter teletype roll of one thousand feet could accommodate the content of 1,500 fully punched IBM cards.

Following the lead of the air corps, many other U.S. military organizations were soon handling stock control at the depot level using electric accounting machines in conjunction with a completely integrated system of telegraphic stock-balance control procedures based on IBM card-to-tape and tape-to-card machines. This application of punched-card equipment may have been IBM's greatest single contribution to the successful prosecution of the war.[18] But it was the innovative "radiotype" that won the highest accolades from many military officers.

The Radiotype

"Every phase of our war effort was affected by your equipment," the chief of army communications told Watson after hostilities had ended. "The setting up of overseas as well as domestic wireless circuits with Radiotype, which sent and received messages automatically and typed them out on the typewriter, was one of the most important contributions."[19]

The activity leading to this contribution began in 1931 when Walter S. Lemmon, president of the Radio Industries Corporation, and his two associates built the first working model.[20] Born in New York City, the thirty-five-year-old Lemmon had studied electrical engineering at Columbia University and had already acquired considerable wealth from his early patents on radio technology.[21] The Radiotype consisted of an electric typewriter coupled with radio transmitting and receiving apparatus. Using the equipment, a person could type a message on one typewriter and cause the identical message to be typed automatically by a second typewriter at a location many miles away. An early version, described as a "crude model," was demonstrated to Watson, who had learned of Lemmon through contacts at Columbia University. Enthusiastic about the concept, Watson agreed to support the research needed to create a product. Thereupon Lemmon and his associates joined IBM.

By 1935 they had a relatively satisfactory model operating. Like all subsequent Radiotype models, it used the IBM electric typewriter for its keyboard and printing mechanism. (IBM had entered the typewriter business in 1933 by purchasing the Electromatic Typewriter Corporation of Rochester, New York.[22] A key motivation for Bryce and Watson was the possible use of electric typewriter elements for input-output equipment and small computing machines.)[23] The Radiotype was designed for shortwave radio hookups to facilitate interoffice communication within large buildings or between factories, home office, and branches. The first significant use of the system, however, was by U.S. military forces during World War II.

Late in 1941 IBM loaned several Radiotype models to the Army Signal Corps to test their applicability for communicating among facilities in Washington, D.C., Dayton, Ohio, and Chicago, Illinois. So successful were these tests that the Signal Corps ordered units for its stations at San Francisco, Honolulu, Panama, and Puerto Rico immediately after the country's entry into the war. More orders followed as additional sites were added. The nerve center for this growing network was the Army Signal Corps radio station WAR, located in the Pentagon in Washington, D.C.

Prior Signal Corps practice had been to transmit messages by radio using Morse code. The incoming messages automatically activated a recorder that printed the dots and dashes on a continuous tape, but it was necessary for a specially trained operator to translate the code and type the messages on a typewriter. With Radiotype the messages were automatically typed and ready for delivery the moment the transmission was finished. Later in the war Radiotype units were coupled to electromechanical encryption and decryption equipment to provide almost instant transmission and receipt of secure messages.[24]

Soon after the Commercial Research Department at corporate headquarters was terminated, Steve Dunwell returned to Endicott to work on the Radiotype. It was just being put into production. The first order was for thirty-eight systems. Dunwell undertook the task of writing the manuals and hiring and training people to maintain the systems. To avoid having to train people in electronics, he hired only those with first-class amateur radio operator licenses. As soon as they completed the month-long training course, the trainees were shipped out with the first Radiotype units and a new class was begun.[25]

Figure 8.1.   Radiotype at WAR
Top: Radiotype units are shown in operation at the Signal Corps radio station
WAR in the Pentagon in 1942. Bottom: The component parts of a Radiotype
unit are labeled. The availability of Radiotype at the beginning of the war
dramatically improved the communications capability of the U.S. military.

Deciphering Enemy Codes

While working on the Radiotype project, Dunwell came in contact with Signal Corps officers who persuaded him and a fellow employee to volunteer for duty in the cryptographic service. They reported for duty in Washington, D.C., in May 1942. Commissioned as officers without any military training whatsoever, they bought their uniforms, pinned on their lieutenant's bars, practiced saluting, and were ready to serve.

To carry out their assigned task of deciphering encrypted enemy messages, they ordered EAM equipment from IBM and installed it in the auditorium of a temporary facility obtained from the Arlington Hall Junior College (for women) in Arlington, Virginia. Their offices were on the stage of the auditorium. Later they moved into two-story buildings built especially for receiving and analyzing enemy messages. Activities involved the German and Japanese languages. Security was tight. A double wire fence surrounded the complex, and there were additional fenced-off areas within it. The greatest fear was that the enemy would learn how successful the group was and, as a result, adopt new encryption methods that might be harder to decode.[26]

Dunwell taught himself cryptography using Signal Corps educational materials assembled before the war. One common cryptographic method used a code book and a key book. The code book contained a list of words or phrases, and beside each was a number selected to represent it. A message encoded in these numbers could easily be decoded by anyone possessing the code book. To make the encoded message more secure, a second cryptographic step was taken. This involved the key book, which contained a large number of random digits running in one long string from the beginning to the end of the book. The sender selected a small portion of the string as his "key" and "locked" (or encrypted) the encoded message by adding the first digit in the selected portion of the string to the first digit of the encoded message, the next digit in the string to the next digit in the message, and so on to the end of the message.

A message so encrypted could be decrypted (deciphered) by anyone who possessed both the code book and the key book and who also knew which key had been selected. The two books occasionally came into enemy hands because they had to be broadly distributed among friendly forces. Without the books, decipherers faced the daunting task of reconstructing them from bits and pieces of information by painstaking processes that defy easy description, but which could be facilitated by punched-card equipment.

Even if one had a copy of the enemy's code and key books, the task of determining what key had been used for a given message was far from trivial. This task was also made easier by EAM equipment. The first step was to transfer all the numbers from the enemy's captured key book onto punched cards in overlapping strings of fifty digits each. These cards were then sorted into numerical order. To decipher an intercepted message, the first step was to guess what some of the words were, based on the origin and context of the message. A guessed word was called a *crib*.

By writing the digits from the enemy's code book corresponding to one of these cribs, it could easily be determined what string of digits, when added to those of the crib, would produce the digits in the intercepted message. Then, using punched-card equipment, a search was made for all keys containing this particular sequence of digits. Next, all the keys that hypothetically might have been used were tried out against the next few words in the message. If one of the keys appeared to be correct, it was used to decipher the entire message. If none of the keys worked, more guesses were made and the process repeated. Because hundreds of guesses (cribs) might be needed to decipher a single message, and because each of these guesses might produce hundreds of plausible keys, the task of finding the correct key would have been nearly impossible without automated equipment.[27]

A deficiency of the automated process, as initially envisioned, related to determining when a hypothesized key was correct. Examination by clerks of the output of processing thousands of hypothesized keys against the encrypted messages was far too time consuming. The solution was to assign a probability of occurrence to each word in the enemy's code book based on linguistic frequency of use. The words of a correctly decoded message segment would have a collective probability of occurrence dramatically higher than words produced by any incorrect key. What was needed was a machine that could rapidly calculate the collective probability of the words in a hypothetically decoded message segment.

Figure 8.2.   Stephen W. and Julia Dunwell
Steve Dunwell is shown with his wife, Julia, at the March 1946 ceremony at which he was awarded the Legion of Merit for his cryptographic work during World War II. He and Julia spent their brief honeymoon at Watson's suite at the IBM Country Club in Endicott in January 1943. In the late 1950s he headed Project Stretch, which produced the most powerful computer of that era.

A Trip to Remember

Dunwell's solution was to obtain a specially designed processor built with electromechanical relays. He first studied the characteristics of relays used in telephone switching systems and found them to be too slow and cumbersome. Then he evaluated the wire-contact relays developed by Clair Lake for the IBM-Harvard Mark I and found them to be quite appropriate. Seeking final approval from Watson to have this special equipment fabricated by IBM, he stopped off in New York City on his way to Endicott. Approval was given swiftly by Watson who said the Signal Corps could have anything it needed.

Then Watson made another decision that provided Dunwell with a trip to Endicott he will never forget. Because of wartime pressures, Dunwell had been allowed only one half day off for his planned wedding. With his normal $6\frac{1}{2}$-day work week, there was no opportunity for a honeymoon. So he had arranged to be married on 18 January 1943, one day before his trip to Endicott, and to have his bride travel with him for their honeymoon. Learning of this arrangement, Watson asked where they were planning to stay. When Dunwell told him, Watson said, "That's an awful place up there. Why don't you stay at my suite at the IBM Country Club?" And so they did—probably the only couple ever to spend their honeymoon in Watson's suite.

A unique feature of the equipment specified by Dunwell and built by IBM was the function of its many plugboards. These permitted the machine to be wired to recognize the sets of code-book digits that corresponded to the most frequently used words and to supply their probabilities. Cards were fed into the machine so that each card that contained part of an encrypted message was followed by one or more cards with a hypothesized key. For each key the machine performed the decryption, assigned probabilities to the resultant words, and calculated the probability that the message segment had been correctly decrypted. The relays were fast enough that the entire analysis could be done between the reading of one card and the next—at the rate of 150 cards per minute. The first unit worked exceptionally well, and more units were put in service.

The process described here is only one example of the great variety of decryption problems encountered and solved during the war. The ready availability of standard IBM equipment and the willingness of Watson to provide modified equipment made

Figure 8.3. Cryptographic Equipment
A relay calculator specially built for cryptographic work by IBM is shown
(left) attached to an IBM Type 405 Alphabetic Accounting Machine (right).
The front gate of the relay calculator is swung open to reveal many rectangular-shaped relay units. These 4-pole, 6-pole, and 12-pole wire-contact relays
had been designed by Clair Lake for use in the IBM-Harvard Mark I. Plugboards for controlling the calculator are behind the five rectangular covers
on the top, and the two covers on the bottom, of the large front gate.

it possible for the Signal Corps to solve new problems quickly. A
typical set-up used at the Signal Corps involved three sorters and
a collator with one operator. At times as many as twenty-five of
these set-ups would be working simultaneously on a single decryption problem.[28]

A critical limitation for the entire operation was the time it took
for keypunch operators to transcribe the intercepted messages.
That limitation became unacceptable "when out of the Pacific, a
full bomber load of intercepts was dumped on us at once," Dunwell recalled. By the time they could have processed all of the
messages, the information would have lost its value. Following this
event, a teletype network was established throughout the Pacific
region. Intercepted messages were keyed in at local sites, transmitted over telephone lines, and recorded on teletype tape in
Washington, D.C. The information on teletype tape was automatically punched into IBM cards using the Type 40 tape-to-card

punch, which had been placed into production only a few months before the attack on Pearl Harbor.[29]

Lusting for Electronics

As supervisor of the electrical laboratory in Endicott, Ralph Palmer participated in many wartime projects. He had the opportunity to go on battleships to observe fire-control systems manufactured by IBM, and he worked on a sophisticated odograph and a simulator for pilot training. He was disappointed, however, on two counts. First, all of his projects used analog rather than digital circuitry. Second, except for his own test equipment, there was little opportunity to use electronics.

His frustration was heightened by the company's lack of interest in using the electronic arithmetic circuits he and Phelps had designed and built in 1942. Not only were these circuits judged to be too fast for any EAM product then under consideration, but there was deep concern that the company's patent department lacked the expertise in electronics needed to ensure that product designs would not infringe patents of others. Furthermore Watson had terminated commercial product development in favor of wartime projects.

Several of Palmer's friends had joined the navy's cryptographic organization, the Communications Supplementary Activity—Washington. This organization was often referred to simply as Naval Communications or as "seesaw" because its initials were CSAW. His colleagues told him about "the fantastic amount of electronic equipment and the computing that was going on there." In Washington on other business, Palmer arranged to meet with leaders of the organization. Wartime security limited the information Palmer could be given, but he was assured he would do a lot of work with electronics. "Probably before I left, I was sold," he recalls. "I almost immediately got orders to report for duty."[30]

The Navy's Task

A primary task of the navy was to ensure that troops, munitions, and other supplies could be shipped from the United States to Great Britain and later to North Africa and Europe. In 1942 German submarines had sunk more tonnage of ships than the

Allies had built. During the first three months of 1943, shortly before Palmer reported for service, the number of ships sunk appeared to be doubling month by month: twenty-nine ships in January, fifty in February, and ninety-five in March. Critical to the German success was their use of an encryption and decryption device for sending messages to and from their submarines. Known as the Enigma, this device contained three rotors, so wired and mechanically interconnected that they converted letters entered on the keyboard into an apparently random set of output letters. Even if the Allies came in possession of an Enigma, the Germans believed they would not be able to decipher messages unless they also knew what key had been chosen for the transmission.[31]

The Allies' ability to protect convoys of merchant ships would depend in part on their ability to read encrypted Enigma messages. Using espionage information and sophisticated mathematics, a Polish cryptographic group in the mid-1930s had reconstructed an Enigma and modified it to run rapidly through key settings to find the correct key for a given message. These devices were called "bombes" because of their appearance and the ticking noise they made.[32] Under increasing military threat from the Germans, the Poles delivered their equipment and information to the French and British. The British refined the methods, and the British Tabulating Machine Company produced numerous bombes to mechanize the decryption process.[33]

Late in 1942 the Germans introduced a four-rotor Enigma that greatly increased the difficulty of finding solutions to encryptions. The Americans, in close cooperation with the British, undertook the task of designing and constructing larger and faster bombes to handle the four-rotor Enigmas. Using a combination of vacuum tube and relay circuits, with mechanical rotors driven by a high-speed motor, each new bombe was said to be equivalent to six of the British-built bombes. Each unit was about 7 feet tall, 10 feet wide, and 2 feet deep and weighed 2.5 tons.

Using these machines, the Allied forces deciphered German naval messages with increasing regularity and speed. By May 1943 the Germans were forced to move many of their submarines out of the North Atlantic to safer areas because of "unbearable" losses: one submarine lost for each 10,000 tons of Allied shipping, versus one submarine lost for 100,000 tons only a few months earlier. During the first three months of 1944, only three Allied merchant ships were sunk—at a cost to the Germans of thirty-six submarines. The Battle of the Atlantic had been won.[34]

For Palmer, as for Dunwell, no time was wasted on military training or indoctrination. Upon reporting for duty in May 1943, he was sent directly to the Naval Computing Machine Laboratory, operated in Dayton, Ohio, by the National Cash Register Company. Bombes and other top-secret electronic equipment were designed and built there for CSAW. Assigned to a nearly completed project, Palmer soon came up with a design that would require far fewer components. "Please don't push the thing too hard," he was told. "It would upset our schedule. What we've got may not be the best, but it will work." In developing special wartime devices, of which only a few units would be made, swift completion was more important than construction cost. The opposite had been true at IBM, where large production runs were anticipated.

Palmer was excited by the opportunity to work on special-purpose electronic equipment. Some units contained over a thousand vacuum tubes and were far larger and more complex than any he had seen before. His strong intellect, good education, and earlier research in electronics quickly put him in a position of leadership. Following a period in which he devised test equipment and servicing methods, he became a technical executive officer, with responsibility for coordinating cryptographic work at Dayton with other military organizations. He learned how Dunwell's group used modified EAM equipment to solve cryptographic problems—often just as effectively as was accomplished in the navy using a combination of special electronic equipment and EAM. There was no doubt in his mind, however, about the long-term potential of electronic circuits in data processing equipment.

Toward the end of the war, Palmer began designing an advanced unit called the full selector—a cryptographic device intended to provide more rapid access to information. A driving force behind this project was Comm. Howard T. Engstrom, who in peacetime had been a professor of mathematics at Yale. More than any other person in CSAW, Engstrom impressed Palmer as an outstanding technical leader. He particularly liked Engstrom's view that anything they designed and built should be "stretching the state-of-the-art in technology." Among the basic elements Palmer set out to devise for the full selector was a magnetic drum storage unit based on research he had done in the IBM Endicott laboratory. Magnetic drum storage devices would become critical elements of postwar electronic computers, but Palmer's project was barely begun when the war ended in the fall of 1945.[35]

A Commercial Venture

Already two men prominent in the hierarchy of CSAW had initiated plans to continue CSAW activities as a commercial venture. One was Howard Engstrom. The other was Lt. Comm. William C. Norris, who in peacetime had been a sales engineer for Westinghouse and was to found the Control Data Corporation in 1957. These two men were soon joined by Capt. Ralph I. Meader, who had interviewed Palmer in Washington and had headed the Naval Computing Machine Laboratory in Dayton. The idea of establishing a commercial company to continue the classified CSAW work gained increasing support within the navy after NCR declined to continue the activity and when it became evident that key technical people were reluctant to accept civil service positions. Among those supporting the concept was James Forrestal, then secretary of the navy and later the first secretary of defense. The navy could not legally help create a private company, however, and certainly could not guarantee that it would receive government business.

The proposal was stymied by these constraints until late in 1945 when a successful investment banker and Annapolis graduate, John E. Parker, was persuaded to raise money to start the company. In January 1946 the company was incorporated under the name Engineering Research Associates (ERA). Ownership was equally divided between two groups: the founding technical group headed by Engstrom, Norris, and Meader, and the investor group headed by Parker. The equity investment was only $20,000, although the investor group also provided a line of credit of $200,000. Six months later the Navy Department, without competitive bidding, awarded to ERA the first of a series of contracts that assured its survival and made it the leading supplier of large-scale electronic computers in the first few postwar years.[36]

Ralph Palmer was under considerable pressure to join the group, but after speaking with Parker, he concluded the man "didn't have the vision to really exploit the technology this group had." Special equipment for the navy was the only business under consideration. To Palmer, the application of electronics in the commercial data processing industry had greater promise.

Discharged from the navy in early 1946, Palmer returned to IBM without any specific commitment concerning his job assignment. Among the factors influencing his decision was that the company had paid him 25 percent of his salary while in the navy. The same had been done for all IBM employees in military service. "I could have survived without it, I suppose, but the thought behind it impressed me," Palmer observes. "This was Mr. Watson's policy. I thought it was pretty unusual and pretty good."[37]

9

Future Demands

"There is no business in the world which can hope to move forward if it does not keep abreast of the times, look into the future and study the probable demands of the future," Watson asserted as he broke ground for the North Street Laboratory in 1932.[1]

Use of the phrase "demands of the future" to connote market requirements for new or not-yet-conceived products has often been considered peculiar to Watson. Like many things associated with him, however, this phrase was acquired while working for John Patterson at NCR. To help assess future market requirements and to review product proposals, Patterson had established what he called the Future Demands Committee. It consisted of key company executives, among them Watson. Another frequent attendee was Charles F. Kettering, the company's leading inventor and a person from whom Watson learned much about the processes of invention and innovation.

Lessons from NCR

Slightly younger than Watson, Kettering had begun working for NCR in 1904, immediately after graduating with a degree in electrical engineering from Ohio State University. He resigned five years later to found the Dayton Engineering Laboratories Company, better known by its acronym, Delco. Its first product, and the invention for which Kettering is best known, was the first practical electric starter for gasoline-powered automobiles. Before Kettering resigned to found Delco, he had already built and tested an operational electric starter with the help of other moonlighting engineers from NCR. In 1916 Delco became a subsidiary of General Motors, a company for which Kettering later served as director of research from 1920 to 1947.[2]

During his five years at NCR, Kettering made many improvements to cash registers. These included the first electrically driven cash register and a means for combining the output from all the registers in a store to provide a continually updated record of total sales. Concerning his NCR years, Kettering said: "I didn't hang around much with other inventors or the executive fellows. I lived with the sales gang. They had some real notion of what people wanted."[3] Top among these salespeople was Watson, who is reported to have been "the first person outside of the Delco group to enjoy a ride in the self-starting automobile."[4]

The rapid growth in customer demand for electrically driven cash registers and other improvements devised by Kettering was an important lesson for Watson. Good salesmanship could increase the demand for existing products and influence customer preferences, but research and engineering could create new products with far more dramatic impact. A means for identifying possible new products of this type was crucial to a company's success.

Lessons gained from Kettering and Patterson increased Watson's respect for the specialized knowledge of engineers. He also learned that he had the ability to bridge the knowledge gap between engineers and salesmen and thus play an important role in defining new products. Arriving at CTR in 1914, Watson took on this role informally as he scrambled to create an engineering organization. By the time he promoted James Bryce to chief engineer and created a small research laboratory in 1922, he was ready to address future demands more formally.

Forming a Committee

"In connection with the appointment of Mr. J. W. Bryce as Chief Engineer of the Computing-Tabulating-Recording Company, please note that a Future Demands Committee has been established," Watson advised the division presidents and other key executives. "We shall expect to have regular meetings of this Committee, and as you are a member, due notices of these meetings will be forwarded to you in time to make your plans to be present."[5]

An important member of the committee was Otto E. Braitmayer, who had been hired as a fifteen-year-old office boy by Hollerith in 1889 and stayed on to serve as secretary and office manager while obtaining a law degree at night.[6] By the time

Watson arrived, Braitmayer was in his early forties and familiar with all aspects of the business. Watson quickly adopted him as his right-hand man. Working directly for Watson, Braitmeyer negotiated contracts with customers and vendors, set and administered salaries and bonuses, gave out engineering assignments, and documented product development objectives. By 1922 Braitmayer had become assistant general manager of the Tabulating Machine Division.[7]

Another member was Clement Ehret, sales manager of the Tabulating Machine Division.[8] Ehret's contributions to the committee's work are typified by a 1927 letter to Watson: "The attached clippings refer to a $60,000 loss by the Waldorf Hotel through the falsification of waiters' checks. I believe one of the first things we should give attention to, as soon as our present engineering program permits, is the restaurant machine. You will recall you had in mind the use of the proposed Railroad Ticket Printing device, with slugs, as a commissary machine as well. We appear to have a good basis to proceed on with this device which would offer all food establishments protection against loss."[9]

Reference to Watson's ideas for new products was common in discussions and correspondence with him. "In accordance with your idea that it is important to study ways and means of getting the primary data on tabulating cards as near the source of information as possible, I have been giving some thought and study to the problem of recording from meters, particularly electric, gas, and water meters," Bryce wrote Watson in 1928. "We have a sample of each of the above kinds of meters. It appears that while it will require some nice design and ingenious work to fit a simple recording device to these, there is nothing impossible about it. . . . The biggest problem in the whole matter I believe to be a business one, and before recommending the expenditure of any money in actual design or experiment, I would like to submit some figures and get your advice."[10]

Neither letter resulted in products at the time, but they are indicative of the far-ranging ideas that were considered and abandoned along the road to products actually developed and marketed. Watson's desire to capture data more directly from utility meters was partially satisfied in the late 1930s, using pencil-mark sensing technologies based on Rey Johnson's test-scoring equipment (see chap. 6). Meter readers made pencil marks on cards, and the marks were later converted automatically to conventional punched holes by a mark-sensing, reproducing card punch.

A Department and Its Demise

By 1929 the committee structure had become inadequate for the task, and Watson established a Future Demands Department. Headed by Clement Ehret, former sales vice president, the department was to study and recommend "the creation and development of new products to cover new fields." A parallel line of inquiry concerned the widening of usage for existing machines. "Our facts will come from a first-hand study of industry and from surveys and analyses made in the field," Ehret asserted.[11]

With a background in sales and finance, Ehret was qualified for some of these activities, but he was not qualified to replace (and certainly not to compete with) Watson in working with the company's engineers to bring about the "development of new products." In recognition of these deficiencies in January 1934, Watson appointed Ehret director of market research, a position he held until his death in 1949.[12]

The Future Demands Department fell dormant for a six-year period during which time Watson personally handled—as he in fact always had—the assignments given to *his* inventors to develop new products. It was not a completely satisfactory arrangement. Watson possessed neither the engineering background to understand the technical problems nor a sufficiently detailed knowledge of customer needs to fully specify new products. Filling this void was an ad hoc responsibility of the Methods Research Department, formed in 1931 to collect, disseminate, and develop EAM methods.[13] Sometimes the department learned of a proposed product soon enough to influence the initial design. More often, however, information became available only after Watson had authorized production. Then followed a frenzied effort to define and make those changes that were absolutely essential. Many desirable changes were thus postponed for incorporation in an "enhanced" product a year or so later.[14]

New Leadership

Although Watson had some appreciation of the problems he was causing, he seemed unable to find anyone to whom he was willing to entrust the future demands function. As he watched the maturing of John C. McPherson, however, a man he had personally hired in February 1930, Watson increasingly believed he

Figure 9.1. John C. McPherson
John McPherson, IBM's director of engineering, is shown addressing a
group of customers in early 1948. He was IBM's principle technical contact
with government agencies during World War II, helped define and get announced the company's most profitable ever accounting machine (the Type
407), and was influential in getting the company into electronics in the early
postwar years.

had found someone to whom he could entrust this critical function.

While at Princeton studying electrical engineering, McPherson had spent his summers working for the chief electrical engineer at the Pennsylvania Railroad shops in Altoona—a position arranged by his father, who was also an electrical engineer. The McPherson home, like Watson's, was in Short Hills, New Jersey. Home for Christmas during his first year at Princeton, McPherson recalls, "Mr. Watson met me at a party at the Short Hills Club and asked me if I might be able to work for him at IBM." McPherson's response was affirmative, and he joined the company soon after obtaining a bachelor's degree in electrical engineering from Princeton. Because of his experience in the railroad business, he soon was assigned to the Transportation Department, which provided technical guidance to salesmen and their customers in the transportation (especially railroad) industry. Similar support groups existed for the insurance, wholesale stores, and oil industries.

That May he attended IBM Sales Class 56. Upon graduation he became a senior sales representative in the Philadelphia office where he specialized in installations for the Pennsylvania and the Reading railroads. Three years later he returned to New York as assistant manager of the Transportation Department, a position he held until January 1940 when Watson had him promoted to manager of the Future Demands Department. His new assignment was to "cooperate with and coordinate the activities of the Engineering, Patent, Market Research, and Commercial Research departments."[15]

McPherson's office at corporate headquarters was adjacent to those of the commercial and market research groups. Among their activities was the handling of customer requests for modified equipment. The headquarters groups worked with customers and with IBM engineers to define appropriate implementations and provide price quotations.[16]

Working in parallel with these groups, McPherson understood his task was "to think longer range, beyond the modification of existing machines, to new ones we should create." It was a small activity that did not grow beyond three people as long as he headed it, but he enjoyed working with the engineers, patent attorneys, and market research people. The work was intellectually stimulating and rewarding. Less than two years after his promotion, the country had entered World War II. McPherson's future demands activities were effectively terminated and replaced by wartime activities.

The Chief Engineer

In February 1943 Watson appointed John McPherson director of engineering. Little explanation for this appointment was given, but it was likely because of the significance of McPherson's role as IBM's principal technical contact with various government agencies. Since 1940, for example, McPherson had served as contact for the U.S. Army Ordnance Corps Ballistic Research Laboratory in Aberdeen, Maryland, where IBM equipment was used for ballistics calculations. He arranged for Lake to build the fastest-ever relay calculator for the Ballistics Laboratory. And he was the person Dunwell and Palmer contacted for their specialized cryptographic needs.[17]

Not announced when McPherson became director of engineering was Watson's plan to assume again full responsibility for product decisions.[18] The Future Demands Department fell dormant (for the second time) until it was reactivated in 1947 as part of the company's move into electronic computing.

As in his previous assignment, McPherson ostensibly reported to Watson. Because those who wanted to see Watson had to wait, possibly for weeks, McPherson submitted written reports from time to time and busied himself making sure that development projects moved ahead in the manner he believed Watson desired. He dealt with sales and manufacturing executives at headquarters and with key inventors in the development laboratories. He was accepted as representing Watson when in the laboratories and as representing the engineers when back at headquarters.

By his nature, McPherson functioned primarily as an analyst and a facilitator. He tried to ensure that the best technical approaches were used to achieve each product development goal established by Watson. It was a delicate task. He needed to know what assignments each inventor had and how the inventor was attempting to achieve them. Simultaneously he had to avoid revealing any of the secrets of one inventor to another. To encourage a free exchange of information between himself and the inventors, he adopted the policy of never filing for patents himself. It was a policy already in force for most technical staff people at corporate headquarters, with the notable exception of Bryce and certain members of his Patent Development Department.

Concerning Watson's relationship with the company's inventors, McPherson says: "Watson challenged them to work on what the business needed. He urged more than one engineer to work on the same kind of project independently. Then he made a choice." Concerning his own role as the first employee to hold the title of director of engineering, McPherson says he always perceived that in fact but not title, "Mr. Watson was the chief engineer."[19]

10

Preparing for Peace

By mid-1943 the tide of battle had shifted in favor of the Allies. The Germans had been defeated at Stalingrad in February and were retreating along much of the Russian front. Severe losses had also forced them to withdraw many submarines from the North Atlantic. The surrender of Italian forces in Tunisia in May had opened the Mediterranean to Allied shipping and paved the way for troop landings in Sicily in July. In September, following the resignation of Benito Mussolini and the surrender of the new Italian government, Allied forces landed on the Italian mainland and began their advance toward Germany. The Japanese, who had suffered their first major naval defeat a year earlier near the island of Midway, were also on the defensive as U.S. troops began working their way toward Japan, island by island.

In the course of three years, Watson had turned IBM into a major supplier for the armed forces. From the end of 1940 to the end of 1943, the company's factory floor space in the United States had increased 140 percent to 1,891,000 square feet, its domestic factory workers had increased 160 percent to 12,238, and its total number of domestic employees had increased 100 percent to 17,262. Approximately two-thirds of the company's production consisted of munitions.[1] Revenues had nearly tripled, although profits had been kept essentially flat by policies devised by Watson to avoid profiting from the war effort. (See chap. 8 and appendix A.)

Now Watson faced the daunting task of continuing to support the war effort for an indefinite time while simultaneously preparing to shift to a peacetime economy. He did not want the company to drop back to its prewar size. But how could he make effective use of his vastly increased manufacturing floor space? And how could he pay for the cost of converting to peacetime production if the government and military organizations began returning EAM equipment rented for wartime purposes?

Planning for Product Improvements

In June 1943 Watson initiated a series of engineering meetings intended to develop plans for improving the product line to meet the anticipated challenges of the postwar era. Among the technical leaders in attendance were James Bryce, Halsey Dickinson, Walter Lemmon, John McPherson, and the patent attorney John Hayward. Other key executives attended, bringing the number to about twenty people. Held twice in June, the meetings continued on a monthly basis to the end of the year and then somewhat less regularly through 1944 and 1945.

At the first meeting, Watson said he hoped to retain all employees hired during the war, but he was even more strongly committed to IBM's employees in military service. "Twenty-three percent of all the men in our organization are in the Service, and we hope they will all come back to us," he stated. "We will lose a few, but the majority of them will come back, and they are going to have jobs when they come back. We have got to create enough business to take care of all of them, or else the rest of us will have to share the work. That is as plainly as I can put it, because we are not going to let any man or woman who has gone into the Service suffer when they get back home."

In an undisguised exhortation for greater effort, Watson said, "It isn't necessary for anybody to make any sacrifice if we are willing to work now and do the things we know how to do." As evidence that the old ways would not be good enough, he reminded them how quickly they had put new products into production for the war. "This war is changing everything," he asserted. "Everybody who makes any progress in business is going to work along different lines than they have ever worked before. The people who do not change in time are going to be sitting on the curbstone waiting for the parade to come by."[2]

Watson then began a brainstorming session that was continued in future meetings. Topics discussed included possible new products and improvements to old ones, the adaptation of special wartime devices to peacetime, new technologies, and the need to hire additional technically trained people even before the war ended. On this latter subject, Watson had particularly strong views. He chided the attendees for not looking hard enough. He read aloud newspaper ads placed by engineers seeking work: for example, "Engineer, 45, experimental or mechanical, electrical, inventive and executive ability; can design and make complete models, parts, and so forth; can do machine hand work." Not all those advertising for work would be good, he noted, but some surely were. "Go to technical schools and hire people," he urged.[3]

To provide structure to the product development discussion, McPherson had been asked to select the five most urgent engineering projects. His choices, in priority order, were a wheel printer to replace the type-bar printer, a new key punch, a multifunction EAM unit, machines for small businesses, and an improved time recording device. The list provoked a lengthy discussion, primarily between McPherson and Watson. Projects were clarified and their priorities reset based on ease of accomplishment and value in the market.

The wheel printer, a long-time favorite of Watson, stayed in first place. For second place, he suggested replacing the improved punch with a machine for small businesses. As the discussion progressed, he came back to this subject saying, "No, I am wrong there. I would put the Electromatic typewriter second—a very low-priced Electromatic typewriter, and redesign the present model in plastic to make it at a lower cost as well." To emphasize the point, he asserted that before long, "Every typewriter is going to be electrical. . . . We pioneered this, now let's not let it get away from us."[4] Of particular interest to Watson was an exploratory project in Endicott that used an electric typewriter as the basis of an accounting machine for small businesses.[5]

Watson's zest for new products to replace wartime revenues was dampening his normal enthusiasm for longer-range projects. Concerned by this, McPherson said, "There is one observation I want to make in connection with the list. I feel that the electronic research should go on regardless of the projects we are rushing to current completion. We must attempt to use vacuum tube circuits in business machines."

"Let's understand this does not mean these are the only things we are going to work on. It means we will concentrate on these five things as being the five most important things," Watson responded. "I want to put electronics in a class by itself because I think it is that important," McPherson persisted. "Can you have something ready in six months that we can go out in the field with?" Watson asked. "No," was the inevitable response. "Well then," said Watson, "it isn't of first importance."[6]

Printer Research

Prior to these discussions, the wheel-printer project had been managed in the manner of most of the company's research. A single engineer, with minimum help, worked on it whenever he found time from more pressing assignments. In this case H. S. (Bud) Beattie had begun research on printing devices, leading to the wheel printer, soon after he joined IBM in 1933.

Beattie had minimized the speed-limiting effect of the type-carrier inertia by mounting the type on the outside surface of a rotating wheel rather than on the front surface of a long, vertically oscillating bar as then used in IBM printers. He also devised an ingenious method for printing in which the motion of the type parallel to the surface of the paper was reduced to zero at the moment of impact. The wheel was rotated at high speed initially to bring the desired character near the print line shortly before impact. Then the speed of rotation was slowed to bring the character into precise position at the moment of impact. The slow rotation speed was chosen to offset exactly the pivoting motion that brought the type in contact with the paper.

Now after ten years of part-time research, Beattie's project became part of an effort to provide an improved accounting machine. The effort was slowed at first by wartime priorities and then by more immediate postwar priorities. These delays were frustrating for Beattie, but they also afforded him time to improve his printer. Using a separate print wheel for each of 120 columns across the paper, he was able to design a printer that achieved a speed of 150 lines per minute with good print quality. Forty-eight numerals, alphabetics, and special characters on each wheel gave the printer outstanding function in addition to its 50 percent greater speed than the fastest previous printer.[7]

In 1947 the proposed accounting machine with its improved printer faced a crucial test. The estimated cost of tooling was so high that the sales department recommended project termination. Watson sought the opinion of John McPherson, who had worked closely with the development engineers. After McPherson explained how its printing speed and other features could give the customer up to eight times the performance of current machines, Watson said: "You go into the meeting tomorrow and tell them that it can do eight times the work of the present machine. At eight hundred dollars [monthly rental], it's a bargain."

McPherson did as instructed, and the sales department withdrew its objections. The machine was introduced in 1949 as the IBM 407 Accounting Machine. Its market reception exceeded expectations, resulting in revenues far larger than any of its predecessors. The 407 is also noteworthy for being IBM's last major electromechanical accounting machine product—and for serving as the printer on the company's first large-scale electronic computers.[8]

During the extensive period devoted to testing and improving the 407, Beattie found time for research on other printing methods. A novel method devised by him used a mushroom-shaped type element whose spherical outer surface held fifty-two raised characters. The desired character was selected by rotating the element about its spherical center.[9] First demonstrated by Beattie in 1946, this mushroom-shaped device was the predecessor of the type element used in the highly popular IBM Selectric typewriter, announced in 1961, as well as in numerous text processors and computer terminals introduced during the 1960s and 1970s.[10]

Watson's decision in the June 1943 engineering meetings to give the second highest priority to improving the electric typewriter line was followed by the transfer of typewriter development and manufacture from Rochester, New York, to Poughkeepsie in 1944. This paved the way for increasing research and development on typewriters and for expanding production when the Poughkeepsie plant shifted to peacetime products. It was a good decision. Revenues from electric typewriter sales, service, and supplies increased fivefold ($11 million to $57 million) during the ten-year period from 1946 through 1955.[11]

Emphasis on Electronics

Stiffening German resistance by the fall of 1943 and continued hard fighting in the Pacific caused Watson to recognize that the end of the war was further away than he had perceived in June. He still wanted new products for rapid release to production, but he was now prepared to focus on longer-term projects as well. In particular he was eager to respond to McPherson's recommendation that research in electronics be strengthened.

"Mr. Watson wants electronics used on the accounting machine and on the printer," the summary of the October engineering meeting records. "He wants Mr. Bryce to get out and visit the various colleges, find the most outstanding Professor on electronics and get him for IBM. If he gets $10,000 with the college, we would be willing to pay him as much as $25,000 and let him keep in touch with his college, going back once a month to give lectures, or perhaps as often as twice a month."[12]

Responding to Watson's mandates on electronics was difficult. All senior electronics engineers were still deeply involved in the war effort. But events associated with the August 1944 dedication of the IBM-Harvard Mark I stimulated Watson and Bryce to more vigorous action. Just prior to the dedication, Howard Aiken of Harvard University had issued a press release describing himself as the sole inventor. The role of IBM was largely ignored. Aiken was willing to acknowledge the intellectual contributions of Bryce, but apparently he could not bring himself to acknowledge the engineering contributions of Clair Lake and others.

Commenting on these issues in a letter to Aiken after the dedication, Bryce wrote: "It was indeed very unfortunate that the mistake was made in the original press statements given out, identifying you as sole inventor of the machine. . . . While I appreciate all that you said about me, I feel that in justice to these other men, it would have been a gracious gesture on your part and very much appreciated by them, if your letter to Mr. Lake had contained an acknowledgement of sincere regret over such unfortunate and erroneous publicity."[13]

Watson himself was enraged by the press release and by Aiken's deportment. Only reluctantly did Watson attend the dedication. He had lavished hundreds of thousands of dollars and IBM's best research and engineering talents in developing the Mark I, and he had donated another hundred thousand dollars for its operation. Now Howard Aiken seemed determined to deprive IBM and its technical people of any credit or benefit from the project. Aiken also indicated he would design and build future machines without IBM's help.[14]

Beyond the emotional pain, there was a very practical consideration for Watson and Bryce. A primary reason for working with Aiken had been to establish with Harvard University a mutually beneficial relationship of the type the company had long enjoyed with Columbia. To foster this relationship, Bryce had encouraged the use of the company's most innovative arithmetic and storage devices in the Mark I. He had viewed the Mark I as a machine IBM would continually upgrade—thus providing a test bed for new devices and computational methods as well as a facility in which customer needs in scientific computation could be assessed. Now the breakdown of cordial relations with Aiken had dashed all hopes for future cooperation.[15]

To fill the void, Watson concluded that IBM should build its own computational facility. He contacted Wallace Eckert with whom he had enjoyed congenial cooperation at Columbia University. During the war Eckert had served as director of the Nautical Almanac at the U.S. Naval Observatory. His first task at the observatory had been to design an air almanac for the expanding air force. Using equipment rapidly installed by IBM, the observatory's personnel were able to compute and compile the data, design the air almanac, and get it approved and into air force training camps in less than a year.

With the war entering its final phase, Watson suggested Eckert should consider peacetime employment. In particular he offered him the opportunity to establish the company's first laboratory devoted to "pure science." A major emphasis, consistent with Eckert's own interests, was to be automatic scientific computation. As part of the assignment, Eckert was to establish specifications for a "supercalculator" Watson proposed to build. Eckert accepted the offer and joined IBM in March 1945.[16]

In describing the supercalculator project to his engineers, Watson said its performance must eclipse the Mark I and any machine Aiken might build in the future. Recognizing that this objective could not be achieved without significant innovation, Bryce urged that a small electronic calculating machine be developed first. The task was assigned to Halsey Dickinson, who had continued his research on electronic arithmetic circuits throughout the war—even in his own basement when wartime pressures made such work inappropriate at IBM. Byron Phelps was assigned to the project, as was an engineer from Dickinson's department. They also had the help of two technicians.[17]

Using circuits developed in Endicott by Palmer and Phelps at the beginning of the war, the small engineering group had a production-prototype electronic calculator operating in April 1946—one year after Phelps joined the project. The prototype and the first four production models could perform both multiplication and division, but market planners concluded the division capability being offered was too limited. Therefore the capability was eliminated entirely before the machine was demonstrated in September at the business show in New York City.

Announced as the IBM 603 Electronic Multiplier, the machine was the first electronic calculator ever placed in production. It contained approximately 300 vacuum tubes. It could multiply two 6-digit numbers read from a card and then punch the 12-digit product into the same card at a speed of 100 cards per minute. Because of unexpectedly good reception for the electronic machine, a decision was made to limit production to one hundred and, as quickly as possible, to develop a more versatile electronic machine to replace it. The replacement machine was the highly successful IBM 604 Electronic Calculating Punch.[18] Exploratory electronic projects encouraged by Bryce before the war, and reestablished by him near the end of the war, had thus resulted in the two most successful electronic calculating machines of the immediate post–World War II era.

The SSEC: A Supercomputer

Meanwhile Watson was busily assembling a team to develop a supercomputer. Engineering responsibility was assigned early in 1945 to Frank Hamilton, who had served as lead engineer under Clair Lake for the Mark I project. In August, Robert R. (Rex) Seeber, a 1932 Harvard graduate with an interest in machine computation, joined Eckert's staff and was assigned to work with Hamilton. As his involvement grew, Seeber became the chief architect.

Previously Seeber had spent a year writing programs for the Mark I, directly under navy commander Howard Aiken. It was not a happy relationship. Their personalities clashed, and Aiken refused to consider Seeber's proposal to endow the next Harvard machine (Mark II) with provisions for modifying its instructions during operation—a feature that later became standard in computers. Seeber gladly joined Eckert, who offered him considerable freedom in defining the capabilities of Watson's proposed machine.

Specifications for the supercomputer were developed by Hamilton and Seeber and approved by Eckert in March 1946. Use of electronic arithmetic circuits like those in the IBM 603 was key to the high performance of the machine. To implement these circuits, Byron Phelps was transferred back to Endicott after finishing his work on the 603.[19]

Completed and tested in Endicott in the summer of 1947, the supercomputer was disassembled and shipped to the company's

Figure 10.1. The SSEC: A Supercomputer
Top: The SSEC (Selective Sequence Electronic Calculator) was dedicated in
January 1948. It occupied the periphery of a room 60 feet long and 30 feet
wide. Along the left wall are panels of vacuum tube circuits for card reading
and sequence control and thirty-six paper-tape readers for table lookup.
Along the back wall are the three paper-tape punches and the thirty paper-
tape readers used for information storage. Along the right wall are the electronic arithmetic and storage units. Card readers, card punches, and printers
can be seen in the center of the room, but the operator's console is ob-
scured by the pillars. Bottom: Standing behind the operator's console are
from left: Robert R. Seeber, Wallace J. Eckert, Thomas J. Watson, and Frank
E. Hamilton. Eckert established specifications for the SSEC, and Seeber and
Hamilton served as the chief architect and chief engineer, respectively.

headquarters at 590 Madison Avenue where it was reassembled, tested, and publicly dedicated in January 1948 as the IBM Selective Sequence Electronic Calculator (SSEC). The SSEC contained 21,400 relays and 12,500 vacuum tubes. Its electronic arithmetic circuits could perform 14-by-14-digit decimal multiplication in 20 milliseconds, division in 33 milliseconds, and addition or subtraction of 19-digit numbers in only 0.3 milliseconds. The SSEC was more than 250 times as fast as the Mark I, whose electromechanical arithmetic unit required 6 seconds for multiplication and 16 seconds for division.

The SSEC could store up to 400,000 decimal digits in a hierarchical memory system consisting of 160 digits of high-speed electronic storage, 3,000 digits of intermediate-speed relay storage, and the remainder in long paper tapes made of standard IBM punched-card stock. About a quarter of the tape storage was in continuous loops mounted on up to 36 tape readers. The loops contained prepunched mathematical function tables, programs, and input data. Three additional storage units used blank rolls of paper tape. Consisting of a punching station followed by 10 reading stations, these units could store intermediate results for later reference.[20]

As in later computers, the SSEC represented, moved, and stored instructions in the same manner as data. Punched-card machines had long been able to sense the sign of the amount in an accumulator and take alternative action when it changed. For the SSEC, Seeber extended the idea (albeit awkwardly) to permit branching to a different subprogram, thus enabling the SSEC to execute program loops. It was the first operational computer capable of modifying its program based on intermediate results.

Although the SSEC was the most powerful computing machine of the time, its influence on later computer designs was limited by external developments (as discussed in chap. 11). It did, however, provide IBM with important patent coverage, and it played a significant role in computer developments by facilitating the early training of programmers inside and outside the company. The programming staff established and directed by Seeber, for example, included John Backus, who later developed FORTRAN, and Edgar F. (Ted) Codd, who later became known as the "originator of the relational model for databases."[21]

Dedicated by Watson "to the use of science throughout the world," the SSEC was operated on a nonprofit basis, with no charge for computations pertaining to "pure science." Wallace

Eckert was, of course, a major user. His accurate calculations of the moon's positions for the period 1952–1971 became the world standard when published in 1949. Fifteen years later his work provided the basis for orbital calculations made to guide the first landing on the moon.[22]

The Watson Laboratory

Wallace Eckert's decision to leave the prestigious position at the Naval Observatory and join IBM in March 1945 was influenced by many years of association with Watson. He knew that Watson was genuinely interested in supporting scientific work and that Watson believed a company that reaped the benefits of science should contribute to science. Eckert was also pleased that Watson urged him to maintain his own credentials as an astronomer so he could retain—and his laboratory could gain—respect and leadership in the scientific community. Eckert, incidentally, was the first IBM employee with a doctorate.

Concerning Watson's desire that the laboratory be devoted to "pure science," Eckert provided the following clarification: "By pure science we mean scientific research where the problem is dictated by the interest in the problem and not by external considerations." Consistent with this objective, Eckert located at Columbia University to facilitate interaction with faculty scientists. Temporarily placed in Pupin Hall, the laboratory moved in November 1945 to a townhouse at 612 West 116th Street where space could be provided for computing equipment, a library, reception lounge, a small machine shop, and two to three dozen professionals. Officially designated the Watson Scientific Computing Laboratory at Columbia University, it was commonly referred to as the Watson Lab.[23]

Among the early employees was Llewellyn H. Thomas, a world-renowned mathematician and theoretical physicist who is best known for the Thomas-Fermi approximation for describing degenerate electron gases and for the Thomas precession of electron spins. Thomas left Ohio State University to join the new laboratory because of his interest in adapting mathematical problems to automatic calculating machines and the promised freedom to pursue other research topics of interest to him. At the Watson Laboratory he continued to be a prolific contributor to science while also finding time to involve himself in practical engineering problems.

Figure 10.2. Watson Laboratory

The Watson Laboratory was located in this five-story townhouse at 612 West 116th Street in New York City beginning in 1945. It was relocated to a larger building on 612 West 115th Street in 1953. There it remained until 1970 when the laboratory's activities were transferred to the Thomas J. Watson Research Center in Yorktown Heights, N.Y.

To identify and attract Thomas and other top talent, Eckert obtained the help of I. I. Rabi, a Nobel Prize–winning member of the Columbia University physics department who had served as associate director of the MIT Radiation Laboratory during the war. Rabi was especially helpful in locating much needed specialists in electronics.[24]

Watson's view of the role of the new laboratory is conveyed by the official news release when it was opened: "The research and instructional resources of the laboratory will be made available to scientists, universities, and research organizations in this country and abroad, and special cooperative arrangements will be made with scholarly institutions." In addition to their primary activities of devising new methods of automatic computation and applying them to scientific problems, laboratory personnel undertook the task of educating others. A course titled "Three-Week Course on Computing" started in 1947 to teach the use of punched-card equipment for mathematical calculations was ultimately attended by approximately 1,600 people from twenty countries.[25]

Because IBM's first laboratory devoted to pure science was established in the same year in which Vannevar Bush issued his report to President Harry S. Truman on *Science, the Endless Frontier*, there is a tendency to link the two events more closely than is warranted.[26] The decision to create the Watson Laboratory in New York City in 1945 appears to have been driven almost exclusively by internal considerations and competitive pressures, including the loss of good relations with Howard Aiken at Harvard and the excellent relationship Watson had enjoyed with Wallace Eckert since long before World War II began.

11

Government-Funded Competition

Watson did not become complacent after World War II, although he had ample reason to do so. The company's gross revenues dropped only about 15 percent during 1946, despite lost sales of munitions. At the same time, profits jumped by 70 percent. During 1947 revenues returned to their peak level and profits were nearly three times those of wartime. (See appendix A.) More secure than ever was IBM's position as the leading supplier of punched-card equipment for record keeping, accounting, and other business applications.

Also strengthened during the war was the company's leadership in digital computation methods and equipment. Some specialized electronic devices for code breaking were in use during the war, but no electronic computing devices were completed in time. The ENIAC, for example, was not ready for test operation until late in 1945. Thus the burden of wartime computational activities fell primarily on IBM equipment. It was used to analyze airframe designs, to predict artillery shell trajectories, to break enemy codes, to support the atomic bomb development, and to perform a range of other tasks that defy easy description.[1]

After the war in September 1946, IBM introduced the industry's first product to employ electronic digital computation, the IBM 603 Electronic Multiplier. Early that same year, upon his return from the navy, Ralph Palmer established an electronic engineering effort in Poughkeepsie. His highest priority was to develop a successor to the 603. The resulting IBM 604 Electronic Calculating Punch was first shipped to customers in the fall of 1948. It provided speed and flexibility of operation unmatched by any calculator in the marketplace for sometime.[2]

Watson's primary competitor was still Remington Rand. Its punched-card equipment business was only one-tenth the size of

IBM's, and it had no experience in electronic computing devices.[3] From where might any significant challenge come?

Sounding the Alarm

The primary postwar challenge was generated unexpectedly by government actions directed by individuals who had been responsible for harnessing advanced technologies during the war. Key among these individuals was Vannevar Bush, a one-time MIT professor whose differential analyzers had been used extensively during the war for calculating ballistic firing tables.[4] President of the Carnegie Institution during the war, Bush also served as head of the Office of Scientific Research and Development (OSRD). His mission was to organize the country's technical resources for military purposes. In fact but not title, Bush was the chief adviser to President Roosevelt on matters of science, engineering, and technology.

At war's end, Bush and his colleagues successfully sought to preserve the country's leadership in technologies crucial to national security. As a result, federal money continued to be spent in postwar years on research and development projects in university and industrial laboratories. This eased the transition from war to peace, contributed to the country's military preparedness, and stimulated economic growth. Bush emphasized electronics—especially its application to automatic computation.[5]

Only gradually did IBM leaders become aware of these events, many of which were shrouded in secrecy appropriate to national security matters. John McPherson, with his technical expertise and federal contacts, was the first to sense the government's new peacetime role. By September 1946 his concern over the size and number of government-funded projects in electronic computing led him to write to Wallace Eckert, urging Eckert to reevaluate the adequacy of his laboratory's program.[6] "In view of the vast program which the government is now sponsoring," Eckert responded, "I feel that the present tempo at the Watson Laboratory is not adequate for IBM, and a greatly accelerated program of development of the various phases of the new electronic techniques should be undertaken."[7]

In November the two of them took the unusual step of writing a joint letter to Watson to advise him of their concerns. "As an outgrowth of the wartime demand for high speed computing," the letter began, "the National Bureau of Standards has embarked on a program of development of electronic digital calculating devices with funds from the Departments of Commerce, War and Navy. Part of this development will be carried on in the Bureau, and part by means of development contracts with outside individuals and organizations. These development contracts are of such nature that they will be very attractive to anyone without previous private experience or patents in the computing field; but the patent provisions make it doubtful if IBM, which has led in the field, can afford to participate in the program."

The army and navy were independently financing major research projects on electronic computing at the University of Pennsylvania, the Institute for Advanced Study, Harvard University, MIT, and other places according to the letter, which further noted that "several commercial concerns in addition to IBM have been developing electronic computing machines."

"Whereas before the war IBM was the only organization able and willing to carry on large scale development of calculators, such development is now taking place on a large scale," they advised Watson. The letter provided disturbing information, but Eckert and McPherson avoided recommending specific action. Instead they observed, "The complete answer to this situation is not obvious since questions of basic policy are involved."[8]

The ENIAC

Among the many government-sponsored activities in digital computers, a project at the Moore School of Electrical Engineering of the University of Pennsylvania achieved the greatest long-term impact. Sponsored by the Army Ballistic Research Laboratory, it had the goal of building an electronic computing machine for wartime ballistics calculations. Work began in the summer of 1943, and the resultant ENIAC (Electronic Numerical Integrator and Computer) was ready for its first test runs in late 1945, some months after the surrender of Japan. The ENIAC was formally unveiled at a dedication ceremony at the Moore School in February 1946.

The senior member of the development team, John W. Mauchly, had proposed the project. His interest in electronic computation began well before his 1941 visit to Iowa State College (discussed in chap. 7) during which he had lengthy discussions with John Atanasoff about the latter's partially completed electronic computer.[9] Second in command was J. Presper Eckert, Jr.,

Figure 11.1.   The ENIAC
Left: Rear view of a small portion of the ENIAC reveals some of its 18,000 vacuum tubes. Right: Front view reveals some of the plug wires and switches used to program the machine. (Courtesy of Smithsonian Institution.)

a twenty-two-year-old graduate student at the Moore School when he first met Mauchly in 1941. Much of the credit for the success of ENIAC belongs to Eckert, who was a brilliant and innovative engineer.[10]

The ENIAC was a huge room-sized machine. Its 18,000 vacuum tubes made it the largest electronic computing device in existence. So many tubes also created a severe operating problem. Seldom did a day go by without replacement of burned-out tubes. Although a faulty tube could be replaced in minutes, locating it often took hours. The ENIAC had 40 percent more vacuum tubes and was somewhat faster in individual operations than IBM's SSEC, which was completed two years later. For diverse calculations, however, the ENIAC was no match for the SSEC because it lacked storage capacity and required time-consuming resetting of many switches and the rewiring of large plugboards to shift from one job to another.[11]

Operation of the ENIAC was described by one early user as follows: "We had about 40 plugboards, each several feet in size. A number of wires had to be plugged for each single instruction of a problem, thousands of them each time a problem was to begin a run; and this took several days to do and many more days to check out. When that was finally accomplished, we would run the problem as long as possible, i.e. as long as we had input data." Reprogramming the machine for a new problem was typically undertaken only after several weeks of operation.[12]

The deficiencies of the ENIAC design became increasingly evident to Eckert and Mauchly, even before John von Neumann became involved in August 1944. A distinguished Hungarian mathematician who emigrated from Germany to the United States in 1930, von Neumann received a permanent appointment three years later to the newly established Institute for Advanced Study in Princeton, New Jersey. During the war he consulted for numerous government organizations and became familiar with the use of punched-card equipment for mathematical applications.[13] Von Neumann shared the feeling that ENIAC's plug-wire control and dearth of internal storage capacity were major deficiencies.

Stored-Program Computers

Through the interactions of Eckert, Mauchly, von Neumann, and others, a design emerged of a more advanced machine called the EDVAC (Electronic Discrete Variable Automatic Computer). The generous support given the ENIAC project can be perceived from the fact that the Army Ordnance Department in January 1945 granted a ten-month supplement of $105,000 just for research and development on the EDVAC. Much of this money was spent for developing a mercury delay-line memory to provide the large-capacity, high-speed internal storage needed to supply data and instructions to the electronic arithmetic units.[14]

While Eckert and Mauchly concentrated on electronic devices and engineering aspects of the machine, von Neumann focused on machine properties of direct concern to a programmer—on what today is called *architecture*. Perhaps more than anyone else to that time, he "gave a logical treatment to the subject, much as if it were a conventional branch of logics or mathematics."[15] By separating the logic of machine operation from matters of practical hardware implementation, von Neumann was able to identify computer design principles that outlived the hardware issues of the day.

Computers adhering to the design philosophy he espoused came to be known, years later, as *stored-program* computers. Using von Neumann's neurological terminology, the critical storage device was called *memory*—and still later *main memory* to distinguish it from larger-capacity and slower storage devices that were also attached to the central processing unit. In stored-program computers, typically a single memory stores both instructions and data so that program sequences can be made available as rapidly as data. Furthermore, by treating instructions as data, the sequence of calculations can be altered automatically during a long computation, based on intermediate results.[16]

The IBM designers of the SSEC had also begun their work in 1945, but they were constrained to use existing technologies in order to complete their machine as quickly as possible. Thus the sequence control of the SSEC made use of an internal memory hierarchy consisting of high-speed vacuum tubes, intermediate-speed electromechanical relays, and paper tape storage devices offering large capacities at relatively low cost.

The SSEC was the first operational computer to satisfy the modern definition of a stored-program computer. Although its architecture lacked the elegance and simplicity achieved by the EDVAC's designers, a patent based on the SSEC and filed in January 1949 provided IBM with primary patent rights on the stored-program computer.[17] All claims in this patent were subsequently upheld during patent-interference proceedings with Sperry Rand.[18]

Designed and built under heavy pressure for rapid completion and without benefit from the Moore School work or the broader intellectual discussions led by John von Neumann, the SSEC was in full operation in January 1948, well over a year before the first computer based on the Moore School design. Ironically the Moore School's EDVAC was not operational until late in 1951.[19]

Promoting the Concept

Long before the first EDVAC-type computer was completed, the influence of EDVAC on future developments was assured by a series of events. The first of these events was the distribution in June 1945 of a "First Draft of a Report on the EDVAC," written by von Neumann. Why this remarkable but unfinished report was distributed with von Neumann listed as the sole author, with no credit to others, is surrounded by controversy. But its initial impact is clear. It ended the productive and harmonious relationship at the Moore School.

Von Neumann's use of neurological analogies and terms outraged Eckert because it enabled von Neumann to give unclassified talks about work at the Moore School "without giving any credit" to anyone else. "I was too young to know how to fight back against this type of behavior," Eckert recalls.[20] Meanwhile Eckert and Mauchly were not able to talk about their work because it was performed under a government security classification of "confidential." Their first detailed engineering progress report on the EDVAC (completed three months after von Neumann's highly abstract, theoretical treatment) was available primarily to project participants and contract administrators.[21]

Herman H. Goldstine, an army officer and mathematician who served as the Ballistic Research Laboratory's representative to the ENIAC project, says the First Draft document was intended as a "working paper for use in clarifying and coordinating the thinking of the group." It was initially distributed only to people closely associated with the project. The content was soon deemed so significant, however, that knowledge of the document spread, and Goldstine gave copies to many who requested them. Thus, according to Goldstine, the document was given broad distribution without von Neumann's knowledge.[22]

The document was not only a significant technical contribution, but it also became an important tool in von Neumann's effort to establish his own computer project at the Institute for Advanced Study (IAS). Seeking support from a variety of sources, he ultimately established his IAS Computer project with $300,000 provided in three equal parts by the institute itself and by the ordnance departments of the army and navy. He also entered into a joint research and development contract with RCA to develop a computer memory. The RCA device, known as the selectron, was based on a specially designed vacuum tube that stored information internally in an array of metallic eyelets, the voltages of which were set to represent logical 1s or 0s by the selective application of electron beam bombardment and electric currents. The selectron was expected to provide even faster access to stored information than the delay-line memory being developed by Eckert for the EDVAC.[23]

Just as important as von Neumann's conceptualization of the stored-program computer was his promotion of it. He attended technical meetings, visited research laboratories, and presented his ideas in private and public forums. Following his initiation of the IAS Computer project, it became a focal point for the exchange of ideas on electronic computing. As a result of his activities, a significant degree of design standardization was achieved, and numerous projects were initiated to design and build stored-program computers. As reported by John McPherson following discussions at the Aberdeen Proving Ground in September 1945, "probably four organizations [are] building machines of this type simultaneously—a machine at the Institute for Advanced Study in Princeton, a machine at the University of Pennsylvania, a machine in England, and probably one at the Naval Ordnance Laboratory in Washington."[24]

A particularly important event was an eight-week Moore School course held in the summer of 1946 on the "Theory and Techniques for Design of Electronic Digital Computers." Jointly sponsored by the Office of Naval Research and the Army Ordnance Department, the purpose of the course was to disseminate information about electronic digital computers and about the opportunities for government funding. Eckert, Mauchly, von Neumann, and others presented lectures. Invitees included representatives from Columbia University, Harvard University, the Institute for Advanced Study, MIT, AT&T, Eastman-Kodak, General Electric, IBM, and National Cash Register as well as from the National Bureau of Standards and other government organizations.[25]

The invitation to IBM was withdrawn shortly before the course began. The official reason given was that the company was not among those receiving government funds to work on electronic computing.[26] A more cogent reason may well have related to recent decisions of two key lecturers. Eckert and Mauchly had decided to leave the Moore School and establish their own company in direct competition with IBM.[27]

Commercial Ventures

A new patent policy of the Moore School was a major factor in the decision of Eckert and Mauchly to leave the University of Pennsylvania. Henceforth, employees would be required to assign to the university all patents resulting from work done while in its employ. Similar policies were common in industry, where employees typically assigned their patents to the company that paid their salaries and the other costs of research.

The primary intent of the university was to maintain the "intellectual purity" of the research it sponsored rather than having research driven by a desire for personal gain. The policy was not, however, acceptable to Eckert and Mauchly. They were motivated by building useful computing devices—and making money—as well as by the purely intellectual aspects of their work. Indeed they had already explored potential funding for the construction of machines for the Bureau of the Census. Refusing to sign the patent release, the two men were forced to resign at the end of March 1946.[28]

In addition to the various opportunities arising from government-funded projects, Eckert and Mauchly received an offer from Thomas Watson. He agreed to establish a computing laboratory for them at IBM. Eckert was very interested because it would have permitted him to develop electronic computer technology independent of institutional constraints, but Mauchly was reluctant. He believed he and Eckert could establish their own very profitable business. In the end Mauchly's view prevailed.[29]

In June 1946 they formed the Electronic Control Company, later called the Eckert-Mauchly Computer Corporation. It was the first company established specifically to design, manufacture, and sell electronic stored-program computers. By the fall of 1949 the company gave the appearance of a thriving organization. It had 134 employees and six contracts for its large, partially developed computer, now called the UNIVAC (UNIVersal Automatic Computer). In fact, however, the Eckert-Mauchly Computer Corporation was in deep trouble.[30]

Initial problems were created when the National Bureau of Standards, which had broad responsibility for government funding of computer projects, received a less than enthusiastic evaluation of the Eckert-Mauchly project from a highly respected expert. As a result, only a study contract for $75,000 was initially offered. A contract for $170,000 to complete the computer design for the Census Bureau was not signed until June 1948, almost two years later. Compounding and contributing to this financial problem, Eckert and Mauchly initially had little comprehension of the difference between developing a commercial product and creating a one-of-a-kind device such as the ENIAC. They also had no business experience.[31]

Running late on their government work and short of funds, they chose to obtain additional money and development experience by entering into a $100,000 contract to build a small com-

Figure 11.2.   Mauchly, Groves, and Eckert with Computer Memory
John W. Mauchly (left) and J. Presper Eckert, Jr. (right), are shown discussing UNIVAC's mercury delay-line memory and its test facility with Gen. Leslie R. Groves (center). The memory is the large metallic cylinder jutting out from the bottom of the rack. (Courtesy of Smithsonian Institution.)

puter (BINAC) for the Northrop Aircraft Company. Delivered in September 1949, the small computer had taken three times longer than the projected eight months to develop, had cost almost three times the contracted price, and fell far short of expectations in reliability and performance.[32]

Already behind schedule on all commitments and out of money in the fall of 1948, the company achieved a temporary solution when the American Totalisator Company agreed to provide approximately $500,000 for 40 percent ownership. The decision was based on the belief that electronic devices might some day replace the relay-operated totalisators used at race tracks. Death in a private plane crash of the American Totalisator vice president who had arranged the deal, combined with escalating development problems, made further fund-raising necessary in the fall of 1949.[33]

Unable to get additional loans, Eckert and Mauchly sold their business to Remington Rand in February 1950. The purchase marked Remington Rand's entry into the field of electronic computers. The Eckert-Mauchly Computer Corporation became a wholly owned subsidiary and functioned as an independent division. In March 1951 the Census Bureau accepted the first UNIVAC, and three more were delivered within eighteen months.[34]

During the years in which Eckert and Mauchly were barely surviving, Engineering Research Associates (ERA) was thriving. Seriously undercapitalized, it nevertheless managed to grow with the solicitous help of the National Security Agency, whose predecessor organizations had helped create it. In fiscal year 1947 employment rose from 145 to 420 as ERA grew its staff to the size needed to develop the top-secret, special-purpose electronic devices needed for code breaking and other national security activities.

In August 1947 ERA was given the task of designing a general-purpose, stored-program computer to carry out many activities previously handled by special-purpose equipment. Seven months later the navy approved the design and authorized construction. Code-named Atlas, after the mental giant in the comic strip, "Barnaby," it was a stored-program computer similar to the EDVAC. Its main memory was provided by a rotating drum with magnetic recording media on the cylindrical surface—a technology pioneered by ERA after the war. Atlas contained 2,700 vacuum tubes and 2,385 crystal diodes. It was delivered to the government in Washington, D.C., and successfully operated in December 1950.

A modified version, called the ERA 1101, was cleared by the navy for sale as a commercial product and announced in December 1951. No commercial orders were received, however, primarily because the computer had very limited input-output facilities, no operating or program manuals were available, and there was no formal marketing effort. Furthermore the company lacked the financial resources to compete in the commercial market.

John Parker, who had arranged ERA's initial financing—$20,000 equity and a $200,000 line of credit—had long recognized the constraints imposed by this meager funding. Accordingly he had been in contact with potential buyers for several years. In December 1951 he announced that an offer had been accepted for the purchase of the company by Remington Rand. Consummation of the deal was delayed until reviews by the Federal Trade Commission and the Justice Department were completed. Approval was granted in May 1952. The value of ERA was set at $1.7 million. Government sponsorship had thus helped ERA shareholders receive an 85-fold return on their investment in only about six years.[35]

The purchase of ERA, combined with the earlier purchase of EMCC, made Remington Rand the undisputed leader in large-scale electronic computers. Government funding of electronic computer development had resulted in a massive concentration of expertise in electronics and digital computing in Remington Rand—a company that would continue to provide IBM with its primary competition for another two decades.[36]

Provocative Terminology

While promoting the stored-program design concept, von Neumann also promulgated his neurological terminology for parts of the machine. The high-speed storage device, for example, became known as "memory." Presper Eckert has suggested this practice was merely a ploy by which von Neumann avoided government classification restrictions. More than likely, however, von Neumann was attracted to a terminology that likened a machine to a human being. In this he was not alone. Eckert and Mauchly, themselves, chose to call their machine a *computer*—a word primarily used at the time to designate a person who did computing with the help of calculating equipment. By calling their machine a computer, Eckert and Mauchly were conjuring up the perception that ENIAC had the intellectual capabilities of a person.

Prominent among those resisting such terminology was Thomas Watson. He well understood the emotional and sales impact of the term, but he was selling products, not ideas. The public had often resisted new machinery that was difficult to comprehend, frightening, or likely to replace people in the workplace. What could be more frightening or likely to replace people than an electronic "computer." Watson wanted to convey the message that IBM's machines were not designed to replace people. Rather they were designed ʌo help people, by relieving them of drudgery.

It was Watson's policy, and therefore IBM's, to refer to such machines as "automatic calculators" or "sequence controlled calculators." Thus the world's first large-scale digital computer, the IBM-Harvard Mark I, was officially named the IBM Automatic Sequence Controlled Calculator, and the first stored-program computer was called the IBM Selective Sequence Electronic Calculator. Even IBM's first electronic product designed and marketed specifically to meet the computing needs of engineers and scientists was called the Card Programmed Calculator rather than the Card Programmed Computer.

The battle for naming computing equipment was not won by IBM, however. The emotional appeal and simplicity of the word *computer* could not be resisted. All that resulted from Watson's effort was a common misperception that early machines that were called calculators must have lacked some important quality of a computer.

12

IBM's Initial Response

"For IBM to keep its position in the business world, it seems to me that we must somehow pass on that spirit of belief in our enterprise and the will to go ahead. Our people must know and believe that they cannot stand still."[1] So wrote James Bryce to Watson in April 1948. It was a time when tensions were mounting between those advocating greater use of electronics in company products and those who favored continuing with electromechanical devices because they were fast enough for most applications, more reliable, less expensive, and—above all—more familiar.

Bryce had worked more than thirty years with Watson to strengthen the product line and to broaden its applications. With Watson he had shared in the success of that endeavor. Having promoted the use of electronics in test equipment and products for many years, Bryce was particularly pleased to witness the 1946 introduction of the IBM 603 Electronic Multiplier, the first commercial product to incorporate electronic arithmetic circuits. Too ill to attend the January 1948 dedication of the SSEC, he could nevertheless take pride in that event as well. Then in March 1949, Bryce died of a cerebral hemorrhage. He was sixty-eight years old.[2]

Attending the funeral at age seventy-five, Watson knew he had little time left to achieve his own final goal—to transfer leadership of IBM to his two sons. It was a goal he had given high priority since the end of the war. The resulting transition profoundly affected IBM's response to electronic computing, and it produced one of the more stressful periods in the company's history.

Grooming Two Sons

Watson's choice of positions for his sons was constrained by their rather different personalities and capabilities. His older son,

Thomas J. Watson, Jr., had not been a good student. Imperfect eye-hand coordination had adversely affected his reading and had also prevented him from doing well at most sports. Overwhelmed by his father's successes and frustrated by his own failures, Tom Watson had suffered periods of depression in his youth. His academic record in high school was poor, causing him to seek recognition in the girls he dated, the expensive cars he drove, and the pranks he played on others.

His first real success was in competitive rowing in which his team qualified for the international regatta in Henley, England. His scores on college admission tests were generally low, except for physics in which he scored remarkably high. With the considerable influence of his father and support from an understanding dean, he was admitted to and graduated from Brown University.[3]

Joining IBM as a sales trainee in 1937, Watson, Jr., enjoyed the informality of being called Tom Watson, or simply Tom. By contrast his father was always addressed as Mr. Watson, even by his closest associates. (Consistent with that practice, this book reserves the less formal name, Tom Watson, for the son.) Graduating from sales school in Endicott, the young Watson was immediately given a prime sales territory in Manhattan. He did well, but he could never get out from under his father's shadow. In his own mind he believed his successes were orchestrated by his father, whereas his failures were his own. Only in flying airplanes, a hobby he took up as a freshman at Brown, did he achieve the personal accomplishment he longed for. Part of the triumph was overcoming his eye-hand coordination limitations.

Eager to escape his father's influence and wishing to fly military airplanes, Watson considered joining the Army Air Corps, but feared he would fail the eye exam. Learning that his civilian flying experience would qualify him for the Air National Guard without attending flight school or taking the eye exam, he signed up immediately and soon obtained his commission as a second lieutenant. When President Roosevelt mobilized the National Guard in September 1940, Tom Watson had achieved his dream. He had become a full-fledged military pilot.[4]

Watson did a lot of flying, and he distinguished himself in a variety of other assignments. He promoted the use of Link trainers to improve pilot training; he served as aide-de-camp to the head of the First Air Force; and he helped establish a ferry route to deliver airplanes to the Soviet Union. In the air corps he became his own man. He achieved the reputation of a self-assertive, strong-willed young officer, capable of accomplishing difficult assignments.[5]

Discharged from the Army Air Corps at the end of 1945, he reported back for work at IBM on the first business day of 1946. His initial assignment was as assistant to Charles A. Kirk, the forty-one-year-old executive vice president who had previously served with distinction as vice president for manufacturing. Kirk's new task was to educate Tom Watson in IBM's business and prepare him for a leadership position. The young Watson found Kirk to be an aggressive executive who had a remarkable grasp of the business and an ability to size up situations quickly and make good decisions. He admired the way Kirk taught him the business without any apparent concern that the two might some-day compete for the top position. Watson by contrast was deeply concerned that his mentor might stand between him and the presidency of IBM.

Figure 12.1. Tom Watson meets Charlie Kirk
While still in the air corps, Tom Watson met Charles A. Kirk for the first time during an unofficial stopover in Endicott. When Tom returned from active duty, his father assigned Kirk to train him for a leadership position in IBM.

"All I could think of," Watson, Jr., recalled, was that "if Dad ever got sick or died, Kirk was the logical successor."[6] He therefore set about to master all the skills Kirk had, to learn all that Kirk knew, and to outperform him in every possible way. Conflicts between the two became common. With young Watson's private track to the top, it was not a fair match. In June 1946, at age thirty-two, Tom Watson was promoted to vice president, and in October he was elected to the board of directors. In May of the following year, Kirk suffered a coronary thrombosis and died while on a business trip with Tom Watson in Europe.[7] In September 1949 Tom Watson was promoted to executive vice president and J. George Phillips, who had served as executive vice president following Kirk's death, became president of IBM. Watson, Sr., still retained ultimate authority as chairman and chief executive officer.[8]

In sharp contrast with his older brother, Arthur K. (Dick) Watson was an excellent student. At Yale he majored in international affairs and did particularly well in foreign languages. When his senior-year studies were interrupted by the war, he applied for European duty but was assigned to the Ordnance Corps in Aberdeen, Maryland, as an instructor. Sent to the Philippines near the end of the war, he was discharged as a major in 1947. Returning immediately to Yale, he earned his bachelor's degree and joined IBM as a sales trainee in the same year.

In 1948 Dick Watson joined his father and a group of executives on a trip to Europe that led to the establishment of the IBM World Trade Corporation in October 1949. The senior Watson's plan was to operate the company's international trade entirely through this new corporation. A national company, wholly owned by the World Trade Corporation, would be established in each country where IBM did substantial business and would be managed and staffed primarily by citizens of that country. The national companies were to provide flexibility for adapting to local conditions and customs, while the World Trade Corporation would optimize global operations and assure the quality of IBM products and services worldwide.

Having served as assistant to his father and translator for the group on the European trip that helped create the World Trade Corporation, Dick Watson was appointed a vice president and director. Thus by the end of 1949 (the year Bryce died) the seventy-five-year-old Watson had placed his two sons, aged thirty-five and thirty, in positions that virtually assured their leadership of IBM.[9]

Assignment in Electronics

While still under Kirk's tutelage, Tom Watson was introduced to two pioneering electronic projects that provided direction to his career. First was the ENIAC, which he and Kirk visited early in 1946. Kirk proposed the visit because he was curious about the machine and wanted to learn more about the patent situation. During the visit, Presper Eckert advised them that he and Mauchly were planning to obtain patents and go into competition with IBM. At the time neither Tom Watson nor Charlie Kirk believed that the huge machine posed any particular threat.

"I never stopped to think what would happen if the speed of electronic circuits could be harnessed for commercial use," Watson later admitted. Fortunately for him, others at IBM had already given that possibility considerable thought. Within a few weeks after seeing the ENIAC, he was brought into Bryce's laboratory by his father to see the company's top-secret electronic project. A product prototype with electronic arithmetic circuits was already in full operation. Unlike the enormous ENIAC, the IBM prototype was a relatively small machine that nevertheless could perform simple arithmetic with electronic speed.

Tom Watson was impressed. Here was an electronic machine that could be used in IBM's business. He recalls urging that the unit, soon named the IBM 603 Electronic Multiplier, be marketed as "the world's first commercial electronic calculator" even if only a few could be sold.[10] The record is replete, however, with reasons to believe that Watson, Sr., needed no urging from his son to market the 603. As early as October 1943, for example, he had expressed concern that IBM was not doing enough in electronics and urged his engineers to use electronics in new products then being developed.[11]

By not emphasizing his own early role, Watson, Sr., provided his son with ownership of the company's thrust into electronics. The master salesman had made one of the more important sales of his life. His son had chosen to be responsible for the company's activities in electronics. The senior Watson could now concentrate on traditional EAM products and a planned expansion of the electric typewriter business.

With his career inextricably tied to electronics, Tom Watson had no intention of letting anything stand in his way, including his father. Those who witnessed the ensuing battles between the two—or made the mistake of getting between them—have concluded that Watson, Sr., resisted the entry into electronics. The record fails to support that view, however. Rather it reveals a father who enticed his son into taking responsibility for a new technology that his technical advisers, James Bryce and John McPherson, assured him had great potential. Having done so, the older Watson had the unenviable task of balancing the company's priorities and tempering his son's otherwise unconstrained drive to make the company's thrust into electronics a resounding success. In recalling his many battles with his father, Watson, Jr., has said, "Electronics was the only major issue on which we didn't fight."[12]

Getting Started in Poughkeepsie

A key element of the senior Watson's postwar strategy was to locate the company's more promising advanced development activities in Poughkeepsie. The resulting new products would be manufactured in the plant established there for wartime munitions production. Strongly committed to expanding the market for electric typewriters and to creating modified versions for use in the EAM line, he had moved the development and manufacture of electric typewriters from Rochester to Poughkeepsie in 1944.[13]

When Ralph Palmer returned from the navy in February 1946, Watson had Charlie Kirk summon him to headquarters to discuss establishing an electronic research and development laboratory in Poughkeepsie. Watson knew the opportunity would appeal to Palmer, who had done pioneering research on electronics in Endicott before the war. Even before he returned from service, Palmer had warned John McPherson and others that wartime advances in electronics were going to put the company at a serious disadvantage.

"I understand you think IBM is falling way behind in electronics," Kirk began their discussion in a somewhat confrontational manner. "That's right," Palmer responded without hesitation. "Why don't you go to Poughkeepsie," Kirk retorted, "and do something about it?" The challenge was accepted. Within a matter of weeks after his discharge, Palmer transferred from Endicott to Poughkeepsie to establish a laboratory devoted to electronics.[14]

He began by hiring electrical engineers and initiating exploratory studies on electronic arithmetic and storage devices likely to

Figure 12.2. Ralph L. Palmer
Ralph Palmer is shown (left) at the head table of a dinner honoring a sales trainee class in Endicott, soon after he was assigned to establish electronic development facilities in Poughkeepsie in 1946.

have value in future products. With Tom Watson's strong encouragement, Palmer soon made his primary task the development of a greatly enhanced replacement for the not-yet-announced 603 Electronic Multiplier. Subjected to closer scrutiny by marketing people, the limitations of the 603 had become increasingly evident.[15] Nevertheless the first production lot of fifty was sold almost immediately. A decision was then made to limit production to one hundred and to introduce the enhanced product as soon as Palmer could develop it.[16]

The resulting IBM 604 Electronic Calculating Punch was delivered to customers beginning in the fall of 1948. It was a major advance over the 603 and provided computational capabilities unmatched by any other commercial product. The 604 offered fifty decimal digits of internal electronic storage, twice that of the 603. It could perform addition, subtraction, multiplication, and division with electronic speed. In its most basic version, it could execute up to twenty plugboard-controlled program steps between reading data from a card and punching out the result. Up to sixty program steps were possible with optional features. Individual program steps could be omitted selectively based on input data or computational results.

The 604 contained over 1,400 vacuum tubes versus 300 in its predecessor. The circuit designs were essentially the same as those devised by Palmer and Phelps before the war, but greater compactness and reduced power consumption was achieved by use of miniature vacuum tubes developed during the war. Recognizing the need for tubes with different characteristics and greater reliability than those used in radios, Palmer established a vacuum-tube research facility. It was located in a small building, affectionately known as the "pickle factory" because it had been used as a specialty food processing plant before the war. Here tubes could be designed and built in sufficient quantity to influence major suppliers such as General Electric, RCA, and Sylvania to meet IBM's special requirements.[17]

Palmer also devised an innovative scheme in which each vacuum tube and its closely associated resistors and capacitors were assembled in a pluggable unit that further increased circuit packaging density.[18] The pluggable unit could be fully tested before insertion, thus facilitating manufacture. It also aided field service. By swapping pluggable units within a machine, rather than individual vacuum tubes or other electronic components, a serviceman could more quickly identify and replace defective units.[19]

The rental for the 604 was under $600 per month, well within the range of sophisticated electromechanical tabulating equipment. So successful was the 604 that annual production peaked at more than 1,000 machines, consuming over 1.5 million vacuum tubes per year. A total of 5,600 machines were built, installed, and serviced during a ten-year period.[20]

A Commercial Electronic Computer

The success of the IBM 604 was due largely to its ability to reduce the number of card passes required by accounting tasks and business analyses, as compared to the number needed in EAM configurations without a 604. It was also attractive, however, to the growing number of customers who wanted to use card equipment for scientific and engineering computations. To satisfy the needs of such customers with the heaviest requirements, the 604 was soon coupled with other EAM equipment in the first IBM product designed specifically for computation centers. Formally announced as the IBM Card-Programmed Electronic Calculator in May 1949, it was universally known simply as the CPC.

The CPC contained fewer than one-tenth as many vacuum tubes as the ENIAC, but it offered more flexibility and ease of use. Whereas the ENIAC's computational sequences could be changed only by laborious rewiring, the CPC's sequences consisted of programmed instructions in a deck of punched cards that could be changed or modified with relative ease. The CPC executed instructions directly from these cards rather than loading them into memory as was subsequently done by UNIVAC and other stored-program electronic computers. A single CPC instruction could initiate rather lengthy computations by calling on subroutines prewired in a plugboard.

The genesis of the CPC can be traced to a cooperative effort between IBM and one of its customers, Northrop Aircraft, Inc., of Hawthorne, California. Among Northrop's many uses for EAM equipment was the calculation of guided-missile trajectories. Initially these calculations were made using a standard IBM 601 electric multiplier and 405 accounting machine. Because many steps in the calculation were dependent on the previous step, the process was slowed by the need to move card decks continually back and forth between the two machines.

Without any help from IBM, the engineers at Northrop speeded this process by interconnecting the two machines so that results of computations completed by one machine could be transmitted directly through a cable to the other without moving cards between them.[21] This arrangement provided considerable improvement. It was woefully inadequate for truly lengthy integrations, however, even when time-saving methods developed by Wallace Eckert of the IBM Watson Laboratory were employed.

Desperate for a better solution, the Northrop group arranged for a discussion of their needs at IBM headquarters in the winter of 1947–1948. They had already concluded the solution should involve the IBM 603 Electronic Multiplier. (The far superior 604 was not yet available.) As described by a member of the Northrop team, "The problem was then taken to IBM Headquarters in New York where Mr. J. C. McPherson went over the problem requirements in detail and agreed with our conclusion with respect to machine requirements. The machine was built. In fact, we received much more than we expected. . . . We received a machine comparable in programming technique to current large computer design—a poor man's ENIAC."[22]

McPherson's ability to understand the Northrop requirements and respond rapidly to them was aided by his knowledge of work at the Watson Laboratory. Here Wallace Eckert had been working since 1946 on what he called "a baby sequence calculator with instructions on punched cards." It consisted of a relay calculator connected with an accounting machine and a specially designed control box in a configuration somewhat similar to that provided to Northrop. Eckert appears to have made no attempt to initiate a product development effort himself. His research activities at the Watson Laboratory, however, were widely disseminated through conferences and publications and may have helped stimulate the Northrop request, although there is no direct evidence for that.[23]

By the end of 1948, IBM had received more than a dozen requests for configurations similar to Northrop's, and the reactivated Future Demands Department had undertaken the specification of a standard product. Leading the effort was Steve Dunwell, who had returned from the Army Signal Corps in June 1946 and had been responsible for specifying the characteristics of the recently introduced IBM 604.[24]

Dunwell began by replacing the 603 Electronic Multiplier in the configuration by the faster and more versatile 604. He also replaced the venerable 405 accounting machine with a recently enhanced version called the 402. As an optional feature he included up to three Type 941 auxiliary storage units, each of which provided electromechanical storage for sixteen numbers of ten decimal digits each and their sign. Preparation for a calculation on the CPC began by writing the sequence of operations to be performed on a "planning chart." Numbers to be entered into the computation at each step were specified by their location either on a punched card or in storage locations within the CPC. This process was similar to that used in preparing a problem for computation by hand except that, with the CPC, the information on the planning chart was punched into a deck of cards.

Then, under control of the punched cards, data were routed over one or the other of two channels to the 604, where desired operations were carried out. These operations could include addition, subtraction, multiplication, division, and more complex functions such as square root, which could be prewired into the 604 plugboard and called for by instructions in the program deck. Using modern terminology one might say the prewired plugboard provided the microcode and the input cards provided the program and data. Computation results were routed over another channel to either storage, card punch, or printer.[25]

Customer deliveries of the CPC began in late 1949, at which time more than twenty had been ordered by premier companies in the airframe industry and by government agencies and laboratories. More than a year would pass before the first UNIVAC was accepted by the Census Bureau. Tom Watson was ecstatic. Nearly 700 CPC systems were delivered during the first half of the 1950s compared to only 14 UNIVACs during the same period.[26]

There is no simple way to compare the computational capabilities of these very different machines. Each could execute a balanced mix of arithmetic functions at an average rate of approximately one thousand per second. But the UNIVAC had an internal memory capacity more than one hundred times greater than the CPC, and it was equipped with magnetic tape storage devices that made it possible to move information in and out of memory rapidly. These storage devices helped keep the arithmetic circuits of the UNIVAC busy doing useful work a greater fraction of the time than was generally possible with the CPC. The UNIVAC's advantage was problem-dependent, however, and could range from no advantage at all to two or more orders of magnitude. In practice a UNIVAC could handle large computational problems that were impractical for a CPC.[27]

In the long run the relative computational capabilities of these machines were less important than the number installed. During the first half of the 1950s, the installed UNIVACs satisfied computational needs at fourteen customer locations, whereas the installed CPCs satisfied the needs at fifty times that many. The company was rapidly creating an infrastructure of knowledgeable customers, salesmen, and servicemen for electronic computers. Contrary to widely held perceptions, IBM had the fastest start in the market for electronic computing capability. It did not have to catch up as most accounts of this era suggest.

The UNIVAC Threat

The real threat of UNIVAC to IBM was not in the relatively small niche market for *computing* but rather in the far larger market for *information processing* equipment. Here IBM's punched cards had long reigned supreme as the means for storing business records such as payroll, inventory, personnel, insurance, or census data. Information stored on cards could be processed in a cost-effective manner using the sorting, collating, and simple arithmetic operations provided by punched-card equipment.

The use of magnetic tape, as proposed by Eckert and Mauchly, to handle many punched-card functions was a major innovation and the primary threat posed by UNIVAC. Initially Watson, Sr., failed to understand this threat because he and his engineering staff believed that data stored sequentially on long magnetic tapes would have limited utility. It was important to be able to enter information in one sequence and then rearrange it into another—for example, to enter information in the sequence in which it was received and then order it alphabetically. Hollerith had recognized this when he chose cards over paper tape. Watson initially believed punched cards would have the same advantage over magnetic tape.

An important insight of Eckert and Mauchly was that UNIVAC would be able to read into memory a sequence of information from magnetic tape, rearrange the information in memory, and then write the rearranged information on another tape. Many passes back and forth between tapes might be needed to rearrange all information, but this could be done automatically under program control. Magnetic tapes could thus replace punched cards for this important function. The sorting of information on tapes and the "sort" programs to perform it were crucial to the success of early business-oriented computers.

The failure of many at the time—and perhaps even more today—to grasp the overarching significance of the use of magnetic tapes on UNIVAC is partly the result of an unfortunate misnomer: all electronic information processing machines are called computers even though they are seldom used for computing. Although ENIAC was the first large-scale electronic computer, it lacked the memory and storage facilities necessary for information processing. In contrast, UNIVAC and other electronic stored-program computers *equipped with magnetic tape storage* were effective information processing machines. Because they were also superior to computers of the ENIAC design for computing, ENIAC had no progeny.

Applied Science Representatives

In responding to the emergence of large-scale electronic computers, IBM initially focused on their application to engineering and scientific computations. Success in the marketplace would require more than equipment. Computation methods suitable for electronic computers would have to be devised, and customers and salesmen would have to be trained.

The Watson Scientific Computing Laboratory at Columbia University played a key role in developing methods and creating knowledgeable customers for automatic computation. Beginning in 1945 Wallace Eckert and others from the Watson Laboratory taught courses in computing machinery and numerical methods as part of the regular Columbia University graduate school program. These courses are believed to be the first "computer science" courses offered by any university. Watson Laboratory personnel also held symposia, published reports, and made their computing resources available to members of the engineering and scientific communities.[28]

To further build the customer base, John McPherson and Wallace Eckert proposed in May 1948 that people with advanced training in mathematics be hired to assist customers in doing scientific computing.[29] In response IBM's general sales manager requested nominations from each sales district of at least three individuals interested in computation. These individuals were to be of "the highest type, from recognized universities or colleges, with a Bachelor's or Master's Degree" in the fields of physics, aerodynamics, chemistry, or metallurgy. The nominations were to be sent for review to John McPherson who had just been promoted to vice president for engineering.[30]

The request produced only four appropriate candidates during the year. This was not adequate. There were already more than fifty IBM installations where the primary activity was scientific and engineering computing, and these were believed to "represent only a fraction of the available business." Furthermore, even people with advanced technical degrees required six or more months of special training with IBM equipment and automatic computation methods before they were ready for assignment to a branch office.[31]

Concluding that success in this endeavor required far greater emphasis, McPherson recommended in August 1949 that a new marketing function be established with the promotion of technical computation as its primary responsibility. The recommendation was accepted, and Cuthbert C. Hurd, recently hired into headquarters from the Oak Ridge National Laboratory, was assigned to serve as director of a new organization, called the Applied Science Department.

Cuthbert Hurd was exceptionally well qualified for the position. He held a bachelor of science degree from Drake University, a master of science degree from Iowa State College, and a doctor's degree in mathematics from the University of Illinois. During World War II he had served as professor of mathematics at the U.S. Coast Guard Academy in New London, Connecticut, where he inaugurated the use of IBM machines for statistical studies. He served as dean of a small college for two years after the war before accepting a position at the Oak Ridge National Laboratory. There he chaired the committee that introduced IBM machines for calculations of gaseous diffusions processes and organized a centralized computing facility to serve twelve divisions.[32]

At IBM Hurd rapidly created a department of highly qualified people, many of whom had Ph.D.s in mathematics, engineering, or science. After receiving training in sales and automatic computing techniques, members of the department were assigned to branch offices where they assisted salesmen in the sale and installation of CPCs and subsequent computers for solving scientific and engineering problems. The unique training and experience of Applied Science representatives enabled them to help customers in understanding and solving problems. They also advised the company's product development groups of new requirements.[33]

Creation of the Applied Science Department to sell machines for scientific and engineering calculations was an important step in developing a market large enough to accommodate not only the CPC but also the more powerful stored-program computers that would soon be available. It also established a second distinct marketing and product development culture in IBM. Up to this point, the company had achieved its commercial success in automatic computing through equipment installed primarily to solve business problems. Now an increasing number of machines would be installed primarily—or even entirely—for scientific and engineering computations.

Supercomputer Strategies

Although IBM enjoyed market leadership in electronic computing, there was a significant missing ingredient: namely, a commercial computer with the capability of a UNIVAC. This was a genuine business need. It was the publicity attendant to UNIVAC, however, that was most painful for Watson, Sr., who was proud of IBM's leadership in automatic computation.

Remington Rand achieved a major publicity coup during the U.S. elections of 1952 by having a UNIVAC featured on national television, programmed to predict the outcome of the election when only a small fraction of the votes were counted.[34] Its spectacular success attracted worldwide attention and made the name UNIVAC almost synonymous with large electronic computers.

Watson, Sr., and James Bryce had established an informal strategy for maintaining leadership in supercomputers. It was to use IBM expertise and money to build and "contribute to science" one-of-a-kind "supercalculators" that could be reproduced for a few customers, if desired, and be used to test improved hardware and computation methods for lower-cost products. This strategy was thwarted in its first implementation by the breakdown of cordial relations between Watson and Aiken during the dedication of the IBM-Harvard Mark I.

To recover from this setback, Watson hired Wallace Eckert to establish the Watson Scientific Computing Laboratory at Columbia University. A primary assignment was to design a supercomputer. The result was the SSEC, dedicated in January 1948. The SSEC provided IBM with engineering experience, valuable expertise in operating and programming computers, and the primary patent on stored-program computers.

Unanticipated by Watson, however, was the vast government program to develop electronic computers. This program created a technical community outside IBM that benefited from many independent engineering projects, simultaneously cooperating and competing with each other. All of these projects were funded by the government and stimulated by von Neumann's intellectual leadership. These activities, rather than IBM's, would define the next developments in large-scale electronic computers.

Watson's insistence on early completion of the SSEC, combined with cost constraints, had forced its designers to limit the use of vacuum tube circuits to a small number of critical functions. Eckert understood, however, that any follow-on supercomputer was to be designed and built on a schedule that would encourage the use of new technologies. To initiate this activity, he hired Byron L. Havens, who had worked at the MIT Radiation Laboratory, where many of the more significant wartime advances in electronics had been made. Havens was recommended by I. I. Rabi, who as associate director of the Radiation Laboratory had himself hired Havens in July 1941.[35]

Arriving at the IBM Watson Laboratory in January 1946, shortly before Palmer transferred from Endicott to Poughkeepsie, Havens began hiring engineers to conduct research studies on electronics. Like Palmer, Havens looked for engineers who had gained practical experience with electronics through their wartime assignments. Unlike Palmer's group which became involved in product development within six months, Havens's group would have several years to conduct research on improved electronic circuits and devices.[36] By mid-1950 Havens was ready to design and build a large stored-program supercomputer. He projected it would be at least two hundred times more powerful than the SSEC and ten times more powerful than any computer then under construction.

In a major change in policy, IBM sought government funding for the project. A prime promoter of this policy shift was Louis H. LaMotte, head of IBM's office in Washington, D.C. LaMotte had become alarmed by a report written by a member of his staff in August 1948. Based on information gleaned at a symposium held at the University of California in Los Angeles, the report advised that at least fourteen organizations in the United States were developing electronic computers. Most of these computers were classed as "large," and all were funded at least in part by the government. Not only was the Bureau of Standards funneling money from various government agencies into computer development, but government-funded organizations were being pressured to purchase machines. According to the report, six organizations were "definitely planning to order large computing machines at the earliest possible moment."[37]

Forwarding this report to Tom Watson and the company's executive vice president, J. George Phillips, LaMotte wrote, "It appears there must be some very fundamental reason why so many outside agencies are intensely interested and active in this field." Then he posed a significant question: "Inasmuch as IBM is the leader in the field of calculating equipment, does it not seem reasonable that it too should be kept abreast of all developments by active participation in this field, either to an equal or greater extent than any of the listed organizations?" LaMotte urged that the company supplement its own funding of research and development by offering to build computers for the government "for any legitimate purpose on a cost-plus basis."[38] The company's strategy of "going it alone" was beginning to crumble under the realities of government-funded competition. McPherson and others began cautiously courting government agencies.

Following receipt of a request for a "high-speed electronic calculator" from the U.S. Naval Ordnance Laboratory in Silver Spring, Maryland, in September 1950, John McPherson responded, "We should be pleased to undertake the development and construction of such a machine for you on a research and development basis, under which we would be reimbursed for our costs plus a fixed fee." The fixed fee was set at one dollar by IBM, whose objectives were not immediate profit, but rather service to a valuable customer, favorable publicity, experience in design, construction, and maintenance of a supercomputer, and patents, which the contract permitted it to retain. The monies ultimately received were about twice the $1.3 million estimated in May 1951 when authorization for the project was received.[39]

Designed and built under Havens's leadership at the Watson Laboratory, the resulting machine became known as the NORC (Naval Ordnance Research Calculator). It was characterized by use of decimal (rather than binary) arithmetic, floating-point operations, automatic address modification, and substantial error detection capability. With a 1-microsecond clock period and a 2,000- to 3,600-word capacity, 8-microsecond access, cathode-ray-tube memory, the NORC reigned as the world's fastest computer for several years after it was publicly demonstrated in December 1954.[40]

The acceptance of government money to pay for developing NORC was evidence of the increasing influence of Tom Watson, who was eager to move into large-scale electronic computing as fast as possible. Through his initiative (see chapter 13) the company embarked on a program to manufacture and sell large-scale electronic computers at the same time negotiations with the Naval Ordnance Laboratory were entering their final phase. As a result, Project NORC was soon relegated to a secondary role in the company's plans. Tom Watson had found an even better way to tap into the country's cold-war funding for electronic computers.

13

Watson, Jr., Takes Charge

In September 1949, not quite four years after he returned from military service, Tom Watson was promoted to executive vice president. He was now next in line for the presidency, which reported to the chief executive officer—his father. Still largely disconnected from the EAM business, he had been given a relatively free hand in electronics. The success of the IBM 603, 604, and CPC had convinced him that customers were ready for the new technology and that IBM had the capability to develop and manufacture it.

He was increasingly frustrated, however, by the relatively low percentage of research and development resources allocated to electronics. Only at his insistence had a plan been made at the end of 1948 to hire twenty-five electronics engineers in 1949, half of whom would be assigned to Ralph Palmer in Poughkeepsie. This was approximately twice the number of engineers of all types hired in the previous year, but it represented only about 5 percent of the company's engineering staff.[1] In his new role as executive vice president, Tom Watson planned to shift resources into electronics even more rapidly. He also planned to benefit somehow from the huge sums of money the government was spending on computers.

Choosing Team Members

To accomplish his objectives, he would first have to assert control over the development of EAM products, which generated most of the company's revenue and consumed most of its R&D funds. A major impediment, as he saw it, was John McPherson, who enjoyed his father's full confidence. McPherson was also well respected by the engineers in Endicott, who had primary responsibility for EAM developments. Learning what the secretive Endicott inventors were doing would have been difficult in any case, but the strong link McPherson provided between them and the older Watson made Tom Watson's task virtually impossible.

Deeper frustration, and indeed anger, was caused by McPherson's support of the senior Watson's view that the company's research was outstanding. Their joint stance thwarted Tom Watson's efforts to increase dramatically the company's expenditures in electronics. McPherson "made a big mistake," the younger Watson later asserted. By remaining loyal to Watson, Sr., who "wasn't going to live very long," McPherson lost any chance of a good relationship with the son.[2]

The person who ultimately provided the rationale for hiring more engineers was Albert L. Williams. With two years of college education, Williams had joined IBM as a student sales representative in 1936. He was elected controller in 1942 and treasurer in 1947.[3] On his own, Williams studied the research and development expenditures of large companies in the electrical equipment and electronics businesses. These companies were typically spending more than 3 percent of their gross income on R&D, whereas IBM was spending somewhat less.[4] It was a simple, yet convincing argument for the older Watson, who was pleased to have a sound business reason for accommodating his son.

Given approval for a significant increase in R&D expenditures, Tom Watson needed a technical leader to carry out the plan. It would not be John McPherson. Although he could not remove McPherson from the position of IBM vice president, he did have an easy way to decouple him from management responsibilities. The position of director of engineering had remained empty following McPherson's promotion to vice president in 1948. Tom Watson filled the position in May 1950 with W. Wallace McDowell, who had served as manager of the Endicott laboratory since 1942.[5] Ironically, John McPherson—the man most responsible for the company's early postwar push into electronics—was to be excluded from any further decision-making responsibilities.

Wally McDowell was just the type of technical administrator Watson needed. After receiving his bachelor's degree in engineering management at MIT in 1930, he had joined IBM and worked briefly as a draftsman and served in several engineering administrative positions in Endicott before becoming laboratory manager. Unlike previous laboratory managers—who primarily provided administrative support for engineers and carried out the wishes of Watson, Sr.—McDowell interacted directly with govern-

Figure 13.1. W. Wallace McDowell
Wally McDowell presided over IBM's rapid growth in engineering, with emphasis on electronics, following his promotion in 1950 from manager of the Endicott laboratory to director of engineering. A 1930 graduate of MIT, he enjoyed the confidence and respect of both Tom Watson and Watson, Sr. This photograph was taken one year before he retired from IBM in 1968.

ment agencies during World War II and made many independent decisions.[6] He lacked the technical capabilities of Palmer or McPherson, but he was a good listener and was well respected for his decisions and follow-through. Of particular note was his support of research on electronic circuits before the war.

McDowell had other important attributes for his new position. He was well respected by both Watsons, politically wise, and able to handle delicate relations between the two. Unknown to Watson, Jr., at the time, for example, his father met privately with McDowell at lunch time almost every day for several months after McDowell was appointed director of engineering. This provided the older Watson with an opportunity to keep informed of his son's activities and to influence them without appearing to do so.[7]

Within five years, under McDowell's leadership, the total number of employees working in R&D increased from fewer than 1,000 to more than 4,000. Approximately 60 percent of these were classed as technical rather than administrative. During the same period, the total number of IBM employees worldwide had nearly doubled to 56,300. (See appendix A.)

Tom Watson found another natural ally in Louis LaMotte, a senior sales executive who had never been cowed by the elder Watson's imperious manner. In 1948 he had warned, from his post in Washington, D.C., of the growing threat of government-funded competition in computers. He had urged that IBM policies be altered so as to accept government development contracts.

In addition to McDowell, Williams, and LaMotte there were two other members of Tom Watson's team in 1950. The first of these was a protégé of Charlie Kirk, James W. Birkenstock, who had been promoted by Watson, Sr., from a minor headquarters sales post to general sales manager in January 1946. Although he was intelligent and capable, Birkenstock was unprepared for this level of responsibility. Twelve months later he was removed as sales manager and made manager of the Future Demands Department, which had been dormant since McPherson vacated its leadership four years earlier.

Despondent over what he considered a demotion, Birkenstock became an adviser to Tom Watson, following a session in which he proposed quitting the company and the young Watson urged him to stay. Soon thereafter Birkenstock became one of the first in IBM to recognize that electronic computers could use magnetic tapes to replace many functions of punched cards. By 1948 he was predicting that electronic computers with magnetic tape storage would take over IBM's traditional markets and that punched cards were doomed. He urged Tom Watson to act quickly.[8]

The final member of Watson's early team was Cuthbert Hurd. With a doctorate in mathematics and extensive experience in digital computation methods, he had already demonstrated his value as head of the Applied Science Department. Now as a member of Watson's inner circle, he provided intellectual leadership that was crucial to the company's entry into the market for large-scale electronic computers.

Even before he selected Wally McDowell to head engineering in 1950, Tom Watson had urged John McPherson to leave IBM, telling him he "would do better elsewhere."[9] But McPherson saw insufficient reason to do so. He still had the support of the older Watson, and he was deeply involved in getting the company into electronics.

Deprived of influence at the top—clearly not a member of Tom Watson's team—McPherson nevertheless continued to play much the same role as he had in the past. He kept abreast of engineering projects. He aided their progress, primarily by making engineers aware of relevant advances of others inside and outside the company. It was an important role in a company in which few technical people had outside contacts and in which the older engineers still kept their work secret from one another.

Ralph Palmer was also left out of the inner circle. Tom Watson recalled his reasons for not appointing him director of engineering as follows: "Putting the leader of the Poughkeepsie mavericks in charge would be an unnecessary insult to Dad's inventors in Endicott. Besides, Palmer was simply too important in the lab."[10] Indeed Palmer's interests were too strongly oriented toward engineering and research to satisfy the needs of Tom Watson, who kept more aloof of detailed engineering decisions than had his father.

The Defense Calculator

An opportunity for action came with the outbreak of the Korean conflict in June 1950, just one month after McDowell's promotion to director of engineering. Recalling his World War II creation of a separate munitions manufacturing organization, Watson, Sr., asked Birkenstock to establish a military products division to provide specialized products for national defense. Watson's motivation was primarily patriotic, but his son seized on the idea as an opportunity to speed the company's development of large-scale electronic computers.[11]

To help Watson, Jr., assess the opportunities, Birkenstock asked Cuthbert Hurd to join him in visiting prospective customers. As director of the Applied Science Department, Hurd already had a list of nearly sixty installations where IBM equipment was being used in defense-related engineering and research applications. Jointly and then separately the two of them visited more than twenty of these. They found people eager to discuss their computation needs, which were growing rapidly because of the military's pressure for significantly improved armaments.[12]

By November Hurd had created his own assessment of the military's needs for computing capability. As submitted to Tom Watson, they were in priority order: (1) atomic energy; (2) guided missiles; (3) strategic planning (cryptanalysis, weather forecasting, and game theory); and (4) jet engines. For a variety of reasons Hurd believed IBM could have the greatest impact by directing its efforts "to the solution of the basic guided missile control problems."[13] Two weeks later, however, Hurd had substantially revised his thinking. He now concluded that the "special needs" of different users could best be served by a single, properly designed machine.

The plan was thus evolving from one in which three or four different computers would be built to the specifications of selected customers to a plan in which only one computer would be designed and manufactured to satisfy the needs of as many customers as possible. As described by Birkenstock, "The machine should be general purpose in concept to permit our duplicating the prototype in the order of 25 to 30 times."[14] It was a riskier strategy because the cost of development would be paid entirely by IBM. If successful, however, the rewards would be greater. Engineering responsibility would rest with Ralph Palmer's group in Poughkeepsie.

Even before completing work on the 604 electronic calculator in mid-1948, Palmer had begun to broaden his group's research activities to encompass all technologies needed for large-scale electronic computers. At the top of his priority list was high-speed memory. His preferred solution (called the Williams-tube memory after its British inventor) made it possible to write and read digitally encoded information electronically on the face of an ordinary cathode ray tube. Not only did the Williams tube provide faster access to information than the delay-line memory planned for UNIVAC, but it had the added advantage that the storage tubes were commercially available. Achieving the desired reliability was, however, a serious problem.[15]

Also under study was diode logic in which vacuum tubes provided power amplification and the lower-power germanium diodes performed the switching function. By mid-1949 information storage by magnetic material on the surface of a rotating drum was under study, using a drum supplied by the Endicott laboratory; and the storage of information on magnetic tape, initially assigned to Endicott, had also become the responsibility of Palmer's group.[16]

That fall Steve Dunwell drew up specifications for an electronic computer using components being developed by Palmer. Intended for business applications, it was called the Tape Processing Machine (TPM) because a key question to be addressed was the appropriateness of magnetic tape for storing business records. By the spring of 1950 the Tape Processing Machine had become the primary focus of Palmer's group.[17] It was to be IBM's most direct response to UNIVAC. To speed the work, Palmer had been authorized to hire more than a dozen additional electronics engineers.[18]

By late in the fall, the possibility of redirecting Palmer's effort to build a computer to meet the needs of military organizations and defense industries was under consideration. To facilitate a decision, Tom Watson established a committee to draw up specifications for the proposed computer. Headed by a member of the sales organization and with representatives from engineering, Future Demands, Applied Science, and the Watson Laboratory, the committee carried out its task between Christmas and New Year's Day.[19]

Hardware component specifications were based on components under development in Palmer's group, but a substantial deviation from the TPM design was required to satisfy the needs of engineering and scientific computing. The most significant change was from a bit-at-a-time serial operation to a data path wide enough to handle an entire word at a time. This increased both the speed and the cost of the computer.

Largely on the basis of Hurd's assertion that he could sell at least six of the machines, Watson made a tentative decision to proceed.[20] Palmer immediately began reassigning engineers to the new project and made preliminary schedule and cost estimates. In February 1951 Hurd was authorized to approach potential customers using an estimated rental of $8,000 per month and delivery in little more than one year.[21]

When more than twenty letters of intent were quickly obtained, Watson gave final approval. By the spring of 1952 firm engineering designs were in place. The projected rental price had doubled, with a range of $11,900 to $17,600 per month, and deliveries were estimated at just under a year. In spite of the higher price, orders for thirteen were confirmed by August and LaMotte (now vice president for sales) had authorized the purchase of materials for a production lot of eighteen machines.[22]

The shift in focus from commercial to defense-related applications for IBM's first large-scale electronic computer was justified by the uncertain market for the former and the well-defined demand for the latter. The shift had also made it easier to sell the project internally. Issues of marketability and profitability could be set aside by arguing its importance to national security.

The name, Defense Calculator, was specifically selected to appeal to the patriotism of the older Watson and to avoid use of the unacceptable word, *computer.*

The internal arithmetic and control features of the Defense Calculator were based, with a few significant departures, on von Neumann's IAS computer, functional plans for which had been circulated in 1946 and again in revised form in September 1947.[23] A principal result of this decision was use of the binary number system rather than the decimal system as in all previous IBM machines. In addition to reducing the design time, the decision was expected to facilitate sales. "I was aware that practically everybody in the country had already been sold on John von Neumann's idea of how to build a machine," Ralph Palmer recalls. Through use of his design, von Neumann inadvertently became "IBM's best salesman."[24]

In January 1952 von Neumann also became a consultant to IBM. Most of the Defense Calculator design decisions had already been made, however, and the engineering work was well advanced. The hiring of von Neumann is best likened to an insurance policy for Tom Watson. No specific contributions can be attributed to him, but the ready availability of his advice bolstered Watson's confidence.[25]

Several significant deviations from von Neumann's IAS design were incorporated in the Defense Calculator. These included the use of 36-bit rather than 40-bit words, the capability to address and process half-length as well as full-length words, and the representation of numbers by their absolute value and their sign rather than by using complements for negative numbers. Probably more significant to users was the emphasis on fast and reliable input-output equipment.

Palmer also determined that each functional unit would be packaged in its own box (frame and covers) made small enough to pass through standard doorways and to fit on commercial elevators. After preshipment testing, a complete system could be disassembled, shipped, and reassembled in the customer's facility simply by disconnecting and reconnecting the cables between the boxes. Repairs and future upgrades would also be easier.[26]

The functional units comprising the Defense Calculator were the electronic analytical control unit, electrostatic storage unit, punched-card reader, alphabetical printer, punched-card recorder, magnetic-tape reader and recorder, and magnetic-drum reader and recorder. Power supplies were also housed in separate

Figure 13.2.   IBM 701
Known as the Defense Calculator during development, the IBM 701 computer is pictured (top) in the Poughkeepsie laboratory in March 1952. Clockwise from the left are two tape units, a magnetic drum storage device, the cathode-ray-tube memory unit, arithmetic and control unit with operator's panel, card reader, printer, and card punch. A panel of the 701 with eight-tube pluggable units is shown (bottom).

boxes. The product type number of the first unit gave the system its widely used informal name, the IBM 701.[27]

Measures of Success

At the April 1952 annual meeting, Watson, Sr., advised stockholders of a doubling of the size of the Poughkeepsie plant to handle defense production, continued growth in demand for the company's "regular products," and rapid progress in electronics. About 35 percent of the laboratory staff was now working on electronics. He also advised stockholders of the effort to develop a large-scale electronic computer, which was twenty-five times faster than the SSEC, yet would occupy less than one fourth the space. He reported that ten of these computers were ordered only two days after it was announced on a limited confidential basis.[28] Watson's pleasure in this announcement was heightened by the evidence it gave of the success of his older son, who had been promoted to president in January.

For Ralph Palmer and the more than 150 people assigned to the 701 development effort, the December 1952 shipment of the first production machine to the company's headquarters in New York City was a major achievement. The shipment occurred just two years after tentative specifications had been proposed for the Defense Calculator and less than eight months after orders for the first ten systems had been confirmed.

An even better measure of success occurred two months later when the second production machine was shipped to the Los Alamos Scientific Laboratory and was installed and operational only three days after it arrived. Debugging to assure satisfactory performance on all customer tasks was continued for another fourteen days before rental payments began.[29] Operated twenty-four hours per day, five days per week, during the first six full months of operation, the system was reported to have been down for errors or maintenance less than 24 percent of the time.[30] Palmer's plan for simplifying installation by shipping functional units in individual boxes was a success. Contributing to that success were engineering designs intended to facilitate manufacturability, reliability, and ease of service of all components.

But IBM did not just design, manufacture, and sell products. It provided a full service that required well-trained employees. More than a year before the first production machine was installed at headquarters, a course was begun for twenty-five recently hired graduate engineers to train them in all aspects of the design, construction, and operation of stored-program computers. These engineers were to assist in constructing, installing, and servicing the machines. Classes were conducted part of each day for a year. The rest of the day was spent on assigned tasks in the 701 development project. Homework was done at night. A second class of fifteen students was begun in May 1952 to train additional servicemen for the 701s. This class consisted primarily of experienced customer engineers who had previously installed or serviced 604 electronic calculators.[31]

The company's primary competition during the 1950s was Remington Rand, which had acquired the Eckert-Mauchly Computer Company (EMCC) in 1950 and Engineering Research Associates (ERA) in 1952. Because ERA had begun its computer developments with a larger cadre of experienced electronics engineers than either IBM or EMCC, it is revealing to compare the IBM 701 experience with that of the ERA 1103.

Several months before ERA delivered its first electronic computer (Atlas) to the government in 1950, its engineers began work on a far more sophisticated computer, code-named Atlas II. Learning in late 1951 that IBM was building the Defense Calculator, the ERA engineers sought permission to announce an unclassified version of their Atlas II computer to compete with IBM. Work on Atlas II continued in mandatory secrecy until their request was granted by the government in the fall of 1952. Then, for the first time, the ERA engineers were able to advise the top management of Remington Rand of the existence of the previously classified computer. None of the top executives had security clearance.

"The astounded executives approved a program to produce two machines and to buy sufficient parts for two more." The declassified Atlas II computer was announced as the ERA 1103 in February 1953. Like the IBM 701, the ERA 1103 used a 36-bit word length and was equipped with a Williams-tube main memory, magnetic drum and magnetic tape storage, and punched-card units for input-output. When all four ERA 1103s were sold within a few months, a decision was made to produce them in quantity. Full-scale manufacturing was underway by 1954, and about twenty were ultimately built. Thus ERA suddenly found itself in the computer business without a business plan. According to two participants, "Questions arose regarding pricing, rental, field service, installation, customer training, and support. The absence of even a modicum of applications and field support became a glaring deficiency."[32]

Engineers at ERA hoped that superior engineering design of the 1103 would offset the company's weakness in applications and field support, but the predicted superiority of the computer over the IBM 701 failed to materialize. A study team commissioned by the Joint Chiefs of Staff to compare the two computers for weather prediction applications in 1954, for example, concluded that the "speeds of the two machines are comparable with a slight advantage in favor of the 701." The input-output equipment of the 701 was significantly faster, causing the study team to recommend it unanimously over the 1103.[33] The marketing problems for the ERA 1103 were exacerbated in May 1954 when IBM announced a substantially improved version of its 701 computer, the IBM 704.

The 700 Series

Heavy emphasis on the 701 project during 1952 brought engineering work on the Tape Processing Machine (TPM) to a near standstill, but the TPM product planners benefited by having more time to improve its specifications. Greater flexibility in attaching input-output equipment was provided by a "common input-output trunk," and a decision to process all bits of a character in parallel rather than one at a time produced a fivefold increase in processing speed that more than offset the cost increase.

These and many other proposed improvements appeared to make the TPM superior to Remington Rand's UNIVAC. Ironically in early 1953, however, careful analyses indicated the company's conventional punched-card equipment would be more cost-effective for most customer tasks. Such analyses failed to take into account new applications that might be made possible with the TPM, and they ignored the huge customer interest already stimulated by four installed UNIVACs and the soon-to-be-delivered IBM 701. Many IBM salesmen were distressed by the company's decision to develop its first electronic stored-program computer for engineering and scientific computations rather than for business data processing. The possibility of losing large data processing customers to Remington Rand threatened affected salesmen with a major loss of sales commissions.

Thus it was that concerns of the sales organization and anticipated future developments—rather than cost-benefit analyses—drove the decision to announce the improved TPM. In September 1953 it was announced as the IBM 702 Electronic Data Processing Machine (EDPM). The name was selected once again to avoid the politically unacceptable word, *computer.* Deliveries were not to begin until early 1955, four years after the first UNIVAC had been accepted by the Census Bureau. In the meantime IBM salesmen had nothing equivalent to offer. Only the inability of Remington Rand to manufacture more UNIVACS—and to provide adequate support services—saved many IBM salesmen from loss of customers.[34]

Customer enthusiasm for UNIVAC and the IBM 702 was also constrained by important business considerations. One consideration was the high cost and long time required to modify business practices and retrain personnel. Another was concern over loss of visual access to data. "Perhaps the most radical idea which business is being asked to accept is the idea that a reel of tape can safely be used to carry information now being entrusted to visual card files," the vice president and chief actuary of the Metropolitan Life Insurance Company observed in late 1953.[35]

Recognizing the various concerns of IBM salesmen and potential customers, and the need to coordinate company activities in electronic computers, Tom Watson turned to T. Vincent Learson for help. A towering personage, mentally and physically, Vin Learson had been a fast-rising member of the sales organization since joining the company in 1935 with a bachelor's degree in mathematics from Harvard University. He had served as sales manager for the EAM Division from 1949 to 1953, when he was promoted to general sales manager. Now in April 1954, six months after the IBM 702 was announced, Tom Watson appointed him director of Electronic Data Processing Machines (EDPM) with a mandate "to coordinate the various aspects of this complicated work."[36]

Moving from the position of general sales manager to responsibility for a tiny new product segment might have been regarded as a demotion, but Learson understood the younger Watson's nearly single-minded dedication to this segment. Working closely with the engineering, programming, manufacturing, sales, and service organizations, Learson moved vigorously to better meet customer needs. That April he created a new Programming Re-

Figure 13.3. Learson, Watson, Jr., and Palmer
T. Vincent Learson (left) was photographed with Tom Watson (center) and
Ralph L. Palmer (right) when he was promoted to the new position of director of electronic data processing machines (EDPM). The term *EDPM* was
chosen to distinguish the new large-scale electronic machines from the earlier electromechanical accounting machines (EAM). Learson's task was to
coordinate all EDPM activities from development through sales and service.

search Department to "develop a library of advanced EDPM programs for the use of customers and [to] assist the sales organization in evaluating customers' potential uses." [37]

With fifty 702s on order in June, he limited shipments to those scheduled for delivery in 1955 and early 1956 so that a number of significant improvements could be made. As a result, only fourteen 702s were built and installed.[38] The remaining orders were to be satisfied (at a higher rental price) by an improved version, which was announced in October 1954 as the IBM Type 705 EDPM. An improved version of the 701 had already been announced in May as the IBM Type 704 EDPM.

That August Learson had expanded an advanced technology effort into a product development program and given it responsibility to provide magnetic-core memories for the IBM 704 and 705 computers. Not wanting to draw attention to reliability problems of the 701 and 702 computers, IBM chose to highlight only the slightly improved processing speed provided by magnetic-core memory. Superior reliability was, however, the primary reason for changing from cathode-ray-tube (Williams tube) memories. For the same reason, magnetic-core memories were retrofitted on installed 701 and 702 computers as soon as shipments of the 704 and 705 computers commenced in January 1956.[39]

The 700 series of computers was capped by the 709 and 705-III, announced in 1957. For scientific and engineering applications, the 700 series offered computers that used binary notation and emphasized fast computation speeds. For business data processing, it offered computers that emphasized alphanumeric notation, magnetic-tape storage, nonstop processing of huge accounting files, and high-quality printing of reports. So successful were these computers that the 700 series evolved into the 7000 series when transistors replaced vacuum tubes. In particular, the IBM 7090 computer, first shipped in November 1959, was made to operate like the earlier IBM 709 in order to facilitate customer migration to the newer machine.[40]

Learson's effectiveness in strengthening the thrust into electronic computers won him a promotion, in only eight months, to vice president in charge of sales. Once again he had responsibility for all of the company's sales activities, but now he was armed with in-depth knowledge of the rapidly growing electronic computer segment—and he was an IBM vice president.[41]

Success of the 700 series was crucial for Tom Watson, who has described himself as being "terribly afraid of failure" and "absolutely panicked" when he first learned that a second UNIVAC had been installed at the Census Bureau.[42] Driving himself and his associates, he was determined to achieve leadership in this part of the industry. By his own count, it was in 1955 that the number of customer installations with 700 series computers first exceeded the number with computers manufactured by Remington Rand. It was then, in Watson's view, that IBM had once again "conclusively asserted its leadership" in the information processing industry.[43]

The Most Popular Computer

At a time when Tom Watson, his close associates, and most outside observers had their attention riveted on large-scale electronic computers, an important story was unfolding in the IBM Endicott laboratory. It was here that Frank Hamilton had set about early in 1948 to carry out the senior Watson's instructions. Using what he had learned from the SSEC supercomputer project, he was to devise a small machine "to meet the requirements of the ordinary businesses we serve."[44]

Advised by the Future Demands Department that the soon-to-be delivered Type 604 electronic calculator would satisfy the foreseeable needs of business applications, Hamilton (with McPherson's support) decided to develop a small computer for scientific applications. His initial approach was to supplement the 604 with a reduced complement of SSEC-like paper-tape devices for storing tabular data and sequence control information, an electromechanical table-lookup unit, and perhaps 200 digits of vacuum tube storage for intermediate results.

Before the end of the summer, however, he had dropped the bulky vacuum tube and electromechanical storage in favor of digital magnetic recording on the cylindrical surface of a rotating drum. Paper-tape storage was also dropped when he recognized that instructions could be read from a rotating drum and executed in the same manner as from paper tape. With a single magnetic drum storage device holding both data and instructions, the architecture of the system had evolved by April 1949 to one having less similarity to its SSEC predecessor than to von Neumann's IAS computer. Unlike the IAS computer, however, it used decimal rather than binary numbers, and it processed information one decimal digit (several bits) at a time, whereas the IAS computer had an internal data path and arithmetic circuits capable of processing an entire forty-bit binary number at a time. Hamilton's proposed machine was now called the Magnetic Drum Calculator.[45]

One month later, Tom Watson redirected the project in the first of a series of corporate-level decisions destined to deprive Hamilton and his Endicott engineers of any opportunity to develop IBM's first electronic, stored-program computer product. Watson's sales manager had found an urgent need for a table-lookup device to support rate table applications on the 604. The Endicott drum was seen as the answer. After three months of work, however, Hamilton's cost and schedule projections for a drum attachment to the 604 were judged to be unacceptable. Negotiations were then undertaken to purchase a magnetic drum storage device from Engineering Research Associates (ERA), which was the recognized leader in magnetic drum technology.[46] Although it normally built devices for classified government projects, its engineers had given unclassified technical presentations on their magnetic storage drums at engineering conferences. The information storage medium consisted of magnetic tape, bonded to the surface of a cylindrical aluminum drum. In operation the drum rotated continuously.[47]

To improve on ERA's crude recording surface, the engineers in Endicott had wrapped magnetic wire tightly around a drum and then ground the outer surface to achieve a smooth cylindrical surface. Despite good results with the Endicott drum, Watson approved the ERA initiative over the objections of Palmer and McPherson. He believed engineers at ERA were superior to those in IBM's Endicott laboratory, whom he described as "a bunch of monkey-wrench engineers" working under the tutelage of his father and John McPherson.[48]

Representatives of IBM were soon convinced by ERA that a drum-augmented 604 would be less desirable than a magnetic drum computer—the very thing Hamilton was working on before Watson redirected the project. The scope of the contact with ERA was accordingly expanded to encompass the design of a magnetic drum computer. Simultaneously Hamilton was allowed to return to his original objective, but now he was in competition with ERA.[49]

An audit of the competing projects was conducted in March 1950. Both machines were judged to have met the functional specifications, and there was no clear winner. A major concern expressed in the audit report was product cost. Neither machine could be built at the desired entry-level rental of $400 per month. Even the upper limit rental of $1,000 per month for a full-function system was in doubt.[50]

Frustration with unachievable cost-performance requirements was compounded for Hamilton by a reduction in engineering resources early in 1951 when major emphasis was given to the Defense Calculator project. The number of people assigned to the Magnetic Drum Calculator dropped steadily, reaching a low of four employees by the fall of 1952. Nevertheless, Hamilton pushed relentlessly forward, trying to complete an engineering model to satisfy specifications established some months after the audit.[51]

Meanwhile IBM's pioneering 604 and CPC were facing increasing competition in the market. By mid-1952, for example, the Remington Rand Type 409-2 calculator, which was described as having "several times the capacity" of the four-year-old IBM 604, was selling well despite its higher monthly rental of $850 versus $550. In addition there were now seven small stored-program computers in the market competing with IBM's three-year-old CPC.[52]

This competition was particularly evident to Cuthbert Hurd who, as head of the Applied Science Department, was responsible for the marketing of computers for scientific and engineering computations. Unlike the better established market for business applications, this market was more sensitive to new function and technologies than it was to price. Accordingly Hurd agreed to assign some members of his department to help tailor Hamilton's computer to satisfy the needs of these customers.

In November 1952 Hurd convinced Tom Watson to give the Magnetic Drum Calculator his full support. Almost immediately Hamilton was authorized to increase his staff from four to fifty.[53] Eight months later Hamilton's group had shown its design to be superior to alternatives proposed by the Poughkeepsie laboratory, had found ways to engineer around certain patents held by Remington Rand, and had readied the machine for announcement. The main memory used a four-inch-diameter drum designed and built in Endicott. Ferromagnetic metal was electroplated on the surface to provide the storage medium. Spinning at 12,500 revolutions per minute, the drum afforded the remarkably short average access time to data of 2.4 milliseconds.

The IBM 650 Magnetic Drum Calculator was announced in July 1953. Rental was $3,250 per month for a machine with one

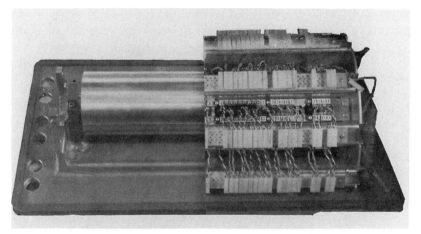

Figure 13.4. IBM 650 Computer
Top: Announced as the IBM 650 Magnetic Drum Calculator in 1953, the 650 became the most popular computer of the 1950s. The woman is sitting in front of the console, which is on the box that housed the processing unit and drum memory. The box behind it housed the controllers and power supply. A Type 533 card read-punch is at left and a higher-performance Type 537 card-read punch is at right. Bottom: The magnetic drum memory is shown with its read-write devices removed at the left to reveal the cylindrical drum on which information was stored.

thousand 10-digit words of memory, and $3,750 per month for a two-thousand-word machine. These rentals were four times smaller than the $15,000 monthly rental for an IBM 701 computer, but they were also four times higher than the original objective for the 650.

Designed and initially marketed primarily for engineering and scientific computations, the IBM 650 was unexpectedly successful for business applications. The first 650 to be shipped was in fact installed at the John Hancock Mutual Life Insurance Company at Boston in December 1954. Part of the product's success can be attributed to punched-card input-output that permitted the 650 to fit easily into established EAM facilities. Of the eight other small digital computers then available, only the machines of the ElectroData Corporation, National Cash Register Company, and the Underwood Corporation offered punched-card input-output comparable to that of the 650, and none of these came within a factor of three of its 2.4-millisecond drum access time.[54]

To satisfy business needs even better, a feature allowing alphabetic information to be read from, and punched into, cards was announced in mid-1954. Another feature added in 1955 permitted attachment of the Type 407 accounting machine to produce reports on-line with excellent print quality.[55]

By the time the last IBM 650 came off the manufacturing line in 1962, almost two thousand had been produced and installed. No other electronic computer had been produced in such quantity. Frank Hamilton—who had learned to build computers by working on the one-of-a-kind Mark I and SSEC supercomputers—had met the senior Watson's challenge. He had developed a machine for "ordinary businesses" that became the most popular computer of the 1950s.[56]

14

Programming Computers

Viewed broadly as the adaptation of general-purpose devices to specific tasks, "programming" was an old data processing concept. So was programming support. From the beginning Hollerith had wired and rewired (programmed) his equipment to handle specific jobs. The introduction of interchangeable, prewired plugboards made it relatively easy for EAM equipment to be shifted from one application to another. An IBM publication called *Pointers* was distributing information about novel plugboard wiring diagrams to customers by the early 1930s. Some of these diagrams were crafted by IBM personnel, others by customers who were willing to share their solutions. (See chap. 5, "Methods Research.")

The first commercially available product to permit more than a few sequential computation steps to be wired on a plugboard was the IBM 604. The forty-step capability initially offered in 1948 was later expanded to sixty. The CPC introduced yet another level of programming methodology to the marketplace in 1949. Program instructions stored in cards could be read sequentially by the CPC and executed. As with conventional EAM equipment, IBM's sales and marketing representatives prepared, solicited, and distributed programs (called solutions) to customers.[1]

Thus a culture of programming support and sharing was well in place among IBM and its customers long before the first 701 computer was installed. The adaptation of this culture to meet the requirements of electronic stored-program computer users would be crucial to the company's continuing success.

Some Early Efforts

The concept of a series of rudimentary processing steps to provide sequence control for automatic computing machines dates back at least to 1843 when Ada Lovelace translated into English a description, written by an Italian mathematician, of Babbage's Analytical Engine. She published the translation together with explanatory notes that contained a list of instructions for directing such an engine to solve assumed problems. Written under Babbage's guidance, these notes may contain the first computer program to be published. Although Babbage worked on the Analytical Engine for many years, his work never reached fruition in an operational device.[2]

The largest electromechanical computer ever built was the Mark I, presented to Harvard University by IBM in August 1944. It was programmed by the staff of the Harvard Computation Laboratory. The electronic ENIAC, which was dedicated in February 1946, was initially programmed by a laborious rewiring process more closely related to the programming of Hollerith equipment than to programming the architecturally advanced Mark I or later computers.[3]

The IBM SSEC, dedicated in January 1948, placed great demands on programmers by offering them more flexibility than did the Mark I. For example, the benefits of large storage capacity, achieved through a multilevel storage hierarchy, were accompanied by increased programming complexity needed to control the flow of data and instructions between storage devices and the arithmetic unit. Other programming challenges arose out of innovative features such as the ability to alter instructions based on intermediate results. Because the SSEC's electronic circuits executed instructions hundreds of times more rapidly than the Mark I, the programming effort to keep it busy effectively limited its use to very large computations.

The benefit of crafting frequently used *subroutines* (i.e., program parts) only once rather than each time a new program needed them gradually became obvious. The kinship to interchangeable plugboards was apparent. Furthermore, as proposed by Eckert and Mauchly in 1945, subroutines used more than once by an application program should be "inserted in the memory only once, and the basic order code must provide for finding these instructions each time they are needed."[4] At about the same time, A. M. Turing, a leading figure in British code-breaking activities during World War II, was planning a computer for the National Physical Laboratory in England. He proposed that frequently used subroutines be stored on punched cards in a manner to facilitate their selection and assembly into a program using standard EAM equipment.[5]

By 1951 Maurice V. Wilkes and two of his colleagues had published a book describing the programming of their stored-program computer (EDSAC) and its library of subroutines. Exhibiting remarkable vision two years earlier, Wilkes had predicted that when a machine was operational, and a number of subroutines were in use, "There would be almost as much capital sunk in the library of subroutines as the machine itself, and builders of new machines in the future might wish to make use of the same order code [i.e., machine language] as an existing machine in order that the sub-routines could be taken over without modification."[6]

The reuse of complete, as opposed to partial, programs also received early attention. The basic concept of a stored-program computer is that an entire program (or its initial portion) is loaded into the computer's main memory before program execution begins. Initiation and control of the program-loading process required a special set of instructions, which could be the same for loading many different programs. Short programs called "program loaders" were therefore among the earliest reusable programs written for the Defense Calculator. One of these was short enough to be held on a single punched card, yet detailed enough to load application programs occupying hundreds of punched cards. Many other short programs were needed to perform a variety of common utilitarian functions.[7]

Such programs, known as "utility programs" or simply "utilities," thrived by 1951 in the UNIVAC environment, where all programs and data files reached the computer in the form of magnetic tapes. The UNIVAC operator was helpless without utilities of various kinds to manage job setups and instructions, debugging sessions, simple copying tasks, and so on, and UNIVAC had no provision for entering data or instructions directly into main memory from a card reader; information transfer between cards and tapes was performed off-line. Unlike UNIVAC, the IBM Defense Calculator could receive data and instructions directly from a card reader as well as from magnetic tape units. This proved to be a significant convenience.

In August 1952, when some thirty representatives of potential customers for the Defense Calculator (already better known as the IBM 701) came to Poughkeepsie to attend a week-long customer training class, IBM programmers described to them three dozen or so utilities written for the 701. These included ones for loading programs into memory, for converting numbers from decimal to binary form, for moving information from magnetic tape to memory, for copying tapes, and for printing results.

The IBM programmers also described two different "assembly programs" that automatically translated instructions from decimal to binary form and combined subroutines and other separately written program pieces into a single program. The latter function relieved programmers of tedious clerical activity such as the renumbering of program instructions. For example, each time a subroutine was incorporated into a program, its instructions had to be given addresses corresponding to the memory locations it would occupy. Subroutines were therefore normally written with symbolic memory addresses such as S1, S2, and S3, which were converted to real memory addresses for each use. Assembly programs automatically handled this conversion.[8]

Sharing Information and Programs

The IBM-hosted training class also provided customers with their first opportunity to test programs they had written, in this case by running them on an engineering model of the 701. For customers, an exciting aspect of acquiring a computer was the opportunity to program it to handle their own jobs in their own way. Programs and subroutines written at IBM initially were viewed as examples of the types of programs that installations might require rather than as programs any installation would actually use. As the magnitude of the programming effort came to be better understood, however, customers were increasingly willing to use IBM-developed programs, particularly in the cases of utilities and standard mathematical functions. Customers also began sharing programs among themselves. Installations took pride in developing programs and subroutines that were particularly effective and used by others.

Activities leading to organized customer sharing of computer programs and other information began when several participants at the August 1952 customer training class decided to continue discussing mutual problems on an informal basis. Their first meeting was held in February 1953 during an AIEE-IRE Computer Conference in Los Angeles. It was then agreed to hold a second meeting after several users had their own 701s installed.[9]

The second meeting was hosted by the Douglas Aircraft Company, in Santa Monica, California, in August 1953. It was attended by representatives from five companies with installed 701s and six customers that had ordered but not yet received theirs.

Representatives of IBM also attended. Among these was Nathaniel Rochester, chief architect of the 701. Upon returning from the conference, he reported that the most "striking feature" of customer activities was the extent to which they were adopting or improving on techniques "to let the 701 aid in problem preparation." Commenting on this "use and extension of the principal techniques in which IBM did pioneering work in New York and Poughkeepsie," he observed, "interpretive programs and assembly programs seem likely to play an important part in the use of any such general purpose machines that we make."[10]

Informal meetings of customers continued. Then following an IBM symposium in Los Angeles in August 1955, the RAND Corporation hosted a meeting of representatives of seventeen organizations that had ordered IBM 704s. During this meeting, the computer industry's first "user organization" was formally created. Given the name SHARE, its purpose was to promote the sharing of information and programs among users of IBM's scientific- and engineering-oriented 704 computer and to influence the company's future developments in hardware and programming support. Nine months later SHARE could boast a membership of forty-seven installations, including all "announced prospective users" of the 704. Among the benefits of membership was a collection of three hundred computer programs, available from an IBM-maintained library.[11]

The benefits of a user organization were soon evident to others. In December 1955 early purchasers of Remington Rand's ERA 1103A formed a user organization called USE, an acronym for Univac Scientific Exchange.[12] User organizations for Remington Rand's UNIVAC, and for Burroughs and Bendix computers, were subsequently formed in 1956, as was GUIDE, the organization for users of IBM's business-oriented computers.[13]

The cooperative nature of a user organization is suggested by excerpts from "Obligations of a SHARE Member" printed in its manual: "It is expected that each member approach each discussion with an open mind, and, having respect for the competence of other members, be willing to accept the opinions of others more frequently than he insists on his own. . . . When it comes to standards, SHARE insists on adherence to them for communication purposes through SHARE channels to the extent that it refuses to distribute material not in SHARE language. Of course, decisions of SHARE can in no way be *binding* on any member installation so far as its internal operation is concerned." The manual also urged that each member be represented at each meeting by at least two people, "one empowered to make basic policy decisions and another thoroughly familiar with techniques, programming and detailed operating matters."[14]

The SHARE organization made numerous contributions to the development of computer programming. Of particular significance was the pioneering work of several West Coast members on *operating systems*—programs that manage and allocate the hardware and software resources of a computer to facilitate the writing and running of application programs. The company's first operating system was a direct outgrowth of the pioneering activities of these members of SHARE. Developed for the IBM 709 computer and introduced in 1959, its origin is suggested by its name, SOS, an acronym for SHARE Operating System.[15]

Customer Support

Support for customers of the IBM 701 had begun more than six months before deliveries, with the August 1952 training class in Poughkeepsie. More hands-on experience was available to customers following delivery in December 1952 of the first production model to the Technical Computing Bureau located at IBM World Headquarters in New York City. Here the day's activities were divided into three eight-hour shifts. One shift was available for program debugging by organizations that had ordered 701s. Another shift was devoted to conventional service bureau work, with personnel and machine time charged to customers. A third shift was reserved for maintenance. Classes on programming the 701 were also offered more or less continually.[16]

A staff of approximately thirty people was responsible for programming and operating the system. This was somewhat fewer than were employed by most 701 installations, but the average experience and education was higher. All members had at least a bachelor's degree in mathematics, about half had master's degrees, and a few had doctor's degrees. Many had experience programming and operating the CPC and SSEC computers.[17]

"Although we ran the 701 seven days a week, 52 weeks a year, it was during the day shift, Monday through Friday, that "spit and polish" prevailed," the manager of the operation recalls. This of course meant the unwritten IBM dress code was in force: white shirts, neckties, and dark suits for the men and office attire for the women. The 701 had replaced the SSEC as IBM's showcase computer.

So proud was Watson, Sr., of this evidence of the company's entry into large-scale electronic computing that he told one of his assistants to get rid of the electromechanical card reader in the same room. As recalled by the manager of the bureau, "When I explained to the assistant that the card reader was the only way we could get information into the 701, he said that made no difference; it had to go. He said Watson felt that the card reader detracted from the rest of the totally electronic aspects of the 701." In a significant departure from the norm, the older Watson's desires in this case had to yield to necessity. The card reader stayed.[18]

Programming and customer support for the 702 developed somewhat differently than for the 701, but the impact on customers was similar. In April 1954, six months after the IBM 702 was announced, Vin Learson ordered the creation of a new department to write application programs for the 702 for demonstration purposes and for use in courses offered to customers. In addition to showing customers how the 702 could handle tasks done with EAM equipment, it was hoped that these model programs could be adapted by customers to satisfy many of their own requirements.

Customers were also given the opportunity to run their own programs on a 702 before their computers were installed. Initially provided on the engineering model, this service was shifted to the first production machine after it was installed in Poughkeepsie in February 1955. IBM 701 and 702 installations were typically doing useful work within a few days or weeks, in part because many customer programs had already been debugged on a system at IBM to assure they could perform satisfactorily.[19] Customer support, of course, went well beyond activities cited here and was a major responsibility of the branch offices.

The importance of customer support can be gauged in part by the experience of General Electric, the first UNIVAC customer with conventional accounting applications. The computer was shipped to its Major Appliance Division in Louisville, Kentucky, in January 1954. Installation and checkout were completed in April, but the first useful results were not achieved until October, when the payroll program was finally operational.[20] Even then, its performance was not satisfactory. According to one account: "Even when the computer was run 24 hours a day, there was not enough time to get out the payroll. The first group who worked on the project at GE was fired, and a new group was brought in. By the time the installation was working, late in 1956, the whole area of automated business computing, and Univac especially, had become very questionable in the eyes of many businessmen." More than six months before the UNIVAC at GE was able to handle its work load, the last-installed IBM 702 was successfully processing a far larger payroll for the Ford Motor Company.[21]

Toward High Level Languages

Among those assigned to the 701 computer operation in New York City was John Backus. He had joined IBM as a programmer for the SSEC in September 1950, soon after earning a master's degree in mathematics at Columbia University. In an early IBM assignment, Backus teamed up with Ted Codd to devise an automated means for locating the source of machine errors during the running of programs on the SSEC. Another early assignment was to study automatic means for converting programs written and debugged on the CPC to operate on the SSEC. The knowledge Backus gained about CPC programming, and his experience in automating SSEC programming and operations, was influential in his later work.[22]

Beginning in January 1953, Backus and five principal colleagues developed a programming system for the 701, called Speedcoding. Its primary purpose was to facilitate the writing of programs using floating-point arithmetic. Floating-point (also called scientific) notation was widely used by engineers and scientists because it expressed very large and very small numbers just as simply as numbers in more common use. To programmers, the benefits of floating-point arithmetic were more mundane, but just as important. A machine performing floating-point arithmetic kept track of decimal-point locations, thus relieving the programmer of this burdensome, error-prone activity.

The inspiration for Speedcoding was a CPC mode of operation devised at the Los Alamos Scientific Laboratory in 1950. Rather than using a differently wired 604 plugboard for each problem, the Los Alamos group had devised a general-purpose, floating-point plugboard wiring pattern that could perform the four basic

Figure 14.1. John W. Backus
John Backus led the development of the FORTRAN language and its first compiler, which was delivered to customers beginning in April 1957.
Awarded the National Medal of Science in 1976 and the Draper Prize for engineering in 1993 for his work on FORTRAN, he was the first IBM employee to receive either of these top-level awards.

arithmetic operations (addition, subtraction, multiplication, and division) and also square roots. When numbers were represented on punched cards in the prescribed floating-point format, and a deck of cards was used to sequence through the desired arithmetic computations, the plugboard carried out the specified operations, automatically maintaining the decimal-point location and the correct power of ten.[23]

To provide this capability on the 701, Backus and his colleagues devised a Speedcoding instruction format that provided simultaneously for one floating-point and one fixed-point operation code. The floating-point operation code was associated with three memory addresses, as had been the floating-point implementation for the CPC. This format allowed the programmer to specify the memory addresses of two floating-point numbers (operands), the operation to be performed, and the memory address to which the floating-point result was to be sent. The fixed-point operation code referenced a single memory address and was used to implement control functions such as "indexing" and "branching."

The Speedcoding system gave the user the illusion of performing all functions of each four-address instruction in one step. Had the instructions been executed on the SSEC, the illusion would have been closer to reality because the SSEC was equipped with two high-speed electronic registers for instructions and six for numerical data.[24] The 701, however, had only one high-speed data register, so a program was needed to break each Speedcoding instruction into a series of steps and also to call on subroutines for performing floating-point arithmetic and other operations not built into the 701. Because this interpretive function had to be performed each time the application program was executed, the time for execution was typically fifteen times longer than for an equivalent program written in machine language. Nevertheless, by the fall of 1953, the ease of programming offered by Speedcoding had attracted several users.[25]

As planning for an improved 701 (the IBM 704) began in 1953, Backus was instrumental in the decision to implement floating-point and indexing capabilities directly in electronic circuits. Speedcoding would thus have little value on the 704. The addition of these and other instructions to the 704 repertoire made assembly language programming easier and more effective, but it did not eliminate the need for more sophisticated tools to reduce the cost of programming.

His work at the Scientific Computing Service Center provided Backus an opportunity to observe the economics and practical problems of computing. At the time, the Service Center had the only stored-program computer installation in the country with a primary function of selling computer services. Thus it was the only installation where cost accounting for equipment, personnel, and supplies was intrinsic to its business. Its second primary function—of helping customers test programs before they received their own computers—provided further insight into customer requirements.

Information from customer facilities, and IBM's own, revealed that the cost of programmers associated with a typical 701 computer installation was at least as great as the cost of the machine itself. Also nearly half of the useful computer time was spent debugging programs. "Thus programming and debugging accounted for as much as three-quarters of the cost of operating a computer," Backus observed, "and obviously, as computers got cheaper, this situation would get worse."[26] The economics of computing provided a compelling rationale for developing easier and more cost-effective means for programming computers.

From his own work on Speedcoding and his observation of other early steps toward "automatic programming," Backus saw the possibility of creating what came to be known as a *high level language*—that is, a computer language whose operational codes and structures are designed to conform to the needs of the user rather than to the machine architecture. A cost-effective means for automatically translating programs written in the high level language to machine code was, of course, mandatory.

For application programs that might be executed repeatedly, Backus believed a fifteenfold penalty in execution time (as experienced with Speedcoding) would be unacceptable.[27] The solution he proposed was to translate the entire program from high level language to machine language before execution rather than *interpreting* each high level instruction individually just before execution. This process, known as *compiling*, caused the time-consuming translation of instructions to be done only once—rather than each time the program was run.

The advantages of a compiler had been advanced a year earlier by Grace Murray Hopper, who had earned a Ph.D. in mathematics at Yale in 1934 and had done her first computer programming on the IBM-Harvard Mark I while serving in the navy. In 1949 she joined the Eckert-Mauchly Computer Corporation as a senior mathematician and did pioneering work on computer programming.[28] Describing her activities at a May 1952 meeting of the Association for Computing Machinery, Hopper provocatively asserted, "It is the current aim to replace, as far as possible, the human brain by an electronic digital computer." A key element of her presentation related to the benefits of a compiler.[29] By late 1953 some UNIVAC customers were making use of her "A-2" language and compiler. The statements in the A-2 language were similar in format to those in Speedcoding, but the language lacked the control and indexing features of Speedcoding.[30]

Backus's objective, by contrast, was to create a high level language far richer and more user-friendly than Speedcoding and still be able to compile its programs into efficient machine language.

The Birth of FORTRAN

By the end of 1953, Backus had won approval for a project to create an "algebraic programming language" that would make use of common mathematical notation. It was to be structured for easy learning and use by mathematicians, scientists, and engineers familiar with standard algebraic notation. A compiler was to be created to translate programs written in the high level language to machine language instructions.

Backus was joined by Irving Ziller, who had been hired into IBM's computing service bureau in 1952 after graduating from Brooklyn College. As part of his initial assignment, Ziller had made use of the similarity between CPC programming and Speedcoding to transfer many customer applications from the CPC to the more powerful and cost-effective 701 computer. The third member of the team was Harlan L. Herrick, who had joined the SSEC programming staff in November 1948. Herrick had a master's degree in mathematics from the University of Iowa and two additional years of teaching and graduate studies at Yale. Crucial support was provided by Roy Nutt, an experienced programmer on loan part time from the United Aircraft Corporation.

By November 1954 these individuals had established the general features of the proposed language. They had also written a descriptive document titled "Preliminary Report, Specifications for the IBM Mathematical FORmula TRANslating System, FORTRAN."

That winter Backus, Ziller, and Herrick visited several customers who had ordered 704 computers, seeking their reaction to the FORTRAN proposal.[31] Most of the customers were skeptical. They shared a concern Backus and Herrick had themselves expressed during a symposium on "Automatic Programming for Digital Computers" in May 1954: "Can a machine translate a sufficiently rich mathematical language into a sufficiently economical machine program at a sufficiently low cost to make the whole affair feasible?"[32] An unexpectedly strong endorsement for the project was provided by United Aircraft, which made Nutt available on a regular basis to help develop the compiler.[33]

The programming and testing of the FORTRAN compiler began early in 1955 and required more than two years. A key problem was to achieve efficient use of index registers as aids to accessing arrays of data during iterative computations. More than a dozen programmers were assigned to the compiler project before it was completed. A programmer's manual was made available in October 1956, and a paper (authored by ten IBM employees and three people on loan to the project from other organizations) was presented at a computer conference two months before shipment of the FORTRAN compiler commenced in April 1957.[34]

So enthusiastic were users of the new language that IBM developed FORTRAN compilers for all its stored-program computers. Most competitors did the same within only a few years. Applications programmed in FORTRAN for one machine could be converted with relative ease for use on another. Thus FORTRAN became the common computer language by which scientists and engineers shared programs and computational processes. So pervasive was the use of the language that most college courses on computing during the 1960s caused students to believe that learning FORTRAN was synonymous with learning to program computers.[35]

"We did expect our system to have a big impact, in the sense that it would make programming for the 704 very much faster, cheaper, more reliable," Backus recalls. "We also expected that, if we were successful in meeting our goals, other groups and manufacturers would follow our example in reducing the cost of programming by providing similar systems with different but similar languages." Beyond that, however, the objectives of the creators of FORTRAN were relatively modest. According to Backus, "We certainly had no idea that languages almost identical to the one we were working on would be used for more than one IBM computer, not to mention those of other manufacturers."[36] Consistent with the practice of the time, IBM made no proprietary claim to the language, and a reel of magnetic tape containing the compiler was provided to customers at no additional charge.

COBOL Arrives

More than a hundred high level languages were developed during the next few years. Many were inspired by the remarkable success of FORTRAN. Most were little used and have been long forgotten. An important exception is COBOL, a language designed for business applications. Its origins can be traced to an April 1959 gathering of six representatives from computer users and manufacturers. Their purpose was to prepare an agenda for a meeting to consider the development of a "common business language." A long-range goal implicit in the word "common" was to forge an industrywide standardization that was not likely to result from the competitive language developments then underway.

The Department of Defense believed such standardization was in the national interest and agreed to host the meeting in the Pentagon in May. In attendance were representatives of Burroughs, GE, Honeywell, IBM, NCR, Philco, RCA, Remington Rand, Sylvania, and ICT, as well as seven government organizations and eleven users. The key decision of the meeting was to proceed with a program having both short-range and long-range goals. A hierarchy of committees, with broad industry representation, was established to carry out the program.

The short-range goal was rapid development of an initial business language, using simple English terms as much as possible. This language was to be used until more sophisticated long-range language goals could be achieved. Two already-defined business languages, IBM's COMTRAN (later renamed Commercial Translator) and Sperry-Rand's Flow-Matic were influential in committee deliberations. In September the short-range language was named COBOL, an acronym for COmmon Business Oriented Language. The initial language definition process was completed by December, although substantial revisions were subsequently made, especially during the first year after its initial availability.

By the end of 1960, RCA and Remington Rand had produced operational compilers. These were used in a public display to demonstrate that the same COBOL program could be run on different computers.[37] Busy with implementing its Commercial Translator, IBM deferred COBOL until the revised specifications (COBOL 61) were developed. Its first COBOL compiler was delivered in January 1962.[38]

Within a few years, COBOL became as dominant for programming business applications as FORTRAN was for engineering and science. The attempt by IBM to achieve broad market acceptance of its own Commercial Translator for business applications had failed. Important to COBOL's success was ongoing support by the industry committee. Originally intended only as a stop-gap measure, COBOL was so successful that it obviated the need for the planned longer-range efforts.

Within ten years after FORTRAN was introduced, it and the subsequently introduced COBOL were used for writing nearly half of all application programs, and their usage was continuing to increase.[39] The cost-effectiveness of high level languages pioneered by FORTRAN had been confirmed. Even a quarter of a century after FORTRAN was first introduced, a survey revealed that "90 percent of all computers—both IBM and non-IBM—doing engineering and scientific work use this programming language more than 70 percent of the time."[40]

15

An Air Defense System

More than a year before the first UNIVAC was accepted by the Census Bureau—at a time when the IBM CPC was the most advanced electronic computer in the market—a government-sponsored study recommended development of an on-line, real-time air defense system. Dozens of large-scale stored-program computers were to be interconnected with each other and with radar units and other specialized input-output equipment dispersed across the country. It was January 1950, five months after the Soviet Union tested its first atomic bomb. Many of the technologies needed for the proposed system did not exist, but no other solution seemed more likely of success in defending the United States against possible attack by Soviet warplanes carrying atomic bombs.[1]

Recognizing the significance of the project when he learned about it in 1952, Tom Watson decided participation was essential to the company's future. "Pulling out the stops" to win an initial contract to work with the Massachusetts Institute of Technology (MIT) in building prototype computers, he was still not assured of getting the really big contract to manufacture, install, and service the dozens of large computers needed for the system. "I worked harder to win that contract than I worked for any other sale in my life," Watson recalled.[2] Ironically the person who initiated IBM's involvement was John McPherson—the man Tom Watson had tried to force out of the company only a few years earlier.

The Whirlwind Computer

The technological basis for the proposed air defense system was Whirlwind, an electronic digital computer under development at MIT since 1946. The genesis of Whirlwind, however, dates back three years earlier when Capt. Luis de Florez, director of the Special Devices Division of the U.S. Navy Bureau of Aeronautics, approached the Bell Telephone Laboratories and MIT (his alma mater) about the possibility of developing a flight trainer capable of simulating many different aircraft. Out of these discussions evolved a navy-funded project to develop an "airplane stability and control analyzer." The project had two objectives: first, a universal trainer, and second, a means for simulating the performance of new aircraft.

The project was officially launched in December 1944 when a $75,000 feasibility study contract was awarded to the MIT Servomechanisms Laboratory. In charge of the project was Jay W. Forrester, a self-assured twenty-six-year-old assistant director of the Servomechanisms Laboratory. Forrester's credentials included a bachelor's degree in electrical engineering from the University of Nebraska and five years' experience as a graduate student and research assistant in electrical engineering. Less than half a year later, Forrester endorsed the replacement of the small feasibility study contract with one calling for completion of the project in eighteen months for nearly twelve times the money, approximately $875,000. As the summer of 1945 wore on, however, he became increasingly concerned that the equipment his group was developing lacked the necessary flexibility and performance.[3]

Seeking alternative solutions, Forrester began considering a shift from traditional analog methods to newer digital methods recommended by Perry O. Crawford, Jr., a fellow graduate student in electrical engineering. Crawford's master's degree thesis (submitted three years earlier) had made the innovative proposal that "automatic control" of "real-time" activities such as directing antiaircraft fire could be carried out by means of numerical computations rather than the analog methods then in use.[4]

When submitted in 1942, Crawford's proposal seemed academic. Computing devices with the speed of electronic circuits were needed, but very little had been done to develop them.[5] By late 1945 the situation had changed dramatically. The ENIAC, whose electronic circuits contained 18,000 vacuum tubes, was being readied for its first full-scale test, and von Neumann's "First Draft of a Report on EDVAC" (distributed that summer) had stimulated additional interest in electronic digital computers.

Eager to participate in the exciting new field of electronic digital computers, Forrester also saw it as the best solution to the problems his project faced. In March 1946, following several months of discussions with the navy, he formally proposed that his project's objectives be revised. Its new tasks would be, first, the design of an electronic digital computer capable of handling the aircraft stability and control analyzer problem, and second, construction and incorporation of the computer in the flight trainer and analyzer equipment.

The cost of the project was now estimated at $2.4 million—approximately three times more than had been estimated for an analog solution. Nevertheless the navy liked what it saw. If the project was successful, it would be the first time digital techniques were used to implement automatic control of a large system. While substantial risks were inherent in such a pioneering effort, there was also the prospect of achieving substantially improved results.

The navy authorized Forrester to undertake research and development of digital technologies for incorporation in a small computer to demonstrate feasibility and to design (but not build) the proposed electronic computer and aircraft analyzer. These two phases of the project were to be completed by June 1948 at a cost of $1.2 million. The newly defined project was named "Whirlwind," consistent with the names Hurricane and Tornado given to other newly funded navy computer projects.[6]

Among those who encouraged the navy to accept the shift from analog to digital methods was Perry Crawford. Having left MIT in October 1945 to join de Florez in the Special Devices Division of the navy, Crawford now included among his responsibilities the review of Forrester's project for the navy. If the use of digital methods for automatic control could be validated by this project, the significance of his thesis and his own reputation would be greatly enhanced. This cozy relationship between project leader and project evaluator helped support Forrester's normal response to difficult problems, which was to seek more resources. By 1947 Project Whirlwind had grown to fifty people, half of whom were highly trained engineers.[7]

Pressure on the navy to reduce expenditures was growing in the postwar era, causing Crawford and Forrester to consider terminating work on the cockpit and ancillary gear. This would free up resources for development of the all-important computer, but it would also cause political problems because the cockpit and ancillary gear represented to many the primary purpose of the project. Nevertheless Forrester, with full support of Crawford, had terminated all such work by June 1948. There was now only one objective for Project Whirlwind: the design of a general-purpose computer capable of handling real-time problems.[8]

A critical evaluation of Project Whirlwind, by an ad hoc panel commissioned in 1949 by the Department of Defense, stiffened the navy's resistance to further cost increases. The cost of completing Whirlwind was projected to be two to three times higher than the *combined* costs of completing von Neumann's IAS computer, Eckert and Mauchly's UNIVAC, and the Moore School's EDVAC. The ad hoc panel commended Project Whirlwind for the excellence of its staff, for the quality of its reports, and for training graduate students. It concluded, however, that the development costs were not justifiable for any known application. It recommended the project be terminated if no suitable application could be found.[9]

Seeking a use for Whirlwind that was sufficiently important to justify its development costs, Forrester undertook a one-year study of its potential use in air traffic control. This study was begun in March 1949 with air force funding.

The New Mission

Five months later the Soviet Union detonated its first atomic bomb. In response to this threat, U.S. military organizations initiated a series of actions that resulted in the selection of Whirlwind as the central element of a nationwide air defense system. Among these early actions was creation by the air force of the Air Defense System Engineering Committee to find "the best solution of the problem of Air Defense." The committee was chaired by George E. Valley, an MIT professor who was also a member of the Air Force Scientific Advisory Board.

The committee's preliminary findings, submitted in January 1950, were consistent with those of a separate study carried out by the Weapon System Evaluation Group (WSEG) of the Department of Defense. Both studies found the existing air defense system to be woefully inadequate. Improvements were needed in radar, antiaircraft artillery, ground-to-air missiles, and fighter aircraft. The most important need, however, was for command and control centers capable of receiving and evaluating information from many sources and of working together to create a coordinated nationwide response to any airborne threat.[10]

Electronic speed would be required for all parts of a modernized system, including observation, evaluation, and communication. Such a system had much in common with the air traffic control system Forrester's group was already studying for the air force. It was also reminiscent of Crawford's 1942 master's degree thesis in which he analyzed the possible use of electronic digital computation methods for "the prediction of the future position of the target" for the "control of anti-aircraft gunfire."[11]

These facts would have made Whirlwind a strong candidate in the thinking of any group asked to consider solutions to the air defense problem. But with MIT professor George Valley as chairman, the committee quickly and decisively endorsed Whirlwind as the "best solution." Informal approval from the air force came almost as rapidly. Fear that Soviet aircraft carrying nuclear bombs were a primary threat to the United States gave the project the highest priority of the Department of Defense.[12] At last an application had been found for Whirlwind with requirements for high performance and reliability—and sufficient urgency—to justify the level of expenditure Forrester had always deemed necessary.

In response to a December 1950 request by the air force, MIT established Project Lincoln and began to construct a laboratory dedicated to the air-defense problem. Located at at the Hanscom Air Force Base a few miles west of Boston, the facilities were called the Lincoln Laboratory.[13] Project Whirlwind continued to be located in Cambridge at the MIT Digital Computer Laboratory, which was directed by Forrester. Activities and persons concerned with Whirlwind and its use in the air defense system were organizationally part of the Lincoln Laboratory Division VI, which was also headed by Forrester.

Forrester did not wait for these complex organizational matters to be resolved before shifting the direction of his project. In April 1950, with full agreement of the air force, he discontinued work on the air traffic control problem and began work on the air defense system. More than a year later (June 1951) a contract went into effect that covered the new project objectives and agreements between MIT and the air force.[14]

Final assembly and test of the Whirlwind computer was underway during the last half of 1950. The most critical component was memory. It consisted of specially constructed cathode-ray tubes, each costing approximately $1,500 and designed to store 256 bits of information in a 16×16 array of electrostatically charged regions on its front surface. The first bank of 16 tubes was installed in Whirlwind in June 1950. All tubes functioned as designed, except that the uniformity and reliability of the storage surfaces were not satisfactory. After three months of intensive effort to solve the problem, Forrester could only report that "final testing and alignment of the first storage bank is moving along steadily."[15]

By early 1951 the memory was functioning well enough that Whirlwind was connected to microwave early warning (MEW) radar for experiments in tracking the course of two airplanes, predicting their future locations, and calculating data for voice transmission to intercepting aircraft. Soon after this capability had been demonstrated in April, a decision was made to construct a feasibility test model of the air-defense system in the region of Cape Cod. Named the Cape Cod System, it was to incorporate at least one of each essential element of the final system so that full-system operation could be simulated.

The Cape Cod System was fully operational by September 1953, less than two and one half years after work on the system began. Its success was made possible by improvements in electronic circuitry, display technology, data handling procedures, methods of analysis, computer programming, and—perhaps most important of all—the use of a new memory technology pioneered by Jay Forrester. Known as magnetic core, ferrite core, or simply core, the new memory technology provided a dramatic improvement in computer reliability.[16]

A Better Memory

Main memory for Whirlwind had been a critical concern for Forrester from the beginning. The high-speed random access capability needed to satisfy real-time response requirements could not be achieved by the magnetic drums pioneered by ERA or by the mercury delay-line memory developed for EDVAC. Of all memory technologies then being developed, only electrostatic storage of information within a cathode ray tube provided adequate speed. But this type of memory occupied a large space, was expensive to build, and was difficult to make reliable.

"Storage tubes do not represent the ultimate in data storage devices," Forrester observed in April 1947. He then put forward his own ideas for "efficient storage," which consisted of individual elements "closely spaced in a 3-dimensional volume." In his first attempt he used gas glow discharge tubes. These possessed a "suitable form of nonlinear impedance," but seemingly uncon-

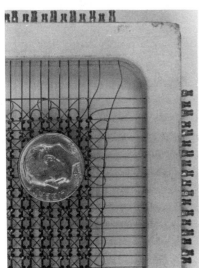

Figure 15.1.   Jay W. Forrester and Memory Devices
Jay Forrester is shown in 1950 (top) with an electrostatic storage tube of the type initially used in Whirlwind. A small corner of a 64 × 64 core plane pioneered by Forrester and used in the XD-1 computer (bottom, left) shows how four wires were threaded through each core: three for reading and writing information and the fourth to detect the output signal. Core size is indicated by U.S. dime; outside diameter was 80 mil (0.2 centimeter). The SAGE computer memory array (bottom, right) contains thirty-six core planes, three of which are spares. (Top photograph courtesy of the MITRE Corporation Archives.)

trollable electrical characteristics forced him to abandon the effort.[17]

Two years later in April 1949, Forrester saw an advertisement for Deltamax, a ferromagnetic metal produced by the Arnold Engineering Company of Chicago. Its remarkably sharp magnetic switching threshold caused him to consider its use for storing information in a compact 3-dimensional array of tiny magnetic rings (cores). The 1s and 0s of binary information would be represented by the clockwise or counterclockwise direction of magnetization of doughnut-shaped cores made of Deltamax.[18]

The idea of storing information in magnetic cores was not new. Several other researchers had considered this possibility.[19] But Forrester's method for wiring magnetic cores into a three-dimensional array and selecting them electrically was new. Fundamental to his proposal was a magnetic material with a well-defined switching threshold. This threshold needed to be sharp enough that coincidence of electric current pulses in two wires through a core would reverse its magnetization direction, whereas one of these pulses alone would be too small to alter the magnetization state of any core through which it passed. Using this concept, Forrester devised a way to wire cores into a three-dimensional array so as to minimize the number of electronic circuits needed to read and write information anywhere in the memory.

Forrester carefully documented his ideas in his engineering notebook and carried out a number of experiments that summer.[20] Simple theory and experiment did not agree as well as he hoped, however, so he selected a graduate student to carry out more detailed experiments as part of the master's degree program. The task was to relate theory to experiment and to find a suitable core material for the proposed memory.[21]

An early suspicion, subsequently verified by experiment, was that metal cores would not switch fast enough because of electric eddy currents induced within the core itself. As a result, Forrester initiated a program at MIT to develop materials with suitable magnetic characteristics that did not conduct electricity. Some of the work on ferrite materials was subcontracted to the General Ceramics and Steatite Corporation of Keasbey, New Jersey. With Whirlwind's huge government funding, Forrester had little trouble paying for activities he regarded as important.

In May 1952 successful operation of a 16 × 16 array of ferrite cores had been demonstrated. One year later the first ferrite core memory with enough storage capacity to serve as a main memory of a computer was assembled and installed in a small computer, specially designed to test memory functions. The memory had a capacity of 17,408 bits of information in a $32 \times 32 \times 17$ array of ferrite cores. By September 1953 two ferrite core arrays of this size had been tested and installed in Whirlwind.

Somewhat faster than the cathode-ray tube memories they replaced, the ferrite core memories were most notable for their superior reliability. The electronic drive and sense circuits sometimes failed, but the tiny doughnut-shaped cores almost never failed. A new memory technology had been developed that could satisfy the speed and reliability needs of Whirlwind.[22]

Selecting IBM

In June 1952, fifteen months before ferrite core memories were installed in Whirlwind, Forrester was already considering problems of manufacturing, installing, and servicing the computers for the proposed air defense system. During a professional society committee meeting in New York City, one of his group leaders had informally discussed the subject with John McPherson. Learning that "McPherson was very interested," Forrester said, "the trouble with IBM would be its traditional secretiveness." Then he cautioned, "A number of companies need to be considered. . . . However, we must avoid indiscriminate discussion of this problem with different manufacturers who might create considerable disturbance in competition and pressure to receive the job."[23]

The "competition and pressure to receive the job" were as intense as Forrester anticipated, but IBM's "traditional secretiveness" was not a problem. Tom Watson wanted the contract in spite of what he considered to be large inherent risks. One of these risks had been identified in a particularly pointed manner by the company's treasurer, Al Williams. Could a mistake in computation, he asked, "result in the accidental destruction of one of our country's own airplanes, with the resultant financial exposure and publicity such an accident might entail?"[24]

Watson believed the contract was so significant that whoever won it would become the kingpin of the emerging electronic computer industry. Knowing he could not obtain the contract without revealing IBM's engineering and manufacturing strengths, he treated Forrester and his colleagues to one of the more open tours of laboratories and plants ever given to outsiders.[25]

During the summer of 1952, Forrester and three of his top technical leaders visited the research, development, and manufacturing facilities of IBM and of other leading contenders. Raytheon was a strong contender because of its wartime activities in electronics and its development of the Hurricane computer under contract to the navy. Remington Rand was an even stronger contender. Under the leadership of James H. Rand, Jr., it had just acquired ERA, and it had acquired the Eckert-Mauchly Computer Company two years earlier.

Jim Rand's methods were different from Tom Watson's, but he was just as eager to win the contract. He personally hosted the MIT evaluation team on the corporate yacht. Also present on the yacht was the new chairman of the Remington Rand board, Gen. Douglas MacArthur, one of the more popular military leaders of World War II. Knowing little about computers, MacArthur entertained the guests with his observations on political and military matters. Leslie R. Groves, who had managed the Manhattan Project in which the first atomic bomb was developed, hosted the group during the days. Recently hired as a Remington Rand vice president and director of advanced research, Groves was an impressive salesman for the company's technical capabilities.[26]

Before the visits were undertaken, Forrester and his team had decided what capabilities a contractor should have, and they had devised a method for quantifying the relative importance of these. Following in-depth reviews, the four of them "were unanimous in their relative placing of the companies and were unanimous in feeling that a wide margin existed between each." First was IBM, followed by Remington Rand and then Raytheon.

Documenting the reasons for selecting IBM over Remington Rand, Forrester wrote: "In the IBM organization we observed a much higher degree of purposefulness, integration, and esprit de corps than we found in the Remington Rand organization. Also, of considerable interest to us, was the evidence of much closer ties between research, factory, and field maintenance in IBM." By contrast, he noted that the Eckert-Mauchly and ERA organizations "had not yet worked with each other or with a Remington Rand factory."

Also cited were the superior technical abilities of key staff members at IBM and the company's leadership in developing, manufacturing, installing, and servicing electronic computing equipment. "At the time of our visit IBM had built much more electronic digital computing equipment. They had some 3,000,000 vacuum tubes operating in their own equipment in commercial service." By contrast Forrester noted, "In the Remington Rand organization suitable factory personnel have not received training, since most of their electronic computer construction has been on an expanded model shop basis connected with the research groups."[27]

Forrester's report did not reveal that IBM had already made considerable progress in developing its own magnetic core memories. However, prior to giving IBM the contract to work with Lincoln Laboratory in defining the computer for the Air Defense System, Forrester sent two of his colleagues to review its research on magnetic core memories.[28]

The lead engineer for this project was Munro K. (Mike) Haynes, who had joined IBM in 1950 after completing his doctoral research in electrical engineering at the University of Illinois. His doctoral thesis was titled, "Magnetic Cores as Elements of Digital Computing Systems." It was primarily devoted to the use of magnetic cores for computer logic, but the last section described a two-dimensional memory array. Without any apparent knowledge of Forrester's prior work, Haynes had independently invented the same type of magnetic core memory using coincident-current selection, albeit for a two-dimensional rather than a three-dimensional array.[29]

Soon after joining IBM, Mike Haynes began seeing General Ceramics advertisements for ferrite cores with sufficiently sharp switching thresholds to be used in his proposed memory. He ordered a variety of these cores, which were typically about an inch in diameter. Teaming up with a more experienced engineer, he built a core memory with just enough capacity to store all the information in an IBM punched card: 960 bits in an 80 × 12 array. In May 1952 it was successfully tested as a data buffer between a Type 405 alphabetical accounting machine and a Type 517 summary punch. This first functional test of a ferrite core memory was made in the same month that a four-times smaller 16 × 16-bit ferrite core array was successfully tested at MIT.

Although Mike Haynes could claim some areas of leadership in magnetic core memory research, the MIT effort was more advanced overall. It had started sooner, had a more clearly defined mission, and benefited from government funding, the breadth of MIT's technical capabilities, and Forrester's inspired leadership.

Particularly significant was Forrester's decision to establish a ferrite materials research effort in 1950 when he learned about ferrite materials with sharp thresholds, produced by General Ceramics. This led to an unwitting cooperation between IBM and MIT that began in 1952 when Mike Haynes ordered smaller ferrite cores than had ever been made by General Ceramics. The cores had 90 mil (0.23 cm) outside diameters and 60 mil (0.15 cm) inside diameters. IBM paid for the special dies to fabricate these cores because there appeared to be no other customer for them. Learning of their existence, the MIT Lincoln Laboratory contracted with General Ceramics to develop improved materials for these smaller cores. Forrester and others at MIT were apparently unaware that IBM had paid for the dies that would soon be used to fabricate ferrite cores for the first magnetic core memory installed in Whirlwind.[30]

Working Together

In October 1952, IBM received a subcontract from the Lincoln Laboratory to assist in the final design of the computer and related equipment for the air-defense system. Off to a fast start, the company had already assigned a few people in September, and by November there were fourteen staff-level employees. An old necktie factory on High Street in Poughkeepsie served as headquarters. It also provided the name, Project High, for IBM's part of the air-defense effort. By July there were 203 technical and 26 administrative people assigned. By November 1953 (only thirteen months after the initial contract was signed) the total number of employees had reached the planned level of about 300.[31]

Assigning qualified people was only the beginning. The newly assigned engineers with their industrial culture had to learn to work with engineers from an academic research environment. Addressing this subject from the MIT perspective in July 1953, Forrester said, "The difficulty in accomplishing the program on time is increased inevitably by the fact that two organizations are doing most of the work together. The relationship between them is new, many of the people in the groups are new to the problem and to the ways of attacking it."[32]

Indeed the two groups had rather different backgrounds and initial expectations. Many MIT engineers believed Whirlwind would require very little modification. They believed IBM engineers would merely have to "do the production engineering, whatever that was, and build the necessary quantity." By contrast many of their counterparts at IBM believed MIT should simply hand over a few pages of specifications so they could redesign the computer the right way. Not surprisingly, "the first meetings of these groups were loud and rancorous," Robert R. Everett (first in command after Forrester) recalled. "After a while, as the two groups began to know and respect each other, the arguments became more cogent and took place between individuals instead of between organizations."[33]

The initial IBM group was drawn heavily from those who had designed the 701 and 702 computers. From January to June of 1953 they thrashed over architectural and hardware designs with MIT engineers. Many meetings were held midway between Poughkeepsie and Boston in a back room of the IBM branch office in Hartford, Connecticut. The first of these meetings was attended by twelve people from IBM and twenty from MIT. Among their conclusions was that "final decisions regarding circuits cannot be made at this time." Of twenty-two different electronic computer circuits already identified for joint development, little was known about ten of them and three of the circuits were described as "complete unknowns."[34]

Decisions hammered out in subsequent meetings included such fundamental things as electronic circuit packaging, the manner in which arithmetic would be handled, and the provision of index registers.[35] These decisions were based on knowledgeable input from both groups, but if agreement could not be reached, the MIT engineers were authorized to make the final decision. "This was a very irksome thing for many of our people," IBM's first project manager recalled. "But it seemed to me that under the urgency of the situation it couldn't have been any other way."[36]

Many more technical decisions were reached at a series of seven closely spaced meetings held during June and July. Known as Project Grind, these meetings were structured to encourage participants to grind away at urgent technical problems until decisions were reached. Committees were formed to deal with specific problems. Then as one engineer described it, "We let the blood flow on the floor until we came to an agreement."[37]

Achieving the required system reliability was particularly challenging, in spite of the substantial contributions already made by the MIT Whirlwind effort. All components were designed for operation under "marginal conditions," that is, when all interacting components were performing in their worst allowable manner—for example, low power supply voltages or low signal levels. The design of circuits to satisfy these conditions and the determination of "realistic" marginal conditions and test procedures required extensive engineering design, followed by lengthy discussions and agreement of both groups.

Forrester believes his management approach was crucial to achieving system reliability. "When a mistake was recognized," he asserts, "it was admitted and fixed rather than evaded or denied." Forrester credits this approach with forcing an early decision to conduct "marginal checking" of critical circuits in service and replacing marginal ones rather than waiting for failures during normal operation. This improved circuit reliability by about a factor of ten. When it was later recognized that the promised reliability could still not be achieved with a single computer, the air force was advised that the original assumptions were wrong. Each computer would require an identical backup computer in case the first one failed. This decision was not made until November 1953, after the air force had established a budget for the entire system. "There was a lot of flak from that," Forrester observes, "but our position was that it had to be done."[38]

To keep the backup computer ready to take over without delay, it had to carry out many of the same tasks in real time as the primary computer. The innovative "duplex" mode devised by the IBM-MIT team permitted the backup computer to carry out certain ancillary functions at the same time, including automatic marginal checking of circuits.

In September 1953 a contract for two prototype computers was awarded to IBM. Shipment of the first prototype to the Lincoln Laboratory was scheduled for August of the next year. Inevitably there were delays. Many of the technical problems were more complex than anticipated. Consider just the tasks of individually fabricating, testing, and wiring 589,824 tiny ferrite cores used by the memory banks of the two computers. Semiautomatic fabrication and test equipment was devised to speed the process, but the designs for these were newer than the designs for the pioneering memory itself. Numerous modifications were required. Even the electrical tests for distinguishing good cores from bad ones had to be modified as more experience was gained.[39]

Remarkably, all of the technical problems were overcome in time to ship the major units of the first prototype computer (XD-1) to the Lincoln Laboratory in January 1955. It successfully replaced Whirlwind in the air defense test system later that year. The second prototype computer (XD-2) was retained by IBM to provide a test facility for modified hardware and to support programming systems development.[40]

The SAGE System

"The first large-scale computer for the nation's vast, new electronic air warning network is being shipped from here to McGuire Air Force Base in New Jersey," the IBM Military Products Division's plant in Kingston, New York, proudly announced in June 1956.[41] An acronym for Semi-Automatic Ground Environment, SAGE had been adopted in 1954 as the name for the air-defense system. The name was chosen to signify the semiautomatic manner in which the system would provide the information environment for operation of the Air Defense Command.[42] Observing that the computer was designed by IBM in cooperation with MIT and that the total "SAGE system was developed by scientists and engineers at MIT's Lincoln Laboratory under contract with the Air Force," the IBM press release continued:

This extraordinary "electronic brain" will become the first of the giant computers to fit into the integrated complex of radar, ships, jet aircraft, communications networks, missiles, and people that is rapidly taking shape as the supersensitive continental air defense system. This immense project is known as the Semi-Automatic Ground Environment (SAGE) system. . . . With a knowledge of flight plans of friendly planes available in the computer, hostile planes can be identified immediately and the most effective defense action taken.

The SAGE system starts with a radar ring—on land, on Navy picket ships at sea, on offshore Texas Towers, and on airborne early warning planes ranging far out over the ocean. These radars are linked by telephone lines or ultrahigh-frequency radio directly to the high-speed computer. Information about aircraft anywhere within the radar area is relayed continuously and automatically to the computer. This IBM-built equipment, called the AN/FSQ-7, digests all of this information plus Ground Observer reports, flight plans, and weather information as fast as it is received and translates it into an over-all picture of the air situation. These TV-like pictures show the air battle as it develops and provide the basis for the necessary human judgments.

The computer automatically calculates for the operator the most effective employment of such defensive weapons as guided missiles,

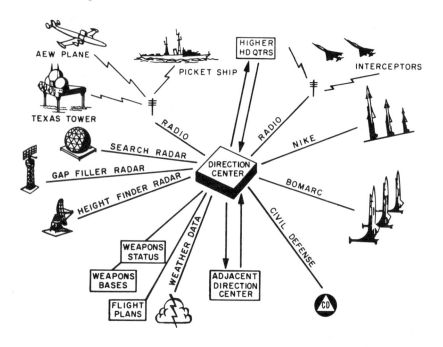

Figure 15.2. SAGE
Top: Schematic reveals the basic elements of the SAGE Air Defense System.
Bottom: Operator sits at a display console using input facilities, including
the light gun held in his right hand. (Courtesy of the MITRE Corporation
Archives.)

antiaircraft batteries, and jet interceptors. In the case of the intercepting jets, the aircraft is controlled by directions fed by radio directly from the computer to the automatic pilot in the plane. Missiles are controlled similarly. At any time, the air battle commander can have the computer display the over-all air situation or whatever part of it he wishes to monitor in detail. As the battle moves, information is transferred spontaneously to an adjacent computer.[43]

Because the SAGE operations seem almost routine in today's world, it is hard to imagine the impact this announcement had in 1956. It was the first time a computer had been used to control a large, geographically distributed system. The size and scope of SAGE was almost unbelievable. When fully deployed in 1963, there were twenty-three direction centers distributed near the northern boundary and the east and west coasts of the United States. Each of these contained an AN/FSQ-7 computer system having almost 60,000 vacuum tubes, weighing 250 tons, occupying an acre of floor space, and using up to 3 million watts of electric power.

Each AN/FSQ-7 computer was actually two identical computers that operated in a "duplexed" mode for greater reliability. They used binary arithmetic, single address instructions, and 32-bit words, and could process approximately 75,000 instructions per second. Each of the two magnetic core memories had a capacity of 8,192 words and had a read-write cycle of 6 microseconds. (These memories were replaced by ones with 69,632 words beginning late in 1957.) Additional high-speed storage was provided by 12 magnetic drums each with a capacity of 12,288 words. Each central processor was capable of handling the operation of 100 display consoles while sending and receiving data from twelve remote sites.[44]

There were also three Air Defense Division headquarters, called combat centers, where military officers had responsibility for supervising the activities of several direction centers. Each of these contained a modified SAGE computer, called AN/FSQ-8, which had fewer display consoles and required far less input processing equipment because it received data previously processed by the direction centers. Its task was to summarize and display air-defense information and to provide alternative actions for the officers in charge.[45]

The first production system was tested and accepted in June 1956 and was declared fully operational within the SAGE system at McGuire Air Force Base in New Jersey in July 1958. The last of these systems was shut down in January 1984, after defending the United States from air attack for more than a quarter century.[46]

Programming

The development, testing, and maintenance of computer programs for SAGE was an enormous task. Primary responsibility for this was given to the Rand Corporation of Santa Monica, California, in part because neither IBM, MIT, nor the Bell Telephone Laboratories could envision using so many programmers once SAGE was completed. Rand was also a very logical choice. Established as a nonprofit corporation in 1948, its origins date back to 1945 when the air force created Project Rand to employ top-quality civilian scientists and advisers to conduct defense research.

A particularly significant project, initiated by Rand in 1950, was the study of group behavior in man-machine systems.[47] For this study an existing air-defense radar station was replicated and pioneering work in simulating battle conditions was undertaken. Several IBM CPC electronic computers were used to perform the millions of computations needed to create the simulated radar scans presented to operators during these studies. The realism achieved was found to improve dramatically the training of personnel within the air-defense system. Even greater realism was achieved when an IBM 701 became available to replace the far less powerful CPCs. In October 1954 the air force awarded Rand a contract to develop, install, and maintain system training facilities in 150 sites nationwide. These activities were excellent preparation for the organization that was to program the computers of the new air-defense system.

Rand's programming activities for SAGE began in July 1955 when five of its programmers arrived at Lincoln Laboratory to work in a "totally integrated, joint organization" with MIT personnel who had already written prototype programs for Whirlwind. Near the end of the year Rand had grown its SAGE programming and system training activities into an independent System Development Division with 450 employees, 75 of whom were at the Lincoln Laboratory. By the end of the next year the division had more than doubled in size and was spun off as an independent company, the System Development Corporation.[48]

The programming of SAGE computers proved to be an even greater task than anticipated. This is not surprising. The programs were, in aggregate, very large, and they controlled the world's first on-line, real-time, geographically distributed system. At the time, however, Bob Everett recalled, "we believed our own myths about software—that one can do anything with software on a general-purpose computer; that software is easy to write, test, and maintain; that it is easily replicated, doesn't wear out, and is not subject to transient errors. We had a lot to learn."[49]

Respect for the size of the programming job was nonetheless evident in a bold decision to build programming tools before starting development of the operational air-defense program itself. A set of programs named the Lincoln Utility System resulted and served to mechanize program development and testing and to impose systematic and efficient standards on those tasks. Consisting of some 40,000 instructions, the system ensured that the 100,000-instruction SAGE operational program was developed in a disciplined manner that facilitated operation, maintenance, and extension. Also crucial to success was the prototype air-defense program already operational on the Whirlwind computer. The SAGE program was, nevertheless, delivered a year later than scheduled and required a far larger memory than initially planned.

"The biggest mistake we made," according to one who worked on both the Whirlwind and SAGE programs, "was that we attempted to make too large a jump from the 35,000 instructions we had operating on the much simpler Whirlwind I computer to the more than 100,000 instructions on the much more powerful IBM SAGE computer." Eventually close to 500,000 computer instructions were written, of which only about 25 percent actually supported operational air-defense missions. The rest were needed to test systems, help generate programs, document the process, and provide various project management functions.[50]

An Assessment

The overall effectiveness of SAGE is hard to assess because it was never used in real combat. Some might argue, however, that that is the true measure of its success. It was a technological marvel, a deterrent to potential aggressors, and a means for simulating attacks and training U.S. military officers and personnel. Sitting in the command-and-control room, armed only with light guns (now called light pens), military officers and personnel could command the computer to provide information on simulated attacks and calculate alternative defensive actions. The system also served as a laboratory for evaluating new designs for command and control systems.[51]

But the importance of SAGE goes far beyond its impact on the cold war. Its pioneering technological contributions were numerous. Among these are magnetic-core memories, a large real-time operating system, highly disciplined program structure and development, overlapping of computation and I/O functions through a rudimentary I/O channel, transmission of digital data via telephone lines, cathode-ray-tube displays with light pens, worst-case designs and marginal testing of circuits and components for high reliability, and duplexed computer operation for enhanced reliability. The system's overall reliability, a crucial design objective, is indicated by two-year performance data compiled beginning in 1978 when only seven centers were still in operation. Both machines in any one center were typically down simultaneously less than 24 hours per year, of which 20 hours were attributed to failures in air conditioning and other noncomputer causes.[52]

Without doubt the most significant technological achievement of Project SAGE was design of the first geographically distributed, on-line, real-time system implemented with digital computers. Inspired by Perry Crawford's master's degree thesis, by the vast number of electronic vacuum tube circuits successfully operated in ENIAC, and by von Neumann's computer design concepts, Jay Forrester moved quickly to use digital computers for system control functions. Development of this hitherto nonexistent field was accelerated by the confluence of several fortuitous events. Particularly significant among these events was the 1949 explosion of the Soviet Union's first atomic bomb. This created an environment in which Forrester's project received almost unlimited technical and financial resources.

There are many examples of Forrester's engineering leadership, but none is more striking than his persistent and successful effort to develop a reliable and cost-effective computer memory. Others had pioneered the use of magnetic cores, but they lacked the insight, clarity of purpose, and challenging requirements that helped Forrester create the first computer main memory implemented with ferrite cores.

Numerous companies were involved in the development of SAGE. Significant among these were the Western Electric Company, with responsibility for overall engineering management and construction of the SAGE centers; the Systems Development Corporation (SDC), with responsibility for programming the SAGE computers; the General Electric Company, with responsibility for developing a variety of radar systems and data links; and the IBM Corporation, with responsibility for the design, manufacture, testing, installation, and maintenance of the SAGE computers.

Each of these companies profited from its involvement, but with the possible exception of SDC whose very existence resulted from SAGE, none profited more than IBM. Although SAGE provided less than 4 percent of IBM's total U.S. revenue from 1952 through 1955, it contributed almost 80 percent of the company's revenue from stored-program computer systems. (See appendix D.) This was a critical period during which the company wrested leadership from Remington Rand in the new market for large-scale electronic stored-program computers. At the peak of its activities in 1957 and 1958, IBM employed over seven thousand people to manufacture, install, service, and improve the SAGE systems.[53]

The skills of its engineers were strengthened and refined through close collaboration with engineers at the MIT Lincoln Laboratory. Its manufacturing organization improved its ability to mass-produce and test large computers, and its service organization gained similar advantages. The benefits of this experience showed up rapidly in the IBM 700 series computers that followed immediately after the 701 and 702. The company also made use of the technical skills of people trained in SAGE to develop, in cooperation with American Airlines, the first commercial airline reservation system, SABRE.

16

Chasing New Technologies

Forrester's emphasis on developing reliable, high-speed memories for SAGE is hardly surprising. A means of storing information for automatic manipulation and analysis by machine is basic to any information processing system. Punched cards introduced by Hollerith in the late 1880s served this function adequately for more than half a century because the time required for arithmetic computations remained in reasonable balance with the time required to handle punched cards.

This relationship was put severely out of balance by the introduction of digital electronics in the 1940s. Electronic circuits could perform arithmetic computations dramatically faster than the data could be read from cards. Finding an adequate solution for the speed imbalance between logic circuits and memory was the primary technological problem facing designers of early electronic computers. Indeed it never ceased being a dominant problem.

The designers of the IBM CPC solved this problem reasonably well by providing a small amount of auxiliary electromechanical memory that fell between vacuum tube and punched-card storage in speed and cost, and by providing the ability to perform many arithmetic operations electronically between the reading of data and instructions from each card. The much larger Remington Rand UNIVAC (operational about a year and a half after the CPC) provided a better solution. Data and instructions were stored on magnetic tape rather than on cards, and they were read into a high-speed mercury delay-line memory before being executed by electronic circuits. This stored-program approach, with some important differences, was subsequently used in the IBM 701 as well as in later computers offered by IBM, Remington Rand, and others.

Among the more significant differences between the IBM 701 and UNIVAC was the 701's use of lightweight Mylar tape, coated with magnetic material, for information storage. Eckert and Mauchly had chosen heavy metallic tape because lightweight tapes broke too frequently during stop-start operation. The breakage problem was overcome by IBM engineers who devised vacuum columns to create long loops of tape at either side of the read-write head; the resulting slack in the tape dramatically reduced the stresses on the tape. This basic vacuum-column design was adopted industrywide and remained the preferred design for decades.

The IBM 701 also featured punched-card input-output capability in addition to magnetic tape storage, and it offered a high-speed magnetic drum to supplement the main memory. The cathode-ray-tube memory used in the 701 was faster but less reliable than UNIVAC's mercury delay-line memory. A truly satisfactory main memory for electronic computers was first provided by the ferrite-core devices pioneered in Project SAGE.

The rapidity with which these and many other technologies were developed and used in products following World War II is remarkable. Even more remarkable is the speed with which yet newer technologies threatened their supremacy. Most important among these was the semiconductor transistor. Invented at the Bell Telephone Laboratories at the end of 1947 and publicly announced the following July, the transistor was devised specifically to replace vacuum tubes in electronic circuits. Next in importance for the future of computers was magnetic disk storage. Invented, implemented, and rapidly improved by IBM, disk storage was destined to take over most functions of punched cards and magnetic tape in computer systems.

Growth of the computer industry was driven for decades by parallel improvements in magnetic disk storage and semiconductor device technologies. Leadership in the product application of these and other rapidly evolving computer technologies was crucial to IBM's continuing success and is the subject of this chapter.

A New Laboratory

Creation of a new laboratory devoted to advanced technologies was motivated in part by "insistent demands of the Sales Department" that had forced postponement of work on nearly all advanced components in the Endicott laboratory. "The only solution," Wally McDowell had advised John McPherson in 1950, "is the establishment of a separate group or groups whose sole function is to work on long range component development."[1] Another motivating factor was the reluctance of many qualified engineers, especially those from California, to relocate to Poughkeepsie or Endicott, New York. This impediment came forcibly to McDowell's attention early in 1951 as he was attempting to double the engineering personnel in Poughkeepsie to 750 by the end of the year.[2]

Out of these considerations a plan evolved to establish a new laboratory in San Jose, California, where the company had operated a card manufacturing plant since the early 1940s. Chosen to head the laboratory was Reynold Johnson, the man Watson, Sr., had hired into the company in 1934 to develop the first automatic test scoring machine (see chap. 6). During the ensuing years, Johnson had demonstrated his technical creativity and management skills on many other projects as well.

Early in 1952 Johnson and four others took occupancy of a small rented building at 99 Notre Dame Avenue and began the task of transforming it into a research laboratory.[3] To their surprise and pleasure, a single advertisement placed in newspapers in the West produced several hundred applicants. The applicants were interviewed and many qualified engineers hired. By June the new laboratory was reported to have a "smoothly functioning organization" with approximately thirty employees.

Wishing to avoid the negative effects of the competition and secrecy that had existed in the Endicott laboratory, Johnson insisted that each engineer be conversant with all projects in the laboratory. To emphasize his desire for a cooperative environment, he established the following priorities for each engineer: "It is your most important assignment in this laboratory to give assistance when you are asked to do so, by any other engineer of this staff, in the form of consultation, experimentation, or suggestions, and the second most important assignment is that of carrying on the project to which you are assigned."[4]

Many projects had been suggested for the laboratory even before it was formally established. Others were identified by newly hired staff members. Several of the more promising projects were launched. Some of these were terminated following unsuccessful initial experiments, and a couple were transferred to Endicott for possible product development. But it took only one project to make the entire activity worthwhile. That project produced the first magnetic disk storage unit, and it provided the primary mission of the San Jose laboratory for years to come. It was formally begun in September 1952 under Arthur J. Critchlow, a 1947 graduate of the California Institute of Technology. According to Critchlow, his initial assignment was to study the manner in which information was organized, formatted, stored, and processed using punched-card equipment—and to seek a better method.[5]

Inventing Disk Storage

Urged by Johnson to learn as much as he could about customer needs, Critchlow turned for help to a special representative in IBM's branch office in San Francisco. Pleased to participate, the representative gave private tutorials and arranged for visits to customer installations.[6] Critchlow learned that punched-card equipment performed customer tasks especially well when processing could be done in batches on sequentially sorted information. Serious problems arose when more nearly random access was needed.

Inventory control was a particularly important application of this latter type. In warehouse operations, for example, each order typically required several cards to be manually located, removed from a stack of cards, the inventory information updated, and the updated cards returned to their original locations. To facilitate this clerical activity, drawers of cards were set out on work tables so that several persons could access cards from the same file. This arrangement was called a "tub file."

Replacement of the tedious and error-prone work associated with tub files soon became the project's objective. Initially considered was every storage configuration "that it was possible for an ingenious staff to think up," Johnson asserts. These included magnetic cards, plates, wires, bands, tapes, twirling rods, and rotating drums and disks, as well as several optical storage concepts.[7] By April 1953 all configurations had been eliminated from consideration except for continuously rotating magnetic disks, spaced along a straight shaft. Proposed by a newly hired engineer only three months earlier, this proposal may seem obvious today, but a related prior proposal lacked its crucial simplicity.[8]

Published in the August 1952 issue of an engineering journal and brought to the attention of Critchlow in December, the earlier proposal had been conceived by a researcher at the National Bureau of Standards. Known as the "notched-disk memory," it stored digital information on magnetically coated disks with pie-shaped notches cut out of them. The disks were mounted on a ring-shaped (rather than straight) axle with their notches normally aligned toward the center of the ring. Read-write heads, mounted on an arm that pivoted about an axis at the center of the ring, could be rotated through the notches of the disks to any desired disk. Information was then written on, or read from, the selected disk by rotating it one full revolution past the read-write heads. Disks not selected for the read-write operation remained stationary.[9] Despite this peculiar arrangement (by today's perspective), the article did help stimulate the IBM engineers to conceive their own successful design.

The new IBM storage unit was publicly demonstrated in May 1955. A press release said in part: "The new electronic device will permit mechanization of accounting and record-keeping previously found impractical owing to costs or procedural problems. Sorting—one of the most costly and time-consuming office machine processes—will be greatly reduced and in some cases actually eliminated."[10]

More technical information was presented at the Western Joint Computer Conference early in 1956: "The information is stored, magnetically, on 50 rotating disks. These disks are mounted, so as to rotate about a vertical axis, with spacing between disks of 0.3 inch. This spacing permits magnetic heads to be positioned to any of the 100 concentric tracks which are available on each side of each disk. Each of these tracks contains 500 alphanumeric characters. Thus, the total storage capacity is 5,000,000 characters."[11] This seemed like an enormous storage capacity at the time, but by the early 1990s two tiny silicon chips could provide as much.[12]

The difficulty of rapidly accelerating and decelerating selected disks, as necessary for the Bureau of Standards design, was avoided by keeping all disks spinning continuously at 1,200 revolutions per minute. Access to both sides of a selected disk was achieved by two read-write heads that straddled the disk. Mounted on a single mechanism, the heads could be withdrawn and reinserted elsewhere in the stack of disks in less than one second. Possible damage to the recording surfaces was avoided by forcing compressed air through orifices in the read-write heads to create a cushion of air between them and the disk surfaces. The resultant head-to-surface spacing was about one-thousandth of an inch.

Known as the IBM 350 Disk Storage Unit, its first use was on the small IBM 305 RAMAC (Random Access Memory Accounting Machine). Fourteen of these were available for field tests beginning in June 1956, and the production version was announced that September. The monthly rental for a basic RAMAC was $3,200, of which $650 was for the disk storage unit, $1,625 for the processing unit and power supply, and $925 for the the console, printer, and card punch. More than a thousand of these vacuum-tube-based computers were built before production ended in 1961.[13]

Important to the success of RAMAC was a novel method for finding stored information when its physical location on the disks was unknown. This first known use of "randomization and chaining" for storing and retrieving records was devised by H. Peter Luhn, who was already an established inventor when hired by Watson, Sr., in 1941. Luhn's application for a patent on the method was rejected by the company's patent review board in Poughkeepsie in 1956 because the concepts were not embodied in hardware. The company had made a policy decision that computer programs and procedures were not patentable.[14]

The most significant competition to RAMAC was provided by the Univac File Computer, which was also first delivered in 1956. The Univac system was equipped with magnetic drum storage that utilized one read-write head per track of information. Thus it could provide far faster access to information than RAMAC, which had only two read-write heads (on one access mechanism) for the entire storage unit. Because information was stored on the cylindrical surfaces of the drums, however, its volumetric storage efficiency was far poorer than for disks. Even when equipped with its maximum of ten drums, the Univac File Computer offered only one-third the storage capacity of RAMAC with its single storage unit.[15] The cost-performance superiority of disks over drums became increasingly evident during the ensuing years, making drum storage obsolete in little over a decade.

Designed as an extension of IBM's punched-card equipment and first offered on the small RAMAC, the IBM 350 Disk Storage Device was the first of a long series of disk storage devices that helped to build the computer industry. By driving the cost of information storage and processing lower with each succeeding

Figure 16.1. RAMAC and Its Development Leaders
Top: Pictured (from left) are William A. Goddard, who led the development
of the disk storage system beginning in April 1953; Reynold B. Johnson, laboratory manager; Louis B. Stevens, who took over development responsibility
in November 1953 and put RAMAC into production; Arthur J. Critchlow,
who did early studies leading to the RAMAC development; and John W.
Haanstra, who had initial responsibility for magnetic recording and electronics. Bottom left: The RAMAC disk storage system, revealing the read-write access mechanism. Bottom right: RAMAC systems undergoing final tests in the
new San Jose manufacturing plant in 1957. (Courtesy of the American Society of Mechanical Engineers.)

disk product, the San Jose engineers made major contributions to IBM's success and to the growth of the industry. Among their many improvements to magnetic disk storage, the following are particularly significant: a dedicated read-write head for each disk surface and self-acting air bearings in 1961, removable disk packs in 1962, voice-coil actuators with servoing to selected tracks in 1970, flexible (floppy) disks in 1971, the "Winchester file" with its lightweight heads in 1973, and thin-film heads in 1979.[16]

In 1984 the IBM 350 Disk Storage Device was designated an International Historic Mechanical Engineering Landmark by the American Society of Mechanical Engineers. As reported in their brochure, "It is difficult to overstate the impact the 350's disk technology has had upon the world in the years since its announcement. . . . it is sufficient to say that fixed and flexible disk drives alone—all derivatives of the basic 350 technology—generated an estimated $12.5 billion in sales worldwide in 1983 for the 72 manufacturers of fixed disk drives and the 52 manufacturers of flexible disk drives."[17]

The Solid-State Challenge

"A device, called a transistor, which has several applications in radio where a vacuum tube ordinarily is employed, was demonstrated for the first time yesterday at Bell Telephone Laboratories . . . where it was invented." Thus began a brief story in the 1 July 1948 issue of the *New York Times*.[18] The invention had been achieved the previous December by John Bardeen and Walter H. Brattain, following years of work with William Shockley and others at the Bell Telephone Laboratories. In 1956 Bardeen, Brattain, and Shockley were awarded the Nobel Prize for their contributions. Except for the brief story in the *New York Times,* the 1948 announcement of the invention was largely ignored by the news media. It was not ignored by scientists working in solid-state physics, however. They avidly read the one-and-one-half-page article published in the July 1948 issue of the *Physical Review.*[19]

Halsey Dickinson, who had succeeded James Bryce as head of IBM's Patent Development Department at World Headquarters, was also keenly interested in the invention. Although he had no prior experience in solid-state theory or devices, he obtained sample transistors from Bell Laboratories within weeks after the announcement. Soon he and others in his department were making their own transistors by attaching additional electrical contacts to commercially available germanium diodes. They designed and patented many transistor circuits, but most of their designs incorporated vacuum tubes as well, to overcome the shortcomings of early transistors.[20]

By the spring of 1950 Tom Watson's newly appointed director of engineering, Wally McDowell, had concluded that the methods of IBM's old-time inventors would not suffice. Believing that modern research methods were needed, he placed all work on solid-state devices under Ralph Palmer in the Poughkeepsie laboratory. Palmer's job was to build the company's expertise in transistors and other solid-state technologies as rapidly as possible while continuing to accelerate the pace of development of new products using vacuum tubes.[21]

Palmer initiated classes to train engineers and hired people with advanced degrees or practical experience in relevant technologies. The world-renowned solid-state physicist, Leon Brillouin, was among those hired to teach courses to the Poughkeepsie engineers.[22] Most courses, however, were taught by people already in the laboratory. Eager to increase their knowledge, engineers spent long hours in the laboratory doing their normal tasks while also attending classes several hours each day. Homework was done at night.

A particularly significant course was conducted in the summer of 1953. Twenty-eight engineers participated. After spending three weeks studying theory, the engineers were divided into six groups for six weeks of laboratory work. Each group was asked to design a practical machine with transistor circuits. One of the groups redesigned the Type 604 Electronic Calculating Punch, using transistor circuits to replace the vacuum tube circuits.[23] So promising was their design that a transistorized 604 was built and demonstrated in October 1954 at the opening of the company's new Research Laboratory in Poughkeepsie. Some 2,200 transistors had been used to do the job of 1,250 vacuum tubes, but the resulting machine occupied less than half the volume and used only 5 percent as much power.[24]

The transistorized 604 became the basis of the IBM 608 Transistor Calculator. First shipped in December 1957, the 608 was the first all solid-state computing machine to be manufactured for the commercial market. The phrase "all solid-state" indicates the machine contained no vacuum tubes or electromechanical devices in its logic, memory, and power-supply circuitry. Not only were its logic circuits implemented with transistors, but so were the support circuits for its small ferrite-core memory. Its advanced circuit technology stood in sharp contrast to its architecture, which was more akin to the EAM equipment it was replacing than to a stored-program computer.[25]

Long before the 608 was completed, Tom Watson became concerned that the use of transistors in company products was progressing too slowly. If each engineering manager was permitted to make his own technology decisions, the more familiar—and still cheaper and more reliable—vacuum tubes would likely remain the technology of choice for many years. Improved reliability and lower costs for transistors could be achieved only through higher manufacturing volumes, which in turn could be achieved only if product development programs were committed to their use.

To force this to happen, Watson took dramatic action two months before shipment of the 608 began. At his behest a corporate policy was established with the following key provisions: "It shall be the policy of IBM to use solid-state circuitry in all machine developments. Furthermore, no new commercial machines or devices shall be announced which make primary use of tube circuitry."[26] The policy was vigorously enforced and achieved the desired results.

Competition in Supercomputers

The engineering resources of the IBM Poughkeepsie laboratory were taxed to their limit during the early 1950s. In rapid succession there had been frantic efforts to gain expertise in vacuum tube circuits, magnetic tape storage, magnetic cores, and transistors. The 700 series of large computers was being developed, and a massive effort had been initiated on Project SAGE.

In spite of these efforts, Ralph Palmer believed his overworked laboratory was at risk of losing a desperate race with engineers in other laboratories. He was only beginning to have the capabilities to push the state of the art in a few technologies. What he wanted was a project with demanding objectives like SAGE, but dedicated to solid-state rather than to vacuum tube electronics. The right project would provide a desirable focus for his research activities as well as essential funding.

Tom Watson was also not satisfied, but for different reasons. He continued to be rankled by Remington Rand's public image. Its UNIVAC had become so closely identified with large-scale electronic computers that the very name, UNIVAC, was often used synonymously for "electronic computer." The public image of Remington Rand as the leading computer company did not change in December 1954 when IBM announced completion of NORC, the most powerful supercomputer of the time. Nor did it change one year later when the number of large-scale computers installed by IBM exceeded the number installed by Remington Rand.

Watson's frustrations were shared by others, among them Steve Dunwell. Returning to IBM from the Signal Corps in mid-1946, he had been influential in the specification and design of many of the company's electronic products, including the CPC, 650, and 702 computers. During part of 1953 and 1954 he had been on special assignment in Washington, D.C., to assess the computer requirements of federal agencies, among them the Federal Bureau of Investigation, National Security Agency, Social Security Administration, Treasury Department, and Weather Bureau.[27] Teaming up with Ralph Palmer in the summer of 1954, Dunwell was enthusiastic about designing a supercomputer for government applications that would also provide Palmer with the focus he wanted for advancing the art in solid-state technologies.

The problem of funding the effort appeared to have a solution in early 1955. The University of California Radiation Laboratory (operated in Livermore, California, for the U.S. Atomic Energy Commission) expressed interest in obtaining a "superspeed computer." The task of seeking the contract fell on Cuthbert Hurd, who had replaced Vin Learson as director of EDPM. Hurd's counterpart in the negotiations was Edward Teller, the physicist who later became known as the "father of the hydrogen bomb." Both men were well supported by technical experts and administrative personnel.

When the two groups met in late January 1955, Teller let it be known that he was serious and in a hurry. All basic decisions about the computer's specifications were to be made and distributed by March. Bids would be due in April, and the winning contractor selected in May. A fixed-price contract in the vicinity of $2.5 million was contemplated for the proposed computer, called LARC, an acronym for Livermore Automatic Research Computer.[28]

The schedule and conditions proposed for LARC precluded the development of significantly improved solid-state devices. Thus what had appeared to be an opportunity to achieve two objectives with one contract suddenly became a divisive issue. Watson, Learson, and Hurd were eager to proceed, whereas Palmer and McDowell were reluctant to commit their limited engineering resources to a project that would not allow time to develop substantially improved device technologies.

A compromise was finally reached that favored the view of Palmer and McDowell. The proposal Hurd submitted in April offered to build and deliver a supercomputer at the desired price in forty-two months. More significantly, the proposal urged that negotiations then be undertaken to modify the contract to substitute a far more powerful computer, on the same schedule, but at a higher price. Not surprisingly, the bid was rejected in favor of Remington Rand's, which promised delivery of LARC in twenty-nine months. Teller had let it be known from the beginning that an early delivery date was of the highest priority.[29]

Loss of the contract was a major disappointment for Palmer. Not only had he lost an opportunity for his laboratory to design and build a supercomputer, but the winner of the contract was IBM's archrival. Unless he could obtain an equivalent or better contract quickly, Remington Rand's leadership in supercomputers would be assured. This outcome would not be acceptable to Tom Watson. Thus began several months of high stress for Palmer as he frantically sought government funding.

Finally in August the National Security Agency (NSA) offered to fund the development of two ferrite-core memories with speeds three and twelve times faster, respectively, than the memory used in SAGE. Funding was also offered for an exploratory study of supercomputer designs to satisfy special requirements of the NSA. "They now believe that we have something spectacular in core memories and very bold and courageous thinking in machine organizations," Palmer enthusiastically reported. He had not been successful, however, in obtaining support for research on transistors. The evidence he offered that IBM "would have a large commercial usage of transistors in the field before the telephone company"—which had invented them—had failed to convince the agency to bet its money on a "newcomer" to the field of transistors.[30]

Project Stretch

The $1.1 million offered by the NSA for eighteen months of research was far too little to finance the development of a supercomputer, but it was an important endorsement of the the company's technical capabilities. It helped Palmer gain approval to establish Project Stretch with considerable IBM funding in August 1955. The name of the project had been selected to connote the intent of Palmer and McDowell to undertake research that would "stretch" all aspects of computer technologies. In January 1956 Steve Dunwell was formally put in charge of the new project.[31]

To obtain additional funding, the project quickly became involved in proposing "the development and construction of a high-speed general purpose computer for the United States Atomic Energy Commission, for installation at the Los Alamos Scientific Laboratory." [32] The proposal called for delivery of a supercomputer for a fixed price of $4.3 million within forty-two months after the contract was signed. Although the AEC appeared reluctant to pay so much for the computer, the cost of its development and construction was estimated by IBM to be over three times higher. The higher costs would have to be recovered from the sale of copies of the supercomputer, research contracts with other government agencies, and use of Stretch-developed technologies in commercial products.[33]

Invitations to submit proposals had been sent by the AEC to twenty firms, of which four were said to be interested. The greatest concern for IBM was that Los Alamos would join its sister laboratory in purchasing a LARC from Sperry Rand. (Remington Rand had merged with Sperry to form the Sperry Rand Corporation in June 1955.) This anxiety vanished in April when IBM representatives were advised informally of the acceptance of their proposal. Formal contract signing did not occur until November, giving Dunwell a much needed extra half a year to get started.[34] Rapid staffing of the project with skilled technical people was a major effort. The number of employees grew from fewer than fifty in mid-1956 to two hundred one year later. It then remained relatively constant until another one hundred were added in 1959 to begin machine construction.[35]

Despite many problems, Project Stretch achieved its primary objective of advancing computer technologies. Among its contributions was a greatly improved ferrite-core memory with a capacity of 131,072 bytes and a read-write cycle of 2.2 microseconds. Equipped with transistor support circuits and other improvements, it was nearly three times faster than the memories used in SAGE, yet less expensive for a given capacity.[36]

Another contribution was the "drift transistor," which was intrinsically faster than the "surface-barrier transistor" used in LARC. By 1958 IBM's "newcomers" to the field of transistors had placed their drift transistors in production and had made arrangements for the Texas Instruments Company to produce additional quantities. Also important was invention of the current-switch, emitter-coupled logic (ECL) circuit by IBM engineer Hannon S. Yourke in August 1956. Quickly adopted for use in Stretch, ECL became the preferred circuit for high-speed switching applications throughout the industry.[37]

The transistor circuits and the cards on which they were mounted were part of a new Standard Modular System (SMS) of

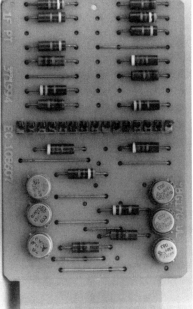

Figure 16.2.   Circuit Cards
The circuit cards shown here were developed as part of Project Stretch and were used in the IBM 7000 series of computers. Six transistors (in cylindrical metal cans) and assorted resistors and jumper wires were mounted on the card (right). Electrical interconnections among these components were achieved by soldering the component leads to copper lines preprinted on the back of the card (left). The cards were known as SMS cards because they were part of IBM's proprietary Standard Modular System of circuit packaging. The cards were 2.5 inches × 4.5 inches and were equipped with sixteen gold-plated tabs for making external electrical contact.

circuit packaging developed in Project Stretch. Designed for automated mass production and low-cost maintenance, SMS was so
reliable and economical that it was used in all IBM electronic
products introduced during the early 1960s and continued to be
used in certain types of new products long after integrated circuits
were introduced.[38]

An unanticipated event caused Stretch-developed technologies
to be used first in a computer other than one for which they had
been developed. This shift in priority followed the October 1957
launching of the first manmade earth satellite, *Sputnik*—a feat
that demonstrated the Soviet Union's ability to deliver atomic
bombs to any target in the United States using rocket-powered
ballistic missiles. To defend against this threat, the U.S. Air Force
undertook development of the Ballistic Missile Early Warning
System (BMEWS). Like SAGE, it would rely on a number of
interconnected computers to receive and analyze incoming information and to determine the appropriate response.

Learning in the spring of 1958 that the air force had mandated
the use of transistorized computers in BMEWS, Ralph Palmer
responded rapidly. He arranged to propose a transistorized version of the IBM 709 computer, which some of his engineers had
already designed in an experimental study. The acceptance of
IBM's proposal in October was heavily influenced by two factors:
first, the components and system design were available; second,
programs could be written for BMEWS and tested on a 709
computer before the first transistorized version was available.

Well before the contract was signed, Learson decided to announce the same transistorized 709 computer in the commercial
market. Christened the IBM 7090 Data Processing System, its
compatibility with the 709 facilitated its rapid acceptance in the
commercial market, as did a performance six times higher and a
price only one-third higher than the 709. The first 7090 was
delivered in November 1959 to Sylvania Electric Products, Inc.,
at Needham, Massachusetts, for incorporation in BMEWS. It was
the first of the highly successful 7000 series of computers.[39]

The Stretch supercomputer (named after Project Stretch) was
not delivered until seventeen months later in April 1961. It was
fully operational the following month—just one year later than
originally specified in the contract. Only one unscheduled maintenance period (which lasted four minutes) was required during
the three-day, forty-hour acceptance test.[40] Subsequently designated the IBM 7030, the Stretch supercomputer was approxi-

mately two hundred times faster than the IBM 701, forty times faster than the IBM 709, and seven times faster than the IBM 7090. It was also substantially faster than LARC, which had been delivered about a year earlier.[41]

Although the 7030 reigned as the world's fastest computer for over a year, its performance was only about half as good as predicted.[42] Performance estimates had been based on the speed of individual components and a system design that provided for a high degree of concurrent operation among internal units. There was considerable uncertainty, however, as to how much concurrency might be achieved in actual operation. To obtain this information, a pioneering simulator had been devised to run on an IBM 704. The simulator proved to be helpful in choosing among different system designs, but its ability to predict actual performance on a customer's job was known to be limited.[43] Even today the prediction of system performance is not a precise science.

The actual performance of the supercomputer was therefore not known until it began to run customer programs, about two months before its shipment to Los Alamos. "With respect to raw operation speeds . . . it appears that the machine executes according to specifications," one observer reported. "However, when the machine executes all of its instructions in complicated programs, the actual efficiency of the system falls below what these raw speeds might indicate."[44]

Tom Watson was embarrassed to announce the less than anticipated performance of the 7030 supercomputer during his keynote address at the May 1961 Western Joint Computer Conference. Worse yet, the performance projections had been given to potential customers. Watson felt obliged to compensate for the lower performance by reducing the computer's price from $13.5 million to $7.8 million. "If we get enough orders at this price, we could go out of business," Watson wryly observed. Because IBM would lose money on each one sold at the lower price, the 7030 was not offered beyond the eight customers with whom negotiations were already underway.[45]

It was several years before Watson could overcome his preoccupation with the failures of Stretch and thereby appreciate its many technological contributions. In addition to advances in solid-state technologies, Stretch pioneered many concepts that influenced the design of later computers, especially the IBM System/360, announced in 1964. Among these were multiprogramming, memory protect, generalized interrupt, interleaving of memories, lookahead, the memory bus, a standard interface for input-output equipment, and the eight-bit character called the byte.[46] Although acknowledging the importance of these contributions in a 1964 letter to Dunwell, Watson reiterated his distress with Project Stretch, saying, "Our customers and the top management of this corporation were led to believe that the performance objective was being achieved when, in fact, we were falling short of it."[47]

Two years later IBM's difficulty in competing with large computers offered by the Control Data Corporation caused Watson to reconsider his position, which had discouraged engineers from taking the necessary risks to compete in large computers. Seeking to right a wrong and to bolster the morale of engineers "working in the big machine area," Watson took the unusual step of devoting most of his remarks at the 1966 IBM Annual Awards Dinner to one award winner. Applauding Steve Dunwell's appointment as an IBM Fellow—the highest recognition for technical achievement in the company—Watson said Dunwell's work on Stretch and many earlier machines had made him "a major contributor to the success of this business." Then noting that "things" had happened during the last few years "that haven't been as fair to Red Dunwell as they might," Watson said, "I just thought I would take the opportunity of publicly trying to correct the record."[48]

It was vintage Watson. Quick to anger and quick to punish, he was also prepared to acknowledge an error and take corrective action.

Reorganizing Research

To carry out the company's rapidly growing research and development activities, the number of employees so engaged had grown from 600 to 3,000 (from 3 to 9 percent of IBM's domestic employees) between 1950 and 1954. Much of this growth had been in Poughkeepsie, where a sevenfold increase from 200 to well over 1,400 had occurred.[49] Although this rapid growth had been managed by McDowell under direct instructions from Watson, Jr., the senior Watson had closely monitored and influenced it. The confidence both Watsons had in McDowell had been crucial to his success in making these dramatic changes.[50]

In recognition of McDowell's achievements as director of engineering and the increased complexity of his assignment, Tom

Watson promoted him to IBM vice president in July 1954. Responding to the younger Watson's challenge that he substantially strengthen the company's research and development programs, McDowell promoted four engineering managers to executive positions at World Headquarters to assist him in managing all corporate technical activities. Chief among those promoted was Ralph Palmer, who was named director of engineering.[51] McDowell also established a task force of about a dozen technical leaders from the Endicott, Poughkeepsie, and Watson laboratories to consider how research should be managed.

Meeting for several weeks at the Fox Hill estate in Connecticut in the spring of 1955, the task force reviewed and compared the research management methods of IBM with those of leading companies such as AT&T, GE, RCA, and Westinghouse. Following its deliberations, the task force recommended that a separate research organization be created, that it report directly to corporate management, and that it be led by a distinguished research executive hired from outside the company.[52]

Ralph Palmer was not sanguine about the proposal. He believed the Poughkeepsie laboratory's success had been achieved in part through close interactions between research and development groups. Development activities provided much needed focus for research, and good research provided a ready source of new ideas and alternative solutions for development. But Palmer was in the minority. Wallace Eckert, director of the Watson Laboratory, strongly favored a separate research organization with close ties to government and university laboratories. McDowell also favored the recommendation. His experience in the Endicott laboratory had caused him to conclude, some years earlier, that research should be separated from development to protect against near-term product pressures.

McDowell's acceptance of the recommendations was signaled by the following announcement in the January 1956 Poughkeepsie Engineering Newsletter: "IBM has established a new independent research organization to develop the business machines of the future. The new group will remain within the company's research and engineering department, but will operate independently of its parent. It will be headed by Mr. R. L. Palmer."[53]

Among the anticipated benefits of a separate research organization, with greater emphasis on basic research, was the ability to attract outstanding college graduates with advanced degrees in science and engineering. Typically these young people were imbued by their professors with the belief that product development was an inferior activity to basic research. As reported elsewhere in the newsletter, "The problem of recruiting top-caliber engineers in sufficient quantity to meet the company's ever-increasing needs is probably the most important single problem facing us today." More than 1,300 additional engineers were to be hired during the year.[54]

What the newsletter failed to reveal was that Ralph Palmer's assignment as head of Research was only temporary. His primary task was to separate research activities in Poughkeepsie from development, thus establishing an interim research organization to help attract a distinguished research executive from outside the company. In September McDowell announced that Emanuel R. Piore had accepted the position of IBM director of research. Palmer's previous position was now officially renamed "acting director." Piore's responsibilities would encompass the research activities Palmer had separated from development in Poughkeepsie; advanced development activities in San Jose that Reynold Johnson had separated from the RAMAC development effort; the Watson Laboratory in New York City; and a laboratory established the previous year in Zurich, Switzerland.

An immigrant from Russia at age nine, "Mannie" Piore had obtained a Ph.D. in physics at the University of Wisconsin in 1935. During World War II he had served as a lieutenant commander on the staff of the deputy chief of naval operations for air. After the war he distinguished himself with the Office of Naval Research (ONR), serving as its chief scientist from 1951 to 1955. Piore was particularly respected for his role in continuing ONR support for research at universities after hostilities ceased, and for shifting the emphasis from short-term military requirements to more basic research. This policy contributed to the preeminence of U.S. universities in science and engineering and strengthened the country's economy in the postwar era.[55]

More a research administrator than a scientist, Piore had a good understanding of strategy and the politics of organizations. At IBM he developed close working relationships with Tom Watson and other key executives. From the Research organization, he initially selected three bright young technical leaders to review ongoing projects. Soon labeled "the three wise men" by their colleagues, they were to help Piore select projects to be dropped or moved out of Research and to identify fields of research the company should enter. Piore also initiated annual research planning conferences to which senior Research members and a few technical leaders from the development laboratories were invited.[56]

An early decision was to move Research from Poughkeepsie to a place with easier access to major universities, cultural centers, and travel facilities. The site Piore selected was Yorktown Heights in Westchester County, approximately twenty-five miles from the northern border of New York City. Here a modern research facility, designed by Eero Saarinen, was built on a 240-acre site overlooking rolling, wooded hills. In honor of Watson, Sr., it was dedicated in April 1961 as the Thomas J. Watson Research Center.[57]

For five years Piore was given a nearly free hand to set the direction of Research. By emphasizing basic research, he attracted an outstanding cadre of bright young scientists with doctor's degrees from leading universities. The newly hired researchers and some of the old-timers rapidly established a good reputation for the laboratory in fields as diverse as solid-state lasers, language translation, integer linear programming, and artificial intelligence. In recognition of these successes, the Research organization was elevated to the status of an IBM division in November 1963.[58]

The new organization's attempts to contribute to the product line were less successful. Thin magnetic films, for example, were vigorously pursued and promoted as replacements for ferrite cores. Transferred to a development laboratory in 1962, magnetic films were successfully used in only one IBM computer model before they became obsolete because of semiconductor memories. Even more disappointing was the outcome of work on cryotrons. Research on these superconducting devices (which operated at very low temperatures) was begun in the hope that they would provide superior performance to semiconductors. Only after the project was transferred to a development laboratory in 1962 were the real limitations of the technology understood. Cryotrons had no chance of replacing semiconductors in any application.[59]

Exciting achievements of the late 1950s in language translation and artificial intelligence were found to be illusory. More than three decades of research—and dramatic improvements in hardware technologies—were required before artificial intelligence or language translation systems began to arrive in the market.

Figure 16.3.   Piore and the Watson Research Center
Top: Emanuel R. Piore is shown in his office soon after being appointed
IBM director of research in 1956. Bottom: The IBM Thomas J. Watson Research Center (named after Watson, Sr.) is shown here about the time it
was dedicated in April 1961. Designed by Eero Saarinen, it is located in
Westchester County about forty miles north of the center of New York City.
Extensions to either end in 1979 and 1984 increased the length of the front
of the building from 1,091 to 1,769 feet and its floor space from 459,000 to
757,000 square feet.

Even more frustrating was the difficulty of achieving any product advantage from outstanding accomplishments of IBM Research in timely fields such as solid-state lasers and integer linear programming.

By the end of the 1960s it had become evident that a change in the emphasis of the Research Division was needed. Contrary to earlier expectations, product improvements were less likely to result from radically new technologies (as had occurred after World War II) than from evolutionary advances in existing technologies. To contribute effectively to this process, the Research Division would have to allocate more of its resources to improving existing technologies, and it needed closer coupling with the product development laboratories. Creating this coupling and nurturing means for transferring improved technologies from research to development were challenging tasks for future directors of Research.[60]

The success of the Research Division should not, however, be measured solely by its contributions to product technologies. From its inception, the luster of its basic science helped promote IBM products and made it easier to hire top-quality technical people throughout the company. Also of importance was the influence the Research director could exert on company-wide product development plans. Piore was particularly adept at this. With his carefully nurtured ties to top corporate executives and easy access to the expertise of Research people, his opinions on the technical adequacy of product development programs could not be ignored.

17

Legacy

The year 1956 marked many significant events for IBM. Among these, the first SAGE computer was installed, the first computer with magnetic disk storage was introduced, the first all solid-state computing machine was readied for production, and research was separated from development to create an independent corporatewide research organization. An antitrust suit was settled with the government, and the senior Watson yielded the post of chief executive officer to his son.

For forty-two years Watson, Sr., had guided the growth of a company and an industry whose origins lay in the inventive and entrepreneurial genius of Herman Hollerith. By 1956 he had achieved his final goal: IBM's future was secure in the hands of his older son, and the company's wholly owned World Trade Corporation was growing rapidly under the leadership of his younger son. Proud of his accomplishments, the eighty-two-year-old Thomas J. Watson, Sr., died of a heart attack on 19 June 1956.[1]

During the three-quarters of a century since Hollerith first sought solutions for handling census data, his inventions and entrepreneurial activities had led to remarkable advances in storing and processing information. Performing mundane record keeping as well as sophisticated engineering and scientific calculations, the progeny of his machines had markedly altered the operations of governments, businesses, and academic institutions throughout the world. The company he founded to tabulate data from the census of 1890 had evolved into the industry-dominating IBM Corporation. This chapter examines IBM's competitive position and reviews some of the events and decisions that had shaped the company Watson now entrusted to his son.

Figure 17.1. Transfer of Authority
Thomas J. Watson, Jr., is congratulated by his father upon his promotion to chief executive officer in May 1956.

Naming the Industry

Somewhat surprisingly a fully satisfactory name for his equipment and the industry he created has never been found. Hollerith referred to his equipment as tabulating machines, and he named his business the Tabulating Machine Company.[2] Others were likely to speak of punched-card machines or Hollerith machines, and the cards were widely known as Hollerith cards.

When IBM introduced its 80-column card with rectangular holes in 1928, Watson insisted that they be called IBM cards. This marketing maneuver was so successful that users of Powers equipment might inadvertently refer to their cards with round holes as

IBM cards. In the late 1930s, customers and then IBM itself began referring to the equipment as EAM, the initials for the company's Electric Accounting Machine Division. The term *EAM* helped distinguish IBM equipment from the mechanical equipment of the company's only significant competitor, Remington Rand. The generic names used for the equipment were *punched-card, tabulating*, or *accounting*, even though its applications were already expanding well beyond tabulating and accounting.

Rapid advances in electronics during World War II and the need to perform vast computations led to the development of electronic computing machines toward the end of the war. These machines were called *computers* because they carried out tasks previously handled by people with the job title of "computer." Using pencil, paper, and mechanical calculating machines, these human computers (mostly women) had carried out lengthy computations that could now be assigned to electronic machines.

Watson, Sr., insisted that the word *computer* should not be used to designate any IBM equipment. He believed that the word had a job-threatening connotation and should be avoided. It was one battle he finally lost. The name *computer* became the primary designation for IBM's equipment and the industry. The names that IBM initially employed, such as automatic sequence controlled calculator, have long been forgotten. Even the carefully chosen name EDPM (Electronic Data Processing Machine) survived only as the formal designation for the IBM 701 computer and a few subsequent offerings of the company. The phrase *data processing* has, however, been widely used to connote the industry and its products.

It is ironic that UNIVAC was officially called a computer even though it was built and marketed primarily for business and government data processing, whereas the IBM 701 was officially called a data processing machine even though it was built and marketed for scientific and engineering computations.[3] It is also ironic that computing has long been a minor application for computers. Most computers are used to perform tasks involving computations that are transparent to the user—one of the more popular tasks being text processing.

General purpose computers are better described as information processing machines. Fundamental to information processing equipment is a means for storing information so it can be processed with as little human intervention as possible. That function was originally handled by punched cards. By the end of the 1970s it was handled primarily by magnetic disks and semiconductor memories.

The phrase *information processing* is widely used and describes today's industry better than does the single word *computer.* Information processing is also an appropriate name for the business Hollerith established in 1889. Nevertheless, it seems likely that the briefer appellation, computer industry, will retain its greater popularity for the foreseeable future.

Some Early Business Practices

Although Hollerith should be remembered primarily as an inventor and entrepreneur, he made many management decisions that survived long after he died in 1929. Perhaps the most important of these was to rent, rather than to sell, his equipment. The renting of capital goods was not a new business concept, but it was particularly appropriate in the embryonic information processing business. Most customers were unwilling to install Hollerith's novel equipment until they were shown how to make effective use of it, and they needed help in adapting their business procedures to it.

These services were provided at no extra charge by Hollerith, who recovered his costs from the rental of installed machines and the sale of punched cards. He also serviced his machines at no extra charge. Indeed his contract with the Census Bureau required him to pay a substantial penalty if the equipment failed to function properly. Partly because of this contract provision, but primarily because of pride in his creation, Hollerith was meticulous in specifying his equipment for manufacture to ensure its reliable performance. He also responded rapidly to any reported malfunctions.

Renting equipment and providing customer service at no extra charge became a cornerstone of Watson's policies after he took over the company in 1914. Many a story is told of IBM servicemen working around the clock to get equipment running. If a fire, flood, or other disaster occurred, IBM was ready to help. Using equipment loaned by another customer, or available at a branch office, or trucked in from a warehouse, the company's personnel were expected to get the customer's work done on time. Reliable service was probably IBM's most valued product, but we can only speculate whether customers would have been willing to pay for it had they known its cost. Equipment was available only for rent, and customers were required to have it serviced by IBM.

The rental-only policy had several other advantages for the manufacturer. First, it assured a nearly undiminished revenue stream in bad economic times when little new equipment was being installed. Watson became acutely aware of this advantage during the brief recession of 1922, and he benefited from it even more during the Great Depression that began in 1929. Second, it was more difficult for others to enter the market because of the longer time required to recover the costs of developing and manufacturing equipment. Third, it was possible for the owner to protect proprietary equipment designs through appropriately devised rental agreements. It will be recalled that Hollerith removed his equipment from the Census Bureau when he learned that the bureau was using it for experimental studies to design its own equipment. Fourth, rental customers were more likely to buy supplies from the manufacturer.

To ensure all of these advantages for themselves, IBM and Remington Rand entered into an agreement in 1931 that (among other things) committed the two companies "to lease and not sell tabulators and sorters" and "to require customers to purchase their card requirements from the lessor or pay a higher price for the rental of machines." Challenging these provisions in 1932, the government filed a complaint charging both companies with violating the Sherman and Clayton acts. The companies voluntarily canceled these agreements in 1934 before the case came to trial, but IBM continued to offer its equipment for rent only—a policy the government later alleged contributed to its dominance of the industry. The requirement that customers pay a higher rental fee if they purchased cards from other suppliers was adjudged to be illegal in 1936.[4]

Although Watson followed many of Hollerith's business practices, his approach to managing the business was quite different. Whereas Hollerith had difficulty attracting and managing top-quality people, Watson was a master at it. Perhaps nowhere was this difference between the two men more evident than in their approaches to selling. Believing the equipment should sell itself, Hollerith relied heavily on word-of-mouth recommendations of satisfied customers and the efforts of independent sales agents. Watson also believed in the importance of satisfied customers, but he was convinced that a well-managed and properly motivated sales force could sell equipment more effectively and keep customers better satisfied.

Borrowing from his experience at NCR, where he had worked for John Patterson, "father of modern salesmanship," Watson created the legendary IBM sales force. Two practices pioneered by Patterson were fundamental. First, each salesman was given exclusive rights to his territory. This increased his commitment to customer satisfaction and to marketing efforts in his territory. It also eliminated disputes among salesmen as to who earned a commission. Second, each salesman was given a sales quota that "had to be met." Based on the estimated number of potential customers and previous sales records for the territory, quotas provided, according to Patterson, "a definite measure of sales efficiency and accomplishment." Quotas also provided a basis for "friendly competition" among salesmen. Those who met their quotas were rewarded by membership in the Hundred Percent Club and an invitation to its emotionally charged annual meeting.[5]

Watson additionally emphasized formal training for his salesmen, who were expected to understand the operation and applications of each machine they sold. He supported them with extensive advertising, and he motivated them with company songs and a sense of being part of the "IBM family." Wearing the mandatory blue suits, white shirts, and neckties, IBM salesmen were taught to look, speak, and feel like winners. Under Watson's tutelage, they became winners.

Salesmen worked closely with customers to ensure that installed equipment performed its tasks as effectively as possible and to identify new sales opportunities. They were instructed to report back to headquarters any information about desirable improvements or competitive innovations. In an important departure from Hollerith's practice, Watson established engineering and manufacturing organizations to respond rapidly to new market requirements, to ensure the quality of products, and to protect proprietary information.

During the depression years of the 1930s, Watson maintained full employment in his engineering and manufacturing organizations by increasing the time employees spent in educational programs and by increasing the IBM content in engineering, tooling, and manufacturing. Consolidating engineering and manufacturing in Endicott, he used these activities as a test-bed for the application of punched-card equipment to the monitoring and control of engineering and manufacturing operations. As a result, the company's equipment and methods were in high demand to help facilitate the country's rapid buildup in the manufacture of war matériel for World War II. Further honing its own manufacturing capabilities through the production of various munitions, IBM had established itself as a premier engineering and manufacturing organization by the end of the war.[6]

Patent Policies

The shock troops of Watson's army were his salesmen. They served in the front lines, representing IBM to its customers. They were the first to learn of, and respond to, new competitive threats. Watson was especially proud of their performance, but of all the things that helped Watson dominate the industry, none was more important than his patent policies and associated research and development activities.

Patents were, of course, the basis of Hollerith's early monopoly of the information processing (punched-card equipment) business. When Watson took over management of the business in 1914, Hollerith's earliest patents had expired, and actions of the Census Bureau had further weakened his patent position. Nevertheless Hollerith still held many critically important patents. Watson planned to use these patents and add to them to strengthen the company's position. He was encouraged in this plan by a consent decree entered into by the General Electric Company in 1912, settling an antitrust case concerning its dominance of the incandescent lamp business. While ruling against mergers as a legal means of gaining a near monopoly position, the court affirmed the legality of competitive advantages based on patents.[7]

When representatives of the Powers Company requested a license to Hollerith's patents in 1914, Watson chose to accommodate them. He liked to represent this decision as magnanimous.[8] But in truth he had good reason to believe that some competition was necessary to avoid antitrust action by the government. Furthermore the licensing agreement with the Powers Company included a royalty payment of 25 percent of gross revenue from equipment sales and rentals and 18 percent of the gross revenue from the sale of cards. Because these royalty payments had to be recovered by Powers in higher prices to customers, Watson enjoyed an enormous price advantage. He could use the large potential profit margin to pay stockholders larger dividends, or to lower prices (and drive Powers out of business), or to invest in his own business by purchasing patents, increasing research and development, and financing equipment on rental. Watson chose to invest in his business.

With the help of James Bryce, he built a strong patent portfolio. He identified and purchased relevant patents. He hired inventors and engineers to create new products and to file for patents. During the brief recession of 1922 Watson took advantage of an opportunity to buy the patents and research facilities, and to hire key personnel, of his most innovative competitor, the J. R. Peirce Company. He also purchased important patents of C. A. Tripp. Then in 1930 he encouraged Bryce to establish the small Patent Development Department to create new ideas and patents in areas likely to be important in future products.

During the recession of 1922 Watson also reduced by half the royalties charged to Powers to help that company out of the receivership into which it had fallen. Once again he chose to help his primary competitor survive rather than risk an antitrust suit. Nevertheless he retained an important provision of the original licensing agreement that diminished that company's prospects. Patents were licensed only for use in mechanical systems. Electrical detection of punched holes, which was basic to Hollerith equipment, was reserved for IBM. The greater flexibility of electrical detection provided a substantial advantage in scientific calculations and in some business applications.

Dominating the Industry

So successful was Watson in dominating the information processing industry, that the U.S. Department of Justice filed an antitrust suit in January 1952 that asserted in part: "IBM now owns all electrical tabulating machines in use in the United States, which comprise 90 percent of all tabulating machines now in use in this country. The remaining 10 percent of such tabulating machines are mechanical machines manufactured by Remington Rand and are either leased or owned by their users. . . . More than 95 percent of the tabulating machines used by the United States Government are owned by IBM."[9]

Deeply distressed by the government's suit, the senior Watson was also proud of the evidence it gave of his own success. When fired from NCR by John Patterson in 1914, Watson had vowed to build a larger and more successful company than Patterson. When Watson left, NCR had approximately 90 percent of the domestic cash register business. Now IBM was reported to have 90 percent of the domestic punched-card equipment business, and its gross revenues and net earnings were substantially larger than those of NCR.

The Department of Justice alleged that IBM was monopolizing "interstate and foreign trade and commerce in the tabulating industry, including new and used machines, machine parts and service, cards and service bureaus." It further asserted that IBM had "entered into contracts, agreements and understandings in unreasonable restraint of the aforesaid interstate and foreign trade and commerce in tabulating machines and tabulating cards." These alleged acts violated Sections 1 and 2 of the Act of Congress of July 1890, "An Act to Protect Trade and Commerce against Unlawful Restraints and Monopolies," commonly called the Sherman Act.[10]

During the six decades since the Sherman Act was passed, its primary function had shifted from protecting the public against "flagrantly anti-competitive activities of the trusts" to an economic policy tool for maintaining competition. A reading of past court decisions revealed that a company was unlikely to prevail against a government suit based on the Sherman Act unless the company could demonstrate either that it did not possess monopoly power or that its monopoly power had been achieved unintentionally— for example, that it had "become a monopolist by force of accident."[11]

Because of the difficulty of convincing anyone that IBM had achieved its market position "accidentally" rather than "intentionally," its first line of defense was to define its industry as one in which it had a relatively small percentage of the market. Defining its industry as the automation of accounting and record keeping, the company said its products competed with adding machines, desk calculators, typewriters, key-operated accounting machines, punched-card accounting machines, addressing machines, marginally punched cards, pegboards and other form alignment devices, visible index equipment, and large-capacity electronic machines.

It was a reasonable position to take. The company's punched-card equipment competed against these products for every new installation and whenever established installations were expanded. Principal manufacturers of these products, with which

IBM said it competed, ranged in size from Remington Rand and the National Cash Register Company, with gross revenues of $236 million and $227 million, respectively, down to R. C. Allen Business Machines, with revenues just over $8 million. Numerous smaller companies were also active in the industry. Listing its own domestic revenues as $334 million, IBM claimed it had less than 20 percent of the domestic market.[12]

Consistent with IBM's position, an independent study done for the Burroughs Corporation revealed that the percentage of sales in the "office machines industry" in 1951 were divided as follows: IBM, 24; Remington Rand, 20; NCR, 19; Burroughs, 11; and all others, 26.[13] Clearly the share of the market held by any company depended on which market was considered and precisely how it was defined.

Adhering to a much narrower market definition that excluded all but punched-card tabulating equipment and related supplies and services, the Department of Justice claimed IBM had 90 percent of the domestic market. Even IBM admitted to having over 80 percent of this more narrowly defined market.[14]

A careful reading of the government's complaint suggests that much of IBM's success, and specifically its gain in market share, resulted from technologically superior products, protected by a strong patent position. The complaint alleged, however, that the company's patent position had been achieved and maintained in part through illegal means and that it was improperly used to restrain trade.

According to the complaint, IBM had (among other things) "systematically acquired developments, inventions, and patents made or owned by others relating in any way to tabulating machines"; "prevented, by its leasing system, the experimental use of IBM leased machines and required compulsory grant backs of inventions which might result from a breach of this condition"; "used its control over experimental use of its tabulating machines to obtain inventions relating to the electrical tabulating system made by others engaged in joint developments with IBM"; and "opposed the procurement by others of patents relating to the electrical tabulating system, by . . . systematically preempting the services of inventors active in the tabulating field by employing them on a long term exclusive retainer basis." [15]

Among allegedly offensive uses of its patent position was introduction of the patented 80-column card with rectangular holes that made IBM equipment incompatible with that of Remington Rand. No longer could equipment of one company handle cards of the other. An organization wishing to standardize its operations now had to select either a fully IBM or a fully Remington Rand system. As reported in the complaint: "The necessity of having uniform records of accounting and statistical data within the Department of National Defense has led the Department to standardize on the electrical tabulating system. . . . Other government agencies and large businesses have, for similar reasons, standardized on the electrical tabulating system." Also presumably offensive was IBM's refusal to license any other company to use its patents for the manufacture and distribution of tabulating equipment using electrical detection of holes punched in cards. Remington Rand, for example, was licensed to use IBM patents only in equipment that detected holes mechanically.[16]

Not all issues raised by the government related to patent practices. For example, the company was said to have acquired foreign businesses that were potential competitors of IBM in the United States; "granted discriminatory concessions to certain of its lessees to forestall the acquisition of business by potential competitors"; and "operated service bureaus to preempt the available demand for tabulating service."[17]

Most of the allegations against IBM, even if proven, would have been legal if undertaken by a minor company in the industry. But in the murky field of antitrust law, actions judged to be legal when performed by a small company could be judged illegal if performed by a larger company. Thus there was considerable uncertainty as to the outcome of the case.[18]

Settling the Antitrust Suit

Incensed that the government was attempting to destroy his hard-won success and convinced he could win the case, the senior Watson insisted that a vigorous defense be mounted. As the pretrial proceedings dragged on, however, the antitrust suit became a heavy burden for his son, who had been promoted to president of IBM just six days before the Justice Department filed the suit.[19] Every business decision now had to be judged by its effect on the legal case.

For reasons similar to those that provoked Hollerith to give up fighting the government in 1910 to concentrate on new business,

Tom Watson now wanted to settle the antitrust suit quickly. But his father, who as chief executive officer still had ultimate authority, was adamant that the case be fought and won. He believed IBM was innocent of any wrongdoing and deserved a complete exoneration by the Justice Department. A settlement out of court would appear to be an admission of guilt. Angry arguments erupted between father and son over this issue—as they frequently had over other issues. Finally in late 1955 the senior Watson capitulated.[20]

The case was settled by a consent decree in January 1956. Titled "Final Judgment," the document asserts that both parties to the suit had "consented to the entry of this Final Judgment, without trial or adjudication of any issue of fact or law herein and without any admission by either party with respect to any such issue." Using such phrases as "IBM is hereby ordered and directed" and "IBM is hereby enjoined and restrained," the document set forth rules under which the company would have to conduct its business.[21]

The most onerous provisions for Watson, Sr., probably related to the manufacture and sale of punched cards.[22] This was the heart of the business he had taken over from Hollerith. It still accounted for approximately 20 percent of the company's gross revenue and 30 percent of its net profits. To help others enter and succeed in the manufacture and sale of punched cards, IBM was to be constrained in its pricing policies, its contracts with suppliers of paper stock, and the type of specifications it could establish for cards used with its equipment. It was further ordered to offer to sell to competing manufacturers "rotary presses in good condition" and "paper suitable for the manufacture of tabulating cards . . . not required for the reasonably anticipated needs of IBM." Finally, if truly competitive conditions had not been achieved within seven years, IBM was to divest itself "of such part of its then existing capacity for the manufacture of tabulating cards as may then be in excess of 50% of the total capacity for the manufacture of tabulating cards in the United States."[23]

The most important provisions for the Justice Department's attorneys appear to have related to IBM's policy of renting rather than selling its equipment. In the future the company would be required to offer to sell its equipment "upon terms and conditions which shall not be substantially more advantageous to IBM than the lease charges." Further, IBM was required to "afford to its salesmen compensation for selling . . . which shall be not less favorable to them than their compensation for leasing the same machines."[24]

By requiring IBM to offer to sell its equipment, the government expected to increase competition in many business areas, such as repair service, secondhand equipment sales, and service bureaus. To facilitate this process, IBM was required (among other things) to provide outside service organizations with service manuals, replacement parts, and personnel training equivalent to that provided to IBM's own employees.[25] The company's service bureau, which offered information processing services to customers, was to be known as the Service Bureau Corporation without any evident tie to IBM. It would not be permitted to use the IBM name, and all dealings with IBM would have to be on the same basis as were available to any other service bureau. Finally, the Service Bureau Corporation would not be permitted to employ people who were also employed by IBM. This final constraint created a serious problem. The company's service bureau employees would have to leave IBM or find entirely new assignments.[26]

A particularly controversial provision of the consent decree was the requirement that IBM "grant to each person making written application therefor an unrestricted, nonexclusive license . . . for the full unexpired term of, any, some or all IBM existing and future patents." This provision applied to patents on electronic data processing machines (computers) as well as to the company's more traditional products. A reasonable royalty could be charged, except that no royalty could be charged for already existing patents on tabulating machinery and cards. The patent licensing requirements were made more palatable by a provision that permitted IBM to refuse to offer a license to any company that would not, in return, offer a license to IBM for its relevant patents.[27]

The requirement that IBM give up its constitutional right to profit from its patents seemed extreme to many. One could argue, however, that if patents were acquired improperly, or used to restrain trade excessively, then that right should be lost. A more pragmatic reason for accepting the government's terms was the political climate. Only one day earlier, the American Telephone and Telegraph Company had agreed to license its past, present, and future patents as part of a settlement of its antitrust suit with the government. In discussing the antitrust settlements with AT&T and IBM, the chief of the Justice Department's antitrust division, said they "supplement each other." These suits and one pending with the Radio Corporation of America should be viewed, he asserted, "as part of one program to open up the electronics field."[28]

The impact of the antitrust settlement on IBM was hard to predict, but it was equally difficult to predict the future without it. Some of the mandated changes were likely to occur with or without the settlement—for example, allowing customers to buy as well as lease equipment. Concerning the patent licensing requirements, the introduction of electronics had already cost the company its dominant patent position. Its patents on magnetic tape and disk drives were more valuable than yet realized, and the company badly underestimated the value of its SSEC patents. Nevertheless IBM would need licenses to patents held by many others to compete successfully in the rapidly evolving field of electronics.

Events soon vindicated Tom Watson's decision to suffer the many constraints of the settlement rather than fight the case in court. He correctly believed the company's future was in electronics and that magnetic tape and disk storage would replace punched cards. His management team had to be free to concentrate on the future and to adapt the company's products and business methods to the onrush of new technologies. The company could not afford to sit still while waiting to be judged.

Domestic Competition

The January 1956 consent decree provided new guidelines and administrative burdens for the conduct of IBM's business, but Tom Watson believed the primary challenge remained unchanged. That challenge was to shift the product line from what the court defined as "tabulators" to what it defined as "electronic data processing machines."

In making this technological transition, IBM's primary competitor would continue to be Remington Rand, which had become a division of Sperry Rand during a June 1955 merger. Tom Watson already knew, however, that the number of installations using large-scale computers manufactured by IBM had finally surpassed the number using Remington Rand computers.[29] In addition to thirty completed installations of IBM 700 series computers at the end of 1955, there were five times that many new orders. Poor cooperation between the ERA and Eckert-Mauchly divisions, poor coupling between engineering and manufacturing, a weak marketing effort, and limited customer support had cost Remington Rand its once preeminent position. But with gross revenues 50 percent larger than those of IBM, the recently formed Sperry Rand Corporation had the financial resources to overcome these problems if its management had the capability and motivation.[30]

A new entrant to the market was the Radio Corporation of America (RCA), which had installed its first BIZMAC in 1955. This large-scale electronic computer in a "typical" configuration was priced at about $1.5 million, although a specially configured system then under construction was reported to have been sold for $4 million. With gross revenues twice those of IBM and substantial experience in military and consumer electronics, RCA was a feared competitor. Another significant entrant was the Datamatic Corporation, which had been formed as a jointly owned subsidiary of the Minneapolis-Honeywell Regulator Company and the Raytheon Manufacturing Company. The combined revenues of these two companies nearly equaled IBM's. Datamatic's first product offering was the DATAMATIC-1000, selling for about $1.8 million. Like recent large-scale computer offerings of IBM, Sperry Rand, and RCA, it was equipped with ferrite-core main memories.

In smaller stored-program computers selling under $300,000, IBM's primary competitors were NCR with 27 machines installed and the Electrodata Corporation with 14 installed at the beginning of 1956. Other entrants with low-end machines were the Bendix Aviation Corporation, Burroughs Corporation, Hogan Laboratories, Inc., Logistics Research, Inc., Marchant Calculators, Inc., Monroe Calculating Machine Company, Sperry Rand Corporation, Technitrol Engineering Company, and Underwood Corporation. These other companies collectively had fewer than 20 operational installations as 1956 began, but the number of machines on order was considerably higher. All but one of the smaller machines had a magnetic drum memory as did the IBM 650, of which over 100 had been installed and 750 were on order.[31]

This brief summary of the domestic competition in electronic data processing machines does not suggest IBM was in difficulty, but it does portray a far more competitive market place than existed for the company's traditional EAM equipment. With so many new competitors and a rapidly evolving market, the outcome was far from predetermined.

The World Trade Corporation

By far the largest part of IBM's revenue from outside North America came from its European operations.[32] Here the World Trade Corporation was busy facilitating the activities of its wholly owned operating companies in each major country. Its tasks included the selection of sites for manufacturing plants and development laboratories to make IBM products available throughout Europe as economically as possible. The patch-work quilt of customs regulations, national standards, and taxes that governed commerce among the many independent countries made this task particularly challenging. Obtaining patent protection in each country was another important responsibility that the World Trade Corporation shared with its national companies.

Particularly important was IBM Germany. This national company had grown out of Dehomag (Deutsche Hollerith Machinen Gesellschaft), which had been established by a German businessman in 1910 to distribute and service Hollerith equipment in Germany and certain other European countries. In 1922 IBM (then called CTR) purchased a controlling interest in the company through a sale by its founder.[33] During World War II the business was devastated, as were most other businesses in Germany. As soon as hostilities ended, the senior Watson arranged to send food to its employees, as well as tools to work with and used equipment to recondition and place on rental. As a result IBM's subsidiary was among the first German businesses to return to full operation after the war.

The situation in Great Britain was quite different and had presented a serious barrier to the creation of the World Trade Corporation in October 1949. It will be recalled that the British Tabulating Machine Company (BTM) had acquired exclusive rights from Hollerith to manufacture and distribute the company's products in all countries of the British Commonwealth except Canada. Because this contract could not be terminated without the consent of BTM, the senior Watson had been forced to offer a nonexclusive license, free of charge, on all existing products as well as on all issued and pending patents. These terms were attractive to BTM. Without the large royalties it was previously obliged to pay, the British company expected to be more profitable and better able to develop new products. All that IBM got in return was the right to compete with BTM.[34]

It was a significant gamble. IBM would now have to compete in Britain (and elsewhere) against its own products and technologies, manufactured and marketed by an established British firm. Among the factors that pushed IBM toward this decision was the threat of antitrust action. The U.S. Justice Department had begun preparing its antitrust case with a series of inquiries at least five years before it filed the lawsuit in 1952. It was known in IBM by 1949 that its agreement with BTM was under scrutiny. Of particular concern was the provision that the two companies not compete in each other's territories.[35]

Beyond the antitrust considerations, the senior Watson had long been distressed by the slow rate at which BTM was developing its market. There had also been continual disputes over royalty payments and other aspects of their relationship.[36] Above all Watson believed his concept of a World Trade Corporation would provide a more effective means for developing and distributing products worldwide.[37]

Competition Abroad

In 1949 when IBM and BTM were reconsidering their agreement, the British-based Powers-Samas company was renegotiating a similar agreement with Remington Rand. Powers-Samas had its origins in the Accounting and Tabulating Machine Company of Great Britain Limited, which was established in November 1915 as a subsidiary of the American-based Powers Accounting Machine Company. Like BTM it began manufacturing some of its own equipment during the 1920s.

In 1929 it eliminated its dependence on sales agencies by establishing its own sales organization under the name, Powers-Samas Accounting Machines Limited. The entire company and its products were soon known by this name. The name Samas had previously been used to designate the company's machines in France, where Remington Rand had refused to allow it to use the registered name Powers.[38]

A clause in their agreement that prevented either company from competing in the other's territory had come to be viewed more as an impediment than an advantage by the Power-Samas company. Among other things it prevented the company from selling equipment to Canada, whose large exports of wheat to the United Kingdom made it a highly desirable and willing customer.

Another disadvantage was the relatively poor performance of Remington Rand's Tabulating Machine Division in competition with IBM. "One wonders how long the unequal struggle can continue," the general manager of Powers-Samas pondered.[39]

Spurred to action by IBM's termination of its agreement with BTM, the Powers-Samas company notified Remington Rand of its intention to end their agreement as well. For Remington Rand there was at least one major incentive for acquiescing, namely, the antitrust implications. Although an agreement not to compete in each other's territories was not illegal per se, Remington Rand had been advised that such an agreement would figure prominently in any antitrust action brought by the government. For this reason, among others, the separation proceeded with little resistance by either party.[40]

In addition to the four punched-card equipment companies already identified in Europe, there was another fully integrated company. Machines Bull of France had grown out of the efforts of Frederik R. Bull, a Norwegian engineer, who undertook in 1918 to make equipment less expensive and more reliable than Hollerith's. More than a quarter of a century after Hollerith's equipment began tabulating the U. S. census of 1890, Bull devised his first tabulating machine. It was a combined tabulator and sorter. When neither function operated efficiently, he began designing separate units. Like Hollerith, he chose electrical rather than mechanical detection of the holes in cards. Following Bull's untimely death in 1925 at age forty-three, his work was continued by another engineer.

Finding a suitable manufacturing location was difficult, in part because the equipment used concepts covered by IBM patents. Switzerland was selected because IBM held no patents there. In 1931 the operation was moved to France (where IBM also held no patents) to take advantage of its much larger domestic market. In 1933 the company took the name Compagnie des Machines Bull.[41] Three years later, it had seventy-two installations in France and six others elsewhere in Europe. It continued to expand its operations until World War II and moved aggressively after the war.[42]

Competing against Remington Rand, Machines Bull, BTM, and Powers-Samas, IBM gained market share at home and abroad. Domestic and foreign revenues both increased an average of 22 percent per year during the 1950s. The United Kingdom was the only significant geographical market in which IBM had less than half of the business.[43] In 1954 when Dick Watson was elected president of the IBM World Trade Corporation, it still had fewer than 600 employees in the UK, whereas BTM and Powers-Samas each had over 5,000.[44]

Both of these British companies gave primary emphasis to strengthening their lines of punched-card equipment, thus leaving the European market for electronic stored-program computers largely to IBM and Remington Rand. The slowness of BTM and Powers-Samas to exploit electronic computer technology is surprising in view of Britain's leadership in electronics during World War II and its subsequent pioneering contributions to electronic computers.[45]

Remarkably the J. Lyons bakery was the first British company to build an electronic computer for business data processing. In 1951 it built the LEO computer in collaboration with Cambridge University, and in 1955 it formed Leo Computer Limited to exploit the market. By then Ferranti, Elliott Brothers, and English Electric had also entered the embryonic computer field. The British computer industry did not begin to take form, however, until BTM and Powers-Samas merged to form International Computers and Tabulators Limited in 1958.[46]

Thus the legacy of Thomas J. Watson, Sr., at the time of his death in 1956, was a company whose primary punched-card equipment business dominated the domestic market and led in all significant foreign markets except Great Britain. In electronic computers, IBM faced stiff competition in the United States, but it had more small-to-medium-sized computers installed by far than all of its competitors combined. Even in large computers, the number of its installations exceeded the number of its nearest competitor, Sperry Rand. Outside the United States there was little prospect of significant near-term competition in electronic computers, except for that offered by U.S. companies and any alliances they might make with European companies. IBM's World Trade Corporation, therefore, faced relatively weak competition and a vast and rapidly growing market for its products.

The senior Watson had provided the initial technical and market base for the company's entry into electronic computers, but the success achieved by 1956 was largely attributable to the team Watson, Jr., had assembled and led. Indeed an important part of the legacy of Watson, Sr., was his older son, whom he had groomed for leadership.

18

Gambling on System/360

Tom Watson took little comfort in IBM's relatively strong position in punched-card equipment and electronic data processing systems. He knew that many companies were being lured into the industry by prospects of profiting from electronics expertise, acquired through military work. Adding to his concern was the antitrust settlement, which had placed enormous constraints and requirements on IBM's normal business operations. Driving himself and his associates to overcome these problems, Watson launched IBM on a development effort that transformed the company and shaped the information processing industry for years to come.

Organizing for Growth

Modernizing the company's archaic organizational structure and putting his most trusted associates in key positions was an early priority. In November 1956 Watson assembled over one hundred IBM executives to announce a companywide reorganization. The structure in which all major decisions had funneled to his father was being replaced by one that emphasized decentralized responsibility.[1]

Some decentralization had already begun with creation of the Electric Typewriter and Military Products divisions in late 1955 and a Supplies Division in early 1956. Now he proposed to consolidate and extend these earlier steps. Particularly appealing to Watson was a reduction in the number of individuals who reported directly to him from seventeen (as it had been in 1954) to only five. These five individuals, who retained their titles of vice president or executive vice president, were given the additional title of "group executive" to signify they reported directly to the president and typically had responsibility for more than one functional unit.

The group executives with assignments most clearly illustrating the new structure were Al Williams, under whom all corporate staff functions had been collected, and Vin Learson, who now had responsibility for the Military Products, Time Equipment, and Special Engineering Products divisions, as well as the proposed Service Bureau Corporation.[2] The other three group executives were L. H. LaMotte, responsible for the newly formed Data Processing Division; H. W. Miller, Jr., responsible for the Electric Typewriter and Supplies divisions; and the younger Watson brother, Dick, who retained responsibility for the World Trade Corporation. Finally a Corporate Management Committee was established, consisting of the five group executives plus Tom Watson as chairman.[3]

Although the broad outlines of this structure survived for many years, a specific failing was observed. Continuing rapid changes in technologies and market requirements were putting major stresses on the Data Processing Division. The organizational structure that treated this business like any other business was not adequate. More significantly, the one person Watson believed could understand the complex technical and marketing issues of the EDPM business had been assigned elsewhere. That person was Vin Learson, the man to whom he had turned for help in 1954 to get the EDPM business started.

Watson's solution was to put Learson in charge of defining, developing, and manufacturing all products for the Data Processing Division. Implementing this decision in May 1959, Watson removed the product development and manufacturing functions from the Data Processing Division and split them into two new divisions. Each of the new divisions was responsible for developing and manufacturing roughly half of the EDPM product line. The Data Systems Division (with plants and laboratories in Poughkeepsie) was responsible for large computer systems, typically renting for more than $10,000 per month. The General Products Division (with plants and laboratories in Endicott, New York; San Jose, California; Burlington, Vermont; and Rochester, Minnesota) was responsible for small systems, typically renting for less than $10,000 per month. The current product offerings of GPD included EAM equipment, RAMAC, and the 650 and 1401 computers; those of DSD included the 700 and 7000 series. For historical reasons DSD had responsibility for magnetic tape storage and GPD for magnetic disk storage.

These two divisions were placed under Group Executive Learson, who was also given responsibility for a newly created Advanced Systems Development Division. This division was to specialize in systems work that was too applied for Research but too exploratory for product development. All divisions that previously reported to Learson were placed under other group executives, except for the Time Equipment Division, which had been sold in 1958. The Data Processing Division, which now had responsibility for sales and service of EAM and EDPM products, was also placed under one of the other group executives.[4]

Impact of the IBM 1401

The new structure put Learson in the middle of a growing rivalry between two laboratories. Engineers in Poughkeepsie had created the company's first electronic products, and they had bested the highly touted Remington Rand engineers in large computers. It was the engineers in Endicott, however, who had built the IBM 650. Although disparaged by Tom Watson as "a bunch of monkey-wrench engineers" and required to compete against ERA for the right to develop the 650, the Endicott engineers had produced the most popular computer of the 1950s.[5]

Now at the time Learson acquired responsibility for defining, developing, and manufacturing all electronic data processing systems, the Endicott laboratory was completing another small computer system. Announced in October 1959 as the IBM 1401 Data Processing System, it used SMS circuit packaging technology developed in Project Stretch. Equipped with ferrite-core memories having capacities of 1400 to 4000 characters, the 1401 could be configured to use punched cards and magnetic tape, and it could be used either as a stand-alone computer or as a peripheral system for larger computers.[6]

The timing of its development was fortuitous. Several important IBM-developed components had just been improved or were available for the first time. In the latter category was the newly devised chain printer. It provided unusually good print quality at a speed of 600 lines per minute. This was four times faster than most printers then available. The chain printer helped to make the 1401 the most popular computer of the early 1960s. The

Figure 18.1. IBM 1401 Computer
The smallest version of the IBM 1401 Data Processing System is shown here
with Type 1402 card read-punch (left), Type 1401 processing unit (center),
and Type 1403 chain printer (right). Announced in October 1959, the 1401
was the most widely used computer for many years. Magnetic tape, and later
magnetic disk, storage units were available as optional equipment.

monthly rental for a 1401 system was $2,500 and up, depending
on the configuration chosen. By the end of 1961 the number
installed in the United States had reached 2,000. This was about
25 percent of all electronic stored-program computers installed
by all manufacturers to that time. The number of 1401s installed
peaked at more than 10,000 in the mid-1960s.[7]

The IBM 1401 announcement sent shock waves through the
information processing industry. In the United States many new
entrants were forced to drop out. Although able to build the basic
electronic central processing unit, they were not prepared to
develop and manufacture low-cost ferrite-core memories or to
match IBM's engineering and manufacturing capability in
punched-card equipment, magnetic tape and disk storage, and
printers. They also lacked appropriate marketing expertise.

Sperry Rand was among the survivors. Its most successful small
computer in the late 1950s and early 1960s was its Solid State
Computer. Using an IBM-compatible 80-column card, this computer was marketed at first only in Europe to avoid making
obsolete the company's 90-column-card equipment in the United
States. When finally released in the United States as the SS-80
computer, it was outclassed by the newer IBM 1401 in cost and
performance and in the variety of configurations available.
Rather than investing in a replacement for the SS-80, Sperry

Rand chose to upgrade the existing product during the early 1960s. The result was not satisfactory. The number installed peaked at about 600, which was only 6 percent of the number of 1401s.[8]

The number of European companies offering computers was smaller than the number of U.S. companies. A lower level of government funding and a less well developed market for punched-card equipment were primary reasons. These factors probably also accounted for the slowness with which Machines Bull of France and the newly formed International Computers and Tabulators Limited (ICT) in Britain entered the field. For example, ICT did not deliver its first electronic computer until a year after the 1401 was available, and significant quantities were not available for yet another year. Thus it was primarily the IBM 1401 that effectively terminated the sale of conventional punched-card equipment there just as it had in the United States.[9]

The overwhelmingly good acceptance of the 1401 increased the rivalry between the IBM laboratories in Endicott and Poughkeepsie. So intense was it that sometimes it seemed to exceed the rivalry with external competitors. Channeling this along beneficial lines was a major challenge for Learson.

The success of the 1401 also increased the need to reassess the company's EDPM strategy. With the 1401 rapidly replacing conventional punched-card equipment, the products of the Endicott and Poughkeepsie laboratories would soon differ primarily in their cost and performance. It should be possible for customers to migrate easily from low-cost to high-cost equipment, but none of the Poughkeepsie machines could run programs written for Endicott machines. In fact, none of the first six IBM computers with transistor circuits could run programs written for another.[10]

The lack of compatibility was serious for customers, but it was even more of a problem for IBM. The company had to train sales and service personnel and provide programming support for each of the incompatible systems. The process was costly and chaotic. Economies of scale in engineering and manufacturing were reduced. For example, peripheral equipment designed for one computer could not be used on any other without modification. As Learson fully understood, these were not simple problems to solve. The engineers who had designed each of the computers and the customers who used them were committed to them and to their extensions.

Seeking Compatibility

In September 1960 the 1401-compatible (and more powerful) IBM 1410 was announced. Immediately successful in the marketplace, it demonstrated how valuable compatibility was. Meanwhile the Poughkeepsie engineers were nearing completion of a plan to create a series of new computers. The series consisted of four separate processors that offered two levels of performance for business applications and two levels for scientific and engineering computing. The most powerful computer was to match the performance of Stretch. Known as the 8000 series and intended to replace the 7000 series, the Poughkeepsie proposal was presented to the Corporate Management Committee in January 1961. The enthusiasm engendered by the presentation convinced Learson he would have to act quickly to achieve compatibility in future products. If he failed, the two laboratories might well battle each other in the marketplace with incompatible product lines.[11]

Only a few days after the 8000 series presentation, Learson acted. He removed the systems development manager in Poughkeepsie and replaced him with Bob O. Evans, who had been engineering manager for the 1401 and 1410 projects in the Endicott laboratory. Evans was thus already committed to compatibility, and he had no vested interest in the Poughkeepsie proposal. Three months after his appointment, Evans recommended that work on the 8000 series be terminated. In its place he urged that an effort be undertaken, with interdivisional participation, "to develop a total cohesive product line."[12]

Acceptance of his recommendation would necessarily delay the availability of new IBM systems. To prevent competitors from replacing IBM's aging equipment, Evans proposed a "temporizing" plan in which the older machines would be upgraded. Further support for a delay in developing new systems was provided by a corporate study on components. It recommended that improved semiconductor devices and circuit packaging technologies be developed to replace SMS. Known as Solid Logic Technology (SLT), the new circuit technologies could not be ready until at least a year later than required to meet the 8000 series schedule. Delay of a year or more in developing new systems could improve their competitiveness through use of SLT.

The proposed change in plan was vigorously opposed by Frederick P. Brooks, Jr., lead designer of the 8000 series. With a 1956 Ph.D. from Howard Aiken's pioneering computer science

Figure 18.2. Bob O. Evans
Bob Evans is shown demonstrating a System/360 model at the time of its announcement in April 1964. Three years earlier he had persuaded management to abandon other product plans in favor of this compatible line.

program at Harvard and experience as a Stretch designer, Fred Brooks was an articulate and knowledgeable opponent. The vigor with which he pressed his views gave no hint of his subordinate position to Evans in the company's hierarchy. To break the stalemate, Learson replaced Brooks's manager with Jerrier A. Haddad, who had most recently served for two years as head of the Advanced Systems Development Division. Previously he had been chief engineer for the IBM 701 development. Haddad's first task in his new assignment was to review the two proposals. He did so and sided with Evans. In May 1961 Learson terminated the 8000 series project.[13]

Bob Evans immediately asked Brooks to lead a search for the "ultimate" family of systems to serve all customers. "To my utter amazement, Bob asked me to take charge of that job after we had been fighting for six months," Fred Brooks recalls. "I was dumbstruck."[14] Brooks eagerly accepted, and his infectious enthusiasm and competence soon won the support of others.[15]

The plan to create an interdivisional product line was not without opposition. The most influential opponent was John W.

Figure 18.3.   Frederick P. Brooks, Jr.
After serving as project manager for System/360 from its inception to near
its announcement, Fred Brooks took over responsibility for development of
the critical operating system, OS/360.

Haanstra, president of the General Products Division. Firmly
committed to the independence of IBM divisions, Haanstra was
insistent on retaining self-determination for his division to develop and manufacture its own products. With the highly successful 1400 series developed in Endicott and the pioneering
magnetic disk storage products developed in San Jose, he was
confident of the capability of his division. His enthusiasm for disk
storage was heightened by his own early experience, working on
disk storage in San Jose during the 1950s. He believed that
developments underway on a low-cost 1401-like processor and on
a low-cost file, with the first removable disk packs, would greatly
expand IBM's customer base.

The SPREAD Task Group Report

To overcome Haanstra's opposition and to secure the cooperation of others, Learson established a corporatewide task group
with Haanstra as chairman and Evans as vice chairman. Code-
named SPREAD (an acronym for Systems Programming, Research, Engineering, And Development), the task group was "to
establish an overall IBM plan for data processor products."[16] Fred
Brooks was one of eleven other members. The SPREAD Task

Group issued its final report at the end of December 1961. One week later it was presented to the company's top executives and their staffs at the new T. J. Watson Research Center. The reaction was mixed, but Learson concluded the report offered the best available plan and ordered that it be implemented.[17]

The report's twenty-six pages contained product recommendations, analyses of their likely impact, and supporting technical and market information. Its primary recommendation was that a new line of "compatible processors " be developed that would span a broad range of performance. A *processor* was defined to be the central processing unit plus main memory and channels for attaching peripheral equipment. Compatible processors were defined as ones "capable of operating correctly all valid machine-language programs of all processors with the same or smaller I/O and memory configuration."[18]

The proposed product line was to consist of five processors spanning a 200-fold range in performance. This range was to be achieved by using SLT circuits of differing speeds, data paths of differing widths, memories of different sizes and speeds, and a variety of other engineering trade-offs. These trade-offs would be the responsibility of each engineering team assigned to develop one of the processors. Each engineering team was also mandated to develop an "economically competitive" processor, rather than depending on the rest of the line to ensure its market success.[19]

Use of a small high-speed memory with permanently stored information to control the action of logic circuits in the processor was strongly urged. Known as a "read-only control store," such a device would obviate the need to wire into the machine the capability to perform each of the programming instructions required of all processors in the compatible line. In Hursley, England, IBM's laboratory had conducted extensive studies of control stores, based on a 1951 proposal by M. V. Wilkes at Cambridge University.[20] Promoted vigorously by the representative to SPREAD from the Hursley laboratory, the proposed use of control stores would be their first commercial application.

In operation, each programming instruction (such as add, multiply, or conditional branch) was equated to an address in control store. When the word at this address was read out, its permanently stored 1s and 0s were used to open or close associated computer logic gates as required to execute the instruction. If an instruction execution required a sequence of such settings (i.e., more than one machine cycle), the first word addressed carried the address of the next control-store word needed to complete the instruction execution.[21]

Noting that many customers were using the same computer for scientific and business applications, the task group carried out a study to determine what instructions (if any) were used by one type of application but not by the other. Only floating-point instructions (used in engineering and scientific computations) were found to be of this type. It was therefore decided that each system in the line would be marketed for both types of applications. At the discretion of the engineering design team for each processor, however, floating-point capability could be offered either as a standard feature or as a field-installable option.[22]

A fundamental and contentious issue related to character size. Prime contenders were 6-bit and 8-bit characters. The 6-bit character was favored because it could represent all 26 letters of the alphabet plus punctuation symbols and because it was used in most computers, including the popular 1401. It was also used to record information in IBM's magnetic tape and disk storage products. It was opposed because it had 2 bits more than needed to represent a decimal digit and thus wasted expensive memory capacity. The 8-bit character was favored because it could be used to store 2 decimal digits efficiently and because the 2 bits more than needed for alphabetic symbols would provide for a wide range of special symbols in the future. The 8-bit character—which had been christened the "byte" when used in Stretch—was selected. Experience indicates it was a good decision. The 8-bit byte continues to be used in almost all computers.[23]

Among other significant architectural decisions was the requirement that standard interfaces be used for input-output (I/O) equipment such as tape and disk storage, card readers, printers, and terminals. As stated in the report, "When one processor is substituted for a slower one, the I/O gear shall not need to be changed."[24] This provision would not only permit customers to upgrade their systems gradually, but it would reduce engineering design and field service costs.

Although supportive of much of the SPREAD report, Haanstra and his Endicott engineers were apprehensive about the lack of compatibility of the proposed computers with any of the company's established products. As stated in the report, "Since such processors must have capabilities not now present in any IBM processor product, the new family of products will *not* be compatible with our existing processors."[25] All members of the task group knew that incompatibility with existing products would be a barrier to sales, but the advantages of the new line were expected to overcome this barrier. It was not until early 1963 that the possibility of competitors marketing machines compatible with IBM's present ones, but having superior cost and performance, appears to have surfaced as a serious concern.[26]

Saved by Emulation

The competitive action that Haanstra feared occurred in December 1963 when Honeywell announced its low-cost H-200 computer. A program, named "Liberator," was announced for use in translating 1401 programs to programs capable of running on the H-200. Prices were not quoted in the announcement, but up to a fivefold improvement in cost-performance over the four-year-old 1401 was indicated. Within two months the IBM sales force had reported 196 losses to the H-200.[27]

The possibility that translators, such as Honeywell's Liberator, could be devised to translate programs from IBM's current machines to run on its new line had been considered and abandoned in IBM well before the Honeywell announcement was made. Studies had revealed that code produced by automatic translation would be inefficient to run unless the two machines were quite similar, as were the H-200 and 1401. Semiautomatic translation was also attempted, but achieving the desired code efficiency required too much human effort.

The well-proven method of *simulating* one computer with another was also explored. In simulation, the "host" computer is programmed to run programs written for the "target" computer by simulating its architectural features. Again the achievable performance was shown to be acceptable only if the two machines were quite similar. Development of a cost-effective means for the conversion of programs written for current machines, to run on those of the new product line, was proving to be technologically more difficult than anticipated.

For some time Haanstra had been quietly working to create his own response to the type of threat Honeywell posed with its H-200. Rather than solving the conversion problem, his approach was to build 1401-compatible computers using SLT. The effort began unintentionally—or perhaps deliberately—in late 1960 with a decision to design a 1401 processor in SLT to provide a "feasibility test" of the new circuit technology. With its schedule tied to the development of SLT, the feasibility model was not fully operational until early 1963. Then, when no means for helping customers convert to the new product line had yet been found, Haanstra transformed the feasibility-model effort into a full-fledged product program. By using a relatively small number of additional circuits in the model, the designers were able to cause it to run programs for two other members of the 1400 series as well. The proposed product, tentatively designated the IBM 1470, was scheduled for announcement in February 1964. It was a blatant challenge to the new product line being developed under the leadership of Evans and Brooks.[28]

Learning of this decision early in January, Bob Evans warned that marketing a 1401-compatible computer, built with SLT and improved memory and storage devices, would inevitably lead to a decision to respond to other competitive threats by taking similar action for 7000 series computers. His vision of a company-wide family of compatible computers seemed to be nearing its end. "I am sad at the consequences," he lamented in a memo that suggested a helplessness uncommon for him.[29]

Almost miraculously, his vision of the new product line was saved by a last-minute technical accomplishment. In mid-1963 engineers in the Poughkeepsie and Endicott laboratories had begun exploring the possibility of adding special microcode to the control stores of computers to improve their performance when simulating earlier IBM computers. The first result of the Poughkeepsie group was exciting. The addition of one particularly well chosen word of microcode had speeded up a frequently used simulation loop by almost a factor of fifty. Additional microcode produced significant improvements in other parts of the simulation process. So dramatic was the improvement in performance of a simulator with microcode (and selected circuitry) enhancements that the Poughkeepsie engineers coined the term *emulator* to describe the concept.[30]

Meanwhile some engineers in Endicott were moving toward an even more ambitious achievement. Because the 1401 instruction set was relatively simple, they planned to implement all of it in an expanded control store of the smallest processor of the new line. To further speed up the simulation, they added a few circuits and made use of high-speed registers (already in the computer) to help translate decimal memory addresses of the 1401 into binary. The result was an emulator with no software portion. Using their emulator, the smallest of the new processors could be run in "1401 mode" to execute programs written for the 1401 more rapidly than the 1401 itself.[31]

It was a salesman's dream come true. The new product line now offered computers that could execute a customer's current programs faster than his present computer and that provided a path into the new world of compatible computers, capable of applications not possible with older equipment. Facing increasing competitive pressures, the IBM sales organization demanded an early product announcement.

Announcing System/360

On 7 April 1964, the new product line was publicly announced as the IBM System/360. To his "Fellow IBMers," Tom Watson said: "Today we are making the most significant product announcement in IBM history—the System/360. In Poughkeepsie, scores of reporters are attending a press conference to hear the news about this new generation of computers. In branch office cities throughout the country, many thousands of IBM customers and prospects have gathered to hear presentations on this new system. The day so many of you have worked so hard for has now arrived."[32]

About two hundred writers and editors had been brought to Poughkeepsie on a train hired by IBM. At the press conference, Watson said: "System/360 represents a sharp departure from concepts of the past in designing and building computers. It is the product of an international effort in IBM's laboratories and plants. . . . This is the beginning of a new generation—not only of computers—but of their application in business, science and government."[33]

The word *system* was chosen to signify that the offering was not just a group of processors with peripheral equipment but rather an aggregation of interchangeable hardware units with program compatibility from top to bottom. The number "360," which is the number of degrees in a circle, was chosen to represent the ability of each computer to handle all types of applications. Except for different costs and performances, all processors in the System/360 line were equivalent and presumably able to handle any anticipated information processing task.

The announcement was unprecedented in its scope. Six processor models, designated the 30, 40, 50, 60, 62, and 70, were announced. Models 60, 62, and 70 were replaced by superior 65

Figure 18.4.   A System/360 Installation
A typical configuration of a relatively small System/360 computer includes
(from left) a card read-punch, four magnetic tape units and controller, two
magnetic disk storage units, and the processor (here a Model 40) with control panel. The operator sits at the printer keyboard within reach of the control panel.

and 75 models before any of the original three were shipped.
Each processor had its own range of memory capacities: 8K to
64K bytes on the Model 30, and 256K to 1024K bytes on the
top-of-the-line Model 75. (K is a binary-oriented multiplier equal
to $2^{10} = 1024$. Thus 8K bytes is 8192 bytes.)

A fiftyfold performance range in processors was achieved, primarily by two design factors. First, data path widths provided a
factor of eight. From one byte wide in the Model 30, the data
path was successively increased, reaching eight bytes in the Model
65 and above. Second, SLT circuits provided almost a factor of
four with operational times ranging from about 8 nanoseconds
to 30 nanoseconds. A variety of other design techniques achieved
an additional factor of about two in performance.[34]

Forty-four different peripheral devices were also announced.
These included several types of magnetic storage devices, visual
display units, communication equipment, card readers and
punches, printers, and an optical character reader. Monthly system rentals ranged "from $2,700 for a basic configuration to
$115,000 for a typical large multisystem configuration." Compa-
rable purchase prices were said to be $133,000 to $5,500,000.[35]

The same general information was provided to an estimated
100,000 customers and prospects at special branch office meet-

ings held in 165 cities in the United States. The response was as unprecedented as the announcement. Orders rapidly exceeded forecasts. Well over one thousand orders were received during the first four weeks, and most orders specified more memory and I/O than anticipated.[36]

Watson had gambled almost all of the company's development resources for more than two years on a single product line. Now the rewards projected by the SPREAD Task Group were at hand, but the early order rate did not ensure success. Another two years of concerted engineering and manufacturing effort were needed before confirmed orders and successfully delivered products would guarantee fulfillment of the promise of System/360.

19

Commitment and Delivery

Successful emulation of a 1401 by the smallest computer of the new product line had failed to change John Haanstra's plans. Believing his division best understood the needs of its customers, he continued preparing to announce a 1401-compatible computer built with SLT. He urged that the marketplace be allowed to decide between it and System/360.

Haanstra was one of IBM's finest engineering managers. Brilliant and self-assured, he pursued his goals with unrelenting vigor. His resistance to the new product line had emphasized the need for a cost-effective means for converting customers to the new system, and he had provided a viable alternative for the low end of the line. Had emulation not been successful, his alternative might have been used. But once the decision was made to announce System/360, opposition had no further value. One month before the product announcement, Haanstra was removed as president of the General Products Division.[1] The message this action delivered was unambiguous: managers and their organizations would be judged primarily by their commitment and contributions to System/360.

Entering the Components Business

Of all the hardware commitments, none posed greater opportunity and risk than IBM's decision to develop and manufacture its own semiconductor devices. It was not an easy decision. Battles had raged for years over whether it was better to make or buy components. Tom Watson, Jim Birkenstock, and other corporate leaders contended that the components business had a lower profit margin than the systems business and should be left to others. Ralph Palmer, Wally McDowell, and several other key engineers believed that leadership in components was essential to leadership in information processing systems. They believed that advances in components would lead to new system concepts and unanticipated product opportunities.

Because the general argument was never resolved, decisions were made on a case-by-case basis. The company had manufactured its own cathode-ray tubes for use in Williams-tube memories because suppliers failed to provide the necessary quality, but it had elected not to manufacture more conventional tubes. Failing to obtain satisfactory patent licensing terms from its primary supplier of ferrite cores, IBM had acquired patent rights to a different process and manufactured its own.[2]

In December 1957 the company had entered into an important agreement with the Texas Instruments Company (TI). The contract called for "exchange of patent licenses, purchasing arrangements, interchange of technical information, and joint development" of transistors and diodes. It made TI the primary supplier of semiconductor devices to IBM.[3] Palmer's initial dislike of the agreement was increased in 1959 when the world's first fully automatic manufacturing line for transistors—developed by his engineers—was taken apart and shipped to TI. Initially used to manufacture transistors only for IBM, the line was soon replicated and used to produce transistors for TI's other customers as well.

There was growing dissatisfaction with the agreement at the corporate level as well. Technical information exchange provided TI with improved devices and manufacturing methods, but the purchasing agreements prevented IBM from buying freely from other vendors to encourage lower prices from TI. Citing these and other problems, Palmer began pressing for a decision to manufacture all critical components in IBM.

To help the corporation address this and other technical issues, a corporate-level Research and Development Board was established in May 1959. Chaired by McDowell until Mannie Piore took over in 1960, the board's nine members included McDowell, Palmer, Piore, and several laboratory managers. Making technological choices critical to IBM and then "deciding the best way to implement these choices" was the board's primary mission.

High on the agenda for the board's monthly meetings were semiconductor device technologies. Almost immediately the board assigned an engineer the task of combining several small projects to establish a companywide program to develop semiconductor circuits and packaging for future products. By the end of

1959 the program had made many technical decisions and was projecting 149 employee-years of development work during the next year.[4]

It was a critical time for this focus. Technical advisers to U.S. military organizations were placing increasing emphasis on the need for smaller and more rugged circuits. Funded by the U.S. Army's Micromodule Program, for example, RCA had made a proposal for achieving over two hundred components per cubic inch. This was more than ten times the density of IBM's SMS technology. The RCA proposal called for mounting discrete transistors, resistors, capacitors, and other electric components on thin ceramic modules a few inches on a side and interconnecting the circuits among many modules in a three-dimensional array.

The IBM Research and Development Board viewed the proposal as a serious threat. Not only was RCA well established in electronics, but it had announced its first fully transistorized computer (the 501) in late 1958 and had installed the first one a year later. Because it was also known to be developing more advanced computers,[5] IBM could not afford to fall behind RCA in circuit technologies.

Adding to the sense of urgency were technical advances throughout the semiconductor industry. In February 1959 Jack S. Kilby filed a patent describing a way to combine all circuit elements and their interconnecting wiring on a single silicon chip. It was the first patent filed for an *integrated circuit*, as that term came to be defined. (Prior to the mid-1960s the term *integrated circuit* was used to describe any densely packed assembly of electric components that formed one or more circuits.)

Kilby was not alone in his ideas. Robert N. Noyce, a founder of the Fairchild Semiconductor Company, was working rapidly to document his ideas. Five months after Kilby filed for a patent and his invention was publicly announced, Noyce filed for his patent. By incorporating advanced processing techniques developed throughout the industry, Noyce in his patent described integrated-circuit structures similar to those that were later developed. In particular it made use of *planar processing*, whereby photographic images created on the flat surface of a silicon wafer delineated where chemical processing steps would create conducting lines and more complex device structures.[6]

These advances toward integrating entire circuits in compact structures supported Palmer's view that IBM could no longer buy individual components and assemble them as it had for SMS. The automated manufacturing of SMS had been achieved by designing circuit cards with the manufacturing process in mind. Palmer believed this concept should now be extended down to the most basic circuit elements. His views were endorsed by the new director of research, Mannie Piore, who established a small task group to study the issue. An important ally and task-group member was Mervin J. Kelly, retired chairman of the Bell Telephone Laboratories, who had been hired by Tom Watson as a "consultant on research and engineering matters."[7]

Within the year the decision was made that IBM would enter the components business to supply most, if not all, of its component needs. A components organization was established in Poughkeepsie in October 1960. Several existing groups were placed in the new organization, and additional people recruited. In July 1961 the new organization became the IBM Components Division. Its manager reported to group executive Vin Learson.[8]

Developing SLT

Technical leaders in the new Components Division had been following developments at TI, Fairchild, and elsewhere. In their judgment, the type of integrated circuits described by Kilby and Noyce were years away from a cost-effective implementation. As events unfolded at IBM, there would not be time for that. The triggering event was approval by the Corporate Management Committee in March 1961 of the 8000-series plan. Learson was opposed to the decision, but he had no alternative to offer. In a first step toward finding an alternative, he asked Bob Evans to establish an interdivisional task group to study "the feasibility of using an advanced [circuit] technology in the 8000-series machines."[9]

Chosen by Evans to lead the task group was Erich Bloch, a native of Germany who had studied at the Swiss Federal Institute of Technology before immigrating to the United States. Working days and studying nights, Bloch had obtained a bachelor's degree in electrical engineering from the University of Buffalo before joining IBM in 1952. Respected for his practical and thorough approach to engineering problems, he was an ideal choice. While serving as engineering manager for Project Stretch, he had gained firsthand knowledge of the development and use of SMS circuits and packaging.[10]

Figure 19.1.   Erich Bloch
Erich Bloch led the efforts that defined and developed SLT. He is shown
here in 1970, reviewing semiconductor manufacturing facilities.

The task force, consisting of Bloch plus eight other highly
qualified engineers, issued their findings within two weeks. "The
TI approach to microminiaturization using the solid circuit is
deemed to have an economical disadvantage, because of the
specifications that must be achieved simultaneously on many
diverse devices," the report opined. "At the present time, it is
contemplated that one transistor per chip will yield optimum
cost." To keep transistor costs low and reliability high, the "use of
planar, glass passivated chip transistors" was recommended. A key
feature of the report, for Learson, was the conclusion that the
tightest possible development schedule would would add an additional year to the development schedule of the proposed 8000
series.[11]
Within three months after Bloch's report was issued, Learson
had terminated the 8000 series, the components group had become an IBM division, and Erich Bloch had been selected to lead
the development of the proposed circuit technology. Early in

August Bloch submitted a forty-two-page report titled "Solid Logic Technology Program—Objectives and Directions."[12] It provided a remarkably accurate description of the semiconductor devices soon to be manufactured. Five months later, in January 1962, Learson endorsed the SPREAD report as the basis for company-wide development of a series of compatible processors. Intrinsic to that plan was SLT.

The SLT chips used with System/360 were little changed in appearance from those proposed in Bloch's report of August 1961. Many novel ideas, patentable and unpatentable, however, were needed to transform the ideas of 1961 into the realities of 1964. Among the patentable ideas was a technique for putting a thin layer of glass over the processed chip surface to protect it from contaminants during subsequent processing steps and years of use in customer facilities. Three tiny holes were etched through this glass layer to permit three small copper spheres to be soldered to conducting lines on the silicon chip. These balls provided the means for making electrical contacts with the next level of the circuit package.

That level was called an SLT module. Its fabrication began with a white ceramic substrate, just under a half inch square. Copper pins were inserted through twelve holes around the perimeter to make electrical connections with the next level of packaging. Conducting lines and resistors were printed on the surface of the ceramic substrate. The ability to fabricate resistors with better precision and lower cost than was then possible on silicon was a key reason for choosing SLT hybrid integrated-circuit technology.[13]

All processes and device designs were intended to facilitate economical mass production. The initial plan for manufacturing SLT modules assumed no human intervention from beginning to end. Ceramic blanks were to enter the line at one end and exit from the other—with lines and resistors fabricated, silicon chips mounted, electrical characteristics tested, capped, and labeled—all at the rate of thirty modules per minute. The design philosophy was similar to that used in the pioneering manufacturing line shipped to TI in 1959.

It soon became evident, however, that greater flexibility was needed. The fabrication of SLT modules required far more processing steps than existed in the previous line. Rather than interconnecting all process steps together in lock-step fashion, it was decided to make each stage operate independently, with its out-

Figure 19.2. Electronic Circuitry Evolution
Top: An SLT card with six attached modules, as announced with System/360, is pictured with an SMS circuit card used on 7000 series computers and the eight-tube pluggable unit introduced on the IBM 701. Bottom: Close-up of an SLT module, without its protective cap, reveals semiconductor chips (1), printed lines (2), and printed resistors (3). The tops of twelve pins (for plugging the module into a card) are evident around the module's periphery.

put stored in racks and manually moved to the next stage. This permitted each process unit to be optimized independently, with several slower units for one process step keeping up with a single faster unit for another.[14]

The next level of SLT packaging was a printed circuit card, the smallest version of which was 1.6 inches square and could hold up to six modules. The cards in turn were plugged into large printed circuit boards. Devising the wiring pattern for thousands of printed lines to interconnect hundreds of circuits on a board was a time-consuming and error-prone activity. Many different board types were needed, and engineering changes would be frequent in the early stages of production.

To automate both the design and manufacturing processes, a computer program was written for the IBM 7090 that generated an engineering description of each board type. This description, which included a detailed wiring layout, was transmitted to an IBM 1401 that converted it into specific commands that operated production equipment. It was just one of many pioneering process tools available when the manufacture of SLT cards and boards was moved into the newly completed Process Technology Building in Endicott in the fall of 1964.[15]

Memory and Storage

The availability of large amounts of reliable main memory on each processor was a major selling point. Equally important was the ability to attach magnetic tape and disk storage via a standard channel interface. Operating systems were provided to allocate memory space among various tasks and to provide standard procedures for moving information between memory and storage and for operating a variety of other peripheral devices.

The choice of ferrite cores for System/360 main memories was obvious. No other memory technology offered such good performance and reliability, and the company had achieved technical leadership through Project SAGE. In November 1961, two months before the SPREAD report was adopted, a task force was established to seek improved memory designs for low-cost manufacture. Members included engineers from development and manufacturing organizations. Among its accomplishments was the design of a wiring pattern that reduced unwanted electrical noise and a manufacturing tool to accomplish the pattern in production.

An inescapable requirement for control stores was speed: they had to supply control words more rapidly than was possible with conventional ferrite-core memories. The solution was to take advantage of the read-only characteristic of control stores. By representing each logical 1 or 0 by the presence or absence of a tiny electrical element, such as a capacitor or inductor, both the time required for a write-back cycle and the cost of write circuits were eliminated. Information could also be read out more rapidly. Corporate responsibility for control store designs was assigned to the laboratory in Hursley, England, where pioneering design work had been done.

By the fall of 1963 the development of main memories and control stores for the smaller processors was progressing reasonably well, but there were severe problems in satisfying the needs of higher-performance processors. To solve these problems, Erich Bloch was given responsibility for the development of computer memories in addition to SLT. By the end of the year, he had authorized several significant changes. A novel "load-sharing matrix switch" was implemented to reduce the current levels required in memory drive circuits. Special SLT circuits were designed for memory use. And a ferrite core with a 30 percent smaller hole diameter was adopted after an engineer, working on his own initiative, demonstrated that improved manufacturing methods would be able to wire the smaller cores into memory arrays.[16]

The redesigned memories achieved read-write cycles even shorter than the targeted 1.0 microsecond. When ways were found to speed up the related control store and logic circuitry as well, processor Models 60, 62, and 70 were withdrawn in April 1965 and replaced by higher performance Models 65 and 75 with 0.75-microsecond cycle memories. Around-the-clock work by engineers made it possible to ship the first Model 65 in November 1965, only three months later than originally scheduled for the earlier models.[17]

Also important to the success of System/360 was the availability of improved magnetic disk storage. The most important technical advance since the 1955 announcement of RAMAC was the self-acting air bearing. Rather than using a jet of forced air to float the read-write head above the disk surface, use was made of a dense layer of air that formed naturally between the rapidly moving disk surface and a properly shaped head structure. An important improvement in access time was was achieved by replacing the single actuator arm (having two read-write heads) with enough arms ganged together to provide a dedicated head for each disk surface.

Both of these advances were introduced with the IBM 1301 Disk Storage in 1961. Compared with RAMAC, it provided a thirteen-fold increase in storage density and three times faster average access to information. An improved version of the 1301, with another fourfold increase in storage density, was announced in September 1963 as the 1302. With little change other than to the attachment interface, it was announced seven months later with the rest of System/360 as the IBM 2302 Disk Storage.[18]

Also available with System/360 was a disk storage system with interchangeable disk packs. The primary motivation for this innovation was to reduce information storage costs by making it possible to store information on disks off-line. System designers, however, also wanted to be able to write information on disks with one system and then read the stored information with another. This required much tighter control of mechanical tolerances in a technology in which tolerance control was already a severe problem.

The first product to provide interchangeability of disk packs was the IBM 1311 Disk Storage Drive, announced in October 1962. Each pack contained six 14-inch-diameter disks in a 4-inch-high stack that weighed ten pounds and held up to 2 million characters. An average access time of 150 milliseconds to information was achieved. The IBM 1440 computer, on which this storage was first offered, did poorly in the marketplace because it was initially offered without the ability to attach magnetic tape units as well.

This mistake was not repeated with System/360. The two types of storage media coexisted on that system for many years, with magnetic tape providing shelf storage at a lower cost than magnetic disks. An improved version of the interchangeable disk storage, having twice the capacity and half the access time, was announced with the rest of System/360 in April 1964 as the IBM 2311 Disk Storage Drive.[19]

The initial System/360 development plan called for no improvement of tape storage products. There were several reasons for this decision: the belief that tape storage would soon be displaced by disk storage, IBM's presumably secure leadership in tape-drive products, and the need to conserve engineering resources in Poughkeepsie. To handle the planned 8-bit byte that was to replace the then conventional 6-bit character, a "tape adapter unit" was proposed. It would convert three 8-bit bytes from the channel into four 6-bit characters for the tape unit, and vice versa, with logic to create appropriate parity bits.

The efforts of a few self-motivated engineers in manufacturing changed this plan in late 1963. They built a head capable of reading and writing nine tracks on conventional half-inch tape and demonstrated that it could be manufactured at reasonable cost. A variety of other improvements were added during product testing in 1964 to meet perceived competitive threats, especially from Honeywell and Sperry Rand. Among these improvements was a read-backward capability that made it possible to sort records more rapidly. Long offered by UNIVAC, this capability previously had been partially compensated for by the superior stop-start and high-speed rewind capabilities of IBM's tape units. Now IBM provided both features.[20]

Again and again during the development of System/360, engineers provided unanticipated solutions for critical problems. Ralph Palmer had motivated this type of activity by challenging more than one engineering group to create "the best solution" for a specific problem and by allowing engineers to spend part time pursuing their own ideas. Many engineers labored long hours on their own time, seeking ways to make better products.

The competition between engineers, which Watson, Sr., had used so effectively in the past, was a key element in the success of System/360. There was, however, an important difference. Competition was no longer "blind." Now information on engineering plans, assignments, and requirements was broadly available. Individual engineers could readily learn what approaches were being tried and what opportunities there might be for improvement.

Achieving Manufacturing Goals

Orders for System/360 computers quickly exceeded the forecast. More than one thousand orders were received in the first month after announcement, and another one thousand were received during the next four months. Adding to production requirements, most orders requested more memory and storage capacity than IBM's product planners had anticipated.[21]

Construction of a 100,000-square-foot manufacturing plant for SLT was begun in September 1962. Located on a newly purchased 450-acre site in East Fishkill (about twelve miles south of

Poughkeepsie), the plant was expanded to three and one-half times its initial size within three years.[22] The number of SLT modules manufactured in East Fishkill in 1963 was 0.5 million. A twelvefold production increase in 1964 resulted in 6 million modules, and plans called for the production of 28 million modules in 1965.

Asked to increase production by yet another factor of two in 1965, the plant manager explained why it could not be done without excessive risk. Ordered to double production anyway, he refused and was replaced by a manager willing to accept the higher commitment. The result was a near disaster. Routine quality control activities during 1965 revealed poor quality in many modules. By September more than 25 percent of the year's production had been impounded by the Quality Control Department, and a decision was made to stop production.

Scientists and engineers from research and development were brought in to help solve the problem. Within a month it was discovered that the higher-volume production equipment caused an undesirable chrome oxide to form when a chrome layer was being deposited on the wafers. Once the problem was understood, it was easily corrected. Production was resumed at the higher level, but IBM had been forced to announce an embarrassing two- to four-month delay in product shipments.[23]

The production of SLT modules reached 36 million in 1965 despite the near disaster, and 90 million were produced in 1966. By then IBM's East Fishkill plant was producing more semiconductor devices than were produced by all other companies in the world combined. Meanwhile production in newly established IBM plants in Burlington, Vermont, and Essonnes, France, had been ramped up to 27 and 26 million modules, respectively.[24]

So frantic was the development of high-volume production equipment for semiconductor devices that little thought was given to protecting proprietary designs. Product innovations were routinely covered by patents, but production equipment was not. As a result much of the production equipment designed by IBM found its way into the general market when vendors, hired to build equipment for IBM, broadened their business by selling essentially the same equipment to others.[25]

The problems encountered in manufacturing ferrite-core memories were less severe because of years of experience. The production of ferrite cores, for example, reached one billion per year in 1963, and there was little difficulty when the rate was increased tenfold during the next four years. The problems of wiring the cores into memory arrays were not so easily solved. So many wire feeders were needed to wire cores into arrays that a department was created in Kingston just to produce them. As quickly as wire feeders were built, they were put on the manufacturing floor. By the end of 1964 there was no more floor space for wire feeders and there were insufficient people to operate them.

A plant was built in Boulder, Colorado, in mid-1965 to alleviate this problem as well as a similar problem in manufacturing tape drives. When this action proved inadequate, an experiment was undertaken to have people in Japan wire core frames by hand. So careful and meticulous were the Japanese workers, and so low were their wages, that memory arrays wired by hand in Japan had the same quality and a lower cost than those produced with automated wire-feed equipment in Kingston.

Core wiring operations were quickly expanded throughout the Orient into what became known as the "Hong Kong Core House." Competitors also established core wiring facilities in the Orient, causing IBM to lose much of the advantage it had gained through automated manufacture. Its memory designs did, hovever, continue to have fewer semiconductor circuits and lower final assembly costs than those of its competitors.[26]

Stress at the Top

The logistical problems of manufacturing System/360 components and products in plants throughout the world were enormous and so was the stress on managers. This can be appreciated best by viewing the scene at the top. To ensure a successful introduction of the new product line, Tom Watson promoted Vin Learson to senior vice president with responsibility for sales. The sales results attest to his success. Watson also promoted his brother to senior vice president with responsibility for research, development, and manufacturing. In preparation for this assignment, Dick Watson had left his World Trade Corporation position and spent half a year as head of the Corporate Staff. Now he and Learson had the two top positions under Tom Watson.[27]

Dick Watson's assignment was intended to prepare him to become the company president at some future date, but its effect was quite different. With little relevant experience, he was unable to cope with all the problems of manufacturing and shipping

System/360. He also had to contend with rising fears of his brother that SLT would rapidly become obsolete because of integrated circuits and that competitive product announcements were undercutting System/360 in the marketplace. Responding to these fears, Learson demanded that new product features be added immediately, even though there were already more problems than could be handled by the engineering groups for which Dick Watson was then responsible. "The friction between Dick and Vin got completely out of hand," Tom Watson said.[28] Rather than creating two complementary positions, Tom Watson had put his brother and Learson into a competition—and Learson was not one who lost easily.

Once the decision was made to announce product shipment delays in October 1964, Tom Watson felt he had no choice but to turn once again to Learson for help. Without formal announcement, Learson returned from sales to replace Dick Watson in running the development and manufacturing organizations. Choosing the head of the corporate manufacturing staff as his top assistant, Learson drafted four senior engineering managers and gave each of them responsibility for operations at selected laboratories and plants. These "four horsemen," as they came to be called, were given companywide authority to decide how System/360 commitments would be met. All other activities had lower priority. Citing the "myriad of typical early manufacturing problems on every box," one of the four horsemen said the situation was "an absolute nightmare." He recalled his own involvement as "a gray blur of twenty-hour days, seven days a week—never being home." But in less than five months, Learson's team had System/360 shipments back on schedule.[29]

In January 1966 Tom Watson advised the board of directors that Al Williams would step down as president at the end of March. Learson was elected president, effective the first of April. Dick Watson was elected to a newly created position of vice chairman of the board. The traumatic events of System/360 that propelled Learson to the presidency had effectively ended Dick Watson's IBM career. In 1970 he undertook a new assignment as the United States ambassador to France.[30]

Software Support

Of all the challenges presented by the System/360 announcement, none was more difficult to accomplish than providing the promised software support. Its importance was never in doubt. General purpose programs, provided "free of charge" by manufacturers, were considered essential to the marketing of computers.[31]

Most computer processing was then done in a *stacked-job* mode in which one program was fully processed before another one was started. Interest was growing, however, in a *multiprogramming* mode in which two or more programs were processed more or less simultaneously. Multiprogramming could improve the overall efficiency of a system by causing the processor to work on one program while waiting for information (from tape or disk storage) needed by another.

Interest was also growing in applications in which people could interact with a computer using terminals at remote locations. This capability had been demonstrated in a few systems. For example, the SABRE airline reservation system, jointly developed by American Airlines and IBM, offered extensive access via remote terminals. But providing such capability for a single system, dedicated as SABRE was to a specific task, was far simpler than providing it as part of a general-purpose operating system. Furthermore each processor of the new line offered many configurations of main memory, magnetic tape and disk storage, and other input-output equipment that had to be supported by the operating system.

Just what type of programming support should be offered was heavily debated following adoption of the SPREAD report in January 1962. It was readily agreed that the smaller processors in the line, especially those ordered with minimum memory capacity, could be given only a rudimentary stacked-job capability. The type of scaled-up support that should (and could) be offered on intermediate to large systems was more difficult to judge, however, because of limited experience with the newer programming concepts.[32]

In January 1963, by which time four levels of programming support had been defined, Fred Brooks established the firm guideline that any application program compiled or assembled at any level must be able to run at any higher level as well. "I should like to be notified at once in the event of any proposed amendment to, or departure from, these ground rules," Brooks admonished the responsible managers.[33] The constraint was essential to full realization of the benefits of a compatible line, but its immediate impact was that no part of an operating system for any one of the processors could be defined without considering its relationship with operating systems for the others. Decision making was impeded.

As 1963 drew to a close, programming activities were in sufficient disarray that Bob Evans requested a technical audit. While highly critical of the "lack of management decision making," the audit report placed some of the blame on the heavy burdens of programming groups that also had to develop software support for the "temporizing" products. Another obstacle had been Haanstra's use of programmers in Endicott to support his proposed 1401-compatible processor rather than the new product line. Of the report's many recommendations, the most important was that a design task force be established to distill months of deliberation into a new set of programming objectives.[34]

Less than one month after the design task force was established, it had hammered out decisions that became the basis for OS/360, the new product line's operating system. Rejecting the plan for a graded set of compatible operating systems, the task force recommended development of a single, full-function operating system, suitable for the largest processor. Its control program was to be comprised of parts that could be selectively omitted to allow for a variety of reduced-function versions for use on processors with smaller memory capacities, down to as little as 16K bytes.[35]

The recommendations of the design task force became the basis for OS/360 as announced with System/360 hardware in April 1964. A stacked-job control-program version of OS/360 was to be available by the end of 1965 and a multiprogramming version was promised for delivery six months later. Also announced were a variety of "special" programming support packages for small systems with as little as 8K bytes of memory.[36]

To help ensure success of the programming effort, Fred Brooks offered to supervise it much as he had coordinated the engineering designs of the processors. His offer was eagerly accepted even though it was understood that he planned to leave IBM in the fall to establish a computer science department at the University of North Carolina.[37]

The magnitude of the task of developing the proposed operating system was grossly underestimated. Over one thousand people (including managers, programmers, manual writers, and those in all support functions) were employed during the peak year. More money was spent to develop System/360 software support during that one year than had been planned for the entire project. At the personal request of Tom Watson, Brooks agreed to remain in charge of the effort for an extra year, while spending one week per month at the University of North Carolina.[38]

Despite a sustained intensive effort, the various parts of OS/360 were delivered months later than announced; they generally used more memory capacity than planned; and their processing times were longer than desired. Improving the performance of critical parts of OS/360 was a key objective of subsequent releases. Brooks attributes the lack of elegance of OS/360 to inadequate vision by its designers, to the difficulty of achieving conceptual integrity in so vast a project, and to the need to subdivide the implementation among so many groups. Concerning his own inability to get the system completed on time despite the use of vast resources, he wryly proclaimed what he called Brooks's Law: "Adding manpower to a late software project makes it later."[39]

The inability to achieve satisfactory performance of OS/360 on processors with less than 32K bytes of memory was particularly serious. This deficiency was not recognized until several months after the April 1964 announcement of System/360. During the intervening months, customers who ordered the System/360 Model 30 with 16K bytes of memory had been assured that they could use the new operating system. The failure to achieve this objective—or perhaps the error in committing to it—resulted from the limited experience of programmers in Poughkeepsie with small systems. In part because of Haanstra's resistance to the new line, the views of the small systems designers in Endicott had not received sufficient consideration.

The situation was so serious in the fall of 1964 that the General Products Division (headquartered in Endicott) was given responsibility for all support required by System/360 processors with 8K to 16K bytes of memory. It was a daunting responsibility. Hardware delivery schedules demanded that all of this support be available within a year. On the last day of 1964 a firm commitment was made, and IBM formally announced three additional operating systems, all of which were to be available by the end of 1965.[40]

The names subsequently given to them were BOS (Basic Operating System), TOS (Tape Operating System), and DOS (Disk Operating System). The minimum storage and memory requirements for BOS were disk plus 8K bytes of memory; for TOS, tape plus 16K bytes of memory; and for DOS, disk plus 16K bytes of memory. The special programming support offered for systems with only 8K bytes of memory became known as BPS (Basic Programming Support).

Long hours of dedicated work by programmers in Endicott and San Jose produced this programming support more or less on schedule—except for DOS, which was finally released in June 1966. Despite the limited time available to define and complete DOS, and despite its late delivery, it became the most widely used operating system in the world. The quality of its conception and implementation contributed to the increasing popularity of disk storage. A multiprogramming version was subsequently released for systems with at least 32K bytes of memory. Some twenty-six releases of DOS, each with enhanced function or performance, had been issued by IBM by the time a decision was made in 1971 to create no more new versions.[41]

Market Impact

When System/360 was announced in 1964, the major companies of the computer industry were often referred to as Snow White and the Seven Dwarfs. Snow White was IBM. The Seven Dwarfs were Burroughs, Control Data, General Electric, Honeywell, NCR, RCA, and Sperry Rand. Of the estimated $10 billion worldwide inventory of installed computers in 1964, the Dwarfs had produced about 30 percent, and IBM had produced the rest. Five years later IBM's worldwide inventory had increased more than threefold to $24 billion and that of the Dwarfs had increased by about the same ratio to $9 billion.[42]

This apparent lack of change, other than dramatic growth, is misleading. The popularity of System/360 made it difficult for others to compete across the broad spectrum of the general purpose computer market. Two of the Dwarfs that attempted to do so failed to make a profit and dropped out of the business in the early 1970s. At the same time, weaknesses of System/360 provided lucrative opportunities in certain parts of the market, and compatibility among processors and modularity of its component parts created attractive opportunities for companies to provide plug-compatible products for attachment to the system.

Among the Seven Dwarfs, RCA pursued the most aggressive and risky strategy. In December 1964 it announced the Spectra 70 product line with four processors covering almost as wide a performance range as System/360. Not only were the four processors compatible with each other, they were designed to be compatible with System/360 as well—a feat presumably accomplished through careful study of IBM's publicly available documentation. Spectra 70 customers would thus be able to use software written for System/360.[43]

Because price was the only obvious differentiation between the two competing systems, RCA planned to offer a 15 to 20 percent price-performance advantage over IBM equipment. Customer response was reasonably good, and RCA's computer revenues during the 1960s increased fifteenfold to $211 million. This was only 3 percent as large as IBM's revenues, however, and represented a very small part of RCA's total revenues as well. In an attempt to preempt IBM's System/370 announcement, RCA announced its RCA series, a price-reduced version of Spectra 70. The result was disastrous. Rather than displacing IBM equipment, the new series primarily displaced RCA's own Spectra 70 computers. This event, coupled with accumulating losses, persuaded RCA to exit the business in 1971 by selling its computer division to Sperry Rand.[44]

General Electric (GE) also moved aggressively in the 1960s to capture a larger share of the rapidly growing computer market. Like Honeywell, its primary strategy was to facilitate the migration to its systems by users of IBM's older computers. General Electric did particularly well with systems for the banking industry, and it expanded in Europe through acquisitions of Machines Bull and the Olivetti computer division. But it had difficulty operating at a profit. Concluding the cost of achieving profitability was too high, GE sold most of its computer business to Honeywell in 1970.[45] With GE and RCA out of the general purpose computer business, five of the Seven Dwarfs remained. These were dubbed the BUNCH: Burroughs, the Univac Division of Sperry Rand, NCR, Control Data, and Honeywell.

The Control Data Corporation (CDC) was one of the more successful companies in the computer industry. Founded by William Norris with other former Sperry Rand employees in 1957, its computers accounted for nearly 5 percent of the value of all computers installed worldwide during the late 1960s and early 1970s.[46] The company's success was based on building computers for scientific and engineering computations. Behind that success was Seymour Cray—a computer designer who became a legend.

A key event was CDC's 1960 proposal to build a Stretch-class supercomputer for the Lawrence Radiation Laboratory. In December 1964 this supercomputer was announced as the midrange computer in the CDC 6000 series, which was to consist of the 6400, 6600, and 6800 computers.

Unwilling to be bested by this tiny company, Tom Watson exhorted his engineers to use the most advanced technologies in the yet-to-be announced System/360 Model 90. The sales organization was similarly exhorted not to lose sales to CDC. Burdened by requirements of compatibility with System/360 and by excessively high development costs, the Model 90 (of which there were several versions) proved no match for the more elegant creations of Seymour Cray.[47]

Fearful of the wrath of Watson should they fail, IBM's marketing organizations used unusually aggressive tactics to sell Model 90s. Alleging that these tactics had been predatory and intended to monopolize the market, the Control Data Corporation filed an antitrust suit in December 1968 against IBM, which viewed the case as risky, given the vagaries of the antitrust law, and settled it before it came to trial. The terms included the sale to CDC of IBM's Service Bureau Corporation at its book value of $16 million—probably only a third of its market value. Other features of the settlement provided CDC with cash and contracts worth $101 million.[48]

At the same time that CDC was exploiting the weakness of System/360 at the top of the line, the Digital Equipment Corporation (DEC) was exploiting opportunities below the bottom of the new line. Kenneth H. Olsen, who founded DEC in 1957, had worked closely with Jay Forrester on Project SAGE at MIT. While assisting IBM engineers with Project SAGE in Poughkeepsie, Olsen had learned a lot about the company's manufacturing and management methods. He began his own business quite modestly by making circuit modules for other organizations. By 1960 these modules had become the building blocks for the company's first "programmed data processor," or PDP-1.

As semiconductor circuit technology improved, DEC was able to provide greater function at lower cost. The PDP-8, introduced in 1965 at a price of only $18,000, was very successful. Stimulated by the then-popular miniskirt, someone called the PDP-8 a "minicomputer," and the name stuck. The company's minicomputers were initially used in scientific apparatus to collect data and to control experiments. Later uses were in process control and communication networks. Gradually minicomputers took their place as general purpose computers. From 1963 to 1969 DEC's worldwide revenues increased ninefold to $91 million. In 1980 its revenues reached $2.4 billion, which was almost 10 percent as large as IBM's $26 billion.[49]

Pressure from the BUNCH and from rapidly rising systems suppliers such as DEC, Scientific Data Systems, and Data General increased as these companies positioned themselves to exploit weaknesses of System/360. But it was price competition from plug-compatible manufacturers of peripheral products and from computer leasing companies that gave IBM its greatest challenge.

The Telex Corporation was the first company to provide plug-compatible products for System/360. Already in the business of manufacturing tape drives, Telex offered its first System/360 tape drives in July 1967. Sold at a 50 percent price discount over equivalent IBM equipment, more than three thousand Telex tape drives had been installed on System/360 computers by the end of 1970. The second company to enter the business was Memorex. Its opportunity was provided by IBM's inability to manufacture the newly invented removable disk packs rapidly enough to satisfy customer demand. Already a leading supplier of high-quality magnetic tape for computers, Memorex began manufacturing the more profitable disk packs in 1966. In mid-1968 it began shipping plug-compatible disk drives as well.[50]

Many IBM employees were lured into the plug-compatible business by companies willing to pay a premium for their knowledge of IBM technology and product plans. Others chose to profit more directly by establishing their own companies. For example, Information Storage Systems was founded by twelve IBM employees in San Jose who resigned en masse in December 1967, and the Storage Technology Corporation was founded by four IBM employees in Boulder who resigned in July 1969. By the end of 1970 the companies supplying plug-compatible products had produced considerably less than 10 percent of the tape drives and only 3 percent of the disk drives attached to System/360 computers, but these percentages were growing rapidly.[51]

Among the noteworthy IBM alumni was Alan F. Shugart. Joining the Memorex Corporation as vice president of product development in 1969, he persuaded more than one hundred IBM employees to join him over the years in keeping Memorex's storage products technologically abreast of IBM's. Shugart subsequently founded two successful storage-product companies: Shugart Associates in 1973 and Seagate Technology in 1978.[52]

The existence of computer leasing companies added to IBM's competitive problems. A typical mode of operation was to offer to buy installed System/360 equipment from IBM and lease it back to the user at a lower rental than was being charged by IBM. To show a profit, leasing companies typically assumed a five- to ten-year life for leased equipment, in contrast to the four-year life IBM assumed. If IBM's estimate proved to be more correct, the leasing companies would be in serious financial difficulty in little more than four years—as indeed many were. Leasing companies also provided a ready market for the lower-priced plug-compatible peripheral products. By early 1968 IBM had come to regard leasing companies collectively as potentially its biggest domestic competitor.[53]

If IBM responded to this competition by cutting its own prices, it would be the primary loser because of its larger market share. But if it failed to respond, the leasing companies and plug-compatible manufacturers would continue to gain market share. The company chose a mixed response—an important element of which was to outrun the competition with technological improvements. Although often impeded by the loss of key employees or by outright theft of proprietary information, the strategy nevertheless helped IBM maintain its high profit levels and was a driving force behind dramatic improvements in computer cost-performance.

20

Onrush of Technology

The introduction of System/360 was so fraught with difficulties that Tom Watson and his engineering managers had little time to celebrate its successes. There had been delays in shipping hardware and software, the performance of the software was below expectations, and competitive announcements threatened the company's installed computers and raised doubts about its new product line.

Nothing caused greater concern, however, than the negative reception accorded SLT. Government agencies that were funding the development of *monolithic* integrated circuits were quick to belittle SLT. Monolithic integrated circuits had one or more circuits fabricated on a single silicon chip, whereas SLT used several chips to make one circuit. Component vendors, whose sales were diminished by IBM's decision to manufacture its own components, were also critical. Gleefully reported by the trade press, these denigrations of SLT unnerved many of IBM's executives.

Concerns that SLT would not be competitive proved to be unfounded. Several years of research and development by many companies would be required before monolithic integrated circuits became as cost effective as SLT. In the long run, however, the concern was valid. Dramatic progress in achieving ever lower costs with integrated circuits was a dominant factor behind decades of growth of the computer industry. Continued success for IBM would depend on its ability to remain at the leading edge of technology—and to adjust its products and marketing methods as new business opportunities were created and old ones were diminished.

Going after Monolithics

A year before the first System/360 computers were shipped, John Haanstra had already concluded that progress in monolithic integrated circuits would rapidly make obsolete the company's new computers. Ousted as president of the General Products Division for opposing System/360, Haanstra saw integrated circuits as an opportunity to regain a leadership position. In a report to management issued in September 1964, he asserted that IBM was more than two years behind TI, Motorola, and Fairchild. He urged an aggressive program to catch up and get ahead. At a time when the leading semiconductor companies were struggling to fabricate fewer than five circuits on a chip, Haanstra boldly set a goal of ten to one hundred.[1]

Pressured by his brother to "make sure the 360 wasn't going to be obsolete before it was even delivered," Dick Watson ordered the technology development divisions to begin working together "to design the next generation machine." Monolithic integrated circuits and other advanced technologies were to be used.[2] To pursue this effort, while at the same time introducing System/360, Dick Watson restructured the company's development and manufacturing organizations in January 1965. The Components Division was abolished; its manufacturing activities were incorporated in a new Systems Manufacturing Division and its development activities, in a new Systems Development Division (SDD). The manufacturing division was to concentrate on producing System/360 while SDD was to create the next generation of machines.[3]

John Haanstra was appointed president of SDD. System and component development had been combined in one division because Haanstra and others believed the ability to put many circuits on a single chip required that systems and components be designed together. Haanstra envisioned the next generation machines to be at least as great a leap forward as System/360 was from its predecessors. To accomplish this, the new machines were to have an entirely new operating system as well.

A firm believer in the "needs-capability" management concept, Haanstra asked his system designers to specify the component needs and the component developers to provide the capability. To minimize the difficulty of achieving their own objectives, the system designers set very aggressive goals for new components. When the hapless component developers complained that the

goals set for them could not be achieved, Haanstra was uncon-
vinced. "You are telling me what *you are capable of* rather than
responding to the *needs*," he admonished them. Managers who
expressed reluctance to accept the goals were advised that others
would be happy to have their jobs.[4]

Semiconductor technology groups were additionally under
pressure to help solve problems in manufacturing components
for System/360. When failure to solve manufacturing problems
fast enough forced Tom Watson to announce a two- to four-
month delay in product shipments in October 1965, he took
quick action. He relieved his brother of responsibility for development and manufacturing and put Vin Learson in charge. By
the time Learson had gotten System/360 shipments back on
schedule, Haanstra had been removed as president of SDD. The
effort to achieve his unrealistic product development objectives
had contributed to the difficulties in getting System/360 products
manufactured and shipped on time.[5]

Operating under more realistic guidelines, the development
groups created integrated circuits that fell far short of the objectives originally set by Haanstra. The circuits were, nevertheless,
equivalent to the best available from outside the company. First
used on the System/360 Model 85 announced in January 1968,
the IBM integrated circuits had one to four circuits on each
silicon chip. Up to four chips were mounted on a half-inch-square
ceramic module similar to an SLT module. The copper balls that
electrically coupled SLT chips to printed lines on ceramic modules had been replaced by a proprietary solder-ball technology
that allowed for higher circuit densities.[6]

The most significant technological advance on the Model 85
was introduction of the first *cache*. This was a small high-speed
buffer (made of monolithic semiconductor memory elements)
that was coupled to the main memory in such a manner that the
combination achieved almost the high speed of semiconductor
devices with the low cost of ferrite-core memories. Whenever a
word was requested from memory during the execution of a
program, a block of many words (containing the requested word)
was moved into the high-speed cache.

For a well-designed cache and memory combination, the frequency with which needed words were found to be already in the
high-speed cache was typically greater than 95 percent—resulting
in an effective memory speed nearly as fast as the cache. The use
of a cache to improve memory performance soon became a

Figure 20.1. System/360 Model 85
Announced in January 1968, the Model 85 was the first computer equipped
with a cache. It also had IBM's first processor to be built entirely with monolithic integrated circuits. The configuration pictured here shows the processor, in which the cache is located (center). Surrounding it (clockwise from
lower left) are data channels, tape drives, printers and control units, disk
drives, card input-output units, and main memory.

standard feature of almost all computers. Even after semiconductor devices replaced ferrite cores as the primary memory elements, computers typically featured memory structures in which
a small high-speed cache enhanced the performance of a lower-
cost main memory.[7]

System/370

The first two of the next-generation computers were announced
in June 1970 as the System/370 Models 155 and 165. The designation 370 was chosen to suggest it was a system for the decade
of the 1970s. Rather than being the dramatic leap forward envisioned by Haanstra, System/370 was an evolutionary extension of
System/360. The use of monolithic integrated circuits and a
cache nevertheless gave the processors a fourfold improvement

in performance over the models they replaced. The reliability of the circuits was ten times better than SLT, which was itself nearly one hundred times more reliable than the SMS it had replaced. Crucial to the success of the new systems was a two-times faster (2,000 lines per minute) printer and a disk storage unit that offered twice the access speed and three times the storage capacity per disk pack. With eight disk packs per unit, the new IBM 3330 Disk Storage, announced with System/370 in June 1970, offered 30-millisecond average access time to 800 megabytes of on-line storage.[8]

An important architectural change was the addition of 6 instructions to the 143 available in System/360. The new instructions provided better performance in certain operations. Their greater significance, however, was from a marketing perspective. They would hasten the obsolescence of the older systems. System/360 processors would not be able to execute System/370 programs that incorporated any of the new instructions, whereas the new processors would be able to execute any old or new program written for System/360.[9]

The two technological advances of System/370 that actually did the most to make earlier computers obsolete were not initially available. The first of these was the industry's first all-semiconductor main memory. Its introduction on the System/370 Model 145 in September 1970 signaled the beginning of years of IBM leadership in semiconductor memories. This leadership was even more important to IBM's success than had been its earlier leadership in ferrite-core memories. Haanstra's early emphasis on developing semiconductor memories during his brief tenure as president of SDD deserves considerable credit. Another important factor was invention of the cache. This gave IBM practical experience in manufacturing semiconductor memory devices (for the cache) long before the low costs needed for main memories could have been achieved.[10]

The second major advance was "dynamic relocation." This permitted programs to be written with "virtual addresses" that were converted to real memory addresses at execution time. A translator built into the system, with a combination of hardware and software, converted the addresses automatically. As described at the time, this provided a "virtual memory that, as far as the programmer is concerned, is directly addressable as if it were main memory. The size of this virtual memory is limited only by the address field and not by installation economics."[11] If the

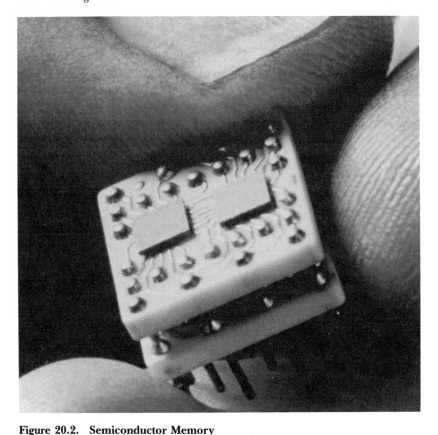

Figure 20.2. Semiconductor Memory
The two-level ceramic module holds four semiconductor memory chips.
Each chip contains 128 bits of memory. These modules were used in the
industry's first all-semiconductor main memory, announced on the
System/370 Model 145 computer in September 1970. Twenty years later
IBM announced its RISC System/6000 workstations with semiconductor
memory chips, having a capacity of 4 million bits each.

virtual memory size required by a program exceeded the amount
of real memory, the system automatically moved "pages" of information between disk storage and main memory to satisfy the
needs of the program.

The concept of enhancing the apparent size of main memory
by "paging" information automatically between it and a slower
storage device was not new with System/370. The first practical
implementation of this was on the Atlas computer, developed by
Manchester University and Ferranti Limited in England. First
operational in a customer's facility in late 1962, Atlas automat-

ically paged information between a ferrite-core memory and a larger-capacity rotating magnetic drum storage device.[12]

Although IBM system designers were well aware of these techniques, they chose not to implement them in System/360 because there was little information on the performance of paging systems on general applications. But when MIT and the Bell Telephone Laboratories began working with General Electric to modify one of its computers to provide this capability for terminal-oriented applications, Learson insisted that IBM also provide it. As a result, the System/360 Model 67 was developed. Delivered to customers beginning nine months after it was announced in August 1965, the Model 67 provided automatic paging between main memory and a magnetic disk storage device. Performance data from Model 67s, handling customer applications, was used in the design of dynamic relocation techniques that implemented virtual memory on System/370.

Bob Evans's role in putting virtual memory on System/370 computers—after the first two were announced—is revealing of the management processes and turmoil in IBM during the 1960s. Evans says he was removed from System/360 leadership in January 1965 primarily because of his failure to offer this capability. An era of conservatism then swept through the development organization following Haanstra's removal as president of SDD. Virtual memory was once again judged to be too speculative for use in mainline products. When Evans returned to the company's mainline activities as president of SDD in October 1969, he "decided not to be punished twice for the same mistake" and immediately reinstated virtual memory in the product plans for System/370.[13]

The FS Failure

The announcement of System/370 in June 1970 coincided with an industrywide business decline. Orders failed to achieve projections. Concern was growing in IBM and the rest of the industry that the financial decline was indicative of more serious long-term problems. In particular, the cost of computer hardware was dropping so rapidly that new customers and applications would have to be found at an alarming rate just to maintain the same dollar value of sales each year.

The situation looked particularly grim in IBM because its technologists were overly optimistic about future achievements. With the first all-semiconductor main memory about to be announced, the research and development groups were projecting the cost per bit would drop thirtyfold during the next five years, and another thirtyfold by the end of the decade. By these projections IBM would have to install 900 times as much computer memory capacity in 1980 as it did in 1970 just to maintain its current revenue. To achieve its traditional 15 percent annual revenue growth rate in memory devices, IBM would have to ship 3,600 times as much memory capacity during the last year of the decade as it did during the first. A similar line of reasoning indicated that 40 times as much disk storage capacity would have to be installed per year at the end of the decade.

Although the cost-reduction projection for memory was about ten times higher than actually occurred, the qualitative message was correct. The industry's success in lowering the costs of its products would greatly reduce its future revenues unless innovative new uses were found for computer power, and especially for memory capacity.[14]

Assessing this situation in December 1970, the Corporate Technical Committee urged that a SPREAD-like task force be established to set goals for what was already being called the Future System, or simply FS. In August 1971 the proposed task force was established with John R. Opel in charge. Opel, who became IBM president in 1974, had joined the company as a sales representative in 1949 immediately after receiving his master's degree in business administration from the University of Chicago. Selected as Tom Watson's administrative assistant in 1959, he rose rapidly and was in charge of the corporate finance and planning staffs when he was put in charge of the FS task force. Other task force members included several of the company's top technical leaders.

A major goal for FS was to reduce the cost of developing application programs. This was considered essential because of the growing shortage of programmers and the high costs involved. Customers at the time were spending twice as much money on programmers and other computing-center personnel as they were on hardware. If FS could be structured to reduce the number of people required to program and operate computers, IBM would receive a higher fraction of the money spent by customers for information processing.[15]

The most promising proposal considered by the task force was based on an exploratory system under study at the company's

T. J. Watson Research Center in Yorktown Heights. Users of the proposed system would not have to concern themselves with the amount or type of main memory and storage or where any particular information might be stored. All physical memory and storage was to be represented to the user as if it were a *single-level store*. Addressing was to be *object-oriented* rather than location-oriented, and information stored anywhere in the system would be addressed by the user in the same manner.[16]

There were insufficient experimental data on automatic, system-managed storage hierarchies to guarantee success in this endeavor. The success of the cache, however, which moved information automatically between main memory and a high-speed buffer, and the success of automatic paging between disk and main memory on the System/360 Model 67, gave considerable encouragement. The potential benefits were sufficiently great that the risk of a major development effort seemed warranted. The single-level store became a central feature of FS.[17]

Development resources were increasingly committed to FS during 1972 in an effort reminiscent of the one that produced System/360. The increased complexities of computers and of the international market they served were reflected in the size and complexity of the FS effort. Intended to provide user-friendly interfaces for professional programmers and novices alike, the internal structure of FS was far from simple. Conflicting views of the many development groups were difficult to resolve because few, if any, understood the entire FS architecture. New problems were uncovered as rapidly as old ones were solved. Schedules slipped so badly that the number of months projected before announcement of FS was forty-five in the spring of 1974, just as it had been in the fall of 1971 when the Opel task force completed its work.[18]

By the fall of 1974 it was clear that the company's System/370 computers would be in serious jeopardy in the marketplace long before FS could be shipped. Following extensive consultations with key technical leaders and top corporate executives, Bob Evans undertook the painful task of seeking the best way to terminate FS and to "extend the architecture of System 360/370."[19] In February 1975 the FS effort was terminated. Although much of the hardware developed for FS could be modified for use in any new computer, most of the system design, microcode, and software were discarded. It was the most expensive development failure in the company's history.[20]

Many causes for the FS failure have been suggested. Frequently cited is the attempt to achieve so many technological advances in a project in which all advances had to be accomplished on the same schedule and had to function compatibly with one another. Other frequently cited causes are the complexity of the FS architecture itself and the complexity of coordinating a development effort among laboratories throughout the world. Returning to IBM from the University of North Carolina as a part-time consultant in June 1973, Fred Brooks summarized the documented description of FS architecture with one word, "Incomprehensible." Concerning the overall project, he observed, "Complexity is the fatal foe."[21]

Another important factor was the change in market conditions. Beginning as a proprietary development, 360-370 architecture had become such a dominant worldwide standard that many of IBM's competitors had a vested interest in perpetuating it. Among these were leasing companies whose profitability depended upon keeping 360-370 computers (purchased from IBM) installed as long as possible. Had IBM developed and introduced FS, the leasing companies would have vigorously resisted its installation by their customers.

Leasing companies were already cutting their costs and upgrading the systems they rented to customers by purchasing magnetic tape and disk storage devices from plug-compatible manufacturers. Yet greater improvements in the performance of these systems could be achieved with the addition of more plug-compatible memories and peripheral devices. Several engineering firms and independent software developers were ready to help leasing companies upgrade their systems. Customers that had chosen to purchase rather than rent systems from IBM would also carefully weigh the benefits of new FS functions against the more easily understood option of upgrading their installed systems.

These impediments to a successful introduction of FS—no matter how good it might have been—were exacerbated by independent manufacturers of 360-370 compatible processors. Among these was Gene M. Amdahl, a key architect of the original System/360 line who had left IBM in 1970 to develop and manufacture large IBM-compatible processors. Significant funding for his company came from Japanese and German computer companies that intended to use the Amdahl Corporation as a means for obtaining advanced computer technology and for entering the

U.S. computer market. Gene Amdahl's technical and management skills, his knowledge of IBM technology and business plans,
and the source of his funding made his corporation a serious
threat.[22]

Only four months after FS was terminated, the first Amdahl
computer was installed. Known as the Amdahl 470 V/6, this
System/370-compatible computer was targeted for the top of the
IBM line. Two agonizing years passed before IBM was able to
complete its shift in development emphasis and announce its first
"post-FS" computer. Not surprisingly it was a high-end computer,
capable of competing with Amdahl's offerings. "The 3033 Processor, a member of the System/370 family, together with extensions to MVS and System/370 architecture, will provide large
systems users with significantly increased data processing capability," the IBM March 1977 announcement asserted. Built under
the leadership of John E. Bertram, who had proposed the plan
for shifting from FS back to 360-370 architecture, the 3033 lived
up to its billing and successfully blocked Amdahl's effort to dominate the high end of the mainframe computer business.[23]

Strategic Concerns

The termination of FS climaxed a decade of uncertainty about
the future of System/360 and its underlying architecture. Fears
that rapid progress in integrated circuits would cause its early
demise were replaced by recognition that it had become an
industry standard in which IBM had the largest investment. Protecting that investment was fundamental to the company's future.

The validity of that strategy is readily confirmed. In 1989, a
quarter of a century after System/360 was announced, products
based on 360 architecture and its extensions still accounted for
more than half of IBM's revenue and a much higher fraction of
its profits. This architecture was also the basis of more than 70
percent of the estimated $160 billion worldwide inventory of all
computers priced over $1 million and more than 50 percent of
the $260 billion worldwide inventory of all computers priced over
$100,000. The vast majority of installed computers based on 360
architecture and its extensions had been manufactured by IBM,
although an increasing number were being supplied by Fujitsu
Limited and Hitachi Limited, frequently through cooperative
arrangements with vendors such as the Amdahl Corporation.[24]

A critical problem faced by IBM was that no computers priced under $100,000 used an architecture based on System/360, and by 1989 these lower-priced computers already accounted for half of the worldwide inventory. Even when System/360 was announced in April 1964, the company's engineers had been unable to achieve compatibility in systems smaller than the Model 30. For this reason the Model 20 (announced in November) was not fully compatible.[25]

In July 1969 the IBM System/3 had been announced in an effort to satisfy the needs of yet smaller businesses. There was no pretense of compatibility with System/360. System/3 even featured a smaller punched card that was $2\frac{5}{8}$ inches high and $3\frac{1}{4}$ inches wide. Six-bit characters were employed, and round holes were used to encode up to 96 characters per card. Designed with the company's new monolithic integrated circuits, System/3 rented for less than $1,000 per month, which was half the typical price of a System/360 Model 20.[26]

In October 1969 the IBM General Systems Division was established to manufacture System/3 and to develop future low-cost systems. A significant accomplishment of this division was revealed by the October 1978 announcement of the IBM System/38, designed to replace the successful but aging System/3. Under development since 1973 in the General Systems Division's laboratory in Rochester, Minnesota, System/38 incorporated many advanced features originally planned for FS. These included a single-level store, object-oriented addressing, and a high-level machine interface to the user. Developing these features for the small system was easier than for FS because of the limited market and simpler applications for which it was intended.[27] System/38 achieved considerable popularity in the early 1980s, and its successor AS/400 series was even more successful. As the decade of the 1990s began, the annual revenue from the AS/400 series and related products exceeded the total annual revenue of the Digital Equipment Corporation, which had the second highest revenue in the computer industry.[28]

As a low-end product, the AS/400 was relatively expensive, however, with prices ranging up to more than $500,000. What IBM needed was a strategy for competing in the market for truly low-cost systems and computer terminals, which had grown rapidly since the late 1960s.

The company's Office Products Division appeared to be well positioned to play a major role in such a strategy. Its products included typewriters, magnetic-tape- and magnetic-card-driven typewriters, communicating typewriters, copiers, and dictating equipment. Previously called the Electric Typewriter Division, it had become a "completely autonomous operation" in 1955 so it could better control its costs and operate in the spartan manner needed in its price-sensitive market.[29] As noted in a memorandum written for the Corporate Technical Committee in 1970, "The data processing world is evolving toward a state in which terminals and office products are virtually indistinguishable." By combining some of the systems design capabilities of other divisions with the manufacturing, marketing, and service capabilities of the Office Products Division, there was "an opportunity to enter this new marketplace while taking advantage of the traditional IBM strengths."[30]

Thus as the 1970s began, IBM appeared to be well structured to prosper in office equipment and small systems. This apparent strength was dissipated, however, by ill-defined and conflicting missions of the Office Products, General Systems, and Systems Development divisions. Furthermore because office products, terminals, and small systems typically had lower profit margins than large systems, it was difficult to get corporate management interested in new product initiatives.[31]

A relatively unsuccessful effort to market the fifty-pound IBM 5100 portable computer, introduced at a price of $9,000 to $20,000 in 1975, confirmed for many that there was little future for IBM in small computers.[32] At the same time, however, several companies (including Apple, Atari, Commodore, and Tandy) successfully introduced personal computers, and industrywide sales of small computers began increasing at a rate in excess of 50 percent per year.

The IBM PC

Determined to overcome all internal impediments to the successful introduction of small computers, the Corporate Management Committee took extraordinary action in 1980. To develop, manufacture, and market an IBM PC, it established an independent business unit (IBU) in the company's laboratory in Boca Raton, Florida. An attractive feature of an IBU was its ability to provide "small-company" flexibility and incentives to groups developing products outside IBM's main line of business. Application of the IBU concept to a product intended to expand the company's traditional business at the low end entailed considerable risk, but it appeared to be the only way to bring about the many changes in business practices that were likely to be needed.[33]

Given considerable freedom to chart its own course, the Boca Raton IBU adopted many policies and practices that were unusual in IBM. To achieve broad market acceptance, for example, the PC was to have an open rather than proprietary architecture. To reduce development time and costs, the operating system was to be purchased from an independent software firm, and hardware components were to be open for competitive bids from inside and outside the company. In perhaps the most dramatic departure from tradition, the PCs were to be sold through retail channels rather than by the company's highly touted (and costly) sales force.[34]

Spurred on by a brilliant advertising campaign that featured Charlie Chaplin's little tramp, sales of the PC soared beyond all expectations. But lacking proprietary control over the PC's basic design elements, the company was soon faced by competition from lower-priced IBM-compatible computers. Manufacturers of these clones often obtained their components from the same vendors that supplied IBM—thus making it difficult to convince buyers that the company's higher-priced products were superior. Even more significant was the company's inability to provide customers with service that was substantially better than that of its competitors. The costs of IBM's traditional service were judged to be far too high, and no satisfactory low-cost alternative was found. The limited service provided to PC customers represented a significant departure from past practice. It will be recalled that Tom Watson had promoted the idea that "IBM means service." His father had insisted on providing the best service in the industry. And Herman Hollerith had refused to install any equipment until he had assured himself that it would handle the customer's jobs effectively.

RISC Architecture

The sustained success of System/360 architecture, combined with the failure of FS, created yet another problem. Product managers in IBM had become resistant to almost any new architectural proposals—including the RISC (Reduced Instruction Set Computer) architecture. Based primarily on ideas of IBM Fellow John

Figure 20.3. The IBM Personal Computer
Announced in August 1981, the IBM Personal Computer (PC) used an Intel
(16-bit, 4.77 megahertz) microprocessor and a disk operating system (DOS)
supplied by Microsoft. Memory capacities from 16 KB to 256 KB were available as were one to two disk drives with capacities of 160 KB each (KB =
1,024 bytes). The IBM PCs were sold through IBM Product Centers, Com-
puterland, and Sears, Roebuck and Company. Prices ranged from $1,565 to
approximately $6,300. The system shown above with the standard 80-charac-
ter-per-second dot-matrix printer, keyboard, system unit (with two disk
drives), and monitor sold for approximately $4,500.

Cocke, RISC architecture gives small computers several times the performance of those designed with earlier architectures. First implemented in the experimental 801 Minicomputer, named after the IBM 801 Building (Watson Research Center) in which it was built, RISC met considerable resistance in a company dedicated to extending the 360-370 architecture. Although IBM used RISC in the input-output processors of its 3090 series of large computers beginning in 1985 and then in its RT PC workstation announced in 1986, it did not fully embrace the architecture until the RISC System/6000 family of advanced workstations was announced in February 1990. By then the power of RISC had been exploited in the marketplace by Sun Microsystems, Hewlett Packard, and others—forcing IBM to catch up with its own technology.

The RISC System/6000, as announced in 1990, exemplified the dramatic onrush of technology during the twenty-six years since System/360 was first announced. Even the most powerful model (POWERserver 540) sat inconspicuously beside a desk rather than filling a large room. It processed 41 million instructions per second, making it five to fifty times more powerful (depending on problem mix) than the most powerful of the early System/360 models. Its electronic logic circuitry had up to 800,000 transistors per silicon chip versus only 1 transistor per chip as first announced with System/360. Its maximum memory size of 256 megabytes was just 256 times more than was offered on the largest of the early System/360 line, and its internal disk storage capacity of 2.5 gigabytes was 25 times the capacity of the 24-inch diameter, 25-disk module of the IBM 2302 Disk Storage announced with System/360 in April 1964.[35]

21

Demands of the Future

The announcement of IBM's RISC System/6000 was made one century after Herman Hollerith won the contract to tabulate the census of 1890. During the intervening one hundred years, dramatic changes had occurred in the technology, operation, and public perception of information processing systems. The public had had little awareness of their existence during the first fifty years, except for Social Security checks printed and issued on punched cards beginning in the 1930s. During the second fifty years, public awareness increased significantly as electronic technologies made possible previously unimagined applications in the exploration of outer space, the production of nuclear power, airline reservation systems, factory automation, medical systems, and many others.

By the end of the 1960s IBM management had determined that continued growth of the industry could be achieved only by making the power of computers more directly available to wider segments of society. The Future System (FS) project was established to accomplish this objective. Emphasis on FS, however, tended to obscure the need for other decisions. The company's inability to achieve adequately low costs in terminals and small systems, for example, had been expected to be offset by FS's control of the entire system. To ensure compatibility, customers were likely to have a strong initial preference for attaching IBM peripheral devices to FS.

With termination of FS and continued reliance on architectural extensions of System/360, customer acceptance of peripheral devices supplied by other vendors was expected to continue to increase. Indeed all the anticipated problems that had triggered the decision to develop FS were unchanged. Product costs and prices were continuing to decline at an exponential rate, and competition was increasing. It appeared unlikely that IBM could maintain for long both its dominant market share and its high profit margins. An upturn in demand for computers had delayed the day of reckoning, but it was only a matter of time before the onrush of technology would force dramatic changes in product strategy.

New Leaders

New decisions and actions were urgently needed, but the "take charge" leaders who had driven IBM into large-scale electronic computers and ushered in the System/360 era were no longer available. Tom Watson had resigned as chief executive officer following a heart attack in November 1970.[1] His typical twelve- to fourteen-hour days and the strain of System/360 had taken their toll. Consistent with his standard approach to any major IBM problem, he had put Learson in charge. This temporary transfer of authority became final when the board of directors elected Learson chairman and CEO beginning in June 1971. Learson's term lasted only until December 1972 because a new IBM policy required senior corporate executives to resign in the year in which they turned sixty.[2]

Speculation abounds that the policy was established to prevent certain individuals from assuming higher positions or from staying in those positions too long. Officially the policy was established to provide advancement opportunities for the large number of competent people who had been hired into the company during the postwar years. Concerning his own successor as CEO, Tom Watson had apparently never believed it should be Learson. Watson's heart attack forced a change in plans, but only briefly.

Watson said he selected Frank T. Cary to be his successor when Dick Watson left the company in 1970 to become the U.S. ambassador to France. Cary, who had a master's degree in business administration from Stanford University, had joined IBM as a marketing representative in Los Angeles in 1948. Rising rapidly in the sales and marketing organizations, he became an IBM vice president and group executive and general manager of the Data Processing Group in 1966 and a member of the board of directors in 1968. "He rarely spoke up at meetings," Watson recalled, "and it wasn't his style to step in and save the day the way Learson and

I did. He didn't make heroic moves and he didn't make glaring mistakes; when he ran into a problem he simply figured out how to fix it."[3]

Fixing the immediate problems caused by the termination of FS was relatively easy. A backup plan for improving System/370 with new hardware and software was put in place. The time lost in developing the new products was costly, but not devastating. Finding a solution for the longer-term problems was not so easy. Conservatism bred in the FS failure and the continuing profitability of extensions to System/360 inhibited decisive action during the 1970s.

Antitrust Issues

Adding to the problems Cary faced was an antitrust suit filed by the U.S. Department of Justice in January 1969. Concluding that IBM's size gave it excessive powers, the department sought to break the company into smaller competitive units

As is often the case in antitrust suits, a key issue was definition of the market that was alleged to have been monopolized. The Department of Justice chose to define the market so as to exclude leasing companies, plug-compatible manufacturers, companies such as DEC whose computers it judged to be not general purpose, and companies that provided only some of the products and services in the government's arbitrarily defined market. By this definition, IBM's share of the revenue was about 70 percent throughout the 1960s and 1970s. If one summed up the revenues for computer products and services of the one hundred top companies in the computer industry, as IBM chose to do in its defense, however, its share would have dropped from nearly 60 percent in the mid-1950s to less than 40 percent by 1969 when the suit was filed.[4]

The antitrust suit droned on for thirteen years. The trial itself did not begin until May 1975, and it lasted six years. The management of the trial is incomprehensible. The judge, for example, required that page after page of deposition testimony be read into the record so he could hear them. Then he routinely absented himself from court while they were being read. The trial called upon 974 witnesses and produced 104,400 transcript pages.[5] Finally in January 1982 the government dropped the case, asserting it had been "without merit."

The decision was long overdue according to most knowledgeable observers. After reading much of the trial transcript and interviewing scores of participants, the editor of *American Lawyer* described the trial as "a farce of such mindboggling proportions that any lawyer who now tries to find out about it so he can explain it to a client or a friend will be risking the same quicksand that devoured the lawyers involved in the case." Concerning the primary issue in the case, he said, "The reality of the 1970s and 1980s is that IBM had and has no monopoly unless one strains, as the government trial lawyers persisted in doing, to gerrymander a bizarre market definition."[6]

In the meantime IBM had spent tens of millions of dollars per year to defend itself. An even greater cost was the involvement of key executives who might better have concentrated on new business. Furthermore, all major business decisions made during those thirteen years had to be analyzed for their impact on the antitrust case. The government's suit also encouraged several companies to file their own antitrust suits against IBM. Every one of these was decided in IBM's favor, but the cost was high.[7]

Recalling that Tom Watson chose to settle the antitrust case of 1952 so he could concentrate on business matters—and that Hollerith finally gave up fighting the government in 1910 for similar reasons—one can ponder the wisdom of fighting the case filed in 1969. Many of the reasons for fighting appear to have vanished with the FS failure. Unable to create a new system architecture capable of dominating the market, IBM could only anticipate increasing fragmentation of its marketplace and a declining benefit from its own size.

Considering the heavy constraints antitrust enforcement placed on IBM's ability to compete, it might have been wiser to break the company into several smaller units as the government proposed. Support for this view is provided by the experience of AT&T. Yielding to government pressure, it agreed to divest itself of its local telephone business in the same year that IBM "won" its antitrust case. After that the value of AT&T stock more than doubled whereas the value of IBM stock declined. "I am convinced," the CEO of AT&T told shareholders in 1994, "that the breakup forced us to make changes in the 1980s that prepared us for the competitive challenges we are confronting in the 1990s."[8]

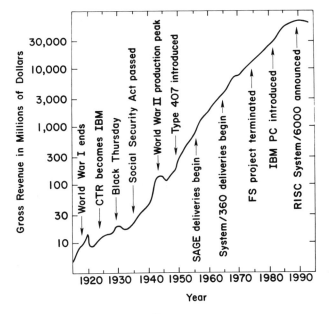

Figure 21.1.   IBM's Gross Revenue
The worldwide gross revenue of IBM increased 15,000-fold from 1915 to
1993 as revealed by this logarithmic graph. Shown in millions of dollars per
year, the revenue is not adjusted for inflation. Some key events in the company's history are indicated.

Coda

From the vantage point of the early 1990s, it is difficult not to
emphasize the recent difficulties IBM has experienced. But in
reviewing the company's history and the dramatic social and
technological changes it has survived, one cannot help but be
impressed more by its successes than by its failures. Its decades
of effective responses to dramatic technological changes, beginning in the 1940s, are particularly noteworthy. Many companies
flourished briefly and then floundered while IBM moved forward
with apparent invincibility. Not until the mid-1980s did the company's financial performance give clear evidence of the difficulties it was experiencing as the cost of computer technology
continued to spiral downward.[9]

Key to IBM's long-term success had been the absolute commitment of Herman Hollerith, Thomas J. Watson, Sr., and Thomas J. Watson, Jr. They understood the importance of technology

and were continually active in the crucial interfaces between technical developments and business strategies. They demanded the best from themselves and their subordinates. They were quick to punish and quick to reward. They insisted on satisfying the needs and desires of their customers. And both Watsons cultivated relationships with people inside and outside the company that kept them alert to changes in technology, competition, and customer requirements.

In words as valid today as they were when spoken in 1932, Watson, Sr., asserted, "There is no business in the world which can hope to move forward if it does not keep abreast of the times, look into the future and study the probable demands of the future."[10]

Appendixes

Appendix A: IBM Worldwide Revenues and Year-End Population

Year	Revenues in $ Million		Year-End Population	
	Gross Income	Net Earnings	U.S.A.	Total
1914	4	1	1,217	1,346
1915	4	1	1,517	1,672
1916	6	1	2,323	2,529
1917	8	1	2,851	3,063
1918	9	1	2,848	3,127
1919	11	2	2,660	3,139
1920	14	2	2,437	2,731
1921	9	1	2,487	3,001
1922	9	1	2,432	3,043
1923	11	2	2,399	3,161
1924	11	2	2,472	3,384
1925	13	3	2,633	3,698
1926	14	4	2,741	3,953
1927	14	4	3,133	4,866
1928	15	5	3,491	5,102
1929	18	7	4,189	5,999
1930	19	7	4,339	6,346
1931	19	7	4,334	6,331
1932	17	6	4,946	6,311
1933	17	6	6,591	8,202
1934	19	7	5,674	7,613
1935	21	7	6,268	8,654
1936	25	8	6,474	9,142
1937	31	8	7,589	10,834
1938	34	9	7,602	11,046
1939	38	9	7,610	11,315
1940	45	9	8,602	12,656
1941	60	10	10,170	14,207
1942	86	8	14,703	18,754
1943	131	9	17,262	21,251
1944	140	10	15,133	21,126
1945	138	11	14,476	18,257
1946	116	19	16,977	22,492
1947	139	24	16,556	22,591

Year	Revenues in $ Million		Year-End Population	
	Gross Income	Net Earnings	U.S.A.	Total
1948	156	28	18,292	24,940
1949	183	33	18,938	27,236
1950	266	37	20,702	30,261
1951	335	32	24,255	35,124
1952	412	34	28,614	41,458
1953	497	39	30,810	46,170
1954	570	59	33,732	50,225
1955	696	73	39,033	56,297
1956	892	87	51,192	72,504
1957	1,203	110	60,281	83,588
1958	1,418	152	61,159	86,736
1959	1,613	176	65,646	94,912
1960	1,817	205	70,050	104,241
1961	2,202	254	75,954	116,276
1962	2,591	305	81,493	127,468
1963	2,863	364	87,173	137,612
1964	3,239	431	96,532	149,834
1965	3,573	477	111,087	172,445
1966	4,248	526	129,023	198,186
1967	5,345	651	144,206	221,866
1968	6,889	871	154,874	241,974
1969	7,197	934	159,976	258,662
1970	7,504	1,018	156,859	269,291
1971	8,274	1,079	149,022	265,493
1972	9,533	1,279	146,895	262,152
1973	10,993	1,575	152,177	274,108
1974	12,675	1,838	160,542	292,350
1975	14,437	1,990	156,938	288,647
1976	16,304	2,398	158,380	291,977
1977	18,133	2,719	170,808	310,155
1978	21,076	3,111	181,057	325,517
1979	22,863	3,011	190,448	337,119
1980	26,213	3,397	194,423	341,279
1981	29,070	3,610	205,230	354,936
1982	34,364	4,409	214,434	364,796
1983	40,180	5,485	218,671	369,545
1984	46,309	6,582	238,955[1]	394,930[1]
1985	50,718	6,555	242,541	405,535
1986	52,160	4,789	237,274	403,508
1987	55,256	5,258	227,949	389,348
1988	59,598	5,741	223,208	387,112
1989	62,654	3,722	215,929	383,220
1990	68,931	5,967	205,421	373,289
1991	64,766	(2,861)	190,666	344,396
1992	64,523	(4,965)	161,980	301,542
1993	62,716	(8,101)	125,000	256,207

1. Includes Rolm Corp. (9,902).

Note: Business Machines of 8 May 1941 reported that there were 250 persons in "this business," presumably EAM, in 1914 and 11,000 persons in 1941; *Business*

Machines of 16 April 1942 reported that there were 250 persons in the business in 1914 and over 12,000 "today." The number of employees worldwide peaked at 407,080 in 1986.

Source: Based on data assembled by the IBM archives and from IBM Annual Reports.

Appendix B: IBM's Early Patents Filed on Tabulators and Time Recorders during Five-Year Periods

Filing Date	All CTR-IBM Inventors	Bryce	Carrol	Ford	Lake	Peirce
1911–15	11	3	0	0	0	7
1916–20	65	30	1	0	7	3
1921–25	143	42	11	7	21	12
1926–30	301	52	29	16	3	20
1931–35	363	45	13	10	24	12
1936–40	305	44	14	8	20	1
1941–45	405	21	10	3	21	0
1946–50	513	7	9	6	11	0
Totals	2106	244	87	50	107	55

Source: Based on data in the IBM Patent Digest of 12 February 1952.

Appendix C: Early Electronic Computing Circuit Patents

Filed	U.S. Pat.	Title	Inventor(s)	Company
1/20/40	2,580,740	Accounting Apparatus	Dickinson	IBM
3/20/40	2,595,045	Calculating Machine	Desch, Mumma	NCR
7/18/40	2,404,739	Calculating Machine	Mumma	NCR
5/23/41	2,402,989	Accounting Apparatus	Dickinson	IBM
5/23/41	2,580,741	Accounting Apparatus	Dickinson	IBM
8/25/42	2,446,945	Electronic Computing Device	Morton, Flory	RCA
11/02/42	2,409,689	Electronic Computing Device	Morton, Flory	RCA

Source: B. E. Phelps, 1980: "Early Electronic Computer Developments at IBM," *Annals of the History of Computing 2*, pp. 253-67.

Appendix D: IBM U.S. Product Revenues by Year (in $ millions)

Year	SAGE	Other Military	604 and CPC	Commercial Stored Program Computers	IBM U.S. Total
1952	1	29	9	0	334
1953	4	49	13	1	410
1954	14	42	17	4	461
1955	47	35	21	12	564
1956	93	28	23	49	734
1957	122	70	26	124	1000
1958	100	111	29	209	1172
1959	97	90	30	306	1310
1960	57	72	31	399	1436
1961	10	173	31	556	1694
1962	13	120	25	797	1925
1963	0	60	20	1045	2060
1964	0	56	16	1305	2288

Note: Revenues from product programs that were significant to IBM's entry into commercial electronic computers are depicted in this table. Particularly important in the early years was the revenue and associated experience gained from the 604 and CPC products. Revenue began in 1948 and exceeded that from commercial stored-program computers through 1955. SAGE development began almost two years after commercial stored-program computer development, but revenue, beginning with design contracts, came earlier; there was no revenue from commercial products until after they were placed on rental. Military products other than SAGE consisted at first of electronic bombing/navigation systems for long-range (B-52 and B-70) aircraft, and evolved into missile guidance systems. All revenues include monies derived from electromechanical as well as electronic devices in the systems. Service revenues are generally included only in the total column, although for rental machines, maintenance service was included in rental. The 604 and CPC revenue is somewhat understated, omitting the accounting machine part of CPC revenue.

Sources: Defendant's Exhibits in *U.S. v. IBM* (1969): DX2609, DX2609A, DX3815, and DX3822.

Appendix E: Top Corporate Officers, 1911–1989

Chairman	President	Chief Executive Officer[1]	Term as Chairman or President
George W. Fairchild			1911 July to 1924 December
	Percy H. Brundage		1911 July
	George W. Fairchild (acting)	x	1911 August to 1912 April
	Frank N. Kondolf	x	1912 April to 1914 December
	None		1915 January to 1915 March
	Thomas J. Watson[2]	x	1915 March to 1949 September
None			1925 January to 1949 September
Thomas J. Watson		a	1949 September to 1956 June
	John G. Phillips		1949 September to 1952 January
	Thomas J. Watson, Jr.	b	1952 January to 1961 May
None			1956 June to 1961 May
Thomas J. Watson, Jr.		x	1961 May to 1971 June
	Albert L. Williams		1961 May to 1966 March
	T. Vincent Learson		1966 April to 1971 June
T. Vincent Learson		x	1971 June to 1972 December
	Frank T. Cary		1971 June to 1974 February
Frank T. Cary		c	1973 January to 1983 February
	John R. Opel	d	1974 February to 1983 February
John R. Opel		e	1983 February to 1986 May
	John F. Akers	f	1983 February to 1989 May

Chairman	President	Chief Executive Officer[1]	Term as Chairman or President
John F. Akers		f	1986 June to 1993 March
	Jack D. Kuehler		1989 May to 1993 February
	None		1993 February–
Louis V. Gerstner, Jr.		x	1993 April–

1. A letter in the Chief Executive Officer column indicates service as chief executive while also serving as chairman or president. Letters other than x indicate that the term as chief executive differed from the term as chairman or president, as follows:
a. Term ended 1956 May
b. Term began 1956 May
c. Term ended 1980 December
d. Term began 1981 January
e. Term ended 1985 January
f. Term began 1985 February

2. Thomas J. Watson joined the Computing-Tabulating-Recording Company in May 1914 as general manager. In February 1924 the company name was changed to International Business Machines Corporation.

Source: All but most recent entries are from E. W. Pugh, L. R. Johnson, and J. H. Palmer, 1991: *IBM's 360 and Early 370 Systems* (Cambridge, Mass.: MIT Press), pp. 649–50.

Appendix F: Computer Improvements

Technological advances have produced dramatic changes in speeds, capacities, and prices of computer systems as illustrated in the tables. Top-of-the-line disk files and low-priced mainframe computers were used for comparison. By the 1980s there was a vast array of lower-priced, lower-performance computers and disk storage units available, which are not revealed below.

All data are as of the announcement; dollar figures are not adjusted for inflation. Data points prior to 1980 are from E. W. Pugh, L. R. Johnson, and J. H. Palmer, 1991: *IBM's 360 and Early 370 Systems* (Cambridge, Mass.: MIT Press), pp. 645–646.

Price of Computer Processing

System	Announcement Year	Purchase Price per Instruction Executed per Second	Price Ratio
650	1953	$242.29	2423
System/360 Model 30	1964	6.13	61
System/370 Model 135	1971	2.71	27
4341	1979	.35	4
ES/9000 Model 190	1990	.10	1

Computer Processing Speed

System	Announcement Year	Speed Ratio[1]
650	1953	1
1401	1959	7
System/360 Model 30	1964	43
System/370 Model 135	1971	214
4341	1979	1143
ES/9000 Model 190	1990	15200

1. Processing ratios are based on selected sample tests run by IBM.

Computer Main Memory Capacity

System	Announcement Year	Maximum Characters	Capacity Ratio
1401	1959	4,000	1
System/360 Model 30	1964	66,000	17
System/370 Model 135	1971	246,000	62
4341	1979	4,194,000	1,049
ES/9000 Model 190	1990	536,576,000	134,144

Price of Computer Disk Storage

Machine	Announcement Year	Purchase Price per Million Characters	Price Ratio
350	1956	$9760	976
1301	1961	3313	331
2314	1965	1243	124
3330-11	1973	191	19
3370	1979	41	4
3390	1992	10[1]	1

1. Substantial discounts were widely available.

Disk Read-Write Speed

Machine	Announcement Year	Characters per Second	Speed Ratio
350	1956	10,000	1
1301	1961	90,000	9
2314	1965	312,000	31
3330	1970	806,000	81
3350	1975	1,198,000	120
3370	1979	1,859,000	186
3390	1992	4,200,000	420

Notes

1 Hollerith: Inventor and Entrepreneur

1. The three patents issued to Hollerith on tabulating equipment on 8 January 1889 were U.S. Patent 395,783, filed 23 September 1884: "Apparatus for Compiling Statistics"; U.S. Patent 395,782, originally filed 23 September 1884, divided and filed 27 October 1885: "Art of Compiling Statistics"; U.S. Patent 395,781, filed 8 June 1887: "Art of Compiling Statistics."

2. G. D. Austrian, 1982: *Herman Hollerith, Forgotten Giant of Information Processing* (New York: Columbia University Press), pp. 1–4, 43. His continuing sensitivity to his poor spelling is revealed by the following sentences in a letter to T. J. Wilson on 7 August 1919: "Please make due allowances for errors of spelling etc. Life is too short to correct type writing." The Columbia School of Mines was the predecessor of the Columbia University School of Engineering.

3. K. S. Reid-Green, February 1989: "The History of Census Tabulation," *Scientific American,* pp. 98–103.

4. Austrian, 1982: pp. 1–4.

5. M. G. Anderson, 1988: *The American Census: A Social History* (New Haven: Yale University Press), especially pp. 9, 83–87.

6. John Shaw Billings first became involved with the U.S. Census in 1870, and he had responsibility for vital statistics in the censuses of 1880 and 1890. As a member of the army, he was not on the census payroll. Beginning in 1876 he also served as medical adviser to the trustees of the Johns Hopkins Fund and helped plan the Johns Hopkins Hospital. He became a full professor of hygiene at the University of Pennsylvania in 1895 when he retired from the army and spent his final years helping to organize the New York Public Library. See L. E. Truesdell, 1965: *The Development of Punch Card Tabulation in the Bureau of the Census,* 1890–1940 (Washington, D.C.: U.S. Department of Commerce), pp. 28–30.

7. H. Hollerith, 7 August 1919: to J. T. Wilson, as reproduced in the IBM document, 1957: "Historical Development of IBM Products and Patents," prepared by J. Hayward, pp. 18–23. Wilson was a former sales agent with the Tabulating Machine Company.

8. Hollerith, 7 August 1919.

9. Austrian, 1982: pp. 11–23.

10. L. E. Truesdell, 1965: *The Development of Punch Card Tabulation in the Bureau of the Census, 1890–1940* (Washington, D.C.: U.S. Department of Commerce), pp. 17–24. Charles W. Seaton, who was chief clerk during the 1870 census, was paid $15,000 for his invention by a special act of Congress in 1872. At the time, Francis A. Walker was superintendent. Seaton replaced Walker as superintendent of the census in 1881 when Walker became president of the Massachusetts Institute of Technology.

11. Reid-Green, February 1989.

12. Manual telegraph systems were in commercial use by the late 1840s. The Wheatstone system, devised in 1858, was probably the first to employ perforated tape to operate the transmitting mechanism. Paper tape–driven automatic telegraph systems were placed in commercial operation during the 1860s and were able to handle about 70 words per minute. Hollerith would, of course, have been aware of these systems as is indicated by Austrian, 1982: p. 13.

13. Hollerith, 7 August 1919.

14. A. Hyman, 1982: *Charles Babbage, Pioneer of the Computer* (Princeton, N.J.: Princeton University Press), pp. 164–66, 254–55; M. Gleiser, September 1979: "The Loom of Lyons," *Datamation*, pp. 216–26.

15. Truesdell, 1965: pp. 38–39. The card used by the Baltimore Department of Health had 192 hole locations, arranged in 6 rows of 32 locations each. Hole locations were positioned near the edges of the card (3 rows on each of the two long edges) to permit punching with the short jaws of a hand-held punch.

16. T. C. Martin, 11 November 1891: "Counting a Nation by Electricity," *The Electrical Engineer 12*, pp. 521–30.

17. J. S. Billings, 1887: "On Some Forms of Tables of Vital Statistics, with Special Reference to the Needs of the Health Department of a City," *Public Health Papers and Reports 13*, American Public Health Association, pp. 203–21, as quoted in Truesdell, 1965: p. 32.

18. U.S. Patent 395,783, filed 23 September 1884: H. Hollerith, "Apparatus for Compiling Statistics"; U.S. Patent 395,782, originally filed 23 September 1884, divided and filed 27 October 1885: H. Hollerith, "Art of Compiling Statistics."

19. U.S. Patent 395,781, filed 8 June 1887: H. Hollerith, "Art of Compiling Statistics."

20. Austrian, 1982: pp. 39–40.

21. Martin, 11 November 1891.

22. U.S. Patent 487,737, filed 10 March 1891: H. Hollerith, "Keyboard-Punch." Hollerith referred to the punch as a "key-board" punch because the large flat plate, with holes into which the stylus was pressed, had a "key" printed near each hole, "indicating the items to be punched into the cards." To further reduce operator effort for the census work, Hollerith created a gang punch that permitted a fixed group of holes in the first four columns to be punched into as many as six cards at a time. These holes represented a given geographical district and were identical for all data from the same district. See, for example, Martin, 11 November 1891. Use of the gang punch for railroad cost accounting applications is discussed in the *American Machinist,* 31 July 1902: pp. 1073–75.

23. H. Hollerith, 19 September 1884: to Albert Meyer, Hollerith Papers, as quoted in Austrian, 1982: p. 20.

24. Austrian, 1982: pp. 20–22, 28.

25. Hollerith's three patents titled "Electro-Magnetically-Operated Air-Brake for Railway-Cars" were filed on 30 April 1885 and issued on 12 January 1886: U.S. Patent 334,020; U.S. Patent 334,021; and U.S. Patent 334,022.

26. Hollerith's cousin in St. Louis was Henry Flad, president of the Mallinckrodt Brake Company, which had been established to promote an improved brake invented by John F. Mallinckrodt. Flad, who was then in his early sixties, had distinguished himself as an engineer and was elected president of the American Society of Civil Engineers in 1886.

27. Austrian, 1982: pp. 27–35.

28. Austrian, 1982: pp. 42–49. Hollerith's equipment was awarded one of the five gold medals received by Americans at the exhibit in Paris.

29. Martin, 11 November 1891. The other two members of the commission were Prof. Henry Gannett and L. M. E. Cooke. Other systems considered were ones proposed by W. C. Hunt and C. F. Pidgen. As described by Martin: "Mr. W. C. Hunt proposed to transfer the details given on the census enumerators' schedules to cards, distinctions being made in part by the color of the ink and in part by writing on them, the results being reached afterwards by hand sorting and counting. . . . The next plan, that of Mr. C. F. Pidgin, contemplated the use of "chips," which should be duly assorted and counted. These chips were to be slips of paper of various colors embracing data printed in different colors so as to indicate the readings of the schedules."

30. Austrian, 1982: pp. 50–54, 67.

31. Martin, 11 November 1891.

32. L. Bodio, December 1893: *The Inventive Age 4,* reprinted in "A Forecast of 1893—and Its Fulfillment," *The Tabulator* (The Tabulating Machine Co.), August 1916, p. 3. Luigi Bodio was director general of Italy's Imperial Bureau of Statistics.

33. In August 1894 the Census Bureau had finished its work and returned all 105 tabulators to Hollerith. On top of the huge loss of revenue was the added cost of storing the equipment for an as yet unknown use. See Austrian, 1982: p. 104.

34. A. D. Chandler, Jr., 1977: *The Visible Hand: The Managerial Revolution in American Business* (Cambridge, Mass.: Belknap Press), pp. 109–21. Although Hollerith's main commercial thrust was in railroads, the Prudential Life Insurance Company had become interested in his equipment even before he won the U.S. Census business. In the spring of 1890 Hollerith installed two machines at the Prudential offices in Newark, New Jersey. See Austrian, 1982: p. 83.

35. Austrian, 1982: pp. 113, 125–26.

36. Cards were fed, nines row first, between a conducting roller and wire brushes, one per column, that made electrical contact with the roller through the holes. Rotation of each wheel was begun when the corresponding brush detected a hole in the card, and all wheels stopped rotating when the 0s row

was reached. Thus each wheel of the accumulator was advanced by the number of digits represented by the corresponding hole in the card. The carry operation was handled within the accumulator by a spring-loaded mechanism that advanced a wheel one position each time a lower-order adjacent wheel rotated from the 9 to the 0 position. See A. H. Dickinson, 2 October 1969: interview by L. M. Saphire.

As early as January 1887 Hollerith had filed for a patent on an integrating tabulator. Issued in June 1890, this patent describes a means for adding numbers rather than simply counting by ones. Intended for use with the stationary pin-box card reader, it consisted of a motor-driven cylinder with nine strips of conducting material of graduated lengths, parallel to the axis of the cylinder and distributed uniformly about its circumference, plus nine electric-contact brushes arranged parallel to the axis of the cylinder. When the cylinder rotated one revolution, each brush made contact with as many of the strips of conducting material as it passed over—the brush at one end making contact with all nine strips, and the others contacting progressively fewer strips as the strips became shorter. When the automatic card feeder was introduced, the concept of measuring the distance of a hole from the zero location to determine its numerical value was a simple extension of this earlier method. See U.S. Patent 430,804, filed 4 January 1887: H. Hollerith, "Electrical Calculating System."

37. Austrian, 1982: pp. 97–98, 138, 153.

38. E. W. Byrn, 19 April 1902: "The Mechanical Work of the Twelfth Census," *Scientific American*, p. 275.

39. M. Campbell-Kelly, 1989: ICL: *A Business and Technical History* (Oxford: Oxford University Press), pp. 13–16.

40. Campbell-Kelly, 1989: p. 8; Austrian, 1982: p. 107.

41. Mrs. R. P. Porter, 5 December 1984: to Mrs. H. Hollerith, Hollerith Papers, as quoted in Austrian, 1982: p. 108.

42. Campbell-Kelly, 1989: pp. 16–19.

43. Campbell-Kelly, 1989: pp. 19–30.

44. J. Connolly, 1967: *History of Computing in Europe* (New York: IBM World Trade Corporation), pp. 10–18. The businessman who successfully established the German Hollerith Company, Dehomag, was Willy Heidinger, previously an agent for adding machines. In 1922 CTR obtained 90 percent of the stock of Dehomag through a sale by Heidinger.

2 Origins of IBM

1. G. D. Austrian, 1982: *Herman Hollerith, Forgotten Giant of Information Processing* (New York: Columbia University Press), pp. 4–5, 38, 47, 74–78.

2. Austrian, 1982: pp. 54–59, 113–14, 160–61.

3. K. S. Reid-Green, February 1989: "The History of Census Tabulation," *Scientific American*, pp. 98–103.

4. L. E. Truesdell, 1965: *The Development of Punch Card Tabulation in the Bureau of the Census, 1890–1940* (Washington, D.C.: U.S. Department of Commerce), pp. 117–21; Austrian, 1982: p. 227. S. N. D. North, who served as director of

the census from 1903 to 1909, was preceded by William R. Merriam from 1899 to 1903.

5. Newcomb, Churchill, and Frey, 1 April 1909: to Senator R. La Follette as quoted in Austrian, 1982: p. 235.

6. Austrian, 1982: pp. 261–302.

7. H. Hollerith, 7 August 1919: to J. T. Wilson, as reproduced in the IBM document, 1957: "Historical Development of IBM Products and Patents," prepared by J. Hayward, pp. 18–23. Wilson was a former sales agent with the Tabulating Machine Company.

8. C. R. Flint, 1923: *Memories of an Active Life* (New York: G. P. Putnam's Sons), pp. 4–10, 85–114, 288–97.

9. A. D. Chandler, Jr., 1977: *The Visible Hand* (Cambridge, Mass.: The Harvard University Press), pp. 315–44.

10. Flint, 1923: especially pp. 244, 286–322. See also *News/34–38*, April 1985: "IBM's Forgotten Founding Father," by Teresa Elms, pp. 64–65.

11. IBM Manual of Instruction, circa 1935: "Development of International Business Machines Corporation," Educational Department, Endicott, N.Y.

12. U.S. Patent 314,717, issued 31 March 1885: J. E. Pitrat, "Weighing and Price Scale."

13. U.S. Patent 393,205, issued 20 November 1888: W. L. Bundy, "Time-Recorder."

14. The card time recorder was based on U.S. Patent 528,223, issued 30 October 1894: Daniel M. Cooper, "Workman's Time Recorder." The dial time recorder was based on a patent issued in 1888 to a Scottish physician, Alexander Dey.

15. IBM Manual of Instruction, circa 1935. It has been noted somewhat humorously that a fourth company involved in the merger, the Bundy Manufacturing Company, is generally ignored because it contributed only the word "Company" to the name.

16. E. A. Ford, 18 July 1911: to H. Hollerith, as quoted in Austrian, 1982: p. 310.

17. Minutes, 15 July 1911: Fifth meeting of the board of directors of the Computing-Tabulating-Recording Company.

18. S. Engelbourg, 1954: "International Business Machines: A Business History," Columbia University doctoral thesis, p. 44.

19. IBM Manual of Instruction, circa 1935. The first president of CTR was Percy H. Brundage.

20. IBM received 100,000 shares of Hobart class B stock. The International Scale Division (heavy-duty scales, etc.) was excluded from this sale, but in 1936 the foreign subsidiaries were also transferred to Hobart. See special stockholder meetings of 25 June 1935 and 20 July 1936.

21. Agreement, 21 October 1958: International Business Machines Corporation and Simplex Time Recorder Company. The gross profit of IBM's Time Equipment Division (i.e., profit before deductions of expenses not distributed by product) had dropped to $7.7 million in 1958, following a rise from $6.7 million

to $9.5 million between 1954 and 1957; see H. W. Trimble, Jr., 10 February 1959: to V. R. Hansen, assistant attorney, General Antitrust Division.

22. Two other events in the company's early history should also be noted here. Both occurred in 1933. IBM was reorganized from a holding company to an operating company, and it entered the electric typewriter business through the purchase of the Electromatic Typewriter Corporation of Rochester, N.Y. See Annual report, 1933: International Business Machines Corporation.

23. The view that IBM was founded when T. J. Watson, Sr., became general manager of CTR in 1914 is broadly accepted. For example, the anticipated announcement of the appointment of Louis V. Gerstner, Jr., as chief executive of IBM was reported by the *New York Times* on 26 March 1993, p. 1D, as follows: "Mr. Gerstner, 51, who is chairman of the RJR Nabisco Holdings Corporation, would be the sixth chief executive in the 79-year history of the International Business Machines Corporation, and the first picked from outside the company's ranks."

3 Watson: A Man with a Mission

1. T. G. Belden and M. R. Belden, 1962: *The Lengthening Shadow* (Boston: Little, Brown), pp. 93–94. See also T. J. Watson, Jr., and Peter Petre, 1990: Father, Son & Co. (New York: Bantam Press), p. 15.

2. T. J. Watson, Jr., and Peter Petre, 1990: *Father, Son & Co.* (New York: Bantam Press), pp. 11–13.

3. A. D. Chandler, Jr., 1977: *The Visible Hand* (Cambridge, Mass.: Harvard University Press), pp. 302–14. Integrated business structures for manufacturers of machinery had first evolved in the sewing machine industry, beginning in the 1850s. By the 1890s the Singer Sewing Machine Company had become fully integrated, with its own timberlands, iron mills, and manufacturing plants, as well as marketing, sales, and service organizations. It dominated its industry at home and abroad.

4. Belden and Belden, 1962: pp. 4–11.

5. Watson, Jr., and Petre, 1990: p. 49. This is a story Watson, Sr., chose not to tell in his official biography; see Belden and Belden, 1962: pp. 12–13.

6. Belden and Belden, 1962: pp. 14–17.

7. Belden and Belden, 1962: p. 33. For background information, see pp. 17–51.

8. R. L. Palmer, 13 September 1991: interview by E. W. Pugh; Belden and Belden, 1962: p. 113.

9. Belden and Belden, 1962: pp. 66–73.

10. Watson, Jr., and Petre, 1990: p. 13.

11. Belden and Belden, 1962: pp. 84–87.

12. Watson, Jr., and Petre, 1990: pp. 13–14.

13. Belden and Belden, 1962: pp. 13, 87. Watson was no doubt also influenced in his decision to ban alcohol at all business functions by the strong objection Charles R. Flint had to its use.

14. Watson, Jr., and Petre, 1990: pp. 49, 141–42.

15. Belden and Belden, 1962: p. 98.

16. Thomas J. Watson was the top executive officer of IBM for forty-one years (from 15 March 1915 until 8 May 1956) when he turned over the position of chief executive officer to his older son, Thomas J. Watson, Jr. The senior Watson died of a heart attack a little more than one month later, 19 June 1956. During those years IBM's gross revenue increased over 200-fold from $4 million to $892 million, the number of employees increased over 50-fold from 1,346 to 72,504, and data processing, which accounted for less than 25 percent of the company's revenue in 1914, grew to 70 percent by 1956. The revenue contributions in 1956 and 1914 are found in B. F. Wiegard, 26 March 1958: to D. Orton, "Questions from Beldens."

17. Belden and Belden, 1962: pp. 126–36 and photo section. The words to IBM's song, "Ever Onward," are as follows:

There's a thrill in store for all,
For we're about to toast
The corporation that we represent.
We're here to cheer each pioneer
And also proudly boast
Of that "man of men," our sterling president.
The name of T. J. Watson means a courage none can stem:
And we feel honored to be here to toast the I.B.M.

First Chorus

EVER ONWARD—EVER ONWARD!
That's the spirit that has brought us fame!
We're big, but bigger we will be,
We can't fail for all can see
That to serve humanity has been our aim!
Our products now are known in every zone,
Our reputation sparkles like a gem!
We've fought our way through—and new
Fields we're sure to conquer too
for the EVER ONWARD IBM.

18. A. H. Dickinson, 2 October 1969: interview by L. M. Saphire.

19. H. Hollerith, 1 December 1914: transcribed remarks to T. J. Watson as quoted by Austrian, 1982: p. 331.

20. U.S. Patent 1,830,699, filed 11 March 1914: Hollerith, "Automatic Control for Tabulating Machines."

21. Belden and Belden, 1962: p. 112.

22. G. D. Austrian, 1982: *Herman Hollerith, Forgotten Giant of Information Processing* (New York: Columbia University Press), p. 346.

4 Building an Engineering Organization

1. *Business Machines*, 1 January 1954: "40 Years of Pioneering," pp. 3–11; see also Watson, Jr., and Petre, 1990: pp. 14–15.

2. M. Campbell-Kelly, 1989: *ICL: A Business and Technical History* (Oxford: Oxford University Press), p. 34; Austrian, 1982: p. 271. Powers emigrated to the United States in 1889 at age eighteen.

3. H. Hollerith, 4 January 1899: to S. G. Metcalf, as quoted in Austrian, 1982: p. 270. Powers also provided a punch in which the operator keyed in all desired

holes before causing the device to punch all holes in a card at once. This permitted operators to check for errors before punching any holes.

4. W. J. Eckert, May 1963: "Early Computers," *IBM Research News*, pp. 7–8, says Clair D. Lake told him this. See also A. H. Dickinson, 2 October 1969: interview by L. Saphire.

5. Campbell-Kelly, 1989: p. 35. A photograph of a Powers connection box may be found in the first group of photographs, between pages 52 and 53, of Campbell-Kelly's book.

6. S. W. Dunwell, 31 July 1991: interview by E. W. Pugh.

7. G. F. Daly, 1953: "Development of IBM Unit Record Equipment, Inventors and Laboratories," p. 3.

8. Austrian, 1982: p. 331.

9. IBM Sales Training Manual, circa 1956: "History and Development of International Business Machines Corporation," Endicott, N.Y. According to this document: "The development and research engineering [of CTR] in 1914 consisted of one engineer and seven draftsmen at the Endicott plant who worked on the development of new time-recording products, and one engineer and three draftsmen in Uxbridge, Massachusetts, who were doing all of the development work on the EAM line of products. The average hourly rate of pay in the manufacturing plants in 1914 was 32 cents and the work week was 54 hours. None of the benefits, such as insurance, hospitalization, and retirement were in existence at that time; and air conditioning, fluorescent lights, and maple floors were either unknown or unheard of for industrial use."

10. Daly, 1953: pp. 3–4. Clair D. Lake had been appointed chief engineer of the Tabulating Machine Division in 1916 when E. A. Ford left the company for a few years to develop his ideas on diesel engines. Lake retained that title in Endicott.

11. IBM document, May 1922: "Suggested announcement for I.B.M. of Mr. Bryce's appointment as Chief Engineer of Computing Tabulating Recording Company." Bryce joined CTR in December 1917.

12. *Think*, April 1949: "The Light He Leaves Behind."

13. T. G. Belden and M. R. Belden, 1962: The Lengthening Shadow (Boston: Little, Brown), pp. 96–97.

14. S. Engelbourg, 1954: "International Business Machines: A Business History," Columbia University doctoral thesis, p. 270; Complaint, 21 January 1952: *U.S. v. IBM*, U.S. District Court, Southern District of New York, N.Y., p. 7.

15. U.S. Patent 1,830,699, filed 11 March 1914: H. Hollerith, "Automatic Control for Tabulating Machines."

16. F. Thomas, circa 1957: "Interference Litigation between Hollerith, Peirce, Tripp, and Powers, 1917 to 1924." Thomas was a member of D. W. Cooper's Law Office: Kerr, Page, and Cooper, the firm that represented the International Time Recording Company and later IBM. This report was included as Chapter 11 in the IBM document, 1957: "Historical Development of IBM Products and Patents" prepared by J. Hayward. As a result of the interference proceedings, the following patents were issued: Tripp (U.S. 1,824,581 dated 9/22/31), Hol-

lerith (U.S. 1,830,699 dated 11/3/31), and Peirce (U.S. 1,930,283 dated 10/10/33).

17. Thomas, circa 1957.

18. Engelbourg, 1954: p. 270; Complaint, 21 January 1952: *U.S. v. IBM*, U.S. District Court, Southern District of New York, N.Y., p. 7. The royalty payments charged to Powers were reduced by half to 12.5 percent of gross rentals and 9 percent of gross receipts from the sale of cards. This reduction followed the reorganization of the Powers company following receivership in 1922.

19. Belden and Belden, 1962: pp. 116–17.

20. T. J. Watson, 1 June 1922: to J. E. Rogers, general manager, International Time Recording Company, and others.

21. E. W. Pugh, 9 March 1993: to file. This memorandum analyzes information prepared by Charles R. Doty for T. J. Watson, Sr. Doty's report describes all projects in the Endicott Laboratory that had been abandoned without resulting in a product, from the time when such records were kept until 1945. Abandoned projects would primarily be a subset of what today are called advanced product development efforts. During the first three years for which comparative data were available, Doty's report lists the cumulative cost of projects terminated in 1928, 1929, and 1930, respectively, to have been (in thousands of dollars) 325, 59, and 186 for accounting machines and only 3, 22, and 14 for time recording equipment.

22. E. A. Ford, 19 February 1924: to T. J. Watson.

23. T. J. Watson, 29 February 1924: to E. A. Ford.

24. E. A. Ford, 1 July 1926: to T. J. Watson. O. E. Braitmayer, 21 June 1926: to T. J. Watson explains the reason for the bonus and describes it as canceling Ford's note for $3,500, which he borrowed when he returned to CTR, plus an extra $1,500. Ford had left CTR in 1916 to pursue his ideas on diesel engines. This development was not successful, causing him to be in debt when he returned to CTR; see Daly, 1953: p. 4.

25. W. W. McDowell, 29 June 1946: to Dwayne Orton.

26. F. M. Carroll, 25 April 1925: to T. J. Watson.

27. Daly, 1953: pp. 5, 13. Watson had also given this assignment to a third inventor (from the Time Recording Division) who soon dropped out of the contest when it became clear that Lake and Carroll had more promising approaches.

28. S. W. Dunwell, 31 July 1991: interview by E. W. Pugh.

29. G. F. Daly, 1953: pp. 15–17; 12 August 1969: interview by L. M. Saphire.

30. C. J. Bashe, L. R. Johnson, J. H. Palmer, and E. W. Pugh, 1986: *IBM's Early Computers* (Cambridge: MIT Press), pp. 10–14.

31. Campbell-Kelly, 1989: pp. 82–83. This reference is particularly interesting because it discusses the response of British companies to IBM's 80-column card in addition to that of Remington Rand.

32. E. J. Rabenda, 20 February 1992: discussion with E. W. Pugh.

33. Bashe et al., 1984: pp. 12–15.

5 *Responding to the Great Depression*

1. *Econostat,* 1 April 1933: "National Cash Register Cleans House."

2. Bashe et al., 1984: pp. 18–19; IBM sales manual, circa 1934.

3. *American Machinist,* 16 June 1937: "From Inventor's Shop to International Corporation," pp. 481–561; see especially pp. 487, 499. The vice president for manufacturing in 1933 was Walter F. Titus, who previously had been the sales manager in Detroit. The manager of engineering (more commonly referred to as the laboratory manager) was Lawrence S. Harrison, who previously had been in charge of IBM's customer engineering.

4. IBM News SDD Endicott, September 1968: "The Future Depends on Engineering," Special edition celebrating 35th anniversary of the North Street Laboratory, p. 4. Endicott laboratory managers from 1933 to 1968, as listed in the article, were as follows: L. S. Harrison, 1933–38; G. H. Armstrong, 1938–42; W. W. McDowell, 1942–50; E. W. Gardinor, 1950–51; E. J. Garvey, 1951–53; J. A. Haddad, 1953–54; F. E. Hamilton, 1954–56; and J. J. Troy, 1956–.

5. S. W. Dunwell, 31 July 1991: interview by E. W. Pugh.

6. IBM Document, 25 November 1957: responses prepared to questions posed by the Beldens on 8 November 1957 for use in *The Lengthening Shadow.*

7. IBM Manual of Instruction, circa 1935: "Development of International Business Machines Corporation," pp. 23–24.

8. G. F. Daly, 1953: "Development of IBM Unit Record Equipment, Inventors, and Laboratories," pp. 8–10. Daly particularly credits C. D. Lake with training many new engineers, including himself, J. M. Cunningham, F. E. Hamilton, W. L. Lewis, W. W. McDowell, and R. E. Page.

9. *American Machinist,* 16 June 1937: pp. 491–92.

10. *Business Machines,* August 1935: "New Field Opened to College Women"; Kristina Brandt, 24 December 1991: discussion with E. W. Pugh; 27 January 1992: interview by E. W. Pugh. The vice president quoted first in the text is F. W. Nichol, the second is O. E. Braitmayer. Information about Ruth M. Leach may be found in *Current Biography 1948,* pp. 373–74. In 1935 Glenn H. Armstrong was in charge of the education program, having previously served as sales manager in Cleveland. In 1938 he replaced L. S. Harrison as laboratory manager in Endicott. See E. J. Rabenda, 20 February 1992: discussion with E. W. Pugh.

11. *American Machinist,* 16 June 1937: pp. 487–88.

12. *American Machinist,* 16 June 1937: pp. 556–58; R. Miller, 27 May 1958: to the Beldens in response to questions asked on 13 September 1957 for use in *The Lengthening Shadow.*

13. *American Machinist,* 16 June 1937: p. 549.

14. *American Machinist,* 16 June 1937: pp. 549–55. The choice of manufacturing tooling was based not only on the operations needed to make the various parts with the specified tolerances but also on the quantities to be produced, the materials used, the quality of the finish, and whether or not heat treatment was required.

15. *American Machinist,* 16 June 1937: pp. 500–502, 539–41.

16. Dunwell, 31 July 1991.

17. F. J. Wesley, 19 May 1955: to L. H. LaMotte with attachment titled, "Accomplishment Summary—25-Year IBM Record of Mr. F. J. Wesley."

18. *Business Machines,* 20 October 1938: "An Interesting Business," by F. J. Wesley. See also Wesley, 19 May 1955. Compendia of Pointer reprints were published periodically. One of the last, "IBM Electric Punched Card Accounting Pointers to Better Service," dated February 1947, included in its preface an echo of the 1920s: "Some 45-column diagrams are still shown . . . because they may be easily converted for 80-column machines."

19. *Business Machines,* 20 October 1938.

20. Dunwell, 31 July 1991.

21. Wesley, 19 May 1955.

22. David W. Rubidge made the changes described in the Social Security collator. See S. W. Dunwell, 5 August 1991: interview by E. W. Pugh; D. W. Rubidge, 11 November 1991: discussion with E. W. Pugh. Rubidge modified the wiring of the single comparing mechanism, which was capable of handling numbers with up to 16 digits, into two portions of 9 and 7 digits each. He assigned the 9-digit portion to making high, low, or equal comparisons on the 9-digit Social Security numbers, as was needed for collating control. The 7-digit portion was used for making an equals comparison on the numeric portion of the name field to ensure that the names on two cards corresponded when the Social Security numbers were equal. If they failed to correspond, the card in the secondary deck was selected by the collator for manual review.

23. *Business Machines,* 20 October 1938.

24. Clarence W. Avery, the uncle of Stephen W. Dunwell, was inducted into the Automotive Hall of Fame in Midland, Mich., in 1990. The plaque honoring Avery reads in part: "Clarence W. Avery (1882–1949)—Credited with developing the moving assembly line in the mass production of automobiles for the Ford Motor Company. . . . This development sparked the beginning of mass production in the automotive industry."

25. Dunwell, 31 July 1991. Dunwell was also given the task of finding ways to reduce the radio interference caused by IBM products.

26. S. W. Dunwell, 15 August 1991: interview by E. W. Pugh.

6 Support for Academic Research

1. L. J. Comrie, 1928: "On the Construction of Tables by Interpolation," Royal Astronomical Society Monthly Notices 88, pp. 506–23. See also H. H. Goldstine, 1972: *The Computer from Pascal to von Neumann,* p. 107.

2. G. W. Snedecor, 1928: "Uses of Punched Card Equipment in Mathematics," *American Mathematical Monthly 35,* pp. 161–69.

3. J. F. Brennan, 1971: *The IBM Watson Laboratory at Columbia University—A History* (Armonk, N.Y.: IBM), pp. 3–4. Wood remained an IBM consultant for twenty-eight years.

4. D. R. Piatt, 19 December 1949: to W. J. Eckert, "Statistical Calculator"; Bashe et al., 1986: p. 23.

5. *Bulletin of Information on the International Test Scoring Machine,* October 1936: published by the Cooperative Test Service of the American Council on Education.

6. R. B. Johnson, 19 May 1977: discussion with C. J. Bashe et al. as summarized on 10 June 1977. Among considerations that caused the IBM board to decide against buying Johnson's test-scoring machine concept was the Patent Department's conclusion that Lasker, of Remington Rand, had invented pencil-mark sensing before Johnson.

7. IBM Document, circa 1944: Employment Record of R. B. Johnson.

8. T. J. Watson, 16 March 1936: to R. B. Johnson.

9. *Bulletin of Information on the International Test Scoring Machine,* October 1936.

10. IBM Document, circa 1944. When company salesmen warned Watson that the Test Scoring Machine would never make money, Watson reportedly responded, "Who wants to make money out of education?"; see Brennan, 1971: p. 5.

11. News Release, 6 January 1946: Columbia University Public Information Office.

12. W. J. Eckert, January 1940: *Punched Card Methods in Scientific Computation,* published by the T. J. Watson Astronomical Computing Bureau, p. 77. John C. McPherson in a letter of 6 January 1982 to E. Nanas says: "Eckert's calculator was an early and primitive 'computer' using punched cards for storage of tables and intermediate calculated results which required a person to move the cards between the punched card accounting machine, summary punch and punched card multiplier, directed by a manual program controller. It was used to carry out highly precise calculations of planetary orbits and other differential equations."

13. W. J. Eckert, May 1963: "Early Computers," *IBM Research News,* pp. 7–8.

14. H. Aiken, circa 1937: "Proposed Automatic Calculating Machine," reprinted in *IEEE Spectrum,* August 1964: pp. 62–69. The origin of this memorandum by Aiken is described in *Spectrum* as follows: "A copy of the unpublished memorandum in which Aiken first outlined his conception of Mark I was recently discovered in Professor Aiken's Harvard files by Mrs. Jacquelin Sanborn Sill, and through her efforts is presented here with the author's permission. The memorandum itself is undated, but an unknown recipient's handwritten notation 'Prospectus of Howard Aiken, November 4, 1937' puts an upper bound on the date for its preparation." The date of receipt by the "unknown recipient" and some specific references to IBM equipment indicate the document was intended for presentation to IBM. Aiken had received a bachelor's degree in electrical engineering from the University of Wisconsin in 1923. From then to 1932 he held various jobs and studied physics at the University of Chicago. He received the M.S. in physics in 1937 and the Ph.D. in 1939 from Harvard University.

15. I. B. Cohen, July 1980: Foreword to "History of Mechanical Computing Machinery" by George C. Chase, in *Annals of the History of Computing 2,* pp. 198–200.

16. H. Aiken, 3 November 1937: to J. W. Bryce.

17. H. E. Pim, 7 January 1938: to J. W. Bryce, "Howard Aiken, Harvard University."

18. F. E. Hamilton, 21 August 1944: untitled report describing development history of the Harvard Machine, which was transmitted to C. D. Lake by J. J. Robbins on 28 January 1949.

19. L. J. Comrie, 1946: "Babbage's Dream Comes True," *Nature 158,* pp. 567–68. See also S. Rosen, 1969: "Electronic Computers: A Historical Survey," *Computing Surveys 1,* pp. 7–36. At about the time Howard Aiken began promoting construction of the large Mark I supercomputer, Konrad Zuse in Berlin, Germany, had begun work on a much smaller unit with a mechanical memory, arithmetic and control units made of secondhand telephone relays, and program control by perforated tape (35mm movie film). His computing device is said to have been operational in 1941. Because it was destroyed during the war, however, there are numerous unanswered questions. With a reported completion date approximately two years before the Mark I, Zuse's machine is credited as a "first" by many historians. It is a rather limited first, however, since the device was too small to do useful work. See, for example, P. E. Ceruzzi, 1983: *Reckoners* (Westport, Conn.: Greenwood Press), pp. 10–40. In contrast, the Calculation Control Switch designed by Wallace Eckert, and operational by 1936, made it possible for standard electromechanical punched-card equipment to operate in a sequence-controlled mode similar to that of Zuse's machine and the Mark I. The Calculation Control Switch was used extensively by Eckert for his work in astronomy, beginning at least four years before Zuse's device is said to have been completed.

20. I. B. Cohen, 1988: "Babbage and Aiken," *Annals of the History of Computing 10,* pp. 171–93, especially pp. 181–83.

21. IBM brochure, 1945: "IBM Automatic Sequence Controlled Calculator." See also C. J. Bashe, 1982: "The SSEC in Historical Perspective," *Annals of the History of Computing 4,* pp. 296–312. Francis E. Hamilton, who reported to Lake, was the engineer responsible for day-to-day direction of the project. Another major contributor was IBM engineer Benjamin M. Durfee.

22. Cohen, 1988: especially p. 178.

23. U.S. Patent 2,616,626, issued 4 November 1952: Clair D. Lake, Howard H. Aiken, Francis E. Hamilton, and Benjamin M. Durfee, "Calculator."

7 Research for Patents and Devices

1. EAM Patent Digest with Use Status, 16 February 1950: an IBM engineering report obtained from the Endicott laboratory in 1981 with the help of J. H. Wellburn.

2. IBM Document, circa 1953: "Bryce Patents by General Subject." This document was found in the files of George F. Daly as part of his materials on IBM patents. Although undated, the last patent on the list is U.S. 2,641,976, dated 06-16-53, and titled, "Photographic Color Recording Machine." A tabular summary of data in this document is provided by E. W. Pugh and C. C. Coppola, 22 April 1991: "Bryce's patents."

3. *Think*, April 1949: "The Light He Leaves Behind." See also E. W. Pugh and C. C. Coppola, 15 and 22 April 1991: to file; these two memoranda provide tabular summaries of data in the documents, "IBM Patent Digest of 1952" and "Bryce Patents by General Subject."

4. IBM document, circa 1949: "James Wares Bryce." This undated and unsigned document was evidently created at the time of the April 1949 article in *Think* and contains identical wording plus additional information.

5. E. J. Rabenda, August 1969: interview by L. M. Saphire.

6. D. W. Rubidge, 11 November 1991: discussion with E. W. Pugh.

7. *Business Machines*, 4 April 1949: "Mr. J. W. Bryce, IBM Pioneer, Inventor, Chief Consultant, Technical Staff Dean, Dies."

8. *Financial Bulletin Service of Dow, Jones & Co.*, 5 May 1930. Bryce's assistant, who replaced him as head of the Patent Department, was W. M. Wilson.

9. A. H. Dickinson, 2 October 1969: interview by L. M. Saphire.

10. J. W. Bryce, 26 January 1939: to T. J. Watson.

11. B. E. Phelps, 1980: "Early Electronic Computer Developments at IBM," *Annals of the History of Computing 2*, pp. 253–67.

12. R. L. Palmer, 13 September 1991: interview by E. W. Pugh. Among the reasons Palmer accepted the IBM job offer was the caliber of those who interviewed him, especially Clair D. Lake, who impressed him very much at the time and in the years that followed.

13. R. L. Palmer, 25 July 1967: interview by L. M. Saphire.

14. H. J. Reich, August 1939: "Trigger Circuits." *Electronics*, pp. 14–17; W. H. Eccles and F. W. Jordan, 1919: "A Trigger Relay Utilizing Three-Electrode Thermionic Vacuum Tubes," *Radio Review 1*, pp. 143–46.

15. A. W. Burks, 1947: "Electronic Computing Circuits of the ENIAC," *Proceedings of the Institute of Radio Engineers*, pp. 756–57; Engineering Research Associates Inc. staff, 1950: *High-Speed Computing Devices* (New York: McGraw-Hill), pp. 12–31.

16. U.S. Patent 2,584,811, filed 27 December 1944: B. E. Phelps, "Electronic Counting Circuit"; B. E. Phelps, 9 December 1971: "The Beginnings of Electronic Computation," IBM Technical Report.

17. Phelps, 1980. The number of additions and the positioning of the column-shift mechanism for multiplication were determined by the number in the multiplier register.

18. G. H. Armstrong, 21 May 1942: to J. V. Atanasoff.

19. M. R. Williams, 1985: *A History of Computing Technology* (Englewood Cliffs, N.J.: Prentice Hall), pp. 266–71.

20. S. Rosen, 1990: "The Origins of Modern Computing," *Computing Reviews 31*, pp. 449–62. See also the "Responses" by H. H. Goldstine, pp. 463–64; A. W. Burks and A. R. Burks, pp. 464–67; J. V. Atanasoff II, pp. 467–69; N. Stern, pp. 469–70; B. A. Galler, pp. 470–71; C. R. Mollenhoff, pp. 471–74; A. R. Mackintosh, pp. 474–75; E. A. Weiss, pp. 475–77; S. Rosen, pp. 477–80.

8 World War II Activities

1. A. L. Norberg, 1990: "High-Technology Calculation in the Early 20th Century: Punched Card Machinery in Business and Government," *Technology and Culture 31*, pp. 753–79, especially 764, 771.

2. Belden and Belden, 1962: pp. 190–217.

3. The Munitions Manufacturing Corporation was incorporated on 31 March 1941. On 1 April 1941 F. H. M. Hart was elected president, and on 7 April 1941 the 215 acres of land in Poughkeepsie were purchased for $201,546. Under Hart's leadership the small food cannery was converted to a munitions factory, the packing plant into offices, and later the residence into a cafeteria. By February 1942 a new 140,000-square-foot manufacturing building (001) was completed and over 250 employees had been hired. On 13 July 1942 the Munitions Manufacturing Corporation was absorbed by IBM and its facilities were designated IBM Plant No. 4. IBM Plant No. 1 was in Endicott, Plant No. 2 was in Washington, D.C., Plant No. 3 was in Rochester, and Plant No. 5 was in Toronto. See *Business Machines,* 16 April 1942, "IBM Employees at Poughkeepsie Hear Mr. Watson," and IBM document, 4 October 1948: "Contractor's Report on Ordnance Manufacture in World War II—Supplement Number One," pp. 9–10. In September 1946 IBM plants in the U.S. were redesignated, with the Poughkeepsie plant changing from Plant 4 to Plant 2. The numbering of company plants lost favor and was discontinued some years later. In 1942 IBM purchased 123 acres on Route 9, just south and east of the main plant, to be used for employee recreation. In 1944 IBM purchased Cliffdale, a 217-acre estate on Boardman Road east of the main plant where research and development facilities were established. See IBM booklets, "Pages from the Past" and "50 years in Poughkeepsie," produced in 1976 and 1991, respectively, for the 35th and 50th anniversaries of the Poughkeepsie facilities.

4. *Business Machines,* 28 September 1950: "Ordnance Group is Told of IBM Production Plans," p. 1; IBM document, 18 December 1950: "Research and Development Facilities," p. 6.

5. The $1^1/_2$ percent constraint on profits voluntarily set by IBM on its munitions production has been widely quoted as 1 percent since at least as early as 1976 when the official IBM corporate publication, "IBM . . . Yesterday and Today," so stated it. Internal documents of the immediate postwar period, however, give the number as $1^1/_2$ percent. An IBM document, circa 1948, "A Resume of the Activities of Mr. Thomas J. Watson from 1939 to 1945," gives the most comprehensive discussion of this policy: "When IBM, in April 1941, entered into its first contract for the production of munitions, slightly more than a year before the enactment of the Renegotiation Act, Mr. Watson, with the approval of the Board of Directors, voluntarily established for IBM a policy of not accepting any profits on war contracts which could in any way be regarded as unreasonable. . . . In conformity with this policy, through forward price reductions and refunds, voluntarily made, IBM has limited its over-all profits on its war contracts with the government to approximately $1^1/_2$% net after taxes, which self-limitation has always been satisfactory to the government." The $1^1/_2$ percent number is also found in the official biography of T. J. Watson; see T. G. Belden and M. R. Belden, 1962: *The Lengthening Shadow* (Boston: Little, Brown), p. 210.

6. *Business Machines,* 22 January 1942: "IBM Engineering Staff Is Devoting Entire Time to Nation's War Program."

7. IBM document, 30 June 1948: "Contractor's Report on Ordnance Manufacture in World War II—Section on Engineering, Research, and Development," submitted by the IBM Corporation to the Chief of Ordnance, United States Army, War Department, Washington, D.C. According to the document, it was "Prepared under the general direction and supervision of the late Mr. C. A. Kirk, Executive Vice President and formerly Vice President in Charge of Manufacturing, and Mr. J. C. McPherson, Vice President in Charge of Engineering, New York, N.Y." Among the ninety-nine separate research and development projects were the development of mobile machine record units, punched-card teletype systems, the Radiotype system for radio transmission of typed messages, an array processor for deciphering intercepted enemy messages, a relay calculator for ballistics calculations, synthetic training devices (or simulators) for pilots, a so-called data repeater that used multiple cathode ray tubes to display relative altitudes and other information on hostile and friendly aircraft, ground and aerial odographs, portions of the analog computer and fire control system for the B-29 bomber, and a mechanical grenade thrower.

8. F. J. Wesley, 19 May 1955: to L. H. LaMotte with attachment titled, "Accomplishment Summary—25 Year IBM Record of Mr. F. J. Wesley."

9. *Business Machines,* 19 February 1942: "Department of Logistics is Formed to Coordinate All IBM Activities." The intimate knowledge of foreign industrial methods and resources that Watson ascribed to F. W. Nichol were undoubtedly acquired when Nichol was in charge of the company's business abroad, an assignment he was given in 1930 when IBM's products were in use in 77 countries; see *Financial Bulletin Service of Dow, Jones & Co.,* 5 May 1930.

10. *Business Machines,* 26 March 1942: "We Must Think in Terms of We-All for Victory, President Watson Tells Members of Organization in Address Heard in All Company's Factories in U.S."

11. *Business Machines,* 28 September 1950. The term EAM was increasingly used to describe all of IBM's punched-card equipment following the change in the name of the responsible division from Tabulating Machine Division to Electric Accounting Machine Division in late 1937. A survey of *Business Machines* during the late 1930s and early 1940s reveals that the division was called the Tabulating Machine (TM) Division in September 1937, the Electric Accounting Machine (EAM) Division in November 1937, the Electric Bookkeeping and Accounting Machine (EBAM) Division in January 1938, and again the Electric Accounting Machine (EAM) Division from April 1939 onward; see L. R. Johnson, 28 February 1985: to file.

12. *Business Machines,* 26 March 1942. Watson's prophecy of increased production by American industry was fulfilled as is described in a retrospective article in *Think Magazine's Diary of U.S. Participation in World War II,* 1950: "The Miracle of Production," p. 185. "Global war demanded a miracle of production. . . . The number of persons engaged in manufacturing establishments jumped from 10,400,000 at the start of the defense program [July 1940] to 17,200,000 at the peak of the war effort [November 1943]. Of this latter number 10,300,000 persons were engaged in munitions work and 6,900,000 in nonmunitions manu-

facturing. The work week was lengthened so production could increase. Workers' hours rose from an average of 37.4 per week to 45.5, though many worked longer hours in critical fields. Weekly earnings naturally increased, rising from an average of $25.52 to an average of $46.00 per week at the end of the war [August 1945]." The increase in worker hours by 101 percent, combined with improved tools and a spirit of cooperation, increased total output by 117 percent.

13. IBM Document, 30 June 1948. Each Mobile Machine Records Unit Detachment was a self-contained military unit. A typical detachment comprised two 10-ton trailer vans, one of which was designed for administrative operations and the other to hold most of the EAM equipment. There were also two $2^{1}/_{2}$-ton, six-wheel drive trucks, two electric generators, and one command car. The personnel of a mobile records detachment at full strength consisted of twenty-nine enlisted men and three officers, all of whom had received basic military training as well as accounting machine instruction. Many mobile units were commanded, operated, and serviced by former IBM employees who had entered the military service.

14. IBM Document, 30 June 1948.

15. C. R. Doty, 15 December 1960: "IBM Tele-Processing Systems and Equipment," IBM Technical Report, p. 11.

16. T. J. Watson, president of IBM, and Walter S. Gifford, president of AT&T, agreed that if any patents were involved between IBM and AT&T, rights thereunder would be waived for the duration of the emergency. Eight U.S. patents were subsequently issued to IBM engineer C. R. Doty on this equipment and modifications thereof; see Doty, 15 December 1960.

17. IBM Document, 30 June 1948.

18. Doty, 15 December 1960, reports the following: "The excellent results obtained by the Air Corps with these machines led to their use during the war by various other branches of the Armed Services, such as the Quartermaster Corps, Signal Corps, the Army Ordnance Department, the Army Transportation Corps, and Naval Air Depots. Also, the Office of Defense Transportation, the U.S. Treasury Department, the Weather Division of the Army Air Forces, the U.S. Weather Bureau and others." The volume of punched-card data transferred from point to point by telegraph during the last two years of the war was estimated to exceed 4 million cards per month.

19. IBM Document, 30 June 1948. Brigadier General F. W. Stoner was the chief of army communications.

20. Walter Lemmon, while at Columbia University, had invented the means by which radio circuits could be trimmed so that all tuning condensers could be on a single shaft. Prior to his invention, the better radios had several dials that had to be aligned individually. Lemmon got a royalty on nearly every radio produced and was quite well off financially. See S. W. Dunwell, 28 May 1991: "Recollections of the IBM Radiotype."

21. *Cue*, 29 March 1941: "People," p. 32.

22. Rochester, N.Y., newspaper, 1 July 1933: "Typewriter Plant Sold to N.Y. Firm." IBM purchased the assets of Electromatic for 2,105 shares of IBM stock; assumed

the entire preferred stock ($72,000 par value) and guaranteed payment of a 6 percent dividend from July 1, 1934; agreed to pay a royalty on the net sales of typewriters at the rate of 5 percent on such sales for the period including 31 December 1938; and assumed the lease on the factory building at Rochester; see R. S. Hansen, 28 May 1958: to A. R. Miller, "Watson Biography." The resulting International Electric Writing Machine Division operated as an independent business unit; it manufactured, sold, and serviced all its products; see *American Machinist,* 16 June 1937: "From Inventor's Shop to International Corporation," pp. 559–64.

23. The possibility of entering the typewriter business had been discussed at least as early as 1928 when Bryce considered using electric typewriter elements as the basis for EAM input-output equipment and in 1929 when Watson pondered the benefits of typewriters that could also perform arithmetic. J. W. Bryce, 25 January 1928: to T. J. Watson; F. J. Tillman, 3 January 1929: to T. J. Watson; J. W. Bryce, 17 January 1929: to T. J. Watson.

24. IBM Document, 30 June 1948. The Radiotype consisted of several units and used holes punched in paper tape for temporary message storage. The first unit was a transcription electric typewriter on which the message was typed by an operator. On the underside of the typewriter was mounted a permutation unit that translated the keyed-in letters and numerals into code by closing one or more of six electric circuits. These circuits operated magnets that caused punches to perforate combinations of up to six holes in the tape. Transmission was automatic, with perforated tapes being fed through a transmitter unit at a speed of 600 characters a minute. If messages were few, the permutation unit could send its signals directly to the transmitter, thus bypassing the tape perforating and reading steps. For receiving messages, similar units were employed.

The Radiotype system was sold by IBM late in 1945 to Globe Wireless, Ltd., with headquarters in New York City. Among the considerations that favored selling the business was that the Radiotype business would place IBM in competition with one of its best customers, AT&T. The potential loss in AT&T business appeared to outweigh any possible gains from marketing Radiotype. As it turned out, Radiotype was not a particularly successful product. See R. G. Canning, circa 1990: "Early Days of Electronics," an unpublished six-page manuscript. The use of Radiotype coupled directly to encryption and decryption equipment, is reported by J. C. McPherson, 8 August 1991: discussion with E. W. Pugh.

25. S. W. Dunwell, 28 May 1991: "Recollections of the IBM Radiotype."

26. James Greene volunteered with Dunwell and served as manager of the operation much of the time. Dunwell served as the technical director. At the end of the war, Dunwell was put in charge of the entire punched-card machine operation, which then employed about 1,400 people. See S. W. Dunwell, 15 August 1991: interview by E. W. Pugh, pp. 4–8.

27. S. W. Dunwell, 1 February 1992: "A description of one way in which punched-card machines with attached relay calculators were used for codebreaking during World War II." In describing this common cryptographic method, Dunwell noted that the "carry" was omitted when the key digit was added to the message digit; e.g., 9 plus 7 was represented as 6 rather than 16.

28. S. W. Dunwell, 15 August 1991: interview by E. W. Pugh; Dunwell, 1 February 1992. Among the modified units ordered by Dunwell was a machine that could read information from a card and punch the result of a computation on that information in the same card at the speed of 100 cards per minute—a capability not previously available. The Type 600 multiplying punch introduced in 1931 could take two factors from a single card, multiply them, and punch the result in a blank field of the same card; however, this was at a much slower speed; see chap. 4.

29. Dunwell, 15 August 1991.

30. R. L. Palmer, 13 September 1991: interview by E. W. Pugh.

31. David Kahn, 1991: Seizing the Enigma (Boston: Houghton Mifflin), pp. 31–48, 245.

32. M. R. Williams, 1985: A History of Computing Technology (Englewood Cliffs, N.J.: Prentice-Hall), pp. 287–90.

33. Kahn, 1991: pp. 49–81, 99, 231. For more information on the role of the British Tabulating Machine Company in building bombes and other military devices, see M. Campbell-Kelly, 1989: *ICL: A Business and Technical History,* pp. 115–23.

34. Decryption of German messages was of course only one of many factors that helped win the Battle of the Atlantic. The introduction of shorter wavelength (9.7 versus 1,500 centimeter) radar by the Allies was another. The various factors that affected the outcome are discussed by Kahn, 1991; see in particular, pages pp. 239–40, 259, 274–75.

35. Palmer, 13 September 1991.

36. E. Tomash and A. A. Cohen, 1979: "The Birth of an ERA: Engineering Research Associates, Inc., 1946–1955," *Annals of the History of Computing 1,* pp. 83–97.

37. Palmer, 13 September 1991.

9 Future Demands

1. IBM News SDD Endicott, September 1968: "North Street Laboratory Celebrates 35th Anniversary," pp. 1–4.

2. S. W. Leslie, 1983: *Boss Kettering* (New York: Columbia University Press), pp. 1–37; T. G. Belden and M. R. Belden, 1962: *The Lengthening Shadow* (Boston: Little, Brown), p. 113. Charles F. Kettering was born in Loudonville, Ohio, in August 1876. He died in November 1958. His partner in founding Delco was Edward A. Deeds.

3. *Saturday Evening Post,* 12 August 1933: "Boss Kettering," by Paul de Kruif, as quoted in Leslie, 1983: p. 36.

4. Leslie, 1983: p. 49.

5. T. J. Watson, 1 June 1922: to J. R. Peirce. Among the members of the Future Demands Committee who received identical letters were S. M. Hastings (president, Computing Scale Company), J. R. Peirce (of Case Peirce Accounting

Machine Company), O. E. Braitmayer (assistant general manager, Tabulating Machine Company), and Clement Ehret (assistant to the general manager, Tabulating Machine Company).

6. IBM Manual of Instruction, circa 1935, p. 5; Austrian, 1982: p. 337.

7. The role of Otto E. Braitmayer is inferred from references to him or letters from him in the files of T. J. Watson. His title in 1922 is given in the letter of 1 June 1922 in which Watson appointed him a member of the Future Demands Committee.

8. *Business Machines,* 26 September 1949: "Mr. Clement Ehret, Head of Market Research, Dies." Ehret had joined the company as a sales representative in 1916 and became assistant to the general manager of the Tabulating Machine Division in 1919. Two years later he became treasurer of the division and soon thereafter sales manager.

9. C. Ehret, 19 February 1927: to T. J. Watson.

10. J. W. Bryce, 17 October 1928: to T. J. Watson.

11. *Sales Management,* 6 April 1929: "International Business Machines Inaugurates a Future Demands Department," C. Ehret as told to A. R. Hahn, pp. 9–10. This publication describes itself as "the weekly magazine for marketing executives."

12. *Business Machines,* 26 September 1949.

13. IBM document, May 1955: "Accomplishment Summary," written by F. J. Wesley with annotations by L. H. LaMotte and M. B. Smith.

14. S. W. Dunwell, 31 July 1991: interview by E. W. Pugh.

15. *Business Machines,* January 1940: "Mr. McPherson Named to Head Future Demands Department"; J. C. McPherson, 11 December 1990: interview by E. W. Pugh. Interestingly both J. C. McPherson and F. J. Wesley, who had headed Commercial Research since 1937, attended IBM Sales Class 56 in Endicott.

16. Special machine requirements had required only occasional engineering support during the 1920s, but by the time the North Street Laboratory was established, special equipment design had become one of two primary duties of the Production Engineering Department. G. F. Daly, 1953: "Development of IBM Unit Record Equipment, Inventors, and Laboratories," p. 12.

17. W. J. Eckert, 1948: "The IBM Pluggable Sequence Relay Calculator," in *Mathematical Tables and Other Aids to Computation 23,* published by the National Research Council, pp. 149–61; H. H. Goldstine, 1972: The Computer from Pascal to von Neumann, pp. 127–30.

18. The manager of Engineering, Glen H. Armstrong, was brought from the Endicott laboratory to headquarters in 1942 to conduct a reduced new products effort now named Special Research; see *Business Machines,* 16 July 1942: "Mr. Armstrong Heads New IBM Research Department."

19. J. C. McPherson, 11 December 1990: interview by E. W. Pugh. See also J. C. McPherson, 17 June 1991: discussion with E. W. Pugh. McPherson's view that Watson was the "chief engineer" takes on greater significance when one recalls that the titled position of chief engineer remained unfilled after Bryce vacated it in 1926 to establish and manage the Patent Department.

10 Preparing for Peace

1. *Business Machines,* 28 September 1950: "Ordnance Group Is Told of IBM Production Plans."

2. IBM document, 10 June 1943: summary of "Meeting of Engineers" called by T. J. Watson, Sr., at 590 Madison Avenue, New York City; IBM document, 6 July 1943: summary of meeting in Mr. Watson's office with J. C. McPherson, K. J. Mackenzie, and G. H. Armstrong.

3. IBM document, 18 June 1943: summary of "Engineering Meeting called by Mr. Watson."

4. IBM document, 18 June 1943: pp. 6–9.

5. The effort to develop an accounting machine for small businesses based on the Electromatic typewriter was managed by R. L. Houston in Endicott from about 1943 to 1947. It was abandoned after an expenditure of approximately $33,000. The machine was designed to operate from three input card decks. The small, 30-column cards ($2^5/_{16}'' \times 3^1/_2''$), were to be punched with a six-hole code. The machine would duplicate or summary punch a new deck, or punch a tape that could be mailed to a remote point for automatic reproduction into standard 80-column cards. All machine operations were controlled by a "sequence card" instead of the conventional control panel. See undated report on "Typewriter Developments," prepared for Watson, Sr., by C. R. Doty, listing research and development projects terminated at Endicott.

6. IBM document, 18 June 1943: pp. 12–13.

7. C. J. Bashe, L. R. Johnson, J. H. Palmer, and E. W. Pugh, 1986: *IBM's Early Computers* (Cambridge, Mass.: MIT Press), p. 481.

8. J. C. McPherson, 11 December 1990: interview by E. W. Pugh. The actual monthly rental of the IBM 407 Accounting Machine ranged from $800 for the least expensive to $920 for the most expensive as listed in a 1957 sales manual.

9. Bashe, Johnson, Palmer, and Pugh, 1986: p. 482.

10. E. W. Pugh, L. R. Johnson, and J. H. Palmer, 1991: *IBM's 360 and Early 370 Systems* (Cambridge, Mass.: MIT Press), pp. 574–75; H. S. Beattie and R. A. Rahenkamp, 1981: "IBM Typewriter Innovation," *IBM Journal of Research and Development 25,* pp. 729–39; F. T. May, 1981: "IBM Word Processing Developments," *IBM Journal of Research and Development 25,* pp. 741–53. The Selectric type element looked much like a golf ball with raised characters on its surface. It twisted, turned, and hammered—moving from left to right as it typed out the message, rather than having the entire paper carriage move from right to left as in conventional typewriters of the time. These innovative features, plus the ability to change type elements easily for different print fonts, contributed to the exceptional popularity of the Selectric typewriter and to the use of the type element in many different computer terminals developed and manufactured by IBM and others.

11. U.S. IBM Year End Book, 1955: A. L. Williams's copy for internal use only; "Pages from the Past," 1976: a booklet produced by IBM to recognize its thirty-fifth year in Poughkeepsie.

12. IBM document, 6 October 1943: "Minutes of Engineering Meeting Held in Mr. Watson's Office."

13. J. W. Bryce, 3 October 1944: to H. H. Aiken.

14. C. J. Bashe, 1982: "The SSEC in Historical Perspective," *Annals of the History of Computing 4*, pp. 296–312.

15. A. H. Dickinson, 18 July 1967: interview by L. M. Saphire, pp. 41–44.

16. W. J. Eckert, 20 July 1967: interview by L. M. Saphire.

17. Carl A. Bergfors was the engineer in Dickinson's group who worked with Phelps to design and build the IBM 603 Electronic Multiplier.

18. B. E. Phelps, 1980: "Early Electronic Computer Developments at IBM," *Annals of the History of Computing 2*, pp. 253–67.

19. Bashe, 1982. Hamilton and Seeber benefited from consultations with Bryce, Dickinson, McPherson, and Eckert in establishing specifications for the supercomputer.

20. IBM brochure, 1948: "IBM Selective Sequence Electronic Calculator"; J. C. McPherson, F. E. Hamilton, and R. R. Seeber, Jr., 1982: "A Large-Scale, General-Purpose Electronic Digital Calculator—the SSEC," *Annals of the History of Computing 4*, pp. 313–26; Phelps, 1980. The SSEC worked with numbers of 19 digits; a 20th digit position in storage units was used exclusively to store the sign (plus or minus) of a number. The digit storage capacities given here follow the lead of most prior SSEC descriptions by reckoning 20 digits per storage unit.

21. Phelps, 1980; Bashe, Johnson, Palmer, and Pugh, 1986: pp. 52–59. The description of Codd's major contribution is taken from a brief biography that preceded his 1981 ACM Turing Award Lecture, published in *Communications of the ACM 25*, 1982, pp. 109–17.

22. J. F. Brennan, 1971: *The IBM Watson Laboratory at Columbia University: A History* (Armonk, N.Y.: IBM), pp. 22–25.

23. W. J. Eckert, August 1946: "Facilities of the Watson Scientific Computing Laboratory," *Proceedings of the Research Forum*, pp. 75–80.

24. Bashe et al., 1986: p. 528.

25. Brennan, 1971: pp. 13–17.

26. V. Bush, 1945: *Science the Endless Frontier: A Report to the President* (Washington: U.S. Government Printing Office).

11 Government-Funded Competition

1. For a description of wartime atomic weapons research using punched-card machines at the Los Alamos Scientific (now National) Laboratory, see N. Metropolis and E. C. Nelson, 1982: "Early Computing at Los Alamos," *Annals of the History of Computing 4*, pp. 348–57.

2. C. J. Bashe, L. R. Johnson, J. H. Palmer, and E. W. Pugh, 1986: *IBM's Early Computers* (Cambridge, Mass.: MIT Press), pp. 59–68.

3. T. G. Belden and M. R. Belden, 1962: *The Lengthening Shadow* (Boston: Little, Brown), pp. 294–95.

4. The Bush differential analyzer is described in M. R. Williams, 1985: *A History of Computing Technology* (Englewood Cliffs, N.J.: Prentice-Hall), pp. 209–12. For

more detail on its origins and place in history, see L. Owens, 1986: "Vannevar Bush and the Differential Analyzer: The Text and Context of an Early Computer," *Technology and Culture 27,* pp. 63–95.

5. An overview of the role of the federal government in supporting research and development activities during and shortly after World War II may be found in A. Hunter Dupree, 1986: *Science in the Federal Government: A History of Policies and Activities* (Baltimore: Johns Hopkins University Press), pp. 369–75. For an account of postwar activities in computers and computing, see M. Rees, 1982: "The Computing Program in the Office of Naval Research, 1946–1953," *Annals of the History of Computing 4,* pp. 102–20.

6. J. C. McPherson, 24 September 1946: to W. J. Eckert.

7. W. J. Eckert, 11 October 1946: to J. C. McPherson, "Development of Electronic Computing Devices."

8. J. C. McPherson and W. J. Eckert, 12 November 1946: to T. J. Watson.

9. N. Stern, 1981: *From ENIAC to UNIVAC* (Bedford, Mass.: Digital Press), pp. 7–65. See especially pp. 33–36 for the relationship between J. W. Mauchly and J. V. Atanasoff.

10. A good account of J. P. Eckert's contribution to the ENIAC is provided by Herman Goldstine who observed it firsthand; see H. H. Goldstine, 1972: *The Computer from Pascal to von Neumann* (Princeton: Princeton University Press), pp. 148–56.

11. M. V. Wilkes, 1968: "Computers Then and Now," *Journal of the Association for Computing Machinery 15,* pp. 1–7 (presented earlier as an ACM Turing Lecture in August 1967); Bashe, Johnson, Palmer, and Pugh, 1986: pp. 55–58. The ENIAC project proposal was for a machine with about 5,000 vacuum tubes and a cost of $150,000. Completed late in 1945, ENIAC had 18,000 tubes and cost about $750,000. Its 18,000 tubes can be compared with 12,500 in IBM's SSEC and with 1,500 tubes in the Colossus, a special-purpose computer built in England to decipher German codes that became operational in December 1943. See, for example, S. Rosen, 1990: "The Origins of Modern Computing," *Computing Reviews 31,* pp. 450–81, especially p. 457.

12. F. L. Alt, 1972: "Archaeology of Computers—Reminiscences, 1945–1947," Communications of the ACM 15, pp. 693–94. The difficulty of rewiring ENIAC for each application was alleviated in 1948 at a sacrifice of machine speed. A permanent wiring was accomplished that enabled the machine to read (and execute) its program as an ordered set of up to several hundred digit-pairs from decimal switch banks originally intended to store 12-digit mathematical function values. Each of some eighty 2-digit numbers caused a particular operation; the set of operations had been chosen to give ENIAC a suitably broad repertoire of instructions and was embodied in the permanent wiring. After that, the ENIAC was programmed by writing a sequence of numbers and setting it into the switches. See also G. W. Reitwiesner, 11 April and 12 December 1986: private communications to J. H. Palmer.

13. W. Aspray, 1990: *John von Neumann and the Origins of Modern Computing* (Cambridge, Mass.: MIT Press), pp. 5–13, 25–34.

14. Stern, 1981: pp. 58–59.

15. Goldstine, 1972: p. 192.

16. John von Neumann, June 1945: "First Draft of a Report on the EDVAC," reprinted in N. Stern, 1981: *From ENIAC to UNIVAC* (Bedford, Mass.: Digital Press), pp. 177–246; E. W. Pugh, 1984: *Memories That Shaped an Industry* (Cambridge, Mass.: MIT Press), p. 3; Goldstine, 1972: pp. 184–210.

17. A stored-program computer is "a digital computer that, under control of internally stored instructions, can synthesize, alter, and store instructions as though they were data and can subsequently execute these new instructions"; see *IEEE Standard Dictionary of Electrical and Electronics Terms*, ANSI/IEEE Std. 100–1988, 4th ed., 8 July 1988, published by the Institute of Electrical and Electronics Engineers, New York, N.Y. Consistent with this modern definition of a stored-program computer, the SSEC could execute sequences of instructions (each encoded as 20 decimal digits) read from its paper tape readers and from its relay memory of 150 individually addressable units. The instruction-alteration capability was typically exploited by a program, stored either on tape or in relay memory, which altered one or two instructions in the relays, after which those instructions were executed. Detailed examples of instruction modification are given in U.S. Patent 2,636,672, filed 19 January 1949: F. E. Hamilton, R. R. Seeber, Jr., R. A. Rowley, and E. S. Hughes, Jr., "Selective Sequence Electronic Calculator." See especially claims 70 and 99 (columns 303 and 309, respectively) and the descriptive material in columns 271–88.

18. The claims of the SSEC patent were particularly broad, covering such concepts as system control of input-output devices and pipelining, as well as the basic Moore School–type of stored-program computer. During an interference between the SSEC patent and the ENIAC patent, then owned by Sperry Rand, according to a 1964 IBM Patent Operations report: "Out of 110 claims contained in this patent, 105 were copied by Sperry-Rand into their ENIAC application [for purposes of the interference process]. In the interference which followed, they were completely unsuccessful and were not granted a single one of the claims which they had copied from our SSEC patent." See E. Lester, February 1964: "History of IBM Systems Patent Coverage," written for IBM Patent Operations; B. E. Phelps, 7 November 1973: to C. J. Bashe "SSEC."

19. Bashe, Johnson, Palmer, and Pugh, 1986: pp. 47–59. The EDSAC, which was built at Cambridge University in England and operational in May 1949, is generally considered to be the first operational full-function computer based on the Moore School design. Delays in completing the EDVAC were unavoidable following the 1946 resignation of Eckert and Mauchly from the Moore School. Kite Sharpless, who took over as head of the project, left with some others to form their own company in 1947. Others left during the ensuing years. With Richard Snyder as chief engineer, EDVAC was ultimately completed in 1951 and joined the ENIAC in 1952 at the U.S. Army Ordnance Corps Ballistic Research Laboratory at Aberdeen Proving Ground in Maryland. The EDVAC contained just over 3,500 vacuum tubes and about 27,000 other electronic components. See M. R. Williams, 1985: *A History of Computing Technology* (Englewood Cliffs, N.J.: Prentice-Hall), pp. 323–34, 349–53.

20. J. P. Eckert, Jr., 1976: "Thoughts on the History of Computing," *Computer 9*, pp. 58–65.

21. J. P. Eckert, Jr., and J. W. Mauchly, 30 September 1945: "Automatic High-Speed Computing—A Progress Report on the EDVAC," Moore School of Electrical Engineering, University of Pennsylvania.

22. Goldstine, 1972: p. 196. The mode of distribution of the document and its impact on knowledgeable readers is revealed by M. V. Wilkes, who recalls that L. J. Comrie (back from a trip to the United States) loaned him a copy of von Neumann's report in May 1946. Not having a means for copying it, Wilkes says, "I sat up late into the night reading the report. . . . I recognized this at once as the real thing, and from that time on never had any doubt as to the way computer development would go." See M. V. Wilkes, 1985: *Memoirs of a Computer Pioneer* (Cambridge, Mass.: MIT Press), pp. 108–09.

23. Stern, 1981: pp. 82–84. A simple description of the Selectron storage device is provided by Pugh, 1984: pp. 14–15.

24. J. C. McPherson, 23 September 1946: to file, with copies to A. H. Dickinson, W. J. Eckert, and F. E. Hamilton. During these discussions, McPherson learned that the EDVAC would be designed to economize its use of vacuum tubes, having perhaps as few as 500. It was estimated that an EDVAC could be replicated, after a few had been built, for less than $20,000. Subsequent experience revealed both of these estimates to be far too low.

25. Goldstine, 1972: p. 241; Stern, 1981: p. 94. The course was held for eight weeks during July and August 1946.

26. J. C. McPherson, 12 March 1971: deposition testimony in *Honeywell, Inc. v. Sperry Rand Corporation*, U.S. District Court, District of Minnesota, pp. 117–22. The reason given for the last-minute exclusion of IBM representatives is highly suspect since some who had no government contracts did attend. Among these was M. V. Wilkes as described by him in 1985: *Memoirs of a Computer Pioneer* (Cambridge, Mass.: MIT Press), chap. 12.

27. In a different context, N. Stern, 1981: *From ENIAC to UNIVAC*, p. 41, notes that during the war "those companies cooperating [in electronics] with the NDRC [National Defense Research Committee] were worried that IBM might gain information and hence a competitive advantage."

28. Stern, 1981: pp. 66–115; see especially pp. 84–85, 88–91, 103.

29. Stern, 1981: p. 92. Based on her 1977 interviews with J. W. Mauchly and J. P. Eckert, Nancy Stern provides the interesting insight that Eckert's wife and father agreed with Mauchly and helped persuade Eckert to attempt the independent commercial venture. Stern also reports that Eckert "expressed some remorse over his decision not to go with IBM"; see Stern, 1981: p. 265, n. 18.

30. Stern, 1981: p. 145.

31. Stern, 1981: pp. 105–06. The evaluation of the proposal was made by George Stibitz, a mathematician at the Bell Telephone Laboratories who designed a number of computing devices using telephone switching relays, beginning with a "partially automatic computer" in 1940. This work began at about the time Howard Aiken and IBM undertook their collaboration on the Mark I. See Goldstine, 1972: pp. 115–20.

32. Williams, 1985: pp. 360–63.

33. The support of EMCC was arranged by the American Totalisator vice president, Henry Strauss, who simultaneously became chairman of the nine-member board of EMCC.

34. Stern, 1981: pp. 116–59; see especially pp. 119–29, 146–51. The first UNIVAC to be installed at a Remington Rand facility was the seventh to be produced and was shipped only two months before the one to GE. The shipment dates and customers for the first eight UNIVACs are as follows: (1) Bureau of Census, Washington, D.C., 3/51; (2) Air Force Comptroller, Arlington, Va., 3/52; (3) Army Map Service, Bethesda, Md., 4/52; (4) Atomic Energy Commission, N.Y.U., New York, N.Y., 4/53; (5) Atomic Energy Commission, Livermore, Calif., 11/52; (6) Bureau of Ships (DTMB), Bethesda, Md., 5/53; (7) Remington Rand UNIVAC, DPC, New York, N.Y., 10/53; (8) General Electric, Louisville, Ky., 1/54. See Sperry Univac's Commemorative Program for the National Computer Conference 1981 Pioneer Day Banquet, 6 May 1981.

35. E. Tomash and A. A. Cohen, 1979: "The Birth of an ERA: Engineering Research Associates, Inc., 1946–1955," *Annals of the History of Computing 1*, pp. 83–97. Functioning as a separate division of Remington Rand, ERA was the responsibility of the director of advanced research, Lieut. Gen. (ret.) Leslie R. Groves, who had served during World War II as head of the Manhattan Project (1942 through 1946). The Atlas computer contained 2,700 vacuum tubes and 2,385 crystal diodes. It was run twenty-four hours a day with 10 percent of the time allocated to preventive maintenance. Reportedly only sixteen hours of unscheduled maintenance were required in the first five hundred hours of operation—an outstanding record for the time.

36. From 1955 to 1970 the value of general-purpose computers shipped by IBM is reported to have accounted for a declining percentage of the market, dropping irregularly from about 80 to 60 percent. During the same time, the value of UNIVAC shipments also dropped (very irregularly) from roughly 12 percent of the market to about 6 percent, when it was overtaken by Burroughs. Honeywell was the third major contender. After GE sold most of its computer business to Honeywell in 1970 and RCA sold out to Univac in 1971, Honeywell and UNIVAC each held 6 to 10 percent of the market for several years. See M. Phister, 1979: *Data Processing Technology and Economics* (Bedford, Mass.: Digital Press), pp. 36–46.

12 IBM's Initial Response

1. J. W. Bryce, 12 April 1948: to T. J. Watson.

2. *Business Machines,* 4 April 1949: "Mr. J. W. Bryce, IBM Pioneer, Inventor, Chief Consultant, Technical Staff Dean, Dies."

3. T. J. Watson, Jr., and P. Petre, 1990: *Father, Son & Co.* (New York: Bantam Press), pp. 31–38, 42.

4. Watson, Jr., and Petre, 1990: pp. 42, 76–87.

5. Watson, Jr., and Petre, 1990: pp. 96–109.

6. Watson, Jr., and Petre, 1990: pp. 130–32.

7. Watson, Jr., and Petre, 1990: pp. 138–46.

8. E. W. Pugh, L. R. Johnson, and J. H. Palmer, 1986: *IBM's 360 and Early 370 Systems* (Cambridge, Mass.: MIT Press), Appen. D, pp. 649–50. The post of Chairman had not been filled since George W. Fairchild vacated it in December 1924.

9. *Fortune Magazine,* November 1960: "Q. What Grows Faster than IBM? A. I.B.M. Abroad"; *IBM Magazine,* September 1970: "For 'Dick' Watson, A New World of Policy and Diplomacy," pp. 3–7; M. Campbell-Kelly, 1989: *ICL: A Business and Technical History* (Oxford, England: Clarendon Press), pp. 139–43. See also *IBM Kingston News,* 23 December 1959, p. 3. In January 1952 Tom Watson was promoted to president of IBM, and in June 1954 Dick Watson was promoted to president of the rapidly growing World Trade Corporation. The final shift in authority occurred in May 1956 when Watson, Jr., replaced his father as CEO. One month later the senior Watson died of a heart attack. A. K. Watson became a corporate vice president and group executive and a member of the board of directors in December 1959.

10. Watson, Jr., and Petre, 1990: pp. 135–37.

11. The eagerness of Watson, Sr., to use electronics in the product line is documented by internal records beginning in 1943. For example, the minutes of the engineering meeting held in Watson's office on 6 October 1943 quotes Watson as saying: "We are not doing enough on electronics. No tests have been made with electronics on the accounting machine. We have done nothing except with two punches at Endicott, and they don't work well." The minutes then assert, "Mr. Watson wants electronics used on the accounting machine and on the printer."

12. Watson, Jr., and Petre, 1990: p. 205. Among the many books and articles that suggest Watson, Sr., opposed the company's entry into electronics is one by R. Sobel, 1981: *IBM Colossus in Transition* (New York: Times Books), p. 121. Sobel says Charlie Kirk showed Watson, Jr., the prototype electronic calculator, and that Kirk and Watson, Jr., subsequently "prodded Watson senior into accelerating the research and then producing the machines." In a letter of 6 January 1982 to Edward Nanas, IBM director of information, John C. McPherson identified this statement as one of many errors in Sobel's book, saying that when Watson, Jr., first saw the electronic multiplier in Bryce's laboratory, "Mr. Watson was there too and needed no prodding to go ahead with immediate production."

13. The enthusiasm of T. J. Watson, Sr., for expanding the electric typewriter business and modifying typewriters to serve as low-cost EAM equipment is discussed in chap. 10; see especially n. 5. The move of typewriter production to Poughkeepsie in 1944 is documented in "Pages from the Past," 1976, a booklet published by IBM to observe its thirty-fifth year in Poughkeepsie.

14. R. L. Palmer, 31 September 1991: interview by E. W. Pugh.

15. C. J. Bashe, L. R. Johnson, J. H. Palmer, and E. W. Pugh, 1986: *IBM's Early Computers* (Cambridge, Mass.: MIT Press), pp. 60–61.

16. B. E. Phelps, 1980: "Early Electronic Computer Developments at IBM," *Annals of the History of Computing 2,* pp. 253–67; see especially page 258.

17. A. L. Samuel, December 1967: interview by L. M. Saphire. See also Bashe et al., 1986: p. 67.

18. Phelps, 1980.

19. Bashe et al., 1986: pp. 62–63.

20. Phelps, 1980.

21. G. J. Toben, 11 June 1968: interview by L. M. Saphire.

22. G. S. Fenn, 1948: "Programming and Using the Type 603–405 Combination Machine in the Solution of Differential Equations," in *Proceedings of the Scientific Computation Forum*, IBM Watson Scientific Computing Laboratory, H. R. J. Grosch, ed., pp. 95–98. See also G. J. Toben, December 1949: "Transition from Problem to Card Program," *Proceedings of the Computation Seminar*, Endicott, N.Y., C. C. Hurd, ed., pp. 128–31.

23. Wallace Eckert had designed and installed a Calculation Control Switch to sequence three interconnected EAM units through lengthy computations at the Thomas J. Watson Astronomical Computing Bureau at Columbia University, in 1937. Although this device was not available as a product, it was described in Eckert's widely read 1940 book, *Punched Card Methods in Scientific Computation*. At an IBM-sponsored forum on automatic computation methods in August 1946, Eckert described the facilities of the new Watson Laboratory and mentioned a plan to go well beyond the Computation Control Switch by connecting a relay calculator with the 405 Accounting Machine and a summary punch. At a similar forum one year later, he again discussed the laboratory's project in which a relay calculator was connected "with an accounting machine and a special control box to operate as a baby sequence calculator with instructions on punched cards." See W. J. Eckert, August 1946: "Facilities of the Watson Scientific Computing Laboratory," in *Proceedings of the Research Forum*, Endicott, N.Y., pp. 75–80; August 1947: "The IBM Department of Pure Science and the Watson Scientific Computing Laboratory," in *Educational Research Forum Proceedings*, Endicott, N.Y., pp. 31–36.

24. S. W. Dunwell, 15 August 1991: interview by E. W. Pugh.

25. C. C. Hurd, November 1949: "The IBM Card-Programmed Electronic Calculator," in *Proceedings of the Seminar on Scientific Computation*, C. C. Hurd, ed., pp. 37–41; J. W. Sheldon and L. Tatum, February 1952: "The IBM Card-Programmed Electronic Calculator," *Review of Electronic Digital Computers, Joint AIEE-IRE Computer Conference*, December 1951, pp. 30–36.

26. The IBM 603 was announced in September 1946 and shipments began before the end of the year. Customer shipments of the IBM 604 began in the fall of 1948 and of the CPC in September 1949. The first UNIVAC was accepted by the Census Bureau on 31 March 1951. See Bashe et al., 1986: pp. 71, 575. On 29 January 1950 the following list of year-end 1949 CPC customers, and their primary applications, was generated by C. M. Mooney at IBM headquarters: University of California (Los Alamos), Albuquerque, N.M. (2 machines for partial differential equations); Argonne National Lab., Aurora, Ill. (partial differential equations); Aberdeen Proving Grounds, Baltimore, Md. (general ballistics, heat transfer, dopler, control of guided missiles, reduction of wind tunnel and Theodolite data); Cornell Aeronautical Laboratory, Buffalo, N.Y. (reduction of wind tunnel data); National Advisory Committee for Aeronautics,

Cleveland, Ohio (reduction of wind tunnel and other pressure gauge data, nuclear shielding); Parsons Corporation, Grand Rapids, Mich. (service bureau on aeronautical design); Fairchild Aircraft, Hagerstown, Md. (vibration and flutter calculations); Penn State College, Johnstown, Pa. (distillation calculations); Carbide & Carbon Chemical (Oak Ridge), Knoxville, Tenn. (2 machines for partial differential equations); Rand Corporation, Los Angeles, Calif. (2 machines for nuclear shielding, partial differential equations); U.S. Dept. of Commerce Bureau of Standards (UCLA), Los Angeles, Calif. (nuclear shielding, reduction of Theodolite data); Telecomputing Corporation, Los Angeles, Calif. (service bureau including vibration and flutter and aerodynamics for Lockheed); Northrop Aircraft, Los Angeles, Calif. (nuclear shielding, vibration and flutter calculations); Douglas Aircraft (Santa Monica), Los Angeles, Calif. (aerodynamics and vibration and flutter calculations); U.S. Dept. of the Interior, Bureau of Mines, Pittsburgh, Pa. (development of explosives); U.S. Naval Ordnance, Riverside, Calif. (2 machines for reduction of Theodolite data); Boeing Aircraft, Seattle, Wash. (vibration and flutter calculations); Reed Research, Inc., Washington, D.C. (service bureau on data reduction and logistic computations); U.S. Dept. of Commerce, Bureau of Standards, Washington, D.C. (Project SCOOP, hydrographic (Loran), optical rate tracing, etc.); IBM Service Bureau, Chicago, Ill. (service bureau); IBM Service Bureau, Los Angeles, Calif. (service bureau); IBM Service Bureau, New York, N.Y. (service bureau); IBM of Canada, Toronto, Canada (service bureau); Navy Hydrographic Office, Washington, D.C. (hydrographic [Loran] tables for maps, stars, etc.); Consolidated Vultee, Fort Worth, Tex. (vibration and flutter calculations); Woodmen of the World, Omaha, Neb. ([application not given]); Air Force, Air Matériel Command, Dayton, Ohio (Project SCOOP establishment of consumption factors).

27. The electronic computation speeds of the CPC were 2,000 additions or subtractions and 86 multiplications or divisions per second. The equivalent speeds for the UNIVAC were 1,700 additions or subtractions, 400 multiplications, or 250 divisions per second. In a problem mix involving an equal number of each arithmetic operation, the UNIVAC would execute 1,012 per second and the CPC, 1,043. The size of the numbers each handled was approximately the same: 10 decimal digits for the CPC and 11 decimal digits for the UNIVAC. The real performance advantage of the UNIVAC came from its one hundred times larger internal memory (12,000 characters) and from its ability to transfer information in and out of memory at speeds up to 9,000 decimal digits per second. The electronic circuits were thus kept busy a higher percentage of the time than on the CPC, which was constrained by the 100-to-150-card-per-minute rate at which program instructions could be entered. However, each of these CPC instructions could result in as many as 60 program steps, consisting of any one of the four arithmetic operations or a number transfer. Thus, in theory, the CPC arithmetic circuits could also be kept busy full time—but it was far less likely. See Engineering Research Associates, Inc., 1950: *High-Speed Computing Devices* (New York: McGraw-Hill), pp. 157–58, 165, 203–06. In discussing the CPC, one authority said: "The limitations of this machine are due to the relatively small size of its memory, and to the small number of subroutines which can be plugged up on it at one time." See B. V. Bowden, 1953: "Computers in America," in *Faster than Thought*, ed. B. V. Bowden (London: Pitman Publishing), p. 177. A computing center could, however, have numerous plugboards

prewired with a variety of subroutines. Prewired plugboards could be taken off the shelf and inserted in the CPC in a matter of minutes.

28. W. J. Eckert, August 1946: "Facilities of the Watson Scientific Computing Laboratory," *Proceedings of the Research Forum,* held in Endicott, N.Y., (New York: International Business Machines Corporation), pp. 75–80; H. R. J. Grosch, 1991: "Early Computing Courses," *Annals of the History of Computing 13,* pp. 306–07; C. C. Hurd, 1980: "Computer Development at IBM," in *A History of Computing in the Twentieth Century* (New York: Academic Press), pp. 389–418, especially p. 400. Describing the course offered by Wallace Eckert as a "fully integrated" part of the Columbia University graduate program, Herb Grosch says, "Starting in the fall term of 1945, he offered a course in machine methods with the assistance of Marjorie Severy Herrick, Lillian Feinstein Hausman, and Eric Hankam." These courses predated those offered by Howard Aiken at Harvard by several years, according to Grosch.

29. W. J. Eckert, 10 May 1948: to J. C. McPherson.

30. C. E. Love, 16 June 1948: to all district managers, "Employment of Men for Scientific Calculating Program"; W. H. Reid, 31 May 1949: to G. P. Lovell, "Scientific Sales Program."

31. W. H. Reid, 1 August 1949: to C. E. Love, "Scientific Computation and Related Activities."

32. *Business Machines,* 28 November 1949: "Dr. Hurd Named Director of Applied Science Dept."

33. *Business Machines,* 13 March 1953: "Applied Science Dept. Is Raised to Division Status." This article gives a good description of the activities of the Applied Science Department. The reported elevation to divisional status was symbolic of its growing importance but had little organizational significance.

34. *Computerworld,* 3 November 1986: "Census led computer age by counting on Univac I," p. 150.

35. When he joined the MIT Radiation Laboratory in July 1941, Havens was a third-year graduate student at Cal Tech, having previously received his bachelor's degree in electrical engineering from the University of Washington. Two others hired from the MIT Radiation Laboratory at the same time were Robert M. Walker and John J. Lentz.

36. B. L. Havens, 31 January 1968: interview by L. M. Saphire.

37. R. Hopkins, 12 August 1948: to L. H. LaMotte, "Digital Computing Machines." The six organizations "planning to order large computing machines at the earliest possible moment" were listed as the Naval Ordnance Laboratory, Washington, D.C.; David Taylor Model Basin, Washington, D.C.; Naval Research Laboratory, Washington, D.C.; University of Illinois; Project Rand, Los Angeles, Calif.; and Naval Test Station, Inyokern, Calif.

38. L. H. LaMotte, 28 August 1948: to J. G. Phillips.

39. J. C. McPherson, 12 October and 3 November 1950: to Commander, U.S. Naval Ordnance Laboratory; A. L. Williams, 7 May 1951: to Department of the Navy. An undated telegram beginning with the phrase "You are hereby awarded letter of intent for contract NORD" authorized reimbursement of "anticipatory

costs incurred by you on and after 1 May 1951 in an amount not to exceed $40,000."

40. Bashe et al., 1986: pp. 181–83.

13 Watson, Jr., Takes Charge

1. W. W. McDowell, 14 December 1948: to T. J. Watson, Jr.; 17 December 1948: to W. L. Lewis, "Hiring of Electronic Engineers."

2. T. J. Watson, Jr., and P. Petre, 1990: *Father, Son & Co.* (New York: Bantam Press), pp. 199–200.

3. *Business Machines,* 12 November 1942: "Mr. A. L. Williams Is Promoted to Comptroller of IBM Corp."; *IBM News Magazine,* 25 April 1969: "Mr. Heart-of-the Matter," pp. 7–11.

4. Watson, Jr., and Petre, 1990: p. 201.

5. *Business Machines,* 12 November 1942: "Mr. W. W. McDowell Heads Laboratory at Endicott"; IBM document, undated: "Employment Record of William W. McDowell."

6. W. W. McDowell, 11 November 1970: interview by L. M. Saphire.

7. Watson, Jr., and Petre, 1990: p. 203.

8. Watson, Jr., and Petre, 1990: pp. 156–57, 196.

9. J. C. McPherson, December 1990: interview by E. W. Pugh.

10. Watson, Jr., and Petre, 1990: p. 201.

11. J. W. Birkenstock, 25 May 1982: interview by E. W. Pugh.

12. C. C. Hurd, 18 October 1950: to W. L. Lewis, "Applied Science Customers Participating in the National Defense Effort"; 3 January 1979: testimony in *U.S. v. IBM,* U.S. District Court, Southern District of New York, N.Y., p. 86339.

13. J. W. Birkenstock, 30 November 1950: to T. J. Watson, Jr.

14. J. W. Birkenstock, 15 December 1950: to T. J. Watson, Jr.

15. E. W. Pugh, 1984: *Memories That Shaped an Industry* (Cambridge, Mass.: MIT Press), pp. 34–38.

16. C. J. Bashe, L. R. Johnson, J. H. Palmer, and E. W. Pugh, 1986: *IBM's Early Computers* (Cambridge, Mass.: MIT Press), pp. 112, 119, 190–95.

17. S. W. Dunwell, 8 November 1949: "Electronic Tape Program"; N. Rochester and W. Buchholz, 24 March 1950: "Preliminary Outline of Tape Processing Machine."

18. W. W. McDowell, 17 December 1948: to W. L. Lewis, "Hiring of Electronic Engineers."

19. Birkenstock, 15 December 1950; N. Rochester, 18 October 1955: to R. K. Richards, "Electrostatic Memory in the 701." The committee was chaired by R. M. Bury of the sales organization. His primary assignment at the time was to help determine how IBM could best contribute to the Korean War effort. Other members of the committee were Stephen W. Dunwell (Future Demands), Wallace J. Eckert and Llewellyn H. Thomas (Watson Laboratory), Cuthbert C.

Hurd and Walter H. Johnson (Applied Science), and Nathaniel Rochester and C. M. Mooney (Engineering).

20. N. Rochester, 3 October 1967: interview by L. M. Saphire; C. C. Hurd, 3 January 1979: testimony in *U.S. v. IBM*, U.S. District Court, Southern District of New York, pp. 86338–44.

21. W. W. McDowell, 22 January 1951: to E. M. Douglas; H. T. Hansfort, 23 February 1951: to J. W. Birkenstock.

22. L. H. LaMotte, 21 May 1952: to internal distribution, "IBM Electronic Data Processing Machine (Defense Calculator)"; IBM document, 4 August 1952: "IBM-EDPM Type 701 Order Status"; H. T. Hansford, 28 July 1952: to L. H. LaMotte, "Electronic Data Processing Machine Delivery Schedule"; L. H. LaMotte, 18 August 1952: to H. T. Hansford, "Electronic Data Processing Machine Delivery Schedule."

23. Bashe et al., 1986: pp. 135–36.

24. R. L. Palmer, 13 September 1991: interview by E. W. Pugh.

25. J. C. McPherson, 5 October 1951: to John von Neumann. This letter formally offered a consulting position with a retainer of $12,000 per year plus travel expenses for up to thirty days of consulting; any additional days were to be paid at the rate of $400 per day. The consulting arrangement was officially terminated by a letter to von Neumann, dated 3 February 1955, signed by T. J. Watson, Jr., and accompanied by a check "representing the final payment." It is interesting to note that Wallace Eckert and John McPherson had attempted to hire von Neumann early in 1945, well before his "First Draft of a Report on the EDVAC" was written. At a fee of $5,000 per year, von Neumann was to have devoted an average of "fifteen percent of his occupational time to this IBM work, and under IBM's direction," according to an unsigned agreement that was dated 1 April 1945. This early contract was not consummated because of perceived conflicts of interest for von Neumann. Further consideration of a consulting arrangement was dropped a year later because von Neumann was undertaking work on an electronic computer at the Institute for Advanced Study in Princeton; see W. Aspray, 1990: *John von Neumann and the Origins of Modern Computing* (Cambridge, Mass.: MIT Press), pp. 241–45.

26. Bashe et al., 1986: pp. 135, 138–41; W. Buchholz, 1953: "The System Design of the IBM Type 701 Computer," *Proceedings of the Institute of Radio Engineers* 41, pp. 1262–75.

27. IBM Principles of Operation Manual, 1953: "Type 701 and Associated Equipment" (IBM Form 22-6042-0); N. Rochester, 26 May 1952: Memo 191, "Availability of the 701." Production of the IBM 701 was at an average rate of one per month from about April 1953 through June 1954 when the eighteenth machine was completed and shipped to Lockheed Aircraft in Burbank, California. A nineteenth machine was assembled from the remaining "spare parts." The nineteen IBM 701s were shipped primarily to companies in the aerospace and other defense-related industries as follows: IBM World Headquarters, New York, N.Y. (12/20/52); University of California, Los Alamos, N.M. (03/23/53); Lockheed Aircraft Company, Glendale, Calif. (04/24/53); National Security Agency, Washington, D.C. (04/28/53); Douglas Aircraft Company, Santa Monica, Calif. (05/20/53); General Electric Company, Lockland, Ohio

(05/27/53); Convair, Fort Worth, Tex. (07/22/53); U.S. Navy, Inyokern, Calif. (08/27/53); United Aircraft, East Hartford, Conn. (09/18/53); North American Aviation, Santa Monica, Calif. (10/09/53); Rand Corporation, Santa Monica, Calif. (10/30/53); Boeing Corporation, Seattle, Wash. (11/20/53); University of California, Los Alamos, N.M. (12/19/53); Douglas Aircraft Company, El Segundo, Calif. (01/08/54); Naval Aviation Supply, Philadelphia, Pa. (02/19/54); University of California, Livermore, Calif. (04/09/54); General Motors Corporation, Detroit, Mich. (04/23/54); Lockheed Aircraft Company, Glendale, Calif. (06/30/54); U.S. Weather Bureau, Washington, D.C. (02/28/55). See *Annals of the History of Computing 5,* April 1983: "Customer Experiences," p. 175.

28. *New York Times,* 30 April 1952: "Watson Reports IBM Expansion," p. 41.

29. *IBM Record,* April 1953: "New IBM Electronic Data Processing Machines Unveiled at World Headquarters in New York." By contrast, UNIVAC was typically not sufficiently operational to earn revenue until several months after shipment. The second UNIVAC, for example, passed its acceptance test and was shipped in late February 1952 to the Pentagon, where the manufacturer's engineers installed it and performed limited operation and checking before it was formally transferred four months later to the air force on 25 June 1952. See R. Kopp, 1953: "Experience on the air force UNIVAC," *Proceedings of the Eastern Joint Computer Conference,* pp. 62–67.

30. W. G. Bouricius, December 1953: "Operating Experience with the Los Alamos 701," *Proceedings of the Eastern Joint Computer Conference,* pp. 45–47.

31. T. A. Burke (undated): "Review—Type 701 Electronic Data Processing Machine Program."

32. E. Tomash and A. A. Cohen, 1979: "The Birth of an ERA: Engineering Research Associates, Inc. 1946–1955," *Annals of the History of Computing 1,* pp. 83–97. The original Atlas (Atlas I) was installed in Washington, D.C., in December 1950; see chap. 11.

33. H. H. Goldstine, 1972: *The Computer from Pascal to von Neumann* (Princeton: Princeton University Press), p. 329.

34. Bashe et al., 1986: pp. 173–78.

35. M. E. Davis, December 1953: "The Use of Electronic Data Processing Systems in the Life Insurance Business," *Proceedings of the Eastern Joint Computer Conference,* pp. 11–18.

36. *Business Machines,* 15 April 1954: "T. V. Learson Named Director of EDPM."

37. *Business Machines,* 3 May 1954: "EDPM Programming Research Department is Organized."

38. O. M. Scott, 25 June 1954: "702 EDPM Equipment." The fourteen installations of the IBM 702 were, in order of receipt of their equipment: IBM Poughkeepsie, Monsanto Chemical, National Security Agency, Aviation Supply Office (USN), State of California, General Electric (Hanford), Commonwealth Edison, Oklahoma City Air Matériel Area (USAF), Pratt & Whitney, Bank of America, Chrysler, Prudential, General Electric (Schenectady), and Ford Motor; see L. R. Johnson, 22 April 1976: to J. H. Palmer, "IBM 702 Original Customers."

39. IBM Product Announcements, 1 October 1954: "IBM Type 705 Electronic Data Processing Machine"; "IBM Type 701–704 EDPM."

40. Bashe et al., 1986: pp. 446–49.

41. *Business Machines,* 1 December 1954: "T. V. Learson Promoted by Board to the Post of Vice-President in Charge of Sales"; 19 January 1955: "Dr. Cuthbert C. Hurd Is Promoted; Becomes Director of EDPM."

42. T. J. Watson, Jr., 13 June 1983: interview by J. B. Rochester in *Computerworld,* pp. 10–17.

43. *Business Machines,* 1 June 1956: "T. J. Watson, Jr., Named IBM Chief Executive," pp. 3–4.

44. T. J. Watson, 10 February 1948: to J. G. Phillips.

45. Bashe et al., 1986: pp. 73–78. At this time a digit was represented in the Magnetic Drum Calculator in the same binary-coded decimal (4-bit) code used in the 603, SSEC, and 604. Engineering considerations later led to the choice of a 7-bit code for processing circuits and a 5-bit code for the magnetic drum. The 7-bit code facilitated economical self-checking and arithmetic circuits. But the cost of magnetic recording heads and circuits worked against its use on the drum, where main memory was implemented in forty bands of five tracks each.

46. C. E. Love, 11 August 1949: to T. J. Watson, Jr., "Magnetic Drum Development."

47. J. M. Coombs, 1947: "Storage of Numbers on Magnetic Tape," *Proceedings of the National Electronics Conference,* pp. 201–09. A photograph of an early ERA drum may be found in E. W. Pugh, 1984: Memories That Shaped an Industry (Cambridge, Mass.: MIT Press), p. 21.

48. Watson, Jr., and Petre, 1990: pp. 199–200; Love, 11 August 1949.

49. IBM document, 8 March 1950: "Agreement, IBM and ERA," signed by T. J. Watson, Jr., for IBM and J. E. Parker for ERA; Bashe et al., 1986: pp. 80–81.

50. IBM document (undated): "Conference on Magnetic Drum Calculators of March 13 & 14, 1950." Twenty members of IBM's engineering staff attended this internal IBM conference, including F. E. Hamilton, W. W. McDowell, J. C. McPherson, R. L. Palmer, and B. E. Phelps. C. C. Hurd represented the Applied Science Department, and S. W. Dunwell represented the Future Demands Department and was instrumental in establishing the stringent cost criteria.

51. Bashe et al., 1982: pp. 95–98.

52. S. W. Dunwell, 30 September 1952: "IBM Calculator Program"; J. C. McPherson, 20 November 1952: "Competitive Drum Computers." The seven small stored-program computers, which sold for prices ranging from $45,000 to $100,000, were offered by Consolidated Engineering Corp., Hogan Laboratories, Marchant Calculators, Inc., Monroe Calculating Machine Co., National Cash Register Co., Remington Rand, and Underwood Corporation.

53. Bashe et al., 1986: pp. 98–101; IBM Development Reports, October 1952 and November 1952: "Magnetic Drum Calculator."

54. J. W. Birkenstock and W. W. McDowell, 24 August 1953: "Magnetic Drum Calculator"; A. J. Perlis, December 1954: "Characteristics of Currently Available Small Digital Computers," *Proceedings of the Eastern Joint Computer Conference,*

pp. 11–16; Bashe et al., 1986: pp. 171–72, 339. When John Hancock in Boston received the first IBM 650 computer in December 1954, more than 450 had been ordered—almost twice the total number projected just before announcement. One of the best discussions of the utility of the 650 is provided by E. H. Dohrmann, 1956: "Data Processing Machine—Business and Industry 'Workhorse,'" in *Punched Card Annual,* pp. 20–23.

55. Bashe et al., 1986: p. 172.

56. The level of success and durability achieved by the IBM 650 is revealed by the "Final Report—IBM Computer Product Line," prepared for the Radio Corporation of America, Advanced Military Systems Division, Princeton, N.J., by Auerbach Electronics Corporation on 12 February 1960. According to the report: "The IBM 650 is an old machine, but is still selling well. Over the years, a host of attachments and accessories have been developed for this machine to increase the range of application. Many of the early installations were for engineering computation. In later years, the machine was primarily used for business data processing. Before the 1401 was introduced, the 650 was a popular "first" machine even for large companies, with the possibility of a step-up to a larger computer later." Tabular data in the report indicate that fifteen hundred IBM 650s had been installed by the end of 1959, compared to only seven of the newly introduced, transistorized RCA 501 computer. For raw arithmetic speed, the IBM 650 was 0.7 times as fast as the RCA 501, but its lower minimum cost give it almost a threefold advantage in arithmetic cost-performance over the 501. The RCA 501 was of course functionally superior because of its larger memory and input-output capability (Auerbach Associates Records, CBI 30, courtesy of the Charles Babbage Institute Archives, University of Minnesota).

14 Programming Computers

1. The first issue of the IBM Applied Science Department Technical Newsletter appeared in June 1950 and contained general purpose control-panel wiring arrangements. Distributed to customers and others until 1957, this informal newsletter played a role for scientific applications similar to that played by *Pointers* for business applications during the 1930s and 1940s. See C. J. Bashe, L. R. Johnson, J. H. Palmer, and E. W. Pugh, 1986: *IBM's Early Computers* (Cambridge, Mass.: MIT Press), pp. 85–86, 618 N. 42.

2. A. Hyman, 1982: *Charles Babbage, Pioneer of the Computer* (Princeton: Princeton University Press), especially pp. 195–98. See also J. Baum, 1986: *The Calculating Passion of Ada Byron* (Hamden, Conn.: Shoe String Press). Ada Lovelace was the daughter of the poet George Gordon, sixth Lord Byron.

3. A new method for programming ENIAC was first tested in September 1948. Proposed by von Neumann, the technique slowed the machine operations by several fold, but it made programming so much easier that the old method was never used again. It provided ENIAC with a set of fifty-one orders (instructions) that could be called on for execution. Within another year, the instruction set had been expanded from fifty-one to ninety-two. See H. H. Goldstine, 1972: "The Computer from Pascal to von Neumann" (Princeton: Princeton University Press), pp. 233–34.

4. J. P. Eckert and J. W. Mauchly, 30 September 1945: "Automatic High Speed Computing—A Progress Report on EDVAC," Moore School of Electrical Engineering, University of Pennsylvania, p. 39. This is a report based on work done under contract to the U.S. Army Ordnance Department.

5. A. M. Turing, 1945: "Proposals for Development in the Mathematics Division of an Automatic Computing Engine (ACE)," reprinted with a foreword by D. W. Davies, April 1972: Report Com. Sci. 57, National Physical Laboratory, especially p. 28.

6. M. V. Wilkes, D. J. Wheeler, and S. Gill, 1951: *The Preparation of Programs for an Electronic Digital Computer* (Cambridge, Mass.: Addison-Wesley Press); M. V. Wilkes, June 1949: summary of his remarks in "Discussion of Plans, Projects and General Ideas," *Report of a Conference on High Speed Automatic Calculating-Machines*, issued by the Cambridge University Mathematical Laboratory, January 1950, pp. 123–33, especially p. 133.

7. F. E. Johnston, 1983: "The One-Card Binary Loader for the IBM 701," *Annals of the History of Computing 5*, pp. 133–35.

8. N. Rochester, 3 August 1952: "Symbolic Programming," an IBM technical report; March 1953: "Symbolic Programming," *Transactions of the Institute of Radio Engineers, Professional Group on Electronic Computers*, EC-2, pp. 10–15, with corrections published in the June 1953 issue of the same journal on p. 27; IBM document, undated: "IBM Applied Science EDPM Assembly Program—IBM SO2." The assembly program SO2 was written by W. F. McClelland of C. C. Hurd's Applied Science Department.

9. J. Morison, August 1953: "701 Symposium Notes," Douglas Aircraft Company, Inc., report.

10. N. Rochester, 10 September 1953: "A Meeting of 701 Customers in Los Angeles on August 17–18, 1953," an IBM report.

11. F. Jones, June 1956: "SHARE—A Study in the Reduction of Redundant Programming Effort through the Promotion of Inter-Installation Communication," *Symposium on Advanced Programming Methods for Digital Computers* (Washington: Office of Naval Research), pp. 67–70. As described in this article, "SHARE is a voluntary, informal organization of the users of the IBM Type 704 electronic data-processing machines. It is devoted to (1) the standardization of machine language and certain machine practices, (2) the elimination of redundant effort expended in connection with the use of the computer, (3) the promotion of inter-installation communication, and (4) the development of a meaningful stream of information between the user and the manufacturer."

12. 1103 Central Exchange, February 1956: Newsletter Number 8. An informal predecessor organization, called the 1103 Central Exchange, reported in its February 1956 newsletter that "the early 1103A purchasers desired to go beyond the Central Exchange with its voluntary exchange of completed routines and actively cooperate in the early stages of program planning and assignment of programming manpower" (USE Inc. Records, CBI 20, courtesy of the Charles Babbage Institute Archives, University of Minnesota).

13. H. S. Bright, August 1960: "Computer User Groups," reprinted in B. H. Bruemmer, 1990: "Early Computer User Groups," *Annals of the History of Computing 12*, pp. 56–61.

14. P. Armer, November 1956: "SHARE," *Proceedings, Second Annual Electronic Business Systems Conference,* pp. 12–17.

15. C. J. Bashe, L. R. Johnson, J. H. Palmer, and E. W. Pugh, 1986: *IBM's Early Computers* (Cambridge, Mass.: MIT Press), pp. 358–61.

16. D. R. Mason, 1983: "The 701 in the IBM Technical Computing Bureau," *Annals of the History of Computing 5,* pp. 176–77.

17. Morison, August 1953.

18. Mason, 1983.

19. During April 1955, for example, IBM allocated 89 hours of machine time (25 percent of all time) on its own 702 for customers to test and debug programs prior to installation of their computers. The first customer to receive an IBM 702 was the Monsanto Chemical Company. It logged 40 hours of machine time at IBM before its own computer was installed and operational. See H. B. Ainsley, Jr., 18 May 1955: to T. E. Clemmons, "702 Installation Progress Report." Installation experience with the IBM 702 is typified by the memorandum, J. J. Kenney, 23 November 1955: to W. J. Mair, "EDPM," which reported as follows: "The Type 702 shipped from Poughkeepsie on October 24 for GE Schenectady was installed and running under testing conditions one week after the shipping date. After installation this machine was operated under normal and marginal testing conditions until November 17, with excellent performance. The machine was released to the customer on November 17."

20. R. M. Petersen, January 1957: "Automatic Coding at G.E.," *Proceedings of the Symposium on Automatic Coding,* held at the Franklin Institute in Philadelphia.

21. G. Schussel, June 1965: "IBM vs. RemRand—Part 2," *Datamation,* pp. 58–66. The computer for General Electric was the eighth UNIVAC to be produced. Unlike IBM that retained the first produced 701 and 702 for customer support activities, Remington Rand waited until two months before General Electric's machine was installed before it placed a UNIVAC at its New York City facilities. The IBM 702 installation at Ford Motor Company was successfully handling a payroll of approximately 70,000 hourly employees in March 1956, as reported by J. Boccomino, August 1957: "The Importance of Program Maintenance," *Systems and Procedures,* pp. 9–12.

22. J. W. Backus, 1981: "The History of FORTRAN I, II, and III," in *History of Programming Languages,* ed. R. L. Wexelblat (New York: Academic Press), pp. 25–74; December 1967: interview by L. M. Saphire; J. W. Sheldon, 12 October 1951: to C. C. Hurd.

23. D. B. MacMillan and R. H. Stark, February 1951: "Floating Decimal Calculations on the IBM Card-Programmed Electronic Calculator," IBM Applied Science Department Technical Newsletter No. 2, pp. 16–26. The floating-point number format for the CPC consisted of ten digits, with the decimal point assumed to be in front of the first digit. The last two digits indicated the power of ten by which the eight-digit fraction was to be multiplied.

24. The SSEC was equipped with eight electronic registers so that various data needed for a computation could be transferred simultaneously from memory. This helped overcome the disparity in speed between the electronic arithmetic circuits and the slower electromechanical memory.

25. J. W. Backus and H. L. Herrick, May 1954: "IBM 701 Speedcoding and Other Automatic-Programming Systems," *Symposium on Automatic Programming for Digital Computers* (Washington: Office of Naval Research), pp. 106–13; IBM Manual, 1954: "IBM Speedcoding System for the Type 701 Electronic Data Processing Machines" (IBM Form 24-6059-0); C. J. Bashe, L. R. Johnson, J. H. Palmer, and E. W. Pugh, 1986: *IBM's Early Computers* (Cambridge, Mass.: MIT Press), pp. 333–38. The programmer had to write each Speedcoding instruction as a string of decimal digits because Speedcoding had no associated assembly program to convert mnemonic operation codes or symbolic addresses to real ones.

26. Backus, 1981: pp. 26–27.

27. J. C. McPherson, 15 February 1954: "Speed Coding." This brief internal memorandum asserts, "It is estimated that the speed ratio between the 701 working normally and in speed coding is approximately 15 to 1."

28. J. E. Sammet, 1992: "Farewell to Grace Hopper—End of an Era!" *Communications of the Association for Computing Machinery 35*, pp. 128–31. Grace M. Hopper died on 1 January 1992.

29. G. M. Hopper, May 1952: "The Education of a Computer," *Proceedings of the Association for Computing Machinery*, pp. 243–49; May 1953: "Compiling Routines," Computers and Automation 2, pp. 1–5.

30. D. E. Knuth and L. T. Pardo, 1977: "The Early Development of Programming Languages," in *Encyclopedia of Computer Science and Technology*, Vol. 7, ed. J. Belzer, A. G. Holzman, and A. Kent (New York: Marcel Dekker).

31. Bashe et al., 1986: pp. 338–42; Backus, 1981; H. L. Herrick, 15 April 1968: interview by L. M. Saphire.

32. Backus and Herrick, May 1954: p. 112.

33. Backus, 1981: pp. 29–33.

34. IBM Programmer's Reference Manual, 15 October 1956: "The FORTRAN Automatic Coding System for the IBM 704 EDPM"; J. W. Backus, R. J. Beeber, S. Best, R. Goldberg, L. M. Haibt, H. L. Herrick, R. A. Nelson, D. Sayre, P. B. Sheridan, H. Stern, I. Ziller, R. A. Hughes, and R. Nutt, February 1957: "The FORTRAN Automatic Coding System," *Proceedings of the Western Joint Computer Conference*, pp. 188–98. Three authors on loan from other organizations to the FORTRAN project were S. Best of MIT, R. A. Hughes of the University of California Radiation Laboratory, and R. Nutt of the United Aircraft Corporation. See also Bashe et al., 1986: pp. 356–58.

35. A. J. Perlis, 6 December 1975: direct testimony in *U.S. v. IBM*, U.S. District Court, Southern District of New York, pp. 1878, 1974. Alan Perlis, a world-renowned professor of computer science at Yale University, presented a strong endorsement of the pioneering significance of FORTRAN in spite of the fact that he testified as a witness for the government. In his testimony he said in part, "FORTRAN was developed by IBM in the middle fifties and as mentioned before, had an enormous impact on a large collection of users and industries and in a certain sense shaped the way the computer would be used to support scientific and engineering research in the United States. . . . Prior to '71 I would say that almost all, that is, 85 to 99 percent, 95 percent of the students were taught that programming and learning FORTRAN were synonymous, and one

has only to look at the set of texts available for student use during that period to observe this effect."

36. Backus, 1981: p. 30.

37. J. E. Sammet, 1981: "The Early History of COBOL," in *History of Programming Languages,* ed. R. L. Wexelblat (New York: Academic Press), pp. 199–278.

38. *Business Week,* 20 January 1962: "Young Team Wins a COBOL Race," pp. 60–62.

39. M. Phister, Jr., 1979: *Data Processing Technology and Economics,* 2d ed. (Bedford, Mass.: Digital Press), pp. 82–83.

40. *Think,* May/June 1982: "Many Are Chosen," pp. 23–25.

15 An Air Defense System

1. K. C. Redmond and T. M. Smith, 1980: *Project Whirlwind: The History of a Pioneer Computer* (Bedford, Mass.: Digital Press), pp. 168–78.

2. T. J. Watson, Jr., and P. Petre, 1990: *Father, Son & Co.* (New York: Bantam Press), pp. 232–33.

3. Redmond and Smith, 1980: pp. 1–4, 14, 22–25. The Servomechanisms Laboratory was established under the direction of Professor Gordon S. Brown, with the help of A. C. Hall, J. O. Silvey, and J. W. Forrester in December 1940. Forrester received his master's degree in electrical engineering in 1945.

4. P. O. Crawford, 1942: "Automatic Control by Arithmetical Operations," thesis submitted in partial fulfillment of the requirements for the degree of master of science at the Massachusetts Institute of Technology, p. 1. To complete his thesis project quickly, Crawford limited his own analysis to "the elements and operation of a calculating system for performing one of the operations in the control of anti-aircraft gunfire, which is, namely, the prediction of the future position of the target."

5. The closest approach to practical implementation of electronic arithmetic circuits had been achieved by Atanasoff and Berry at Iowa State College and by Palmer and Phelps at the IBM laboratory in Endicott shortly before these researchers moved on to their World War II assignments in 1942. Little publicity was given to the work at Iowa State, and the proprietary IBM results were not disclosed outside the company (see chap. 7).

6. Redmond and Smith, 1980: pp. 41–44.

7. E. W. Pugh, 1984: *Memories That Shaped an Industry* (Cambridge, Mass.: MIT Press), p. 64; Redmond and Smith, 1980: p. 27.

8. Redmond and Smith, 1980: pp. 58–59. As early as December 1947, Perry Crawford had recommended to the Special Devices Division that work on the cockpit be discontinued because it was "not essential to the program."

9. Redmond and Smith, 1980: pp. 109–11, 120, 151–67. The estimated costs to completion in 1949 of the four computers were as follows: Whirlwind, $3 million to $5 million; IAS, $0.65 million; UNIVAC, $0.45 million; and EDVAC, $0.47 million.

10. Redmond and Smith, 1980: pp. 128, 171–73.

11. Crawford, 1942.

12. M. M. Astrahan and J. F. Jacobs, 1983: "History of the Design of the SAGE Computer—The AN/FSQ-7," *Annals of the History of Computing 5,* pp. 340–49, especially p. 341.

13. The first director of Project Lincoln was F. Wheeler Loomis, on leave from the University of Illinois.

14. M. Rees, 1982: "The Computing Program of the Office of Naval Research, 1946–1953," *Annals of the History of Computing 4,* pp. 102–20, especially p. 114; Redmond and Smith, 1980: pp. 173, 191–92, 199.

15. Redmond and Smith, 1980: pp. 186, 195.

16. C. R. Wieser, 1983: "The Cape Cod System," *Annals of the History of Computing 5,* pp. 362–69. The early aircraft-tracking demonstrations that justified creating the Cape Cod System were known as Project Charles.

17. J. W. Forrester, 29 April 1947: "Data Storage in Three Dimensions," Servomechanisms Laboratory Memorandum, No. M-70 (courtesy of MITRE Corporation Archives).

18. Pugh, 1984: pp. 66–69.

19. Pugh, 1984: pp. 81–89.

20. J. W. Forrester, June 13–30, 1949: MIT Computation Notebook, No. 47, pp. 15–27.

21. The graduate student was William N. Papian. Born in 1916, Papian worked as an electrician's apprentice and radio mechanic before going to the RCA Institute to become a radio technician. After serving as a radio intelligence officer during World War II, he entered MIT as a freshman at age thirty. See W. N. Papian, 18 June 1982: interview by E. W. Pugh.

22. Pugh, 1984: pp. 76–81.

23. D. R. Brown, 11 June 1952: "Group Leaders' Meeting June 9, 1952" (courtesy of MITRE Corporation Archives). The person who met with J. C. McPherson in New York City was Norman H. Taylor.

24. C. C. Hurd, 1981: "Early IBM Computers: Edited Testimony," *Annals of the History of Computing 3,* pp. 163–82, especially p. 174.

25. J. C. McPherson, 17 June 1952: to J. R. Shipman; Watson and Petre, 1990: pp. 230–31. As reported by McPherson, "They [the MIT representatives] visited our various laboratories at Poughkeepsie, Endicott, and the Watson Laboratory, and were given demonstrations of the Defense Calculator, the Tape Processing Machine, the Eastman Printer, the Wire Printer (with but a single feed), Hamilton's Drum Calculator, and Xerographic continuous printing. They spent some time at the Vestal Laboratory discussing the BDASA Project, and at the Watson Laboratory we reviewed the NORC Calculator plans, the Havens delay unit design (old), and were shown the cathode ray tube test apparatus, the operation of the tape reader and controls, and electronic components test unit."

26. J. F. Jacobs, 1986: *The SAGE Air Defense System–A Personal History* (Bedford, Mass.: MITRE Corporation), pp. 43–44. According to Jacobs the scores of the three top contenders, based on the weighting scheme agreed to by the evalua-

tors before the visits, were as follows: IBM, 1816; Remington Rand, 1374; and Raytheon, 1067.

27. J. W. Forrester, 12 May 1953: to A. G. Hill, "Selection of a Company to Work with the Lincoln Laboratory on the Transition System." According to Forrester, this memorandum expands on information provided in an earlier memorandum of 5 November 1952. The four representatives from MIT who evaluated and ranked IBM, Remington Rand, and Raytheon were Jay W. Forrester, Robert R. Everett, Norman H. Taylor, and C. Robert Wieser. The Bell Telephone Laboratories and RCA were also among the top five contenders, but they "chose to withdraw from being considered after the preliminary meeting, on the basis that their existing commitments did not allow them to undertake the work." Several secondary sources cite Sylvania as a leading contender, but Forrester's May 1953 memorandum indicates it was not among the top five.

28. The two individuals sent by Forrester to review IBM's work on magnetic core memories were William N. Papian and Kenneth H. Olsen. Both were graduate students working on different aspects of magnetic core memories as thesis projects. In 1953 a number of MIT staff members were assigned to IBM's Poughkeepsie laboratory to help with the final testing of the prototype computers; one of them was Kenneth Olsen, who in 1957 founded the Digital Equipment Corporation (DEC).

29. M. K. Haynes, 28 August 1950: "Magnetic Cores as Elements of Digital Computing Systems," a thesis submitted in partial fulfillment of the requirements for the degree of doctor of philosophy in electrical engineering in the graduate college of the University of Illinois.

30. M. K. Haynes, 26 March 1952: to C. L. Snyder, vice president, General Ceramics and Steatite Corporation; Pugh, 1984: pp. 45–57, 105. The experienced engineer who worked with Mike Haynes on the early ferrite core memory was Edward Rabenda.

31. Pugh, 1984: p. 95.

32. J. W. Forrester, 15 July 1953: to AN/FSQ-7 Engineers, "Planning, Scheduling and Administering the AN/FSQ-7 Program."

33. R. R. Everett, 1983: "Editor's Note," *Annals of the History of Computing 5,* p. 340.

34. A. P. Kromer, 26 January 1953: to all conferees, "Minutes of Joint MIT-IBM Conference Held at Hartford, Connecticut, January 20, 1953" (document, courtesy of the MITRE Corporation Archives, Bedford, Mass.). That the meetings were held in a back room of the IBM branch office in Hartford is related by R. P. Crago, in H. S. Tropp et al., 1983: "A Perspective on SAGE: Discussion," *Annals of the History of Computing 5,* pp. 375–98, see p. 384.

35. M. M. Astrahan, 12 June 1968: interview by L. M. Saphire.

36. J. M. Coombs, 20 October 1967: interview by L. M. Saphire. John Coombs worked on navy electronics projects at the National Cash Register Company during World War II and joined ERA when it was formed in 1946. He joined IBM in 1952 and initially organized a school for teaching newly hired engineers about computer technologies and methods. He was given the job of administrator in charge of IBM's engineering work on SAGE. Later Robert P. Crago

became the engineering leader with both administrative and technical responsibilities.

37. A. P. Kromer and R. P. Mayer, 29 June 1953: to AN/FSQ-7 Planning Group, "Project Grind Meeting of June 25, 1953 (Second Day)" (document courtesy of the MITRE Corporation Archives, Bedford, Mass.). See also M. M. Astrahan, 12 June 1968: interview by L. M. Saphire, especially tape 1, p. 41.

38. J. W. Forrester, in H. S. Tropp et al., 1983: "A Perspective on SAGE: Discussion," *Annals of the History of Computing 5*, pp. 375–98, especially pp. 382–83. Henry S. Tropp served as moderator of a discussion among Herbert D. Benington, Robert Bright, Robert P. Crago, Robert R. Everett, Jay W. Forrester, John V. Harrington, John F. Jacobs, Albert R. Shiely, Norman H. Taylor, and C. Robert Wieser. The discussion was held at the MITRE Corporation on 26 October 1982. The date of the decision to use a duplex system is provided by M. M. Astrahan and J. F. Jacobs, 1983: "History of the Design of the SAGE Computer—The AN/FSQ-7," *Annals of the History of Computing 5*, pp. 340–49; see p. 348.

39. Pugh, 1984: pp. 107–15.

40. M. M. Astrahan and J. F. Jacobs, 1983: "History of the Design of the SAGE Computer—The AN/FSQ-7," *Annals of the History of Computing 5*, pp. 340–49.

41. IBM press release, 30 June 1956: "IBM-Built Computer Is Heart of Electronic Air Defense System," date-lined Kingston, N.Y. Characterization of the SAGE computer as an "electronic brain" would probably not have been permitted by Watson, Sr., but he had died earlier that month.

42. It has often been suggested that the name SAGE was chosen to match that of Nathaniel Sage, the director of MIT's Division of Industrial Cooperation, who had shepherded Project Whirlwind and its predecessor project through the government contract processes. See, for example, J. W. Forrester, in H. S. Tropp et al., 1983: p. 394.

43. IBM press release, 30 June 1956. The designation AN/FSQ stood for Army-Navy/Fixed Special Equipment.

44. *IBM Kingston News,* 9 October 1957: "New Array Increases Memory 8-Fold"; IBM brochure, circa 1958: "The SAGE Computer"; IBM Advanced Systems Sales Manual, 15 October 1962: "Ground Based Data Processors"; R. R. Everett, C. A. Zraket, and H. D. Benington, 1983: "SAGE—A Data-Processing System for Air Defense," *Annals of the History of Computing 5*, pp. 330–39, adapted from a paper presented at the 1957 Eastern Joint Computer Conference.

45. Astrahan and Jacobs, 1983: pp. 347–49.

46. J. F. Jacobs, 1983: "SAGE Overview," *Annals of the History of Computing 5*, pp. 323–29.

47. The study of group behavior in man-machine systems was proposed by John L. Kennedy, a psychologist and consultant to Rand.

48. C. Baum, 1981: *The System Builders: The Story of SDC* (Santa Monica, Calif.: System Development Corporation), pp. 23–27. Wesley Melahn, who was in charge of the first five Rand programmers to work on SAGE, later became the second president of the System Development Corporation. The first president was Melvin O. Kappler.

49. R. R. Everett, editor's note on paper by H. D. Benington, 1983: "Production of Large Computer Programs," *Annals of the History of Computing 5*, pp. 350–61.

50. H. D. Benington, 1983: "Production of Large Computer Programs," *Annals of the History of Computing 5*, pp. 350–61. This article contains a long foreword by Benington, followed by a paper adapted from one presented in Washington, D.C., in June 1956 at a symposium on advanced programming methods for digital computers, sponsored by the Navy Mathematical Computing Advisory Panel and the Office of Naval Research. Benington describes the paper as "a description of the organization and techniques we used at MIT's Lincoln Laboratory in the mid-1950s to produce programs for the SAGE air-defense system." The cost of programming was estimated by Benington at about $55 per instruction. The importance of the 8.5-fold increase in SAGE computer memory size to the operating program is highlighted by Benington in H. S. Tropp et al., 1983: p. 377.

51. G. Burck and the editors of *Fortune*, 1965: *The Computer Age and Its Potential for Management* (New York: Harper & Row), chap. 2, "'On Line' in 'Real Time'."

52. Astrahan and Jacobs, 1983: pp. 347–49.

53. Defendant's exhibit 2609A in *U.S. v. IBM* (1969), U.S. District Court, Southern District of New York, pp. 34–150; R. P. Crago, 19 December 1978: testimony in *U.S. v. IBM*, U.S. District Court, Southern District of New York, pp. 85963–64. IBM's revenue from SAGE in the years 1952 through 1959 was $478 million. During the same time IBM's worldwide revenue from electronic stored-program computer systems was $1,321 million and its total worldwide revenues were $7,301 million.

16 Chasing New Technologies

1. W. W. McDowell, 4 January 1950: to J. C. McPherson.

2. The engineering personnel in Poughkeepsie reached 359, 750, and 1,040 by year end 1950, 1951, and 1952, respectively. See Yearbook, 1952: IBM Engineering Laboratory, Poughkeepsie, N.Y.

3. The four individuals who joined Reynold Johnson in establishing the new laboratory in San Jose were as follows: James Hood, from the administrative staff of the Endicott laboratory, was chosen to help establish administrative procedures; Harold F. Martin, a recent graduate of the California Institute of Technology, became Johnson's administrative assistant; Louis D. Stevens, an experienced engineer from the Poughkeepsie laboratory, served as Johnson's technical assistant; and William H. Reid, from World Headquarters, was assigned by W. W. McDowell to assist in other organizational matters. See R. B. Johnson, 15 December 1957: "Remarks on IBM San Jose Story."

4. R. B. Johnson, 15 December 1957: "Remarks on IBM San Jose Story."

5. A. J. Critchlow, September 1952, as quoted by D. W. Kean, 1977: *IBM San Jose: A Quarter Century of Innovation* (San Jose: IBM), p. 21.

6. The special representative from the San Francisco branch office was Glen E. Perkins, who had joined IBM as a systems service man in New York City in 1925; see Business Machines, 1963 Christmas issue: pp. 14–17.

7. Johnson, 15 December 1957.

8. G. A. Hotham was the first to propose storing information magnetically in a stack of disks continuously spinning on an axle. He documented this proposal in his engineering notebook on 14 January 1953. Because of the cooperative mode of operation encouraged in the laboratory by R. B. Johnson, it is difficult to identify specific contributions of individuals. A chronology of the project reveals that development of the random access file was assigned to W. A. Goddard in April 1953. Goddard assigned D. D. Johnson to develop the air bearing head in early May and J. W. Haanstra to develop the magnetics for the disk and recording head in late May. In August J. J. Lynott was assigned the task of developing a servo-drive system for moving the read-write head, and a method devised by him and T. Noyes was adopted in January 1954. In October 1953 J. J. Hagopian developed a spin-coating method for achieving the desired magnetic layer on the aluminum disks. In November 1953 L. D. Stevens was promoted to development engineer and put in charge of the random access disk project, while R. B. Johnson increasingly devoted himself to newer advanced technology concepts. See L. D. Stevens, December 1957: "Chronological Summary—Evolution of the RAMAC."

9. J. Rabinow, August 1952: "The Notched-Disk Memory," *Electrical Engineering*, pp. 745–49.

10. IBM Press Release, 6 May 1955.

11. T. Noyes and W. E. Dickinson, February 1956: *Proceedings of the Western Joint Computer Conference*, pp. 42–44.

12. In 1991 IBM began manufacturing 16-megabit memory chips that were used in computers beginning early in 1992. Each chip had about half the storage capacity of RAMAC. See the *Wall Street Journal*, 14 June 1991: "Two U. S. Firms Outpace Japan Rivals—IBM Has Lead in Producing Latest Chip."

13. IBM sales manual of electronic data processing machines, 4 September 1956; C. J. Bashe, L. R. Johnson, J. H. Palmer, and E. W. Pugh, 1986: *IBM's Early Computers* (Cambridge, Mass.: MIT Press), p. 300.

14. B. E. Phelps, 15 May 1956: to H. P. Luhn, "RAMAC Addressing Scheme."

15. *Digital Computer Newsletter 8*, October 1956: p. 402; R. P. Daly, February 1956: "Integrated Data Processing with the Univac File Computer," *Proceedings of the Western Joint Computer Conference*, pp. 95–98.

16. E. W. Pugh, L. R. Johnson, and J. H. Palmer, 1991: *IBM's 360 and Early 370 Systems* (Cambridge, Mass.: MIT Press), pp. 246–59, 261–70, 495–521, 774n39.

17. "The IBM 350 RAMAC Disk File," 27 February 1984: brochure produced by The American Society of Mechanical Engineers to commemorate their selection of RAMAC as an International Historic Landmark.

18. *New York Times*, 1 July 1948: "The News of Radio," as quoted in C. Weiner, January 1973: "How the Transistor Emerged," *IEEE Spectrum*, pp. 24–33.

19. J. Bardeen and W. H. Brattain, July 1948: "The Transistor, A Semi-Conductor Triode," *Physical Review*, pp. 230–31.

20. A. H. Dickinson, 18 May 1950: "Transistors in IBM."

21. C. J. Bashe, L. R. Johnson, J. H. Palmer, and E. W. Pugh, 1986: *IBM's Early Computers*, p. 377. Ralph Palmer assigned the task of developing IBM's expertise

in solid-state technologies to Arthur L. Samuel, who had joined IBM from the University of Illinois in September 1949. Samuel was best known at the time for his work on electronic vacuum tube design at the Bell Telephone Laboratories, where he had spent more than fifteen years prior to joining the University of Illinois in 1946.

22. Leon Brillouin was hired by Columbia University from Harvard with the help of T. J. Watson, Sr., who arranged for him to have an office at the Watson Laboratory and to be paid as an IBM consultant. See H. Fleisher, 1 November 1982: discussion with E. W. Pugh.

23. J. C. Logue, April 1968: interview by L. M. Saphire. Joseph C. Logue organized the course that produced the transistorized 604 and educated many engineers in the new solid-state technologies. Logue had graduated from Cornell in 1944 with a bachelor's degree in electrical engineering. He joined IBM in 1951 after teaching at Cornell, earning his master's degree, and working for two years at the Brookhaven National Laboratory.

24. *New York Times,* 8 October 1954: "IBM to Expand Laboratory, Shows Transistor Calculator," p. 1; IBM press release, 8 October 1954.

25. Bashe et al., 1986: p. 386.

26. W. W. McDowell, 2 October 1957: to L. H. LaMotte, J. A. Haddad, H. R. Keith, H. W. Miller, and E. R. Piore, "Solid State Components."

27. S. W. Dunwell, March 1968: interview by L. M. Saphire.

28. C. C. Hurd, 21 January 1955: "High Speed Data Processing Machines"; 31 January, "Project Whitney"; Bashe et al., 1986: pp. 423–25.

29. C. C. Hurd and W. W. McDowell, 20 April 1955: to D. A. Bruce, purchasing agent, "Proposal, Computer"; D. A. Bruce, 10 May 1955: to C. C. Hurd, "Livermore Computer"; Bashe et al., 1986: p. 127. Bruce advised Hurd on 10 May 1955 that the decision was based upon "lowest overall cost" in which the "predominant" factor was delivery schedule.

30. R. L. Palmer, 13 September 1955: to file, "Project Stretch."

31. For a detailed account of Project Stretch, see Bashe et al., 1986: pp. 416–58. The name "Stretch" had been adopted in August 1955 to signify the intent of Palmer and McDowell to stretch well beyond the state of the art in specifying components for IBM's next supercomputer. See C. C. Hurd, 31 August 1955: to L. H. LaMotte.

32. C. C. Hurd and B. F. Wiegard, 29 February 1956: to W. H. Brummett, Jr. This six-page letter accompanied IBM's 53-page proposal to the Atomic Energy Commission's Contracts and Procurement Branch in Albuquerque, N.M.

33. H. A. Faw, 29 February 1958: to file, "Project Stretch."

34. H. A. Faw, 20 January 1956: memorandum of meeting, "Project Stretch—AEC"; C. C. Hurd, 30 March 1956: to A. L. Williams, "NSA"; United States Atomic Energy Commission, 20 November 1956: Contract No. AT(29-2)-476.

35. P. K. Spatz, 1 May 1959: "The STRETCH Development Program," IBM staff report, p. 26.

36. E. W. Pugh, 1984: *Memories That Shaped an Industry* (Cambridge, Mass.: MIT Press), pp. 127, 166–75. A particularly important innovation was the load-shar-

ing matrix switch that greatly reduced the number of memory drive circuits and the power required from each circuit.

37. Bashe et al., 1986: pp. 390–98. Cost-effective designs that facilitated manufacture and service were emphasized in all Stretch components with the expectation that they would be used in commercial computers as well. Rather than using "worst-case" circuit design methods pioneered in SAGE, the Stretch engineers devised computer-implemented statistical designs that achieved good reliability with a significantly better speed/cost ratio.

38. Bashe et al., 1986: pp. 406–14. Component lead wires were automatically inserted in predrilled holes in SMS printed-circuit cards, under guidance of an electronic controller directed by instructions read from punched cards. Reliable electrical interconnections were achieved by an automated process that soldered all component leads simultaneously to preprinted copper lines on the back of each card. Back-panel wiring that interconnected circuits between cards was automatically performed by a paper-tape-controlled wire-wrapping machine. It was one of the earliest examples of digital design information being generated in a form directly applicable to the manufacturing process.

39. Bashe et al., 1986: pp. 446–49. The IBM 7080, announced in January 1960 as a higher-performance replacement for the IBM 705 III, was the second member of the 7000 series. It used the same components as the 7090.

40. *IBM Poughkeepsie Laboratory Newsletter,* 12 May 1961: "Stretch at Los Alamos"; E. Bloch, 15 May 1961: to file, "Summary of Stretch Acceptance Test in Los Alamos."

41. E. W. Pugh, 20 July 1965: "Scientific Compute Factor versus Processor Installation Date," prepared as background for the "IBM Corporate Memory Strategy" of 1965.

42. The first computer to challenge the performance of Stretch was Atlas, which was developed in a cooperative effort between Manchester University and Ferranti Limited in Great Britain. Completed in 1962, it is reported to be "probably the most powerful machine available in the early 1960s"; see S. H. Lavington, 1978: "The Manchester Mark I and Atlas: A Historical Perspective," *Communications of the ACM 21,* pp. 4–12.

43. The simulator was devised by H. G. Kolsky, a former LASL mathematician who joined IBM in 1957, and John Cocke, a Stretch planner; see Bashe et al., 1986: pp. 442–43. John Cocke achieved considerable fame in the 1980s as the inventor of RISC architecture.

44. C. R. DeCarlo, 2 February 1961: to W. B. McWhirter, "STRETCH."

45. *Datamation,* June 1961: "The Shrinking of Stretch."

46. S. W. Dunwell, 8 April 1964: to T. J. Watson, Jr.

47. T. J. Watson, Jr., 20 April 1964: to S. W. Dunwell.

48. T. J. Watson, Jr., 24 March 1966: remarks at the IBM Annual Awards Dinner. The IBM Fellow program was initiated in 1963 to reward creativity of engineers, programmers, and scientists by allowing them freedom to define and carry out their own research programs.

49. Ford, Bacon, and Davis, Inc., 22 April 1954: "Report on Organization, Engineering Department, International Business Machines Corporation."

50. Unknown to the younger Watson at the time, his father had even arranged for private lunchtime meetings with McDowell almost every day for several months after McDowell was promoted to director of engineering in 1950. See Watson, Jr., and Petre, 1990: p. 203.

51. *Business Machines,* 1 October 1954: "R. L. Palmer Is Named Director of Engineering in Departmental Expansion Program."

52. G. L. Tucker, 31 October 1977: interview by M. J. Schiller.

53. IBM Poughkeepsie Engineering Newsletter, 17 January 1956: "IBM Engineering Reorganizes—Research to Be Independent under Palmer; Beattie Heads Product Development Here."

54. IBM Poughkeepsie Engineering Newsletter, 17 January 1956.

55. *Business Machines,* 22 October 1956: "For IBM: A New Director of Research"; 28 December 1956: "A New Plan for Corporate Organization Is Announced."

56. M. C. Andrews, 2 February 1983: interview by E. W. Pugh. The "three wise men" selected by E. R. Piore to advise him were M. Clayton Andrews, John W. Gibson, and Gardiner L. Tucker.

57. *IBM Research Magazine,* November/December 1981: "25 Years of Innovation." This entire forty-page issue is devoted to the history of research in IBM, with emphasis on the twenty-five years since an independent corporate research organization was formed.

58. In 1956 Arthur L. Samuel, of the IBM Poughkeepsie laboratory, programmed an IBM 704 to play checkers, using a method in which the machine could "learn" from its own experience. It is believed to be "the world's first self-learning program, and as such a very early demonstration of a fundamental concept of artificial intelligence." See G. Wiederhold and J. McCarthy, May 1992: "Arthur Samuel: Pioneer in Machine Learning," *IBM Journal of Research and Development 36,* pp. 329–31. Significant IBM research achievements in solid-state lasers began in 1960 when Peter P. Sorokin and Mirek J. Stevenson created the second and third operational solid-state lasers. The first was created by T. H. Maiman of the Hughes Aircraft Company in June 1960. Considerable publicity was accorded the IBM Mark I language translator when its translation of Nikita Khrushchev's speech of May 1960 to the Supreme Soviet was submitted, just ten days after it was delivered, to the Congressional Committee on Science and Technology. The speech dealt with the flight of the U.S. U-2 spy plane over the Soviet Union. The Mark I and Mark II translators were developed by a research group headed by Gilbert King. The field of integer linear programming was initiated by Ralph E. Gomory at Princeton University. After joining IBM in 1959, he continued to lead this new field until he became IBM director of research in August 1970. See Bashe et al., 1984: pp. 559–65.

59. E. W. Pugh, 1984: *Memories That Shaped an Industry* (Cambridge, Mass.: MIT Press), pp. 214–18. The company's first magnetic film memory was shipped on a System/360 Model 95 to NASA in New York City in February 1968. One month later the second and last Model 95 was shipped with its film memory to the NASA Goddard Space Flight Center. Its 120-nanosecond read-write cycle made it the fastest multimegabit memory in operation for several years. See Pugh et al., 1991: pp. 469–75.

60. Research was elevated to the status of an IBM division in November 1963. Directors of IBM Research have been Emanuel R. Piore, 1956–1960; Gilbert W. King, 1961–1962; Gardiner L. Tucker, 1963–1967; Arthur G. Anderson, 1967–1970; Ralph E. Gomory, 1970–1986; John A. Armstrong, 1986–1989; and James C. McGroddy, 1989–.

17 Legacy

1. Giving the eulogy at the Presbyterian church on Park Avenue, New York City, where Watson had been an elder, the Reverend Paul Austin Wolfe provided insight into Watson's success, saying: "He had a peculiar singleness of mind, and he saw things simply. It was because of that simplicity of mind that he could make decisions." The minister also observed, "Even though he made machines, he never forgot that they were made by people and for people." See *Fortune,* September 1956: "Tom Jr.'s I.B.M.," by Robert Sheehan, pp. 9–12, 113–17.

2. Herman Hollerith incorporated his business as the Tabulating Machine Company in December 1896, three months after he signed a contract to supply equipment to the New York Central Railroad.

3. UNIVAC was an acronym for UNIVersal Automatic Computer. The Defense Calculator, which was introduced to the public on 7 April 1953 as the "IBM Electronic Data Processing Machines," was already better known simply as the "701." See *IBM Record,* April 1953: "New IBM Electronic Data Processing Machines Unveiled at World Headquarters in New York."

4. A brief discussion of the relations between IBM and Remington Rand, and their agreement of 1931, may be found in Complaint, 21 January 1952: *U.S.* v. *IBM,* U.S. District Court, Southern District of New York, N.Y., pp. 7–9. Permitting users to purchase cards from other suppliers, without paying a rental penalty, had little effect on IBM's business, in part because the rotary press invented by Fred Carroll made the company the lowest-cost producer of cards. During the next two decades, the company's share of the sales of punched cards continued to match its increasing share of installed equipment.

5. J. W. Cortada, 1993: *Before the Computer* (Princeton: Princeton University Press), pp. 68–70, 118–25.

6. Supporting information for much of the material in the first three sections of this chapter may be found in previous chapters. The strengthening of IBM's engineering and manufacturing operations during the depression of the 1930s and World War II, for example, may be found in chapters 5 and 8, respectively.

7. A brief summary of the settlement of the antitrust case against General Electric may be found in G. Wise, 1985: *Willis R. Whitney, General Electric, and the Origins of U. S. Industrial Research* (New York: Columbia University Press), p. 138.

8. T. G. Belden and M. R. Belden, 1962: The Lengthening Shadow (Boston: Little, Brown), pp. 96–97.

9. Complaint, 21 January 1952: *U.S.* v. *IBM,* U.S. District Court, Southern District of New York, N.Y., p. 9. The complaint noted that Remington Rand machines were available for purchase or rent, whereas IBM machines could only be

rented. The estimated annual rental paid by the government in 1951 was $25 million, up from $15 million two years earlier.

10. Complaint, 21 January 1952: p. 15.

11. A. D. Neale and D. G. Goyder, 1980: *The Antitrust Laws of the U.S.A.: A Study of Competition Enforced by Law,* 3d ed. (Cambridge: Cambridge University Press), pp. 1–33, 90–117; especially pp. 20, 108. The last quotation in the paragraph is from Judge Hand in *United States* v. *Aluminum Company of America* (decided in 1945) as quoted in Neale and Goyder, p. 108.

12. "The General Market for Accounting Machines," 21 September 1953: draft stipulation of fact prepared by IBM for *U.S.* v. *IBM,* District Court of the United States, Southern District of New York, pp. 8–25. The principal companies with which IBM said it competed were R. C. Allen Business Machines, Inc., Burroughs Corporation, Clary Multiplier Corporation, Elliott Addressing Machine Co., Felt and Tarrant, Inc., Friden Calculating Machine Co., Marchant Calculating Machine Co., Monroe Calculating Machine Co., McBee Co., National Cash Register Co., Remington Rand, Inc., Royal Typewriter Co., L. C. Smith & Corona Typewriters, Inc., and the Underwood Corporation.

13. Lehman Brothers, 19 May 1952: "Burroughs Adding Machine Company: Study of Company and Its Position in the Business Machine Industry," Table 14 as summarized in Cortada, 1993: p. 256, Table 17.11.

14. *Newsweek,* 4 February 1952: "Monopolies: IBM on the Spot."

15. Complaint, 21 January 1952: pp. 17–18.

16. Complaint, 21 January 1952: pp. 6, 14.

17. Complaint, 21 January 1952: pp. 19–21.

18. A good overview of U.S. antitrust law is provided by Neale and Goyder, 1980.

19. T. J. Watson, Jr., was appointed president of IBM on 15 January 1952, and the Justice Department filed its antitrust suit on 21 January 1952.

20. T. J. Watson, Jr., and Peter Petre, 1990: Father Son & Co. (New York: Bantam Press), pp. 216–20, 268–70; Belden and Belden, 1962: pp. 291–313.

21. Final Judgment, 25 January 1956: *U.S.* v. *IBM,* U.S. District Court, Southern District of New York, N.Y., pp. 1, 6–29.

22. Belden and Belden, 1962: p. 309.

23. Final Judgment, 25 January 1956: pp. 16–18.

24. Final Judgment, 25 January 1956: pp. 6–7.

25. Final Judgment, 25 January 1956: pp. 8–15.

26. Final Judgement, 25 January 1956: pp. 12–14.

27. Final Judgment, 25 January 1956: pp. 18–24.

28. *New York Times,* 26 January 1956: "IBM Trust Suit Ended by Decree—Company Agrees to Sell Its Electronic Computers and License All Patents." Stanley N. Barnes was the chief of the Justice Department's Antitrust Division.

29. *Business Machines,* 1 June 1956: "T. J. Watson, Jr., Named IBM Chief Executive," pp. 3–4.

30. The Electronic Data Processing Industry, 1956: a study prepared by Arthur D. Little, Inc., Cambridge, Mass., with the cooperation of White, Weld & Co., members of the New York Stock Exchange. This document reported that all 19 planned installations of the IBM 701 were completed, and that 11 of the planned 14 installations for the IBM 702 were completed. There were 44 orders for the recently announced IBM 704 and 114 orders for the recently announced IBM 705. The report did not give the number of Sperry Rand systems installed or on order.

31. The Electronic Data Processing Industry, 1956. A typical IBM 650 system rented for about $3,500 per month. An equivalent sales price of fifty times monthly rental would have been about $175,000.

32. In 1960 the gross revenue of the World Trade Corporation reached $360 million, or 20 percent of IBM's total revenue. Most of World Trade's revenue came from Europe (67 percent). The remainder came from Canada (14 percent), South and Central America (11 percent), and the Asia-Pacific area including Japan (7 percent). See *Fortune*, November 1960: "Q. What Grows Faster than I.B.M.? A. I.B.M. Abroad," by R. Sheehan.

33. J. Connolly, 1967: *History of Computing in Europe* (New York: IBM World Trade Corporation), pp. 10–18.

34. M. Campbell-Kelly, 1989: *ICL: A Business and Technical History* (Oxford, England: Oxford University Press), pp. 128, 141–43.

35. Belden and Belden, 1962: p. 298; Campbell-Kelly, 1989: p. 140.

36. Two letters provide insight to the nature and intensity of the dispute between IBM and BTM over their relationship. In January 1936 Watson, Sr., wrote to Sir G. E. Chadwyck-Healey of BTM saying in part: "Mr. Braitmayer informs me that your competitor has more machines in use than your company. When we compare your business and the potentialities of your territory with the business done in other countries, it prompts me to respectfully suggest that you and Mr. Phillpotts, who, I understand, are the largest stockholders, come to the United States, and we will go into the matter." Chadwyck-Healey responded quickly, saying in part: "I have to repeat that we cannot afford to continue to pay you Royalties and, in addition, income tax on their amount. As I have said to you before, English law makes any agreement to do so null and void, and there is, indeed, a penalty enforceable here on any person who refuses to allow the deduction to be made." Excerpts from these letters from the BTM Board Papers are here quoted from Campbell-Kelly, 1989: pp. 93, 94.

37. Many believed that Watson's fondest dream had been realized when a low-priced accounting system called the 3000 series was developed in the laboratories of the German company for the worldwide market. Representatives from twelve countries had participated in setting its specifications. It was the first major product from the World Trade laboratories. Renting for only $340 per month and using smaller punched cards than IBM's conventional equipment, it was expected to compete with small-card systems already offered by Powers-Samas, BTM, and Machines Bull. Over 800 sales were recorded in the first six months after its introduction in the spring of 1960. See *Fortune*, November 1960: "Q. What Grows Faster Than I.B.M.? A. I.B.M. Abroad," by R. Sheehan. Powers-Samas had introduced low-priced machines using small cards of two

different sizes (4.75 × 2 inches and 2.75 × 2 inches) in 1932, and BTM had attempted to match this with a half-length IBM card in 1936; see Campbell-Kelly: pp. 85, 99. Despite its initial success, the 3000 series became an embarrassment in the marketplace because it was introduced half a year after the more versatile and cost-effective IBM 1401.

38. Campbell-Kelly, 1989: pp. 43–47, 73–76.

39. W. Desborough, 7 June 1949: "Remington Rand Tabulating Machine Division: General Impressions," Powers-Samas Board Papers, as quoted in Campbell-Kelly, 1989: p. 140.

40. Campbell-Kelly, 1989: pp. 139–41.

41. L. Heide, 1991: "From Invention to Production: The Development of Punched-Card Machines by F. R. Bull and K. A. Knutsen, 1918–1930," *Annals of the History of Computing,* pp. 261–72.

42. Connolly, 1967: pp. E-12, E-15.

43. *Fortune,* November 1960.

44. Campbell-Kelly, 1989: p. 149. Arthur K. (Dick) Watson succeeded H. K. Chauncy as president of the World Trade Corporation in June 1954.

45. The head of BTM's research, Doc Keen, was said to be "openly hostile towards the new technology"; see Campbell-Kelly, 1989: p. 157.

46. After BTM and Powers-Samas merged in 1958 to form International Computers and Tabulators Limited, a decade of mergers followed before a stable state was reached in 1968 with the creation of International Computers Limited (ICL). Strongly encouraged by the British government, ICL was the country's response to the dramatic success achieved by IBM System/360, announced in 1964. See Campbell-Kelly, 1989: pp. 144–264.

18 Gambling on System/360

1. *IBM Business Machines,* 28 December 1956: "Special Issue on Williamsburg Conference."

2. The staff functions reporting to Al Williams included finance, legal, personnel, communications, and commercial development, as well as marketing, manufacturing, and research and engineering support services. Creating the autonomous Service Bureau Corporation (mandated by the antitrust settlement of 1956) was probably Learson's most challenging assignment because of the profound impact it had on the way IBM worked with customers and because of the problems associated with transferring employees to an independent business unit.

3. R. L. Palmer was promoted to product development manager of the Data Processing Division.

4. E. W. Pugh, L. R. Johnson, and J. H. Palmer, 1991: *IBM's 360 and Early 370 Systems* (Cambridge, Mass.: MIT Press). Appendix E, pp. 651–69, provides several organization charts for the IBM Corporation from 1956 through 1976. The newly formed Advanced Systems Development Division (ASDD) was headed by Jerrier A. Haddad. He had been engineering manager of the IBM 701 development project. More recently he had headed the Special Engineering Products

Division, most of whose activities were included in ASDD. The Data Processing Division, with its manufacturing and development responsibilities removed in 1959, reported to Orland M. Scott, who also had responsibility for the Federal Systems Division. The Time Equipment Division was sold to the Simplex Time Recorder Company in October 1958. Its profit in 1958 was about $8 million or roughly 6 percent of IBM's total profit.

5. T. J. Watson, Jr., and P. Petre, 1990: *Father, Son & Co.* (New York: Bantam Press), p. 200; chap. 13 of this book.

6. C. J. Bashe, L. R. Johnson, J. H. Palmer, and E. W. Pugh, 1986: *IBM's Early Computers* (Cambridge, Mass.: MIT Press), pp. 465–74. Charles E. Branscomb had primary responsibility for developing the IBM 1401 computer, the design of which had resulted from a competition between IBM engineers in France, Germany, and the United States beginning in mid-1955. The objective had been to develop an accounting machine capable of competing in the world market with low-cost machines offered by Machines Bull of France and others. Francis O. Underwood, of the Endicott engineering group, first showed that conventional accounting machine functions of relatively small businesses could be implemented with a stored-program computer more effectively than by any other electronic means.

7. F. M. Fisher, J. W. McKie, and R. B. Mancke, 1983: *IBM and the U. S. Data Processing Industry: An Economic History* (New York: Praeger Publishers), pp. 52–53, 101. Final Report of SPREAD Task Group, 28 December 1961, reprinted in *Annals of the History of Computing 5* 1983: pp. 6–26; see p. 24. The numbers of installed computers listed in these two references are not in full agreement. Those from the SPREAD report are used here. Development of the 1403 chain printer, used on the 1401 computer, is discussed in Bashe et al., 1986: pp. 489–93.

8. Fisher et al., 1983: especially p. 60.

9. M. Campbell-Kelly, 1989: *ICL: A Business and Technical History* (Oxford: University of Oxford Press), pp. 201–03.

10. Bashe et al., 1986: p. 119. The first six computers to be announced with transistor circuits were the 7070, 7090, 1401, 1620, 7080, and Stretch. No two of these were compatible with each other.

11. Bashe et al., 1986: pp. 474–80.

12. B. O. Evans, 23 March 1961: to W. B. McWhirter, "DS Product Line."

13. Pugh et al., 1991: pp. 114–22. This book provides detailed accounts of the development of SLT and IBM System/360 and of the creation of the IBM Components Division.

14. F. P. Brooks, Jr., 1983: "Discussion of the SPREAD Report, June 23, 1982," *Annals of the History of Computing 5*, pp. 27–44.

15. The 8000-series design team, which included Gerrit A. Blaauw, was augmented in August 1961 by several others from Research, including Gene M. Amdahl, John Cocke, and Elaine M. Boehm. See Brooks, Jr., 1983: p. 30.

16. Final Report of SPREAD Task Group, 28 December 1961: J. W. Haanstra, chairman, B. O. Evans, vice chairman, with J. D. Aron, F. P. Brooks, Jr., J. W. Fairclough, W. P. Heising, H. Hellerman, W. H. Johnson, M. J. Kelly, D. V.

Newton, B. G. Oldfield, S. A. Rosen, and J. Svigals. Reprinted in *Annals of the History of Computing 5,* 1983: pp. 6–26.

17. Pugh et al., 1991: pp. 122–24.

18. Final Report of SPREAD Task Group, 28 December 1961: p. 7, 11.

19. Final Report of SPREAD Task Group, 28 December 1961: p. 11.

20. M. V. Wilkes, July 1951: "The Best Way to Design an Automatic Calculating Machine," *Manchester University Computer—Inaugural Conference,* pp. 16–18.

21. John W. Fairclough was the Hursley laboratory representative to the SPREAD Task Group. So promising was his proposal that the report commanded, "Microprogram controls using a read-only memory shall be employed unless the cost performance of a conventional control system is less than 2/3 that of a microprogram control system." See Final Report of SPREAD Task Group, 28 December 1961: p. 12.

22. The study of instruction repertoires from across the industry to identify instructions used solely for business or scientific applications was led by J. W. Haanstra. See Pugh et al., 1991: pp. 127–28.

23. Chief antagonists in this debate were Gene M. Amdahl, who favored a 6-bit character and Gerrit A. Blaauw, who favored the 8-bit byte. See Pugh et al., 1991: pp. 148–49, 634.

24. Final Report of SPREAD Task Group, 28 December 1961: p. 12. Another important architectural decision was to provide the capability to address up to 2^{24} or 16,777,216 characters in memory. A so-called base register addressing scheme was adopted that reduced the bits required in each address from 24 to 16. This reduction was particularly helpful to designers of the smaller machines. See Pugh et al., 1991: pp. 145–48.

25. Final Report of SPREAD Task Group, 28 December 1961: p. 9.

26. Pugh et al., 1991: pp. 157–58.

27. IBM document, undated: "Analysis of H 200 Activity as of January 27, 1964." The document lists various types of orders for the H-200 in IBM's eastern, midwestern, western, and federal sales regions. Altogether 196 orders for H-200 systems were listed, involving 126 IBM accounts.

28. Pugh et al., 1991: pp. 157–64. Announcement of the upgraded 1401 computer was scheduled for 15 February 1964; see G. F. Daly, 10 January 1964: to D. E. Slattery.

29. B. O. Evans, 8 January 1964: to P. W. Knaplund, "IBM Future Products."

30. S. G. Tucker, 1965: "Emulation of Large Systems," *Communications of the ACM 8,* pp. 753–61. The first emulator was devised in 1963 by Stuart G. Tucker and Larry M. Moss in the IBM Poughkeepsie laboratory. It permitted programs written for the IBM 7070 to be run on one of the larger System/360 computers.

31. By showing that the smallest of the new computers could emulate the operation of the 1401 economically, some of Haanstra's own engineers had defeated his effort to have Endicott retain control over its product line. See E. W. Pugh, 1984: Memories That Shaped an Industry (Cambridge, Mass.: MIT Press), pp. 203–04. See also Pugh et al., 1991: pp. 160–62.

32. T. J. Watson, Jr., 7 April 1964: "A Letter from the Chairman," published in *IBM News*, 7 April 1964.

33. *IBM News*, 7 April 1964: "IBM Announces System/360."

34. Pugh et al., 1991: pp. 83, 156. The 200-fold performance range, projected by the SPREAD report in December 1961, was not achieved until the Model 91 (announced in November 1964) was shipped in October 1967 with three to ten times the performance of the Model 75. The System/360 Model 20 is not included in the performance range because it was not fully compatible with other System/360 processors. It had, for example, only 37 instructions rather than 143. See A. Padegs, 1981: "System/360 and Beyond," *IBM Journal of Research and Development 25*, pp. 377–90; Pugh et al., 1991: pp. 420, 643.

35. IBM press release, Technical Information, 7 April 1964: "Forty-four Devices Announced for IBM System/360"; IBM press release, 7 April 1964: "for release from Poughkeepsie at 12 Noon."

36. *IBM News*, 7 April 1964; J. T. Ahlin, 7 May 1964: to C. E. Branscomb et al., "System/360 Orders"; L. L. Horn, 14 May 1964: to J. T. Ahlin et al., "System/360 Requirements."

19 Commitment and Delivery

1. E. W. Pugh, L. R. Johnson, and J. H. Palmer, 1991: *IBM's 360 and Early 370 Systems* (Cambridge, Mass.: MIT Press), pp. 162–64. The referenced book provides substantially more information about most topics found in this chapter.

2. Pugh et al., 1991: pp. 62–63.

3. P. N. Whittaker, 23 January 1958: "IBM–Texas Instruments Agreement Summary," with attachment. A producer of electronic equipment during World War II, Texas Instruments had begun developing and producing transistors soon after they were invented. Among IBM's reasons for selecting TI was its reputation as a technical leader.

4. Pugh et al., 1991: pp. 46, 62–64.

5. Minutes of the Eleventh Meeting of the R & D Board, 10 March 1960: presentation by B. N. Slade; F. M. Fisher, J. W. McKie, and R. B. Mancke, 1983: *IBM and the U.S. Data Processing Industry—An Economic History* (New York: Praeger Publishers), pp. 71–75.

6. Pugh et al., 1991: pp. 56–58.

7. E. W. Pugh, 29 October 1957: "Report of First Meeting." In attendance were M. J. Kelly, H. T. Marcy, R. L. Palmer, E. R. Piore, and E. W. Pugh. See also *Business Machines*, April 1959: "IBM Engages Top Consultant," p. 5.

8. R. H. Bullen, 8 December 1964: to A. K. Watson, "History of the Components Division."

9. E. Bloch, 18 April 1961: to B. O. Evans, "Advanced Technology Study." The task group was established on 3 April 1961 and reported to B. O. Evans.

10. E. W. Pugh, 1984: *Memories That Shaped an Industry* (Cambridge, Mass.: MIT Press), pp. 57, 172.

11. Bloch, 18 April 1961. The eight engineers who served on Bloch's task force were selected from the General Products and Data Systems divisions and Group Staff.

12. E. Bloch, 1 August 1961: "Solid Logic Technology Program—Objectives and Directions."

13. The printed lines and resistors had a unique pattern for each circuit type, with different sizes and numbers of resistors and different locations for mounting silicon chips. Each circuit type comprised only four basic electric elements: transistors and diodes fabricated on silicon chips, and resistors and conducting lines printed on the ceramic substrate. The ceramic substrates were 0.455 inch square and 0.06 inch thick, and the silicon transistor chips were 0.025 inch square. A newly devised slurry saw cut more than one thousand fully processed chips out of each 1.25-inch-diameter silicon wafer. See Pugh et al., 1991: pp. 74–81.

14. E. L. Fritz, 13 March 1986: interview by E. W. Pugh; W. J. Schuelke, April 1967: "Modular Approach to System Design," *Automation.* The new design philosophy also provided for easier repair of individual production units without shutting down the entire line.

15. *IBM News,* 25 May 1964: "MRL Pioneers SLT Production" and "New Design Concepts Will Offer Maximum Flexibility in New Manufacturing Facility"; Pugh et al., 1991: pp. 83–92. The decision to manufacture SLT cards and boards internally had been made to protect proprietary information, to accommodate engineering design changes more rapidly, and to ensure quality control.

16. Robert L. Judge, a manufacturing engineer, had already demonstrated that cores with 19 mil inside diameter and 32 mil outside diameter could be wired by creating work-hardened bullet-shaped ends of the wires to act as their own needles as they were driven through the holes in the cores in an array. Cores of this size were used in the memories being developed for System/360 Models 62 and 70. On his own, Judge extended this capability to the 30 percent smaller cores with 13 mil (0.33 mm.) inside diameter and 21 mil (0.53 mm.) outside diameter. These smaller cores helped make it possible to operate the memories at an 0.75 microsecond read-write cycle. The inventor of IBM's load-sharing switch was Gregory Constantine, Jr. See Pugh, 1984: pp. 231–36.

17. Pugh, 1984: pp. 230–37. The Model 60 had been designed to use a 2-microsecond cycle memory and the Models 62 and 70 were designed for a 1-microsecond memory that was in serious technical difficulty before responsibility for memory development was transferred to Erich Bloch in the Components Division. A crucial change in the Model 65 from the Models 60 and 62 was the use of a control store rather than wired-in logic for control as used in the Model 75. The Model 65 was thus able to *emulate* the older IBM 7070 computer, which was important to customers who wanted the greater performance of System/360 but had a large investment in software written for the 7070. The self-motivated effort of the IBM engineer, Fernando (Fred) Neves, who made possible the use of a control store on the Model 65, is described in Pugh, 1984: pp. 225–29.

18. Pugh et al., 1991: pp. 247–61. The IBM 1301 Disk Storage provided 50 tracks per inch and 520 bits per inch on a track, compared to 20 and 100, respectively,

on RAMAC. Average access time had been reduced to less than 0.2 second from 0.6 second. A single 1301 storage unit could have one or two modules of 25 disks each. Each 25-disk module had capacity for up to 28 million 6-bit characters—nearly six times the 5-million-character capacity of the 50-disk RAMAC storage unit.

19. Pugh et al., 1991: pp. 261–68. Disk packs were given the product designation of IBM 1316. When used on the IBM 1311 Disk Storage, a track density of 50 per inch was achieved. A track density of 100 per inch was achieved on the IBM 2311 Disk Storage.

20. Pugh et al., 1991: pp. 228–31.

21. J. T. Ahlin, 7 May 1964: to C. E. Branscomb et al., "System/360 Orders"; 28 May 1964: to L. L. Horn, "System/360 Requirements"; P. W. Knaplund, 11 September 1964: to C. E. Frizzel and G. F. Kennard, "System/360 Order Position."

22. *IBM News,* 16 July 1971: "CD Observes Its Tenth Anniversary This Week." Development facilities built on the same site were larger than the manufacturing facilities.

23. IBM news release, 26 October 1965. Noting that 300 systems had already been installed, the release said in part: "International Business Machines Corporation announced today that its customers are being advised that during 1966 most System/360's will be delivered 60 to 120 days later than originally scheduled. The delays will result from problems in building up the rate of production of the System/360 as rapidly as necessary to meet the unprecedented customer demands for the new equipment."

24. Pugh et al., 1991: pp. 99–103. The person who took over responsibility for SLT production from Bernard N. Slade was Edward J. Garvey, one of IBM's most respected manufacturing managers. Previously he had been in charge of manufacturing in Endicott.

25. E. L. Fritz, 13 March 1986: interview by E. W. Pugh. Elliot Fritz believes that the slurry saw designed for cutting silicon wafers into chips is the first tooling invention to be patented by IBM; see U.S. Patent 3,241,265, filed on 27 June 1963 by H. Wing.

26. Pugh, 1984: pp. 245, 249–51; W. Newman, 29 April 1982: interview by E. W. Pugh. Construction of the Boulder plant began in March 1965.

27. IBM news release, 27 May 1964: "Executive Promotions Announced." Just as A. K. Watson had half a year as head of the corporate staff before being promoted in May 1964 to senior vice president (a newly created position), so Vin Learson was put in charge of sales half a year before he was promoted to senior vice president. See Pugh et al., 1991: pp. 165, 169–73.

28. T. J. Watson, Jr., and P. Petre, 1990: *Father, Son & Co.* (New York: Bantam Press), pp. 342–60, especially p. 355.

29. H. E. Cooley, June 1987: interview by E. W. Pugh. The "four horsemen" were John W. Gibson, John W. Haanstra, Clarence E. Frizzell, and Henry E. (Hank) Cooley. Lincoln L. Horn, an IBM vice president, served as Learson's first assistant in getting System/360 manufactured and shipped.

30. IBM news release, 25 January 1966: "Executive Elections and New Corporate Office Announced"; *IBMagazine,* September 1970: "For 'Dick' Watson, a New World of Policy and Diplomacy."

31. General purpose software support offered "free of charge" by IBM and other systems manufacturers by the early 1960s typically included *utilities* that performed routine tasks such as copying records from magnetic tape onto printed pages; *sort* routines that rearranged records from one sequence to another; *assemblers* that translated a machine-specific language with mnemonic user aids into actual machine language; and compilers that translated high-level languages like FORTRAN and COBOL into machine language for specific computers. Also provided were sequences of instructions for operating input-output devices. By the time System/360 was being defined, most large computing systems were supported by an *operating system* that combined all of these support programs with a *control program* that controlled system operation by initiating general purpose programs as needed to process a set of application programs.

32. Pugh et al., 1991: pp. 298–12.

33. F. P. Brooks, Jr., 23 January 1963: to G. A. Grover, "Software Design."

34. L. C. Wood, 23 January 1964: to C. H. Reynolds, "NPL Programming Review." New Processor Line (NPL) was the designation of System/360 during its development. Carl H. Reynolds managed the programming activities of the Data Systems Division.

35. Report of the Strategy Committee of the NPL Programming Task Force, 5 March 1964: to C. H. Reynolds. Members of the committee were R. P. Case, C. L. Foster, M. deV. Roberts, W. P. Simonet, and E. F. Wheeler. The use of a single operating system (with modular functional levels) had not previously been embraced because it added yet another level of technical challenge. Introduction by IBM in 1963 of operating systems for two small disk-based computers with memory capacities of only 16K characters gave reason to believe that reduced-function versions of the proposed operating system could be used on computers with as little as 16K bytes of main memory.

36. IBM Product Announcement, 7 April 1964: System/360, Letter 264-26; IBM Programming Announcement, 7 April 1964: IBM System/360—Programming Support Package, Letter P64-56. See also Pugh et al., 1991: p. 320.

37. It was during this time that Fred Brooks introduced the term "architecture" to the software development process; see Pugh et al., 1991: p. 318.

38. F. P. Brooks, Jr., 6 December 1993: "The Design of Design," a talk presented at the IBM T. J. Watson Research Center in which he spoke briefly about his early years at IBM. See also Pugh et al., 1991: p. 343.

39. F. P. Brooks, Jr., 1975: *The Mythical Man-Month: Essays on Software Engineering* (Reading, Mass.: Addison-Wesley), especially p. 25. In the preface, Brooks says, "This book is a belated answer to Tom Watson's probing questions as to why programming is hard to manage."

40. IBM Programming Announcement, 31 December 1964: IBM System/360 Programming Support, Letter P64-201. During November Earl F. Wheeler agreed to accept the commitment to develop the three new operating systems on the schedule announced in December. The plan for these developments

had been devised by James H. Frame, whom Wheeler had replaced as top programming manager in the General Products Division in October.

41. Pugh et al., 1991: pp. 321–31.

42. M. Phister, Jr., 1979: *Data Processing Technology and Economics,* 2d ed. (Bedford, Mass.: Digital Press), pp. 36–45.

43. *Datamation,* December 1964: "RCA's New Spectra 70 Series," pp. 34–36.

44. IBM's Proposed Findings of Fact, January 1982: pp. 4103, 4125, 4145, 4156–66, 4196–4202. This 5,979-page document was prepared by IBM for *U.S. v. IBM,* filed 17 January 1969: United States District Court for the Southern District of New York. Intent on becoming second only to IBM in the computer industry, RCA hired L. E. Donegan, Jr., and J. Rooney from IBM in 1969 to become vice presidents of sales and marketing, respectively, of the RCA computer division.

45. K. D. Fishman, 1981: *The Computer Establishment* (New York: Harper & Row), pp. 164–65. General Electric retained an 18.5 percent interest in the just-formed Honeywell Information Systems, and it continued to offer time-sharing services with its own equipment.

46. Phister, Jr., 1979: p. 39. The Control Data Corporation was founded in 1957 by William C. Norris, who had been one of the founders of Engineering Research Associates (ERA) in 1946.

47. B. Elzen and D. MacKenzie, 1994: "The Social Limits of Speed: The Development and Use of Supercomputers," *IEEE Annals of the History of Computing,* pp. 46–61; IBM's Proposed Findings of Fact, January 1982: pp. 4281–88. Control Data was unable to produce the CDC 6800, scheduled for delivery in May 1967, because of technical problems in achieving the promised high performance in a machine compatible with the 6600. The CDC 7600 was announced in 1968 as a replacement for the never-delivered 6800. First delivered in January 1969, the 7600 was not compatible with the 6600.

48. Watson, Jr., and Petre, 1990: pp. 383–87; IBM's Proposed Findings of Fact, January 1982: pp. 4233–35, 4271.

49. Fishman, 1981: pp. 209–16; IBM's Proposed Findings of Fact, January 1982: p. 4513.

50. Pugh et al., 1991: pp. 233–34, 269–70. By the end of 1970, IBM had installed 110,000 tape drives on System/360 computers. A particularly attractive target for plug-compatible manufacturers was the IBM 2314 Direct Access Storage Facility. It provided up to eight disk drives (plus a spare) and a storage capacity of 29.2 million bytes per disk pack. Announced in April 1965, its cumulative revenue in the United States was $1.2 billion by 1972. This was more than the cumulative revenue of either of the two largest revenue-producing System/360 processing units, the Models 30 and 40.

51. Pugh et al., 1991: pp. 289–95, 522–30. Prominent in the formation of the Storage Technology Corporation (STC) was Jesse I. Aweida who had led the development of the most advanced of the IBM 2400 tape drive series on which STC's first plug-compatible product was based.

52. *Electronics Week,* 14 January 1985: "Award for Achievement," pp. 40–44.

53. F. M. Fisher, J. W. McKie, and R. B. Mancke, 1983: *IBM and the U.S. Data Processing Industry* (New York: Praeger Publishers), pp. 307–16. The Greyhound Corporation, Boothe Computer Corporation, and Itel were among the primary computer leasing firms. IBM identified 250 leasing firms in 1970, up from 92 in 1966. The popularity of System/360 and certain economic factors facilitated their spectacular growth. Leasing companies purchased a total of $2.5 billion of IBM equipment in 1969, up from $200 million in 1965.

20 Onrush of Technology

1. J. W. Haanstra, September 1964: "Monolithics and IBM," IBM Technical Report.

2. T. J. Watson, Jr., and P. Petre, 1990: *Father, Son & Co.* (New York: Bantam Press), p. 354; A. K. Watson, 9 October 1964: to J. W. Gibson and E. R. Piore. Design of the "New Generation Systems," which were to be built entirely with NGT (variously called Next or New Generation Technology) was underway by early 1965; see P. Fagg and E. S. Hughes, 27 January 1965: Minutes of meeting on the "New Generation Systems."

3. *IBM News,* September 1965: Special Edition, "Systems Development Division, Emphasis on Technical Excellence and Leadership"; *IBM News,* 16 July 1971: "Components Division Tenth Anniversary This Week."

4. This quotation is based on the author's own recollections of Haanstra's statements upon several occasions. To survive in this environment, technical managers had to agree to achieve objectives they believed were impossible. The result was distrust of one another and reduced ability to work together to achieve common goals.

5. See chap. 19, "Stress at the Top." John Haanstra was one of the "four horsemen" selected by Learson to help solve the System/360 manufacturing problems. Getting expert technical help to solve problems in component manufacturing had become more difficult because creation of the Systems Development Division (SDD) had organizationally separated the component development and component manufacturing functions. Removed as president of SDD, Haanstra was assigned to the Federal Systems Division under Bob Evans. Haanstra remained there until August 1967 when he joined the General Electric Company to become general manager of the GE Information Systems Equipment Division eight months later. He died in the crash of a small plane he was piloting in August 1969.

6. E. W. Pugh, L. R. Johnson, and J. H. Palmer, 1991: *IBM's 360 and Early 370 Systems* (Cambridge, Mass.: MIT Press), pp. 432–40. IBM's proprietary solder-ball technology for attaching semiconductor chips to printed lines on ceramic modules was known as controlled-collapse chip connections, or simply C-4. The integrated circuit technology on which it was first introduced was MST, which stood for monolithic systems technology.

7. Pugh et al., 1991: pp. 406–21.

8. IBM Product Announcement, 30 June 1970: "IBM System/370—Powerful New Computing System," letter 270-52; Pugh et al., 1991: pp. 109, 482–84, 495–96. The System/370 models that replaced the earlier lower-performance

System/360 models were offered at a price increase of about 25 percent. This was about equal to the inflation during the intervening years.

9. A. Padegs, 1981: "System/360 and Beyond," *IBM Journal of Research and Development 25*, pp. 377–90, especially pp. 379, 380. IBM's ability to modify the standard, as it did in moving from 360 to 370 architecture, was especially objectionable to companies whose business plans had been devised to profit from the market for System/360 products. From a broader perspective, however, privately created standards (such as IBM's) induce more rapid technological progress than do traditional industry standards that are typically achieved through years of intense negotiations. The creator of a private standard has an incentive to modify it continually for his own benefit, but if these modifications do not generally benefit customers as well, the standard will lose its appeal and its value. See, for example, C. R. Morris and C. H. Ferguson, March-April 1993: "How Architecture Wins Technology Wars," *Harvard Business Review*, pp. 86–96.

10. E. W. Pugh, D. L. Critchlow, R. A. Henle, and L. A. Russell, 1981: "Solid State Memory Development in IBM," *IBM Journal of Research and Development 25*, pp. 585–602.

11. R. P. Case, 29 April 1970: "Relocation: Its Meaning and Value," IBM SDD technical report, especially p. 3. Dynamic relocation was particularly beneficial in a computer used to service remote terminals that might initiate new programs or request infrequently used data. To keep such information in main memory was impractical, but to require users to move it into low-cost storage between uses was not convenient. The solution was to provide automatic paging of information between disk and main memory.

12. *Data Processing*, October-December 1961: "ATLAS—Europe's Largest Data Processing System," pp. 255–60.

13. Pugh et al., 1991: pp. 355–67, 481–85. Bob O. Evans was "ostracized" to the position of president of the IBM Federal Systems Division from January 1965 to October 1969. He then replaced Charles E. Branscomb as president of SDD in October 1969.

14. E. W. Pugh, 1971: "Research Storage Study," a task-force report prepared for the director of Research; E. W. Pugh, 1985: "Technology Assessment," *Proceedings of the IEEE 73*, pp. 1756–63. Inherent in this analysis was the realistic assumption that the ratio of revenue received to manufacturing costs would change very little compared to the projected change in manufacturing costs. The optimistic cost-reduction projections for semiconductor memories correctly assumed a switch from bipolar devices to FETs.

15. Pugh et al., 1991: pp. 538–42. Richard P. Case was selected to work with John R. Opel to organize and manage the FS task force. Beginning his IBM career as an electrical engineer in the Endicott laboratory in 1956, Case had advanced to engineering manager for a mid-range 1400 series computer before he moved into programming in 1962 to participate in the development of software support for System/360. He had recently been appointed director of advanced systems for SDD when he was asked to assist Opel with the FS task force.

16. G. Radin, 26 March 1990: interview by E. W. Pugh. The term "single-level store" was used to distinguish the broad concepts embodied in FS storage

management from the simple "one-level store" implemented by the British designers of ATLAS. George Radin was the lead architect for FS.

17. E. W. Pugh et al., 8 April 1970: "Storage Hierarchy White Paper," a task-force report prepared for the Corporate Technical Committee; 9 December 1970: to the Corporate Technical Committee, "Storage Hierarchy White Paper—Eight Months Later."

18. R. P. Case, 19 June 1973: "FS Project—Schedule History."

19. B. O. Evans, 16 November 1974: to file, "A Potential Systems Direction."

20. B. O. Evans, 19 February 1975: to distribution, "Product Plans"; R. P. Case, 27 January 1994: private communication. IBM spent approximately $1 billion per year on research and development during the three years 1972 through 1974. Expenditures on FS increased from about $100 million in 1972 to more than $400 million in 1974. Probably somewhat less than half of the FS expenditures were a complete loss.

21. F. P. Brooks, Jr., 20–22 June 1973: hand-written notes made during a two-day review of the FS project; R. P. Case, 18 August 1973: summary of the comments made by F. P. Brooks, Jr., during the FS project review in June.

22. G. M. Amdahl, February 1979: "The Early Chapters of the PCM Story," *Datamation*, pp. 113–16. The Heizer Corporation, a venture capital firm, made an initial $2 million investment in the Amdahl Corporation. Subsequent funding of $6 million each was provided by Fujitsu, Ltd., of Japan and Nixdorf Computers of Germany.

23. IBM Product Announcement, 25 March 1977: "Large Systems Announcement Overview," Letter 277-20; "3033 Processor Complex Offers Growth, Improved Price/Performance and New Function," Letter 277-21. John E. Bertram, who had earlier headed the Advanced Computer Systems (ACS) project in Los Gatos, was president of the relatively small Advanced Systems Development Division when he made the proposal to revert from FS to 360-370 architecture. He was promoted to the newly created position of vice president for development and manufacturing of the Systems Products Division to lead the development of the post-FS systems. In recognition of his contributions, IBM established the internal John E. Bertram Award for Sustained Technical Excellence. The first recipient of the award was John Cocke in 1990. See IBM Research Magazine, Fall 1990: "John Cocke: Gentleman, Scholar and Super Computer Scientist," pp. 7–9.

24. Pugh et al., 1991: pp. 641–42. It is common to refer to a "System/390 architecture" to emphasize its new features. Nevertheless System/390 architecture is an evolutionary improvement on that of System/370, just as System/370 architecture was an evolutionary improvement on that of System/360.

25. Besides using only a subset of the System/360 instruction set, the Model 20 had a reduced register set and a different treatment of I/O. See Padegs, 1981, especially p. 379.

26. IBM Product Announcement, 30 July 1969: "System/3, Featuring New Size Punched Card and Low Price Disk Capability, Introduced for Small Business Use"; *IBM News*, Rochester, Minn., 10 September 1969: "System/3 Uses Monolithic, SLD—IBM's Most Advanced Circuitry." Lawrence A. Wilson transferred

from IBM's Endicott laboratory to San Jose to lead the development of low-cost products—an effort that produced the System/3; see Pugh et al., 1991: pp. 443–51.

27. IBM Product Announcement, 24 October 1978: "IBM System/38 Announced"; D. N. Reynolds and G. G. Henry, August 1979: "The IBM System/38," *Datamation*, pp. 141–43; G. G. Henry, 20 April 1990: interview by E. W. Pugh.

28. *Datamation*, 15 July 1991: "Can IBM Recast the AS/400?" pp. 28–31. The estimated annual revenue from the AS/400 and related products according to this reference was $14 billion. The annual revenue of the Digital Equipment Corporation was $12.9 billion in 1990 and $13.9 billion in 1991.

29. The Electric Typewriter Division had become a "completely autonomous operation" in 1955. See *Business Machines*, 24 October 1955: "The Division That Won a Promotion," pp. 3–5.

30. A. Myers, 6 May 1970: to Communications Products File, "Terminal and Office Products."

31. Myers, 6 May 1970.

32. IBM News Release, 9 September 1975: "Portable Computer Announced by IBM"; the IBM 5100 was described as being "slightly larger than an IBM typewriter."

33. William C. Lowe, laboratory director of IBM's Entry Level Systems Unit in Boca Raton, Florida, directed the activities that (with Frank Cary's strong support) established the IBU in which the personal computer was developed. The development was led by Philip D. (Don) Estridge, who had joined IBM in 1958 with a bachelor's degree in electrical engineering. Estridge worked as an engineer on Project SAGE and as a systems programmer on the Apollo moon mission at IBM before he undertook development responsibility for the personal computer.

34. IBM Product Announcement, 12 August 1981: "The IBM Personal Computer"; IBM News Release, 12 August 1991: "IBM Celebrates 10th Anniversary of the IBM Personal Computer, a Decade of Industry Leadership"; J. Chposky and T. Leonsis, 1988: *Blue Magic* (New York: Facts on File Publications).

35. *IBM Research Magazine*, Spring 1986: "The 801 Minicomputer," pp. 1–5; Spring 1990: "The Second Generation of RISC," pp. 2–4. The term RISC (Reduced Instruction Set Computer) was coined at the University of California at Berkeley. The comparative data on System/360 may be found in Pugh et al., 1991.

21 Demands of the Future

1. Thomas J. Watson, Jr., died on the morning of 31 December 1993 at age seventy-nine. The cause of death was attributed to complications from a stroke he suffered earlier in the month.

2. T. J. Watson, Jr., and P. Petre, 1990: *Father, Son & Co.* (New York: Bantam Press), pp. 392–96. During his brief term as CEO, Learson settled the antitrust case filed by the Control Data Corporation (CDC) in December 1968. A crucial part of the settlement allowed CDC to purchase IBM's Service Bureau Corporation for considerably less than its generally estimated market value. The

purchase involved the transfer of 1,700 people. To ensure that these people would receive "their existing IBM major benefit plans," the company contributed $26 million to support these benefits "not for any limited period, but throughout their careers in SBC." See Frank Cary, 1973: to IBMers, "Letter from the Chairman," *Think 39*, inside cover.

3. Watson, Jr., and Petre, 1990: p. 395.

4. F. M. Fisher, J. J. McGowan, and J. E. Greenwood, 1983: *Folded, Spindled, and Mutilated* (Cambridge, Mass.: MIT Press), pp. 1–17, 110–21. As in the antitrust case settled in 1956, a key issue was market definition. The reference cited here provides an excellent discussion of these issues, although it may be considered biased because the authors served as economic consultants to IBM during the antitrust case.

5. IBM's Proposed Findings of Fact, January 1982: pp. 2–3. This 5,979-page document in four large volumes was prepared by IBM as part of its defense effort in *U.S.* v. *IBM,* filed 17 January 1969: United States District Court for the Southern District of New York.

6. S. Brill, April 1982: "What to Tell Your Friends about IBM," *American Lawyer.* The magazine's publisher said, "The Justice Department pushed on foolishly with a case it never defined, never could manage, and therefore couldn't hope to win." The trial judge in the *U.S.* v. *IBM* suit that ended in 1981 was David N. Edelstein, who had previously presided over the earlier antitrust case that ended in a consent decree in 1956.

7. IBM's Proposed Findings of Fact, January 1982: p. 8. In the first private antitrust case initiated after the Justice Department filed its case, the Greyhound Computer Leasing Corporation (in November 1969) charged IBM with monopolizing a "market consisting only of leased computers." In a directed verdict in mid-1972, the judge found in favor of IBM, saying IBM had gained its position through "superior skills, foresight, and industry." The second private case, brought in January 1972 by the Telex Corporation and Telex Computer Products, Inc., charged IBM with monopolizing the electronic data processing market. In an amendment to the case, Telex defined a narrower market consisting only of certain types of peripheral equipment designed by IBM, copied by others (including Telex), and attached only to IBM processors. The federal district court in Tulsa, Oklahoma, found in favor of Telex in September 1973 and awarded it $352.5 million (later corrected to $259 million) in trebled damages and injunctive relief. Simultaneously the court awarded IBM $21.9 million damages for theft by Telex of trade secrets on which the copied equipment was based. The antitrust decision against IBM was reversed by the Court of Appeals for the Tenth Circuit in January 1975. The parties agreed to terminate further legal action, without payment of money by either party, when IBM agreed not to pursue damages for theft of trade secrets. Adverse ramifications of the initial verdict in favor of Telex included encouragement of more private antitrust suits by Calcomp, Hudson General, Marshall, Memorex, and Transamerica—all filed before the end of 1973. All cases were settled in IBM's favor. See D & C Publishers, 1974: *Telex Plaintiff Versus IBM Defendent* (Campbell, Calif.: D & C Publishers); Fisher, Gowan, and Greenwood, 1983: pp. 13–17; R. J. Siegel, January-February 1974: "Where We Stand on the Lawsuits," *Think,* pp. 17–21.

8. R. E. Allen, 9 February 1994: letter to shareowners, AT&T 1993 Annual Report, pp. 2–3. The outcomes of the AT&T and IBM antitrust cases were announced on the same day by Assistant Attorney General William Baxter.

9. Gordon E. Moore in 1993 suggested that the end of the exponential increase in the number of devices on a silicon chip, predicted by his own "Moore's Law," was finally at hand. From the mid-1960s to the end of the 1980s, the number of circuits per chip had doubled every one to two years. See *Electronic News,* 5 April 1993: "Statute of Limitations on Moore's Law?"

10. IBM News SDD Endicott, September 1968: "North Street Laboratory Celebrates 35th Anniversary," pp. 1–4.

Index